Dafydd ap Gwilym: Influences and Analogues

HUW M. EDWARDS

CLARENDON PRESS · OXFORD
1996

Oxford University Press, Walton Street, Oxford OX2 6DP

Oxford New York
Athens Auckland Bangkok Bombay
Calcutta Cape Town Dar es Salaam Delhi
Florence Hong Kong Istanbul Karachi
Kuala Lumpur Madras Madrid Melbourne
Mexico City Nairobi Paris Singapore
Taipei Tokyo Toronto
and associated companies in
Berlin Ibadan

Oxford is a trade mark of Oxford University Press

Published in the United States
by Oxford University Press Inc., New York

British Library Cataloguing in Publication Data
Data available

Library of Congress Cataloging in Publication Data
Edwards, Huw M.
Dafydd ap Gwilym: influences and analogues / Huw W. Edwards.
p. cm.—(Oxford modern languages and literature monographs)
Includes bibliographical references and index.
1. Dafydd ap Gwilym, 14th cent.—Knowledge—Literature.
2. Welsh poetry—1100–1400—French influences.
3. Poetry, Medieval—History and criticism.
4. Wales—In literature. I. Title. II. Series.
PB2273.D3E28 1996 891.6'611—dc20 95-51240
ISBN 0–19–815901–3

1 3 5 7 9 10 8 6 4 2

Typeset by Hope Services (Abingdon) Ltd.
Printed in Great Britain
on acid-free paper by
Bookcraft Ltd,
Midsomer Norton, Bath

I

Meinir ac Efa

Acknowledgements

I am truly grateful for all the help and advice I received while preparing this book. Special thanks are due to Professor D. Ellis Evans, Professor Dafydd Johnston, and Professor D. A. Trotter, and also to Mrs Beryl Wyn Jenkins and Mrs Julie Jones.

Contents

Abbreviations

APDG	Rachel Bromwich, *Aspects of the Poetry of Dafydd ap Gwilym* (Cardiff, 1986)
BBBGDd	Dafydd Johnston (ed.), *Blodeugerdd Barddas o'r Bedwaredd Ganrif ar Ddeg* (Llandybïe, 1989)
BBCS	*The Bulletin of the Board of Celtic Studies*
BDG	Robert Ellis (Cynddelw) (ed.), *Barddoniaeth Dafydd ab Gwilym o grynhoad Owen Jones, William Owen ac Edward Williams, yn nghydag amryw gyfieithiadau i'r Seisnig* (Liverpool, 1873)
BT	J. Gwenogvryn Evans, *Facsimile and Text of the Book of Taliesin* (Llanbedrog, 1910)
CIGE	Ifor Williams, Henry Lewis and Thomas Roberts (eds.), *Cywyddau Iolo Goch ac Eraill* (rev. edn., Cardiff, 1937)
CLlC	J. H. Davies (ed.), *Cymdeithas Llên Cymru*, i–vi (Cardiff, 1900–5)
CMCS	*Cambridge Medieval Celtic Studies*
CMOC	Dafydd Johnston (ed. and trans.), *Canu Maswedd yr Oesoedd Canol / Medieval Welsh Erotic Poetry* (Cardiff, 1991)
CRhC	T. H. Parry-Williams (ed.), *Canu Rhydd Cynnar* (Cardiff, 1932)
CSTB	P. Donovan (ed.), *Cywyddau Serch y Tri Bedo* (Cardiff, 1982)
DCRh	Brinley Rees, *Dulliau'r Canu Rhydd 1500–1650* (Cardiff, 1952)
DGChSOC	John Rowlands (ed.), *Dafydd ap Gwilym a Chanu Serch yr Oesoedd Canol* (Cardiff, 1975)
DGEC	Helen Fulton, *Dafydd ap Gwilym and the European Context* (Cardiff, 1989)
DGG	Ifor Williams and Thomas Roberts (eds.), *Cywyddau Dafydd ap Gwilym a'i Gyfoeswyr* (Bangor, 1914)
DGG²	Ifor Williams and Thomas Roberts (eds.), *Cywyddau Dafydd ap Gwilym a'i Gyfoeswyr* (rev. edn., Cardiff, 1935)
EWGP	Kenneth Jackson (ed.), *Early Welsh Gnomic Poems* (Cardiff, 1935)
G	J. Lloyd-Jones, *Geirfa Barddoniaeth Gynnar Gymraeg* (Cardiff, 1931–63)
GDG	Thomas Parry (ed.), *Gwaith Dafydd ap Gwilym* (2nd edn., Cardiff, 1963)
GDG¹	Thomas Parry (ed.), *Gwaith Dafydd ap Gwilym* (Cardiff, 1952)
GCBM	Nerys Ann Jones and Ann Parry Owen (eds.), *Gwaith Cynddelw Brydydd Mawr*, vol. 1 (Cardiff, 1991)
GIG	Dafydd Johnston (ed.), *Gwaith Iolo Goch* (Cardiff, 1988)
GLlLl	Elin M. Jones and Nerys Ann Jones (eds.), *Gwaith Llywarch ap Llywelyn 'Prydydd y Moch'* (Cardiff, 1991)

GP   G. J. Williams and E. J. Jones (eds.), *Gramadegau'r Penceird-
            diaid* (Cardiff, 1934)
GPC   *Geiriadur Prifysgol Cymru* (Cardiff, 1950–   )
H   John Morris-Jones and T. H. Parry-Williams (eds.), *Llawysgrif
            Hendregadredd* (Cardiff, 1933)
HB   T. H. Parry-Williams (ed.), *Hen Benillion* (2nd edn., Llandysul,
            1956)
LlC   *Llên Cymru*
LlDC   A. O. H. Jarman (ed.), *Llyfr Du Caerfyrddin* (Cardiff, 1982)
LlRMG   T. H. Parry-Williams (ed.), *Llawysgrif Richard Morris o Gerddi*
            (Cardiff, 1931)
MA   Owen Jones, William Owen Pughe, and Edward Williams
            (eds.), *The Myvyrian Archaiology of Wales* (2nd edn., Denbigh,
            1870)
MLRELL   Peter Dronke, *Medieval Latin and the Rise of European Love-
            Lyric*, 2 vols. (Oxford, 1965–6)
NLWJ   *The National Library of Wales Journal*
OBWV   Thomas Parry (ed.), *The Oxford Book of Welsh Verse* (Oxford,
            1962)
Origines   Alfred Jeanroy, *Les Origines de la poésie lyrique en France au
            moyen âge* (3rd edn., Paris, 1925)
Recherches Theodor Max Chotzen, *Recherches sur la poésie de Dafydd ab
            Gwilym* (Amsterdam, 1927)
Roman   Daniel Poirion (ed.), *Le Roman de la Rose* (Paris, 1974)
RP   J. Gwenogvryn Evans, *The Poetry in the Red Book of Hergest*
            (Llanbedrog, 1911)
SC   *Studia Celtica*
SP   Rachel Bromwich, *Selected Poems of Dafydd ap Gwilym*
            (Bungay, Suffolk, 1985)
THSC   *Transactions of the Honourable Society of Cymmrodorion*
TYP   Rachel Bromwich (ed.), *Trioedd Ynys Prydein, The Welsh
            Triads* (Cardiff, 1961)
YB   *Ysgrifau Beirniadol*
ZCP   *Zeitschrift für celtische Philologie*

Introduction

The work of the first generation of *Cywyddwyr* constitutes a remarkable body of verse. With the cessation of princely patronage following the Edwardian conquest of Gwynedd in the late thirteenth century, the qualified poets became entirely dependent for their livelihood on the increasingly powerful *uchelwyr* class, the landed gentry. There was now a more widespread demand for entertainment as well as praise, and the challenge was most effectively met by Dafydd ap Gwilym and a group of contemporaries who developed the new and comparatively flexible couplet-based *cywydd* metre. Their poems have a creative vitality, an exciting freshness and diversity in theme and treatment, which make this one of the most innovative periods in the history of the Welsh literary tradition.

Social and political factors were certainly conducive, but the development was also made possible by the convergence in fourteenth-century Wales of various cultural and literary influences to which Dafydd ap Gwilym, the most innovative of all medieval Welsh poets, was especially receptive. From the Continent came the pervasive influence of the poetry of 'courtly love', to be modified and renewed according to native tastes. Within Wales itself, an important source of inspiration is likely to have been provided by an indigenous undercurrent of popular verse, made more accessible to the established bardic hierarchy by the collapse of the old order. The term 'popular' requires definition. It will be used here to describe verse which was not a product of formal bardic training, and the great bulk of which was deemed unworthy of preservation in medieval manuscripts. It is therefore by and large synonymous with 'sub-bardic'. It refers not only to folk-poetry of the kind sung by the populace at festive periods, but also to the similarly submerged compositions of the unqualified wandering performers of medieval Wales, collectively known as *Clêr*, which must inevitably have reflected to a considerable extent the popular culture of the time. That is not to say that some of Dafydd ap Gwilym's poems, although he belonged to an essentially learned aristocratic tradition, could not also be enjoyed outside the confines of a nobleman's hall. Indeed, the line between his less elevated pieces and those of the *Clêr* must have been somewhat vague at times. One of the aims of this study is to highlight the enriching effect of increased interaction between the 'popular' and 'aristocratic' traditions in the post-Conquest period.

The first to appreciate fully the significance of the early *Cywyddwyr*'s debt both to the native popular tradition and to Continental literature was the Dutch scholar T. M. Chotzen. The shortcomings of his ambitiously wide-ranging *Recherches sur la poésie de Dafydd ab Gwilym* (Amsterdam, 1927) are all too evident, caused not least by the fact that it preceded by a quarter of a century the publication of the established canon of Dafydd's poetry. Even so, it remains for the researcher an invaluable study in comparative literature laden with a wealth of textual analogues, and my indebtedness to it will be apparent throughout. It would be equally difficult to overstate Rachel Bromwich's contribution to our understanding of the subject. In a series of articles conveniently gathered together in her *Aspects of the Poetry of Dafydd ap Gwilym* (Cardiff, 1986) she argues convincingly that Dafydd had access to a thriving sub-literary verse tradition, and considers its likely influence on some aspects of his poetry. My objective is largely to broaden the discussion to include a greater variety of thematic and stylistic elements in the early *cywyddau* which may owe something to the popular sub-culture of medieval Wales. I accept Bromwich's theory that the hidden verse tradition acted as a channel for the transmission of some of the conventions of the Continental love-lyric, and in Chapters 4 and 5 an attempt is made to develop her view that comparison with free-metre poetry might help to point to some affinities between the *cywyddau* and the verse of the *Clêr*. Mention must also be made of D. J. Bowen's perceptive articles (listed in the Bibliography), which show a constant awareness of the various influences—native and external, literary and sub-literary—that were at work in fourteenth-century Wales.

Finally, Helen Fulton's recent study, *Dafydd ap Gwilym and the European Context* (Cardiff, 1989), has enabled us to view Dafydd's poetry with greater clarity from a wider European perspective. By placing the poems in their socio-historical context she shows that their affinity with certain types of French love-poetry can be seen to arise in part from a similarity in social function and poetic stance. Although she does touch upon some specific elements which are likely to derive ultimately from French or Anglo-Norman, that is not her main concern. The comparative study which forms the final chapters of this enquiry is primarily textual. Some of the analogues identified may appear less significant than others, and only in exceptional cases is it suggested that any given text can be considered a possible 'source' for early *cywydd* poetry. I believe, however, that the cumulative weight of the evidence compiled in these chapters is strongly indicative of Dafydd's receptiveness to external literary trends which had become the common currency of western Europe.

Any discussion of literary influences is by its very nature a perilous venture. But if this book succeeds in giving the reader some impression of the cultural complexity which underlies the fascinatingly inventive verse of Dafydd ap Gwilym and his contemporaries, it will have achieved its end.

1

Popular Entertainers in Medieval Wales

For the professional poets of medieval Wales the fourteenth century was a time of redefinition and innovation. The *cywydd* poetry of this period owes its remarkable richness to a happy fusion of creative genius and a variety of formative influences, not the least of which is likely to have been an indigenous undercurrent of popular verse. Before going on to evaluate the nature of the early *Cywyddwyr*'s debt to the sub-literary verse tradition of their time, it will be useful to establish what exactly we mean when we speak of the popular poets of medieval Wales. The present chapter will be concerned with the evidence relating to the existence of a class of entertainers of inferior status who, unlike their bardic counterparts, have been doomed to an almost unbroken, but deceptive silence until the close of the Middle Ages.

The sudden increase from the fourteenth century onwards in the number of references to such minstrels, collectively known as *y Glêr*, indicates an enhanced awareness of their activities on the part of the learned classes, both secular and religious. However, although the term *Clêr* is in most cases overtly derogatory when applied to a class of inferior poets and musicians, it often has the more neutral meaning of 'poets in general', a peculiar semantic dichotomy which has to do with the etymology of the word itself. In 1914 Ifor Williams questioned the direct derivation of *clêr* from Latin *clerus*, since this would have given the diphthongal form *clwyr*.[1] The form is in fact attested, but the meaning is obscure in all cases.[2] It was Ifor Williams's opinion that *clêr* is derived from the collective form *clerus* through the intermediacy of Old French *cler(s)*. However, the Dutch scholar T. M. Chotzen, writing in 1927,[3] rejected this on the basis that *cler(s)* is not in fact attested in a collective sense in Old French, the collective noun which bears this meaning being *clergie*. Chotzen goes on to consider the possibility of a borrowing from the plural *clerc/clers*

---

[1] 'Dafydd ap Gwilym a'r Glêr', *THSC* (1913–14), 141.
[2] See J. Lloyd-Jones, *G* 151. [3] *Recherches*, 75 ff.

or even a late semi-learned borrowing from *clerus*, which would have followed the formation of the regular form *clwyr* in an earlier period. Although, as he says, the validity of these etymologies is not disproven, he rejects these also, preferring to seek the origin of *clêr* in a non-diphthongal collective form derived from Latin *clerus*. Such a form is found in the Irish *cléir* which, like *clêr*, is feminine (though the diphthongal form *clíar* is also derived from *clerus*). His attempt at tracing the semantic evolution of *cléir* is as follows: priests > officiating priests > a troupe of itinerant musicians > a metaphorical term for birds as minstrels > poets in general.

The theory proposed by Chotzen, though by no means conclusively proven, represents the orthodox view of the etymology of *clêr*.[4] Thomas Parry compares the usage of the word with the various meanings of *cléir* and *clíar* attested in Irish, and discovers striking similarities. Having cited Meyer's definition of *cléir*, 'a chorus, a band', and *clíar*, 'clergy; a company, band, train', and Dinneen's definition of the latter, 'a band, a company; the clergy; the bards, strolling singers; a chorus; *clíar na n-éan*, the feathered choir',[5] he observes:

Yr ystyron a geir yn Gymraeg yw'r ddwy a nodwyd uchod ynglŷn â'r beirdd, a hefyd yr ystyr o fintai yn canu neu gôr yn y cwpled yn IGE² 102.23–4 . . . am yr angylion yn canu pan fu farw Dewi Sant. Ac wrth gwrs fe'i defnyddir gan DG, fel y sylwodd Chotzen . . . am aderyn, 'clerwraig nant' (122.29). Y mae'r ystyron hyn yn cyfateb yn bur agos i ystyron *cléir* mewn Gw., ac o blaid tybio mai benthyg sydd yma.[6]

(The meanings which we find in Welsh are the two which are noted above concerning the poets, and also the meaning of a company singing or a choir in the couplet in IGE² 102.23–4 . . . of the angels singing upon the death of St David. And of course, it is used by DG [Dafydd ap Gwilym], as Chotzen has remarked . . . of a bird, *clerwraig nant* (122.29). These meanings correspond fairly closely to the meanings of *cléir* in Irish, and support the assumption that borrowing has taken place.)

⁴ GPC (497), gives: '*clêr* [?bnth. Gwydd. C. *cléir* 'mintai, cwmni; offeiriaid; beirdd neu gerddorion crwydrad; côr', adding: 'a dyl. H. Ffr. *cler*, *clers* arno]'. Rachel Bromwich also suggests a later French influence: 'It appears to have been an early borrowing from Irish *cléir* . . . and was later influenced semantically by French *clers*, which gave it a pejorative colouring' (SP 162). Cf. also her remarks in *Dafydd ap Gwilym* (Cardiff, 1974), 27–8.

⁵ Kuno Meyer, *Contributions to Irish Lexicography*, vol. 1, pt. 1 (Halle, 1906), 383, and see also 386–7; Patrick S. Dinneen, *An Irish–English Dictionary* (Dublin, 1927), s.v. *clíar*.

⁶ GDG, pp. 439–40.

The basic meaning of *cléir*, then, when not used in the religious sense, is an itinerant band, or chorus, comprised mainly of poets and musicians.[7] It should be noted that the pejorative connotation of *clêr* when applied to inferior minstrels from the fourteenth century onwards has not been shown to exist in Irish, though this does not affect Parry's central argument. It is his contention that, probably during the reign of Gruffudd ap Cynan (1081–1137), when relations between Wales and Ireland were at their closest, *clêr* was borrowed from Irish to refer to a class of wandering minstrels, and could, therefore, if the pejorative meaning was not already present, have become a term of contempt among the established court bards of the Welsh princes and in the eyes of the Church. But when most, if not all, bards were forced to undertake circuits after the loss of political independence in 1282–3, the term could then have come to embrace all poets, irrespective of status, while retaining its original meaning according to the context. As Parry points out, the very fact that the word has two distinct meanings by the fourteenth century suggests that it had entered the language early enough for such a semantic development to take place.

The main objection to this theory is, of course, the fact that *clêr* is not attested until the late thirteenth century, at the earliest. It will be seen, however, that the qualified bards of pre-Conquest Wales had little reason to refer to their inferiors, and if terms such as *gofeirdd* and *beirdd ysbyddaid* (poetasters) have been preserved it is only by chance. Chotzen is persuaded by the evidence available to suggest a late borrowing, in the late thirteenth or early fourteenth century, but the cultural and political ties with Ireland to which he refers in this period are convincingly dismissed by Parry as being insignificant compared with the links forged at the time of Gruffudd ap Cynan. Furthermore, if we are to accept such a theory, we must assume that the semantic dichotomy which characterizes the term *clêr* would have been inherited directly from Irish *cléir*. Beside the fact that such a clearly defined distinction does not appear to be reflected in Irish, it will be argued that *clêr* may only have become current as a term for poets in general in the second quarter of the fourteenth century,

---

[7] One of the definitions of *clíar* in the Royal Irish Academy's *Dictionary of the Irish Language*, compact edn. (Dublin, 1983), 121, is ' "company, band, train, troop" (especially of a poet's following)'. The meaning of a poet's troupe of entertainers does not appear to be attested in Welsh, although D. J. Bowen does infer a similar interpretation of *clêr* in GDG 85 (see pp. 32–4 below).

so that its assumed semantic development may actually have occurred during the course of that century.

Despite the rather loose application of the term *clêr* to certain fourteenth-century satirical poets, there is no indisputable evidence of their verse before the latter part of the fifteenth century.[8] This lack of concrete evidence is hardly surprising given the selective nature of the manuscript tradition, and even less so when one considers the exclusivity and fierce pride of the official bardic order. Bardic verse was highly formalized in style and content, a strict alliterative verse boasting a wealth of acquired lore and technical expertise which was passed on to each generation of pupils. The Welsh court poets and their successors, the *Cywyddwyr*, regarded themselves as guardians of an essentially aristocratic tradition which stretched back to the days of Taliesin in the sixth century, and as such they had to be seen to regard the relatively unsophisticated pronouncements of mere minstrels with suitable disdain. There can be little doubt that a vigorous popular verse tradition once formed part of the rich oral and, therefore, sub-literary culture of medieval Wales. One need only consult the work of the twelfth-century cleric Giraldus Cambrensis to realize that even the anonymous common folk had their own songs which were a natural accompaniment to everyday life. One reads, for instance, that the people of Wales and the north of England (across the Humber and in Yorkshire) used to sing in harmony,[9] though we can only guess at the nature of these songs. And although the *Clêr* are known to have been entertainers at court and at the homes of noblemen as well as at the humble market-place, it was inevitable that their once-vibrant songs should suffer the same fate as the folk-poetry of the period.

The laws of Hywel Dda, originally codified in the tenth century but the earliest manuscript versions of which date from the twelfth and thirteenth centuries, speak of three kinds of poet: *pencerdd* (*musicus primarius* or *princeps poetarum*), *bardd teulu*, and *cerddor*

---

[8] The rather artless eulogies and request poems of the late-15th-cent. poet Y Nant (or 'Dafydd Nant'), contained in Peniarth MS 54, i, are clearly not the work of a qualified bard. Some of these have been edited by G. J. Williams, 'Cerddi'r Nant', *BBCS* 17 (1957), 77–89. His important cursing poem is discussed in Ch. 2 below.

[9] Lewis Thorpe (trans.), *The Journey Through Wales and The Description of Wales* (Harmondsworth, 1978), 242. On the 'rich tradition of popular songs' which must have existed in Europe from an early time, see Peter Dronke's introduction to his *The Medieval Lyric* (London, 1968), 13 ff.

(*joculator*).[10] It appears that a bard became a *pencerdd* by winning a chair in a poetic contest, and this gave him the right to take pupils, who were allowed to solicit within his territory only with his permission. The *pencerdd* was head of the bardic guild in his particular area, and thus his status at court was not as one of the twenty-four court officers but as a guest of honour. As the power of the political units, especially that of Gwynedd, increased in the time of the so-called *Gogynfeirdd* or Poets of the Princes, it seems that the *penceirddiaid* were gradually drawn into the ruling hierarchies, taking, as it were, honorary posts at the royal courts. There were still presumably *penceirddiaid* who functioned independently within the bardic community, though they are likely to have become fewer with the growth of central authority. It was the *pencerdd*'s duty to present two poems, 'the first to God and the second to the king'. The third song was to be sung by the *bardd teulu* or Household Bard, who is named as a court officer. He should also sing 'Unbeiniaeth Prydein' ('The Chieftainship of Britain') when the king's followers prepared for battle, and if he sang to them during a raid he was entitled to the finest beast. His other function was to entertain the queen 'in a quiet voice, so as not to disturb the court', and according to the Demetian version of the laws three songs should be sung to her in her own room (which accounts for the name *bardd stafell* in one of the Latin texts). It would appear, then, that the status of the *bardd teulu* diminished as a result of the increased importance of the *pencerdd* at the royal court. The king's following is said to consist of thirty-six men on horseback—namely, his twenty-four official ministers and twelve guests—as well as his retinue, noblemen, servants, dependants, and *cerddorion*. Here, as elsewhere, this term is rendered in the Latin texts as *joculatores*. The context of the Latin word in most cases clearly shows that it is used as a generic term for poets and musicians, rather than in the more specific sense of 'jester' or 'buffoon',[11] so that there is no reason to identify these poets with

---

[10] For a summary and evaluation of references to the bardic hierarchy in the legal tracts see, in particular, Dafydd Jenkins, 'Pencerdd a Bardd Teilu', *YB* 14 (1988), 19–46; also id. (ed. and trans.), *The Law of Hywel Dda* (Llandysul, 1990), 8–10, 20, 38–40; Stephen J. Williams and J. Enoch Powell (eds.), *Llyfr Blegywryd* (Cardiff, 1942), pp. xxvi–xxviii; J. E. Caerwyn Williams, 'Beirdd Y Tywysogion: Arolwg', *LlC* 11 (1970–1), 30 ff.; id., 'Cerdd a Phencerdd', *LlC* 16 (1990–1), 205–11.

[11] The term is used with its familiar pejorative connotation by Giraldus Cambrensis of the monks of Canterbury, whom he criticizes for being over-expressive, as if they were 'ad ludos scenicos aut inter histriones et joculatores' (J. S. Brewer (ed.), *Giraldi*

the inferior class of minstrels known in the fourteenth century as *Clêr*.[12] All that we can reasonably deduce is that they were one of three kinds of poet officially recognized at the royal court, of more humble status than the *pencerdd*, who was entitled to a payment of twenty-four pennies from each *cerddor* upon completion of his training. Yet in one instance the Latin *joculator* corresponds to the term *croessan* in all three Welsh versions, which is cognate with and probably derived from Irish *crosán* (buffoon). It is stated that the chief groom should present each horse given by the king, and for each he shall receive four pennies, except three: those given to the household priest and the court judge: '. . . a'r hwnn a rodher y'r croessaeneit (canys rwymaw troet kebystyr hwnnw a wneir wrth y dwygeill, ac velly y rodir).'[13] ('. . . and that given to the *croesaniaid*, for the end of its tether should be tied to its testicles, and it is thus that it is given.') This would appear to be related to the ribald nature of the *croesan*'s particular brand of entertainment, though his repertoire may have included the kind of satirical or scurrilous verse associated with his Irish counterparts as well as the clowning and mimicry which one usually identifies with a court jester.

In stark contrast to the frequent allusions to the *Clêr* from the fourteenth century onwards, when the bardic order had lost its former legal status with the disappearance of the royal house of Gwynedd, references to itinerant minstrels are few and far between in the work of the Poets of the Princes. There would be little reason for the court bard, secure in his standing, and in the knowledge of his innate superiority, to tarnish his eulogy, elegy, or religious verse with the mention of such lowly rhymesters. However, in the few instances that have been preserved there is no mistaking that implacable arrogance which, in the wake of the Conquest, turns to scorn and vituperation as the professional bards are challenged from below in their quest for noble patronage. In the early twelfth century Meilyr, generally regarded as

Cambrensis: Opera, Rolls Series 21, London, 1861, i. 51). On this type of entertainer see J. D. A. Ogilvy, 'Mimi, Scurrae, Histriones: Entertainers of the Early Middle Ages', *Speculum*, 38 (1963), 603–19; E. Faral, *Les Jongleurs en France au Moyen Âge* (Paris, 1910); J. Southworth, *The English Medieval Minstrel* (Woodbridge, 1989).

[12] *Gogynfeirdd* usage shows *cerddor* to be a term for poets and/or musicians in general. For examples see D. J. Bowen, 'Y Cywyddwyr a'r Noddwyr Cynnar', *YB* 11 (1979), 82–3.

[13] *Llyfr Blegywryd*, 19.7–10. The passage is discussed by Brinley Rees, 'Tair Cymhariaeth', *BBCS* 28 (1979), 390–1, where it is suggested that the custom may originally have been part of a fertility rite, which would provide a parallel for one of the likely functions of the Irish *crosán*.

the first of the *Gogynfeirdd* whose work has been preserved, speaks haughtily, it appears, of 'manfeirdd' ('minor' or 'worthless poets') and 'cychwilfeirdd' ('wandering poets'), a term which calls to mind Cynddelw's 'treiglfeirdd' a generation later.[14] In the early thirteenth century two *awdlau* or odes composed by Phylip Brydydd to Lord Rhys Ieuanc (d. 1222) at Llanbadarn Fawr, discuss a contention between the *pencerdd* himself and poets of an inferior status as to who should first present a poem on Christmas Day. The headings of the poems in the Hendregadredd manuscript refer to Phylip's adversaries as 'beird ysbydeit', and 'gofeird yspydeit',[15] poetasters, and the bard himself refers twice to 'gofeird', and also to 'geuueird' and 'gwagueird', 'vain' or 'empty poets'. It might conceivably be a question of a contest with lesser poets within the bardic order, possibly pupils, especially as Phylip speaks of a dispute between young and old, 'heneint ac yeuegtyt'. His terminology and tone, however, are those of a superior bard dealing with lowly minstrels, and the phrase 'y gofeird ar beird' ('the rhymesters and the poets') in the second *awdl*, is reminiscent of distinctions such as 'y beirdd a'r glêr' in the following centuries. Significantly, during the course of this poem he invokes the authority of 'hengerd telessin', 'the ancient verse of Taliesin', protesting that no man has the right to deprive the bard of God's gift ('diwreinaw dawn duw nyt dyn ae med').[16] This concept of divine inspiration as the sole privilege of the *pencerdd*, along with the bards' traditional learning and exclusive knowledge, was to be reiterated

[14] *H* 6.1; 4.1; *GCBM* 11.75. Cf. the reference in the third branch of the *Mabinogi* (composed *c*.1050–1120) to a clerk (*yscolheic*) who has been singing in England, where he received a pound for begging (*cardotta*): Ifor Williams (ed.), *Pedeir Keinc y Mabinogi* (Cardiff, 1930), 61–2. The editor identifies this poet with the *clerici vagantes*, the Latin wandering scholars of medieval Europe (ibid. 245); cf. his remarks in 'Dafydd ap Gwilym a'r Glêr', 157–8.

[15] *H* 226–9; cf. *H* 208.2 (Llywelyn Fardd, *fl. c*.1230–80). John Davies's *Dictionarium Duplex* (1632) gives 'Beirdd ysbyddaid, Poëtæ parasitici' (s.v. *Ysbyddad*); cf. also the spurious triad: 'Tri chorn enllib ac athrawd: puten pen fordd [*sic*], bardd yspyddaid, a meddwyn' (*MA* 901). R. Geraint Gruffydd regards the poems of Phylip Brydydd as an indication of a thriving sub-literary tradition in Deheubarth throughout the Middle Ages ('The Early Court Poetry of South West Wales', *SC* 14/15 (1979–80), 101).

[16] *H* 228.25. Cf. *H* 229.13–16, where Phylip boasts that his inspiration, the bardic *awen*, will never fail him. T. Gwynn Jones argues in the context of these poems, which he somewhat fancifully interprets as 'important evidence of the struggle between the bards and the romancers in the thirteenth century', that the Christianization of the bardic order, apparent in the legal definition of the *pencerdd*'s duties, caused the inferior poets to be despised for their satire and untruth, earlier material being 'tolerated only as the mere buffoonery of the Clerwyr' ('Bardism and Romance: A Study of the Welsh Literary Tradition', *THSC* (1913–14), 290–8).

many times by the upholders of the professional hierarchy in the post-Conquest period in order to distinguish themselves from the *Clêr* and the various other popular entertainers of medieval Wales.

The *awdlau* of Phylip Brydydd are significant in that they suggest that minor poets, as did the *croesaniaid*, had the privilege of appearing at court along with the established bards and that, by the early thirteenth century, at least, there was a certain interaction between poets from very different backgrounds. Entertainment at court and in the noble halls was doubtless more varied and colourful than is suggested by the stately and rather monochrome *awdlau* of the period. The *pencerdd*, for all his aloofness, could not fail to rub shoulders with other kinds of entertainers, a point which is vividly grasped by Chotzen in his fascinating study of the poetry of Dafydd ap Gwilym. The princes, he suggests, having listened with interest and no little pride to the stately and artistically accomplished *awdlau* performed in their honour, would sometimes feel the need for entertainment of a lighter nature; they would then call the *croesaniaid* with their 'vulgar farces', and the *clerwyr*, who might 'satirize their host's enemies or insult one another to the great delight of the noble audience'.[17] Taking the thesis a step further, D. J. Bowen, having alluded to the work of Phylip Brydydd, remarks that 'before the end of the festivities, and as the evenings drew to a close, it is likely that each grade within the poetic brotherhood would have become intermingled'.[18] Though it would perhaps be unwise to over-emphasize such interaction in the *Gogynfeirdd* period, the process would certainly have been accelerated after 1282.

The scant evidence surveyed so far affords little insight into the sub-literary entertainment of pre-Conquest Wales. It may, however, be instructive to compare the more detailed and suggestive evidence of early Irish literature, if only for two reasons. First, the Irish court bards, like their Welsh counterparts, belonged to a closed corporation which prided itself on its status, tradition, and learning. But as Proinsias MacCana has pointed out, particularly from the ninth century onwards: 'The learned ascendancy was always keenly sensitive to any danger of professional competition from the lower orders of poets and entertainers',[19] a danger which, in the Welsh context, is

---

[17] *Recherches*, 156.   [18] 'Y Cywyddwyr', 77.
[19] 'The Rise of the Later Schools of Filidheacht', *Ériu*, 25 (1974), 138 n. 47. On the various grades of poets in early and medieval Ireland see Liam Breatnach, *Uraicecht na Ríar: The Poetic Grades in Early Irish Law* (Dublin, 1987).

more immediately relevant to the post-Conquest period. Secondly, it has been seen that the word *croesan* probably derives from Irish, and that the term *clêr* is itself likely to be an Irish borrowing, possibly dating from the time of Gruffudd ap Cynan. In sixteenth-century Wales, at least, there was a strong tradition which maintained that when Gruffudd landed from Ireland in 1075 and again in 1081 he brought with him musicians and poets, and authorized a revision in the arts of poetry and music. This is presented as fact in the document known as 'Statud Gruffudd ap Cynan', which was drawn up in 1522 in preparation for the first Caerwys eisteddfod in the following year.[20] Its chief purpose was to regulate the activities of poets and musicians, and it is in order to lend weight to its largely fictional account of the bardic tradition that it appeals to the authority of Gruffudd and other Welsh princes and lords from the eleventh to the fourteenth centuries. It is A. O. H. Jarman's opinion that the host which accompanied Gruffudd from Ireland would almost certainly have included artists as well as soldiers, and that, in any case, the circumstances of his reign favoured Irish influence whether the 'statute' is to be believed or not.[21] He shows too that, mainly through the intermediacy of the Church, literary relations between the two countries had existed since the latter centuries of the Dark Ages, though it cannot be proven that Irish poets or musicians visited Wales in that period.

The functions of the Irish *crosán* are of particular interest since it is implied in the laws of Hywel Dda that his Welsh counterpart was an entertainer at the royal courts. In Irish sources the *crosán* is usually connected with other minor poets and minstrels in the chieftain's court. In the Latin originals on which some of the Irish saints' lives are based the word that corresponds most frequently to *crosán* is *scurra*, meaning 'a buffoon, a jester', especially a professional jester, a word which is also used to gloss Irish *drúth* and *óinmhid*, which both have the meaning of 'jester, buffoon or idiot'. As Alan Harrison has shown, in one instance it is the Latin *praeco* ('a herald, a crier') which corresponds to *crosán*, and a *praeco*, as well as leading church processions, could in fact take part in 'pantomime-type entertainments' along with

---

[20] A text of the 'Statute' has been edited by Thomas Parry, 'Statud Gruffudd ap Cynan', *BBCS* 5 (1929), 25–33. See also T. Gwynn Jones's introduction to *Gwaith Tudur Aled*, vol. 1 (Cardiff, 1926), pp. xxix–xxxvi.

[21] 'Telyn a Chrwth', *LlC* 6 (1960–1), 170; cf. D. Simon Evans, *Historia Gruffud vab Kenan* (Cardiff, 1977), pp. lix ff.

the *scurra*. He concludes that: 'The *crosán/scurra/praeco* was therefore probably cognate with the *mimi/histriones/menestrelli* (and *scurrae*) that were to be found in other countries and towards whom the church authorities often had an ambivalent attitude.'[22] In an attempt to explain the attitude of the Church, Harrison suggests a role for the early crosáns and other popular entertainers who were 'already anathema to the church' as representatives of the devil and the powers of evil in medieval religious drama. In support of this theory, he goes on to infer from various sources a strong connection with primitive drama, which would be in keeping with the traditional image of the *crosán* as a mimic or buffoon. These include references to features such as long shaggy hair, blackened faces, and head-dress, which find striking parallels in surviving popular customs, such as those enacted by the biddyboys, mayboys, and wrenboys. The first carry a straw effigy of a cross (or a saint), and in all cases disguise, demonic character, and general horseplay and misrule are prominent. The occurrence of these activities on calendar days and at rites of passage certainly suggests an origin in ancient ritual, in which the powers of evil and chaos might have been expiated through enactment by special entertainers, though with the passing of time the humorous antics of the buffoon would have been stripped of their symbolic function.

A triad from the Yellow Book of Lecan which states that: 'A *crosán* is identified by three things, a stretched mouth, a stretched stomach, and a stretched bag',[23] is reminiscent of the kind of dwelling on sexual organs and the like as a source of vulgar humour which has already been encountered in the brief reference to the *croesan* in the Welsh laws. (The first feature seems to refer to abuse, possibly in the form of verse, while the second implies gluttony and physical grotesqueness.) Certain texts imply that the *crosán* was

---

[22] 'Tricksters and Entertainers in the Irish Tradition', *Proceedings of the First North American Congress of Celtic Studies*, Ottawa, 1986 (Ottawa, 1988), 293–307. He disputes the conventional explanation of the term *crosán* (first suggested by J. H. Todd in *The Irish Version of the Historia Brittonum of Nennius* (Dublin, 1848), 182 n.), namely that the *crosáns* were originally cross-bearers in religious ceremonies who also satirized those who incurred church censure. He believes this to be based solely on the sense of *praeco* as a leader of church processions, and suggests, rather, that the crosáns (< Lat. *crux*) 'could have "borrowed" the cross in their activities as a pagan/secular reaction to the missionary church or there may already have been the form of the cross in their activities, either in their dancing or other antics, or in the form of an artifact that they used as part of their entertainment' (pp. 299–300). For a more detailed study see Harrison's *An Chrosántacht* (Dublin, 1979).

[23] 'tréde neimhthigedar crossán: rige óile, rige théighe, rige bronn' (R. Atkinson, *The Yellow Book of Lecan*, facsimile (Dublin, 1896), 416).

expected to perform other forms of entertainment as well as buffoonery and abuse. In the tale known as *Séanadh Saighre* it is said
that 'nine shaggy jet-black crosáns came and they were chanting over
the grave as is the custom of crosáns from that time',[24] and that this
performance consisted of 'duan agus oirfideadh', verse and minstrelsy. The *crosán*'s verse was, no doubt, for the most part satirical
or, at least, of a scurrilous nature. A passage from the eleventh-
century saga *Immram Ua Corra* (The Voyage of the Ui Corra)[25] is
even more enlightening. Here, the jester or clown (*fuirseoir*) from a
troupe of crosáns, having abandoned his distinctive costume (possibly worn by each member of the group), goes on a pilgrimage during which he provides entertainment (*oirfideadh*) which, according to
Harrison, may be rendered as 'minstrelsy', and 'probably incorporated music, storytelling, dancing, singing and perhaps, juggling and
acrobatics'. Although little is known of many of the minor professional minstrels of medieval Ireland, the list provided by Harrison
makes interesting reading. He enumerates the *glámh* (lampooner),
the *cáinte* and *bancháinte* (satirist and female satirist), *drúth*,
óinmhid (both jesters or buffoons), *mear* (fool), *cornaire* (piper),
fuirseoir (clown), *cearrbhach* (gambler), *geocach* (jester), and *crosán*.
He notes, however, that in his opinion each of these names refers to
a certain kind of entertainment rather than to any strict categories,
and that: 'Any single entertainer or troupe of entertainers could be
expected to be proficient in one or more of these elements.'[26]

The diversity of non-bardic entertainment in medieval Ireland,
then, is well attested, and it appears that the repertoire of the *crosán*
was varied to a degree hardly imaginable from the fleeting reference
to the Welsh *croesan* in the laws of Hywel Dda. Although we cannot assume that each type of minstrel mentioned here necessarily had
its counterpart across the water, it is reasonable to postulate that a

[24] 'táncatar nōnbhar crosān ciabhach cīrdhubh co mbātar forsan uaigh ac
cliaraighecht amhail is bēs do chrosánaibh ó sin anall' (A. Harrison (ed.), 'Séanadh
Saighre', *Éigse*, 20 (1984), 142).

[25] Whitley Stokes (ed. and trans.), 'The Voyage of the Húi Corra', *Revue Celtique*,
14 (1893), 38–40. Harrison argues that the passage connects the *crosán* with various
other itinerant professionals such as story-tellers, gamblers, tradesmen, and prosti-
tutes. ('Tricksters and Entertainers', 301).

[26] Ibid. 298. Compare the tale *Togail Bruidne Dá Derga*, which contains references
not only to court harpers and poets (*filed*), but also to 'the chief juggler (*rígdruith*) of
the King of Tara', 'the King's three conjurers' (*clesamnach*), his 'three lampooners'
(*anmed*), 'the King of Erin's three jesters' (*fursiri*), and 'the nine pipers' (*cuslennach*)
(W. Stokes (ed. and trans.), 'The Destruction of Dá Derga's Hostel', *Revue Celtique*,
22 (1901), 9–61, *passim*).

similar diversity would have been an inherent part of courtly and popular entertainment at this time, despite the silence of Welsh texts on the subject in the pre-Conquest period. At a major festival, such as the so-called eisteddfod reputed to have been held by Lord Rhys in his newly built castle at Cardigan during Christmas in 1176, there would surely have been performers other than the bards and the harpists, crowthers, and pipers who are said in the manuscripts to have competed for chairs.[27] In an albeit late account of doubtful authenticity, there is indeed mention of such a festival, namely that said to have been held by Gruffudd ap Rhys at Ystrad Tywi about the year 1135:

Gwedi adynnill ei diroedd fe wnaeth Gruffydd ab Rhŷs wledd anrhydeddus yn Ystrad Tywi . . . a pharattoi pob moethus o fwydydd a diodydd, a phob ymryson doethineb, a phob diddanwch cerdd arwest a cherdd dannau, a chroesawi [sic] prydyddion a cherddorion, a chynnal pob chwareuon hud a lledrith, a phob arddangos, a phob campau gwrolion . . .[28]

(Having regained his lands, Gruffydd ap Rhys held a magnificent feast at Ystrad Tywi . . . and all manner of fine food and drink were prepared, contests of intellect, harp-playing and other musical entertainment; poets and musicians were invited, and various plays of sorcery and illusion were held, along with representations and feats of strength.)

Whether this is fact or fiction, it is quite likely that such gatherings, encompassing the whole spectrum of medieval entertainment, from *pencerdd* and rhymester to juggler and acrobat to 'plays of sorcery and illusion, representations and feats of strength', were not uncommon in medieval Wales. A century-and-a-half later an account of payments for Edward I's entertainments in 1284 states that 10s. was paid to the 1,000 Welsh minstrels who visited the king and queen at Overton (compared with the more generous sum of 20s. paid to Sir Thomas de Clare's organist, and 1 mark to his Tom Fool).[29] Were we to come across an account of the nature of these minstrels' activ-

---

[27] On the tradition concerning this festival see J. E. Caerwyn Williams, 'Aberteifi 1176', *Taliesin*, 32 (July 1976), 30–5.

[28] Cited by T. Gwynn Jones, 'Bardism and Romance', 226 n. 2, from the so-called 'Gwentian Brut' (published by the Camb. Arch. Assoc., 1863). Cf. the 'wrestlings and miracle plays' which are denounced in England around 1300 as being harmful to fields and crops (R. M. Wilson, *The Lost Literature of Medieval England* (London, 1952), 227.

[29] A. J. Taylor, 'A Fragment of a *Dona* Account of 1284', *BBCS* 27 (1977), 253–4. See also Constance Bullock-Davies, 'Welsh Minstrels at the Courts of Edward I and Edward II', *THSC* (1972–3), 104–22; id., *Menestrellorum Multitudo: Minstrels at a Royal Feast* (Cardiff, 1978), esp. 68 ff.

ities, we might well recognize the same kind of wide-ranging entertainment as has been seen to exist in medieval Ireland.

These anonymous minstrels stand at the beginning of the next period under review, which opens with the English conquest of 1282–3. The closing years of the thirteenth century provide no certain references to poets or minstrels of inferior status, but by the fourteenth century learned texts, secular and religious, as well as the work of the bards themselves, are more enlightening. The terms *clêr*, *clerwr*, *clerwriaeth*, and the like appear for the first time, though it is difficult to date the earliest instances with any certainty. The singular form *clerwr*, along with the abstract noun *clerwriaeth*, are prominent in the Bardic Grammar believed to have been compiled or edited by Einion Offeiriad (Einion the Priest) around 1330.[30] At roughly the same period the collective noun *clêr* and derivative forms appear in verse. In the Grammar, at least, the terms used display none of the ambiguity of meaning which is often found in bardic verse from the fourteenth century onwards. Its terminology refers explicitly to an inferior class of poets or entertainers, never to 'poets in general'.

The first of three key passages, which occurs, with minor variations, in all three of the earliest manuscripts,[31] is taken here from the Red Book of Hergest:

Teir keing yssyd o gerd dafawt, nyt amgen, klerwryaeth, teulwryaeth, a phrydydyaeth. Teir keing a berthynant ar glerwryaeth: ymsennu, ac ymdaualu geir tra geir, a danwaret. Teir keing ereill a berthynant ar teulwryaeth: testunyaw, ac ymdyualu gwers tra gwers, a gorderchgerd o gywydeu teulueid drwy eireu amwys. Teir keing ereill a berthynant ar brydydyaeth: eglynyon, ac odleu, a chywydeu kerdwryeid, anhawd eu kanyat a'e dechymic. (*GP* 6.34–41)

(There are three branches of poetry, namely, *clerwriaeth*, *teuluwriaeth*, and *prydyddiaeth*. There are three branches belonging to *clerwriaeth*: lampooning, descriptive abuse in alternate lines (?), and mimicry. There are three other branches belonging to *teuluwriaeth*: ridiculing, descriptive abuse in alternate stanzas (?), and love-poems in the *cywydd* metre composed in the

[30] On the dating of the Grammar see J. Beverley Smith, 'Einion Offeiriad', *BBCS* 20 (1964), 339–47.

[31] Jesus 1 (the Red Book of Hergest), Llanstephan 3, and Peniarth 20. These versions, along with various later grammars, have been edited by G. J. Williams and E. J. Jones, *Gramadegau'r Penceirddiaid* (Cardiff, 1934). The other early text of the Grammar, the incomplete version of Bangor MS 1, is edited by John T. Jones in *BBCS* 2 (1925), 186–200.

manner of the *teuluwr*, with verbal conceits. There are three other branches belonging to *prydyddiaeth*: *englynion*, *awdlau*, and intricate *cywyddau*, of difficult composition and invention.)

It is immediately apparent that the compiler has adopted the same kind of tripartite structure as that implied by the laws of Hywel Dda. It appears that the term *prydydd* has been substituted for *pencerdd*, *teuluwr* for *bardd teulu*, and *clerwr* perhaps for *cerddor* or *croesan*. Such a dogmatic partitioning of poetic functions makes one wary of accepting the Grammar as an accurate reflection of contemporary practice, just as the precepts of the laws are not fully relevant to *Gogynfeirdd* poetry. This view is confirmed by a glance at the work of the fourteenth-century *Cywyddwyr*, where vicious satire, the love theme, and great technical complexity exist side by side; indeed, they are often intertwined. Besides, the term *teuluwr* is often applied by these poets to themselves and to each other, along with the more common labels of *prydydd*, *pencerdd*, and the like.[32] That there was any significant distinction between the functions of *prydydd* and *teuluwr* by the fourteenth century is unlikely. The close connection between the two disciplines is, in fact, apparent in the Grammar itself, where it is stated that it is proper for the *prydydd* to involve himself with *teuluwriaeth* as distinct from mere *clerwriaeth* since, unlike the latter, it is reducible to rule; moreover, it is implied in the same passage that the *prydydd* is the teacher of the *teuluwr*.[33]

As regards the functions of these poets as defined in this section of the Grammar, it may be noted that the kind of 'ymddyfalu' associated with *teuluwriaeth* is apparently more complex than that of *clerwriaeth*, and that 'testunio', as opposed to 'ymsennu', appears to represent a legitimate form of satire in the compiler's view. In later sources the term is associated with the abuse of a *pencerdd* by other accomplished poets, a bizarre practice connected chiefly with wedding feasts. It was the custom on these occasions that the satire should be patently untrue, and thus a source of humour rather than injury, and it will be seen in the next chapter that some fourteenth-century satire is probably comprised of this type of verse, as well as

[32] See Dafydd Johnston's discussion of *teuluwr*/*teuluwas*, GIG, p. 308. To the examples noted there may be added Iolo's description of Ithel Ddu as a *teuluwr* (GIG XXXVI.6); GDG 31.52, 56 (of Madog Benfras and of DG's companions or fellow poets); GDG 55.9 (DG of himself).

[33] GP 35.15–17; cf. ibid. 57.3–7 and 133.21–2. Cf. also Iolo Goch's elegy to Llywelyn Goch Amheurig Hen—'Nis gŵyr Duw am deuluwas, | Yn athro grym aeth i'r gras' (GIG XXII. 9–10), and see Johnston's note, p. 308.

genuine attacks on the lowly *Clêr*. The Grammar does not condemn satire as such, as long as it is skilfully expressed in bardic style, never combined with praise or addressed to 'that which is good'.[34] The 'ymsennu' attributed to *clerwriaeth* is no doubt meant to convey reciprocal abuse of the most disreputable and indiscriminate kind.[35] The phrase 'ymdaualu geir tra geir' is less clear. It is perhaps best interpreted as a form of descriptive vituperative verse, possibly akin to riddling, in the form of lampooning contests between two or more poets.[36] 'Danwaret' is also problematic. The term has been explained as referring to the mimicry of a buffoon or to play-acting, which are both quite feasible given the compiler's apparent wish to associate the *Clêr* with the most disreputable kinds of entertainers. But since this passage is concerned specifically with poetry (*cerdd dafod*), the sense of 'mocking verse' is perhaps nearer the mark.[37]

The compiler's intention of vilifying the *Clêr* as a class unworthy of bardic status is more clearly illustrated in the following passage, which (again with slight variations) forms part of the 'Trioedd Cerdd' (Triads of Poetry) section in the Red Book of Hergest and the Llanstephan 3 manuscript. Once more, it is the Red Book version which is given here:

---

[34] 'Mydr neu brydyat yw kyuansodyat ymadrodyon kyfyawn o eireu adurn arderchawc . . . a arwydockaont molyant neu ogan, a hynny ar gerd dafawt ganmoledic' (*GP* 6.31–4; cf. ibid. 15.4–5; 16.30–1; 148). Cf. also Gruffudd Gryg's preference of DG's 'dychan glanbryd' to the praise of others (*DGG* LXXXII.9–10).

[35] In *BDG* CLXV.27 'ymsenu' describes an argument between a hag and the poet's beloved.

[36] One of the meanings of *dyfalu* was 'to mock, deride, ridicule, mimic; call names, nickname' (*GPC* 1122); cf. Madog Benfras in 'Cywydd yr Halaenwr' (*DGG* LXXIX.31–4):

> Cyfodi rhifedi rhaith   Yr iangwyr anwreangwaith.
> Cynhafal fy nyfalu   Cyfarth lef cŵn buarth lu.

Dyfalu was also used for the *Cywyddwyr*'s characteristic descriptive device consisting of a cumulative sequence of metaphors and similes, often in a satirical context. The relationship between this device and both bardic satire and riddling is discussed in Ch. 4 below.

[37] Ifor Williams asks: 'Pa enw gwell ellid gael ar *play acting* na "dynwared"?' and adds: 'Am y ddwy gainc arall o glerwriaeth, "ymsennu" ac "ymddyfalu gair tragair", cyfeiriant hwythau hefyd at gellwair y *buffoons*, neu'r croesaniaid, yn gwaradwyddo ei gilydd i greu chwerthin ymhlith yr ynfyd: gwaith *clowns*, neu ffyliaid ffair' ('Dafydd ap Gwilym a'r Glêr', 156). Chotzen compares *danwaret* with the imitation of animal noises practised by some of the less sophisticated entertainers of medieval France (*Recherches*, 70 n. 5); for a similar practice in 14th-cent. England see Richard Barber, *The Life and Campaigns of the Black Prince* (Woodbridge, 1986), 85.

Tri ryw gerdwr yssyd: clerwr, teuluwr, a phrydyd.

Tri pheth a berthynant ar glerwr: ymbil, a goganu, a gwarthrudaw.

Tri pheth a berthynant ar deuluwr: kyuanhedu, a haelyoni, ac eruyn da yn deulueid heb rwy ymbil amdanaw.

Tri pheth a berthynant ar brydyd: clotuori, a digryfhau, a gwrthneu gogangerd. (*GP* 17.6–12)

(There are three kinds of poet: *clerwr*, *teuluwr* and *prydydd*.

There are three things which become a *clerwr*: begging, and satire, and defamation.

There are three things which become a *teuluwr*: entertainment, generosity, and soliciting money in the manner of the *teuluwr* (i.e. pleasantly?) without excessive begging.

There are three things which become a *prydydd*: praise, the bringing of pleasure, and the refusal of satire.)

Vulgar satire, then, along with what appears to be a rather unsubtle form of begging poem, is again presented as the preserve of the *clerwr*, and is expressly forbidden to the *prydydd*. One is inevitably reminded of the groups of minstrels in medieval Ireland which specialized in lampoon and satire, which again raises the question whether the compiler is deliberately identifying the *Clêr* in general with a particularly disreputable class of minstrels in order to dissipate their threat to the established bardic order. This may be the reason for the very inclusion of the *Clêr* in an essentially artificial hierarchy, alongside, but greatly inferior to, the qualified poets, and presented in such a light as to make competition with these bards for noble patronage seem close to blasphemy. It will become apparent that the bards' bitterly hostile reaction to the *Clêr* from this period onwards does imply that the threat presented by these minstrels to their innate sense of superiority was in fact very real following the loss of royal patronage.[38] One would, therefore, expect that *Clêr* poetry boasted subject-matter other than satire, vituperation, and begging poems. It may have included an alternative form of eulogy more akin to Dafydd ap Gwilym's innovative *cywyddau* to Ifor Hael of Glamorgan than to the majestic *awdl*, which still flourished in the fourteenth century but was more in keeping with the courtly ceremony of days gone by than with the relative intimacy of the *uchelwr*,

---

[38] On the crisis facing the bardic order in the post-Conquest period, and on the intermingling of various grades of poets, see in particular Ceri W. Lewis, 'The Content of Poetry and the Crisis in the Bardic Tradition', in Jarman and Hughes (eds.), *A Guide to Welsh Literature*, vol. 2 (Swansea, 1979), 189 ff.

or nobleman's, hall.[39] The repertoires of some of these poets may
also have included more diverting elements such as love-poems,
accounts of humorous incidents, drinking-songs, and the like—
cruder, less artistically accomplished expressions of some of the
themes which provide much of the freshness and vitality of early
cywydd poetry.

The third of the key passages from the Grammar, which is
strangely lacking in the Red Book version, is taken here from
Llanstephan 3:

Ni pherthyn ar brydyd ymyru ar glerwryaeth, er aruer ohoni, kanys gwrth-
wneb yw y greffteu prydyd. Kanys ar glerwr y perthyn goganu, ac agloduori,
a gwneuthur kewilid a gwaradwyd, ac ar prydyd y perthyn kanmawl, a chlo-
duori, a gwneuthur clod, a llewenyd, a gogonyant. A chyda hynny, ny ellir
dosparth ar glerwryaeth, kanys kerd anosparthus yw, ac am hynny, nac
ymyred prydyd yndi . . . trech y dyly vod molyangerd prydyd no gogangerd
klerwr. Swynogleu, a dewindabaeth, a chwaryeu hudolyaeth, ny rwy berthyn
ar prydyd ymyru yndunt, nac arver ohanunt. Hengerd, ac ystoryaeu
yscriuenedic . . . da yw y prydyd eu gwybod . . . Kanys kyffran o doethineb
anianawl yw prydydyaeth, ac o'r Yspryt Glan y pan henyw, a'e hawen a
geffir o ethrylith a cheluydyd aruer. (GP 35.9–26)

(The *prydydd* should not dabble in *clerwriaeth*, in order to practise it, since
it is contrary to the skills of the *prydydd*. For it becomes the *clerwr* to satirize, defame, and bring shame and dishonour, while it becomes the *prydydd*
to commend and eulogize, and to bring praise and mirth and glory.
Moreover, *clerwriaeth* is not reducible to rule, for it is a disorderly art, and
thus a *prydydd* should not involve himself with it . . . the eulogy of a *prydydd* should be superior to the satire of a *clerwr*. Charms, divination, and
plays of magic—it does not become the *prydydd* to dabble in these, or to
practise them. Ancient verse, and written tales . . . it is good that a *prydydd*
should be conversant with these . . . For *prydyddiaeth* is a portion of natural wisdom, and emanates from the Holy Spirit, and its inspiration stems
from ingenuity and artistic assiduousness.)

The author proceeds to list the seven virtues which characterize the
prydydd, and the 'Seven Deadly Sins' which defile the inspiration of
his art ('a lygrant awen prydydaeth'), by implication the distinguish-
ing marks of the *clerwr*.

Besides the usual allusions to abuse and satire, then, the *clerwr* is
associated here, again implicitly, with 'charms, divination, and plays

---

[39] Cf. the relatively informal and often humorous eulogies and begging-poems of
the 15th-cent. *clerwr* Y Nant, referred to above, n. 8.

of magic'. Once more, in the absence of any explanatory detail, the terminology used is difficult to decipher. T. Gwynn Jones[40] has suggested a connection between these 'charms' and a repetitive, almost incantatory cursing-poem composed by a *clerwr* known as 'Y Nant' in the late fifteenth century. For 'plays of magic', which resembles the phrase 'chwareuon hud a lledrith' cited above in the account of the festival reputed to have been held at Ystrad Tywi in 1135, he suggests the meaning of 'miracle plays'.[41] Whatever the precise meaning, the general context of magic, which is no doubt condemned as a survival of the old paganism, points to forms of entertainment which have little to do with poetry, and it appears that the *Clêr* are again associated with certain groups of disreputable entertainers. The reference to the Holy Spirit as the source of the *prydydd*'s inspiration[42] is familiar enough, and the allusion to 'Hengerdd' ('early poetry'), which harks back to Taliesin at the dawn of the bardic tradition, further sets him apart from the uncultured *clerwr*. The most striking divergence in the Peniarth 20 version of the passage is the substitution of the term 'klerwr kroessan' twice for 'clerwr' (though the latter also occurs), and of 'croessangerd' for 'gogangerd' ('mocking verse').[43] It has been shown that this text was written in the mid- or late fourteenth century, while the Red Book and Llanstephan 3 belong to *c.* 1400 and Bangor 1 to the mid-fifteenth century.[44] Though all these versions are ultimately based on a common prototype, it may be that some of the significant variants in Peniarth 20 reflect the insecurity of the bardic order at the time of its composition. It is curious that the invention of three new *awdl* metres is attributed in the Red Book and Llanstephan 3 to Einion Offeiriad, who flourished in the first quarter of the fourteenth century, whereas in Peniarth 20 the inventor is said to be Dafydd Ddu Athro, who

---

[40] 'Bardism and Romance', 298–9. (The translation of the phrase is his, ibid. 273.) The poem in question is discussed in Ch. 2 below.

[41] *GPC*, however, renders *chwarae hudoliaeth*, 'to juggle, delude' (p. 842); cf. 'chware hvdolieth' in *CRhC* 35.56 (16th cent.?), in the sense of 'illusion' or 'trickery'.

[42] See A. T. E. Matonis, 'The Concept of Poetry in the Middle Ages: The Welsh Evidence from the Bardic Grammars', *BBCS* 36 (1989), 1–12.

[43] *GP* 56.43–5; 57.2. The singular *clerwr croesan* may be compared with the Irish *cliar crosan*, a collective term for 'a party of jesters', in 'The Voyage of the Húi Corra' (n. 25 above), 38.

[44] See Bromwich's discussion of the relationship between the texts, *APDG* 106. On the Peniarth 20 version see Saunders Lewis, *Gramadegau'r Penceirddiaid* (Cardiff, 1967).

probably belongs to the second half of the century.[45] It is thus tempting to view this qualification of *clerwr* as an indication of the development of the term during the course of that century to embrace
poets in general as well as inferior minstrels. Whether such an interpretation is valid or not, here we have yet another instance of the
identification of the *Clêr* with lowly entertainers such as buffoons
and jesters.

The moralizing tone of the Grammar suggests strong clerical
influence. The name of its compiler, Einion Offeiriad, identifies him
as a priest, but he was also an accomplished poet, and whether his
work is meant to reflect the official attitude of the Church we cannot be sure. As one would expect, the few references to the *Clêr* in
fourteenth-century religious texts display the same intolerance.[46] In
the Welsh version of the Latin text known as the *Elucidarium*, *clêr*
corresponds to *joculatores*: 'Pa obeith yssyd yr gler. nyt oes yr vn.
kannys oe holl ynni ymaent ȳgwassanaethu ydiawl.' ('Habent spem
joculatores?—Nullam: tota namque intentione sunt ministri Satanae
. . .')[47] In the *Hystoria o uuched Dewi* ('The Life of St David') which,
like the *Elucidarium*, is contained in the compilation known as *The
Book of the Anchorite of Llanddewifrefi*, probably written in 1346,
the *croesan* is paired with the *putain* (whore), though it should be

---

[45] GP 51.26–8. On Dafydd Ddu Athro see ibid., pp. xvii–xxii; Brynley Roberts,
Gwassanaeth Meir (Cardiff, 1961), pp. lxxv–lxxx.

[46] On the attitude of the Church towards poets in general see Glanmor Williams,
The Welsh Church From Conquest to Reformation (Cardiff, 1962), chs. 2, 5, and 12.
On Church hostility to secular song in Europe from an early time, see F. M. Warren,
'The Romance Lyric from the Standpoint of Antecedent Latin Documents',
Proceedings of the Modern Language Association of America, 26 (1911), 280–314;
Helen Waddell, *The Wandering Scholars* (6th edn., Harmondsworth, 1932), 182 ff.
and App. E: 'Councils on the *Clericus vagus* or *joculator*', 264 ff.

[47] John Morris-Jones and John Rhŷs (eds.), *The Elucidarium and Other Tracts in
Welsh from Llyvyr Agkyr Llandewivrevi* (Oxford, 1894), 40, 203. Given the ambiguity
of *clêr* the term may, of course, refer here to poets in general. Indeed, this is how the
passage was understood by Gruffudd Llwyd (*fl.* 1380–1420), who in a *cywydd* composed no later than 1399 is at pains to distinguish between the cultured *prydydd* and
the *croesaniaid* and 'worthless *clêr*', the inferior class condemned in the Grammar
(*CIGE* XL. 7–22):

Liwsidariws wiwdlws waith	A ddywod ymy ddwywaith
Y mae baich ym o bechawd	Oedd brydu a gwerthu gwawd . . .
Dan bwyth nad anobeithiwyf,	Nid un o'r glêr ofer wyf:
Nid wyf ry ddifoes groesan,	Nac wyf, a mi a wn gân.
Hefyd nid wyf, cyd bwyf bardd,	Bastynwr ffair, bost anardd.

On the meaning of *bastynwr* see pp. 25–6 below. The poet goes on to claim the Holy
Spirit as the source of his inspiration.

remembered that the word *croesan* also developed the general meaning of 'fornicator' or the like.[48] Particularly informative is a passage
from *Chwedlau Odo*, the fables of Odo de Chériton, translated from
Latin probably around 1400. Echoing the language of the Bardic
Grammar, the writer complains that many monks, clerics, and lay-
men gain little benefit from saints' lives or 'other laudable edifying
tales wich increase man's wisdom and provide sustenance for the
soul', preferring to frequent taverns to converse with whores,

ac ymdyualu, a gwarandaw clerwryaeth orwac ac ouergerd y leihau y syn-
hwyr ac y achwaneckau pechawt, a gwahawd diawl yn gynhorthwy yn lle
angel goleuni . . .[49]

(and mock each other and listen to vain *clerwriaeth* and frivolous verse, thus
decreasing wisdom and increasing sin, and inviting the aid of the devil
instead of the angel of light . . .)

Moral censure is also prominent in the poetry of the period. In a
pious *awdl* the Glamorgan poet Casnodyn, composing in the early
part of the fourteenth century, couples the sins of arrogance ('traha')
and defamation ('gogan'), and the references in the Grammar and in
contemporary verse, especially satirical verse, point to the *Clêr* as
being among the likely 'sinners' in these particular stanzas. This view
is made more tenable by a specific reference later in the poem, where
Casnodyn, who admits his own sinful past, states that it is better to
renounce 'the utter vacuousness of the frivolous, boozing *Clêr*'
('gorwacter y gler ouer ayf').[50] As in the passage from *Chwedlau Odo*
and in the triads of the bardic grammars, the tavern is seen as the

[48] Morris-Jones and Rhŷs, *Elucidarium*, 116.20–1. The editors suggest the meaning
'fornicator'. The sexual meaning is appropriate for *groesaneth* in GDG 55.16 (see
Parry's note, p. 489), but in GDG 52.30 where DG refers to himself as a *croesan*, it is
the meaning 'digrifddyn, cellweiriwr' (in the non-professional sense) which is most
apt. When 'croesanaeth' is applied to the inferior poets Rhys Meigen and Tudur Goch
(GDG 21.19; 154.49) the original meaning of 'a professional jester' may also be present. Compare also the *Pum Llyfr Cerddwriaeth* (16th cent.) triad: 'Tri pheth annweddvs ar gerddor: ffrost, a gogangerdd, a chroessanaeth' (GP 135.42–3).
[49] Ifor Williams (ed.), *Chwedlau Odo, gyda rhagymadrodd, nodiadau a geirfa*
(Wrexham, 1926), 6.2–6. Cf. 'Tri pheth a dyly prydyd eu gochel: llynna, a gwrageda,
a chlerwryaeth' (GP 17.13–4). See also the 15th-cent. translation *Ffordd y Brawd
Odrig*, ed. Stephen J. Williams (Cardiff, 1929), 40.23; 53.12, 24, where *cler* corresponds to Latin *histriones*.
[50] RP 1,233.29–35; 1,236.34–7. Cf. the apparently clerical critique of the *Clêr*'s
moral laxity in the so-called 'Bustl y Beirdd', which begins: 'Cler o gam arfer a ymar-
ferant | Cathlau aneddfol fydd eu moliant . . .' (MA 29). The poem probably belongs
to the second half of the 14th cent.; see Ifor Williams, *Chwedl Taliesin* (Cardiff, 1957),
16–18.

natural haunt of the *Clêr*, and the words 'y gler ouer' may be compared with the term 'ofergerdd' which is coupled with 'clerwriaeth' in the same passage. It will be seen that this adjective, 'ofer' ('worthless' or 'frivolous'), features regularly in the depiction of these minstrels from this period onwards. The same poet, in his eulogy to Ieuan Llwyd of Glyn Aeron in Ceredigion, contrasts his own 'perfect' verse-craft with 'sothachiaith beirdd caith Caeaw', 'the base pronouncements of the villein-poets of Caeo'.[51] Nothing is known of the poets in question, but it may be conjectured that they were of an inferior order and that they had angered the proud *pencerdd* in some way, perhaps through the invective of their verse. D. J. Bowen has drawn attention to the fact that the commote of Caeo borders on the commotes of Mabwynion and Pennardd, the area associated with Einion Offeiriad, which may be significant in view of Einion's attitude towards the *Clêr* and the bards' pride in their knowledge of the classical art of grammar.[52] Another important early reference to the *Clêr* occurs in the opening lines of a poem by Casnodyn's contemporary, Gruffudd ap Dafydd ap Tudur,[53] requesting the gift of a bow:

> Eruit newit nwyf. aruer cler am cwlyf. [*leg*.clwyf]
> ervynnyeit ym rwyf yd wyf y da.
> Arwydwawt eruyn. ar oet vn vlwydyn
> a warawt toppyn velyn vwla.

(RP 1,253.30–3)

(Passion of exchange of fists: it is the practice of the *Clêr* that afflicts me; it is my lord whom I solicit for his wealth. A request in meaningful verse at an appointed time with a year's notice has seen off a yellow-scalped bull [of a man].)

---

[51] *BBBGDd* 4.7–8. D. Myrddin Lloyd suggests that the reference may be to the author of the satire of Casnodyn in *RP* 1,340–2 (possibly Hywel Ystorm, see Ch. 2, n. 15 below) and composers of similar lampoons (*A Guide to Welsh Literature*, ii. 43). According to Eurys Rowlands Casnodyn may even be alluding to the early *Cywyddwyr*, with their new metre and subject-matter ('Iolo Goch', in J. Carney and D. Greene (eds.), *Celtic Studies: Essays in Memory of Angus Matheson 1912–62* (London, 1968), 140).

[52] 'Dafydd ap Gwilym a Datblygiad y Cywydd', *LlC* 8 (1964), 8–9.

[53] His *floruit* is usually given as the first quarter of the 14th cent. However, Dafydd Johnston has recently suggested that one of his poems (*BBBGDd* 1) was composed as early as *c*.1284, though he does admit 1318 as a possibility ('Tri Chyfeiriad at Lywelyn ap Gruffudd', *BBCS* 36 (1989), 97–8). In view of the description of the English king as 'breiniawg Cemais' (l. 18), and in particular the well-developed *cynghanedd* in Gruffudd's poems in general, the latter seems to me the more likely. His importance as one of the *Cywyddwyr*'s most significant predecessors is discussed in Ch. 3 below.

That *clêr* does not apply here to poets in general is implied by the sharp invective of the fourth line, and also by the suggestion that the poet in question has flaunted bardic etiquette by presumably refusing to confine his soliciting to the traditional festivals of Christmas, Easter, and Whitsun. Like Phylip Brydydd's *beirdd ysbyddaid* a century earlier, these poets are seen to be competing for patronage with their bardic counterparts.

The threat posed by this competition from below is strikingly illustrated in a poem by Iorwerth Beli in praise of a bishop of Bangor—probably Anian Sais, who held the position between 1309 and 1327—'and to reproach him for neglecting bards and honouring musicians'.[54] Once more, it is the poet's claim that a patron has honoured inferior entertainers at the expense of a qualified bard, leaving the great poets naked while musicians are provided with fine garments. Despite the name of one of their number—Tudur Wion—these musicians clearly include young Englishmen ('iangwyr Saeson'). It is not the traditional art of the Welsh musicians to which Iorwerth is opposed, but foreign instruments such as the crowd of willow (*crwth*) with its strings of gut and the loud, tightly strung harp which are both vilified in his poem; drums ('tabyrddau') are also mentioned. The sound produced by such a harp would have differed considerably from the soft drone of the 'telyn rawn' mentioned in the laws, the traditional harp strung with twisted horsehair.[55] It is Caerwyn Williams's opinion that this music was performed as accompaniment to lyrics which were sung, so that Iorwerth was protesting also against the favour shown to a poetry which was new and had no tradition as far as Wales was concerned.[56] The fact that it is said of the aforementioned Tudur Wion that he received a long green garment for being able to speak English suggests that some English lyrics may have been sung at such gatherings. In the face of such an affront to his dignity by these so-called 'dregs of song' ('gwehilion cerddau'), Iorwerth Beli, like Phylip Brydydd before him, recalls the glory of his illustrious predecessors—Llywarch (ap Llywelyn), Cynddelw, Gwilym Ryfel, and Dafydd Benfras—bards who epitomized the classical tradition of *Cerdd Dafod* to which he belonged.

[54] *MA* 317. The poem has been edited by Dafydd Johnston, *BBBGDd* 2.

[55] Compare Iolo Goch's 'Cywydd Moliant i'r Delyn Rawn a Dychan i'r Delyn Ledr' (*GIG* XXXII); both are discussed by Jarman, 'Telyn a Chrwth', 159 ff.

[56] 'Cerddi'r Gogynfeirdd i Wragedd a Merched, a'u Cefndir yng Nghymru a'r Cyfandir', *LlC* 13 (1974–81), 95–6.

It will have been noted that none of the early-fourteenth-century instances of *clêr/clerwr/clerwriaeth* discussed above can be said to apply to 'poets in general', only to an inferior class of minstrels. In his theoretical account of the development of the term *clêr* to embrace all poets in post-Conquest Wales because of the need to undertake bardic circuits (the practice described by the verb 'clera'), Thomas Parry does not propose that this evolution actually took place during the course of the fourteenth century. Admittedly, the two verse references by Casnodyn and Gruffudd ap Dafydd provide insufficient evidence, but it is not altogether unlikely that the stigma attached to the word *clêr* prevented its use as a general term until the second quarter of the century. And as one might expect, the use of the word in its derogatory sense is particularly striking in the satirical verse composed by contemporaries of Casnodyn, and in the little-known corpus of fourteenth-century satire as a whole. The important evidence of the Red Book satires, in which we catch fleeting glimpses of certain *clerwyr* as abusive rhymesters and worthless musicians who peddled their wares to all who cared to listen, will be discussed in greater detail in the next chapter. We will confine our attention here to a couple of poems from the Red Book corpus which warrant particular attention in relation to the term *clêr*.

The first is by Iocyn Ddu ab Ithel Grach, the only surviving example of his work.[57] Because of its leisurely narrative style and humorous subject-matter, which includes the poet's sexual exploits but consists mainly of a comic account of his maltreatment at an Englishman's hall in Chester, Iocyn Ddu has inevitably been classified as one of the *Clêr*.[58] The very first line of the poem seems to confirm this view, where he says of himself: 'Rhodiwr fydd clerwr, clau ei adlais', 'the *clerwr* is a wanderer whose cry is heard aloud'. However, the court steward places him to sit among the *Clêr*, whom he despised—'A'r ystiward llys . . . | A'm rhoes gyda'r glêr a ddigerais'—and things go from bad to worse. He vomits for lack of food

---

[57] BBBGDd 70; for a translation ('A Minstrel's Boast'), see Dafydd Johnston, CMOC 18. See also H. M. Edwards, '"Rhodiwr fydd clerwr": Sylwadau ar Gerdd Ymffrost o'r Bedwaredd Ganrif ar Ddeg', Y Traethodydd (Jan. 1994), 50–5.

[58] Cf. Saunders Lewis, Braslun o Hanes Llenyddiaeth Gymraeg (Cardiff, 1932), 74–5. Although it seems doubtful whether Iocyn should be identified with the lowly *Clêr* of the Bardic Grammar, his work is certainly *clerwraidd* in spirit and content and 'the tone of his poem and the metrical laxity suggest that he did not belong to the highest rank of poets, despite his contempt for the common minstrels' (Johnston, CMOC, p. 87).

and drink, and assures us that 'no man fully knows how I did curse because of the harm and the scowling and the affliction of a *clerwr*':

> Ni ŵyr dyn yn llwyr llwrw y ceblais
> Herwydd drwg a gwg a goglais—clerwr . . .

Clerwr, in the first instance, then, is surely to be understood as a term for itinerant poets in general (from the verb 'clera'), since the poet sets himself apart from the inferior *Clêr*. In the second instance, *clerwr* is clearly synonymous with the latter, so that both fourteenth-century meanings of the word would seem to be represented within the same poem. This ambiguity does not arise in the second poem, by Madog Dwygraig, which bears the grandiose title *Ystorya Deykyn*.[59] These *englynion*, which again have a strong narrative quality, tell of a man who loses his wealth through his arrogance, and resorts to the sordid life of a beggar. His wandering is described as 'clera', which essentially involves travelling from one place to another in search of reward, but there is no mention of verse or of any other form of entertainment. The word 'croessan' seems to refer to his ridiculous condition rather than to any actual buffoonery, and if he is described as 'Luciffer y gler glorya'[60] (*lit*. 'Lucifer of the arse-*Clêr*') it is presumably because they too are regarded by Madog as no better than undignified beggars. The words 'y gler glorya' are significant. Such a qualification of *clêr* recalls the 'clerwr croesan' of the Grammar, and more specifically various other disparaging epithets which leave us in no doubt as to the meaning of the term. Apart from the ubiquitous 'clêr ofer', which first appears in the work of Casnodyn, the most common of these from the fourteenth to the sixteenth century is 'clêr y dom'[61] ('*clêr* of the dung[-heap]'). Others

---

[59] *RP* 1,272. This accomplished poet, because of the unedifying nature of much of his verse, has also been misleadingly referred to as a *clerwr*. Chotzen, *Recherches*, 280, speaks of the 'terminologie ordurière dans les satires du *clerwr* Madog Dwygraig'; cf. Meirion Pennar, 'Dryll o Dystiolaeth am y Glêr', *BBCS* 28 (1979), 410 n. 3, and see his remarks in 'Teuluaeth a Maswedd', *YB* 16 (1990), 52–3.

[60] *RP* 1272. 17–18. This seems to be an irreverent pun, playing on *cloria* ('arse')/*Gloria* and the religious connotation of *clêr*. Cf. Iolo Goch's description of priests as 'Cain glêr yn canu gloria' (*GIG* XXIX.92), and the ambiguous 'Klorya pla' in a scurrilous *englyn* to a cleric in *GP* 53.8 (see Ch. 2, p. 53 below). The plural form 'cleroed' (*cleroedd*) (*RP* 1,272.14)—'hosts of poets'—is well attested, never in a pejorative context (cf. *RP* 1,260.15; 1,281.30–1; 1,336.5).

[61] Examples include *DGG* LXXXV.50; John (Tegid) Jones and Walter Davies (eds.), *Gwaith Lewis Glyn Cothi* (Oxford, 1837), p.281.54; E. D. Jones (ed.), *Gwaith Lewis Glyn Cothi*, vol. 1 (Cardiff and Aberystwyth, 1953), 25.37 (since going to press, this poet's work has been re-edited by Dafydd Johnston, *Gwaith Lewys Glyn Cothi*

include 'tin y glêr'[62] ('arse [i.e. the lowest] of the *clêr*'), 'clêr fân' or 'mangler'[63] ('petty *clêr*'), and so on. In the Red Book satires, 'gwtter cler' ('gutter of the *clêr*'), and 'cler wadawt' ('dregs of the *clêr*'), serve the same purpose.[64]

The satirical verse of the *cywyddwyr* Dafydd ap Gwilym and Iolo Goch, both contemporaries of Madog Dwygraig, draws to a large extent on the same conventions of theme, diction, and metaphor that are exploited by the Red Book satirists. This is particularly true of Dafydd's famous satire of the *clerwr* Rhys Meigen (*GDG* 21). Among the expected references to mindless abuse, boasting, begging, unskilled verse, and the like, there are certain aspects of the poem which are particularly significant. Rhys Meigen is described as 'taer flawdfardd tai' (l. 20) (*lit.* 'insistent meal-poet of houses'). The term was evidently current for an inferior poet, since 'beirdd y blawd' is used by Iolo Goch in a similar context (*GIG* XXXVII.53), and in the sixteenth-century grammar known as the *Pum Llyfr Cerddwriaeth* the 'meal-poet', *clerwr* and conjurer are named as 'three worthless entertainers': 'Tri ofer gerddor: klerwr, a bardd y blawd, a hvdol' (*GP* 136.12). It probably denotes a poet who sang for flour from house to house, as elsewhere Rhys is described as one who begs for flour ('blotai'), as well as wheat, broth, and meat (ll. 27–47). It appears, then, that as in other satires of this period, the *clerwr* is once more seen as an entertainer of peasants. In the phrase 'Croesanaeth croyw a seiniai' (l. 19), 'Loud-voiced buffoonery did he proclaim', the term *croesanaeth* probably alludes to the *clerwr*'s frivolous or ribald verse (though the physical connotation of buffoonery may also be present). The rare form 'bastynwas' (l. 33) is echoed elsewhere in Dafydd's work in the phrase 'Llawenaf . . . | Yw'r

(Cardiff, 1995)); Ifor Williams and J. Ll. Williams (eds.), *Gwaith Guto'r Glyn* (Cardiff, 1939), LXXXIII.32; Gruffydd Aled Williams (ed.), *Ymryson Edmwnd Prys a Wiliam Cynwal* (Cardiff, 1986), 10.15; 20.98.

[62] T. Roberts (ed.), *Gwaith Tudur Penllyn ac Ieuan ap Tudur Penllyn* (Cardiff, 1958), 30.32. Cf. 'llygad tin clêr holl wŷr Dyffryn Clwyd' from the 16th cent. (Cennard Davies, 'Robin Clidro a'i Ganlynwyr', unpublished MA thesis, University of Wales (1964), 56). Compare also 'clêr clorya', and 'tin-kerddiaid kerddav' (E. Bachellery (ed.), *L'Œuvre poétique de Gutun Owain* (Paris, 1951), LXIV.24). In the *Pum Llyfr Cerddwriaeth* 'tinkerddiaidd' (or 'isselradd', 'of low status') describes one of the three classes of *cywydd* (i.e. *traethodl?*), the other two being 'pennkerddiaidd' and 'dysgybliaidd' (GP 131.4–6).

[63] *Gwaith Lewis Glyn Cothi* (1837), p. 299.39; *Gwaith Tudur Aled*, vol. 2, p. 733.14; Eurys Rowlands (ed.), *Gwaith Lewys Môn* (Cardiff, 1975), XC.26.

[64] *RP* 1,355.5; 1,359.35–6.

bastynwyr . . .' (*GDG* 76.31–2), which clearly refers to poets of some kind since the 'bastynwyr' are compared with the blackbird which sings its song without a care in the world. Gruffudd Llwyd, who belongs to the next generation of *Cywyddwyr*, contrasts himself with the 'croesan' and the 'bastynwr ffair'.[65] In the second half of the fifteenth century an *englyn* by Gutun Owain describes a 'boastful' poet as 'pastwn ffair y gwleddav', his contemporary Tudur Penllyn refers to a boastful adversary as 'bastwn drain', and in the sixteenth century 'bastwn-glêr' is used by Wiliam Egwad to describe a fellow poet, again in a satirical context involving abuse and boasting.[66] In Siôn Dafydd Rhys's sixteenth-century grammar, the 'datgeiniad' 'Penn Pastwn' (i.e. the reciter who used the end of his staff, or baton) is defined as follows:

un a fo yn datcanu heb fedru dim canu tant ei hunan; a hwnnw a ddyly sefyll yng nghenawl y neuadd a churaw ei ffon, a chanu ei Gywydd neu ei Owdl gyd â'r dyrnodiau.[67]

(one who recites without being able to play the harp himself; and he should stand in the centre of the hall and beat his staff, and sing his *cywydd* or *awdl* [in time] with the beats.)

Ifor Williams has suggested that the grammarian, rather than describing actual practice, is perhaps attempting to explain another less familiar meaning of *bastwn*, 'a stanza of verse', which may have developed in the fourteenth century from Middle English *baston*, *bastoun* (< Old French *baston*). Thus 'bastynwyr' would simply mean 'versifiers'.[68] However, Siôn Dafydd Rhys's explanation does seem logical when applied to an unskilled poet or reciter, and is unlikely to have been invented out of thin air. Tudur Penllyn's 'bastwn drain' would appear, then, to be a reference to a *clerwr*'s staff made of thorn-wood.[69]

In Iolo Goch's satire of Gwyddelyn (*GIG* XXXVII), who seems to have been one of the stock figures of satire among the bards, the *clerwr* is described as the servant of an old ostler, and Iolo states sar-

[65] *CIGE* XL.19–22 (see n. 47 above).

[66] *Œuvre poétique*, LXIV.14; *Gwaith Tudur Penllyn*, 26.10; H. Ll. Jones and Eurys Rowlands (eds.), *Gwaith Iorwerth Fynglwyd* (Cardiff, 1975), 31.29.

[67] *Cambrobrytannicæ Cymræcæve Linguæ Institutiones &c.* (1592), 304 (cited in *DGG* 220–1).

[68] *DGG* 220–1. It is this explanation which is given by Parry, *GDG* 506.

[69] Bachellery accepts the grammarian's definition (*Œuvre poétique*, 332). With 'bastwn drain' compare 'A phastwn du-ddraenen' in *Hen Benillion*, ed. T. H. Parry-Williams (Aberystwyth, 1940), no. 196.

castically that it would be far easier for him to dry the horse of the poet Ithel Ddu than to compete with him in verse, or with Madog Dwygraig (ll. 39–48). He is referred to as a tinker of song ('Tincer gwawd') and a beggar of meat ('cicai') (ll. 86, 22), and the metaphor of a tithe carriage at a gathering of peasants ('Car degwm côr daeogau' (l. 8)), suggests the nature of his audiences. The *cywydd* includes a striking passage where Iolo emphatically distinguishes between himself, Ithel Ddu, and Madog Dwygraig, and the kind of minstrels which Gwyddelyn represents:

> Nid synnwyr ffôl wrth ddolef,
> Nid clêr lliw'r tryser llawr tref,
> Nid beirdd y blawd, brawd heb rym,
> Profedig feirdd prif ydym.[70]
>
> (ll. 51–4)

([We utter] no cries of foolish nonsense, we are not the *Clêr* of the market-place, of the colour of the three stars(?), not meal-poets—an unfounded judgement—but qualified *prifeirdd* (chief poets).)

The *Clêr*, as is implied in a few of the Red Book satires, are clearly seen here to be popular entertainers at the market-place or centre of towns. The need to draw such a distinction arose, perhaps, from the ambiguity of the term *clêr* in this period, and from the fact that, despite appearances, there was inevitably some interaction between the various classes of poets. This may well be reflected in the broadened subject-matter of the *Cywyddwyr* themselves.

One form of intercourse between *prifardd* and *clerwr*, it will be seen, is discernible in the kind of satirical contests hinted at in the Red Book of Hergest, and the *cyff clêr* convention may be significant in this respect. Judging from certain references in their verse, it appears that the fourteenth-century *Cywyddwyr* indulged in the satirizing of the *Clêr* to an extent which is not reflected in the manuscripts. Iolo Goch, in his mock-elegy to Ithel Ddu, lists among the poet's feats the satirizing of the Gwyddelyn mentioned earlier, and of a certain Brem (*GIG* XXIII.25–8). Similarly, Gruffudd Gryg bids farewell to one Tudur Goch, whom he greets as 'glowrllyd froch glêr', 'scabby badger of the *Clêr*', since he must concentrate his poetic energies on his famous contention with Dafydd ap Gwilym (*GDG* 153.17–22). Also, Llywelyn Goch Amheurig Hen lists among

---

[70] With 'Profedig feirdd prif' compare Hywel Ystorm's 'prifveird profyedic' and Dafydd Y Coed's 'heird brydydyon prifyon pryff', which occur in similar satirical contexts (*RP* 1,338.9; 1,361.10–11).

his bardic functions at the home of his cultured nephews, after reading 'Brut hen y Brutaniaid':

> Clau ddychanu llu lledffrom,
> Clywir ei dwrf, cler y dom.
> (*DGG* LXXXV.49–50)

(Loudly satirizing a wrathful mob—its tumult is heard [far and wide]—the *Clêr* of the dung-heap.)

Iolo Goch implies that Gwyddelyn may have been involved in wrangles with both Ithel Ddu and Madog Dwygraig, and tradition has it that Dafydd's vilification of Rhys Meigen was occasioned by the *clerwr*'s mocking verse.[71] It is therefore logical to assume that satire of this kind was often a two-way affair which was bound to bring minstrels and bards into close contact with each other.

Iolo Goch's work contains only two certain examples of *clêr* in relation to inferior poets, both in the satire of Gwyddelyn (*GIG* XXXVII.12,52). A possible third instance occurs in the satire of the *clerwr*'s mother, nicknamed Hersdin Hogl, where it is said that after her funeral her flour, her huskless oats, her apron (?), and her stick should be divided among *clêr* (*GIG* XXXVI.91–2).[72] Dafydd Johnston, the most recent editor of Iolo's work, admits this as a possibility but, especially as these *clêr* are said to pray for the woman's soul, thinks it more likely that the word refers to priests in this case. This meaning of *clêr* is probably present also in Iolo's elegy to Ithel ap Robert and in his *cywydd* to St David[73] (*GIG* XV.79–82; XXIX.91–4). On the whole, however, Iolo's use of *clêr* and its derivatives is consistent with fourteenth-century usage in general, in *cywyddau* and *awdlau* alike. That is to say, when the meaning is not overtly derogatory, he is referring to poets in general.[74] Phrases such

---

[71] See *GDG* pp. xl–xli, and the *englynion* attributed to the two poets, ibid., p. 419 (no. xix).

[72] For a similar satirical list of a hag's possessions see *RP* 1,347.25–32 (Hywel Ystorm?); and in the 15th cent., *Gwaith Tudur Penllyn* . . ., pp. 95–6 (Ieuan Brydydd Hir).

[73] See Johnston's notes on *clêr* in this sense, *GIG* 271–2, 344, 368–9.

[74] Apart from Llywelyn Goch's 'clêr y dom', the *cywyddau* in *DGG* contain only two instances of *clêr*, both referring to poets in general—*DGG* LXX.8 (Madog Benfras); *DGG* LXXIX.46 (Gruffudd Gryg). In the large corpus of 14th-cent. *awdlau* (with the exception of the satirical poems and the references by Casnodyn and Gruffudd ap Dafydd ap Tudur, mentioned earlier), *clêr* is again a general term for poets—e.g. *RP* 1,302.31; 1,307.36; 1,308.31; 1,309.17 (Llywelyn Goch); 1,271.1, 23, 39 (Madog Dwygraig); 1,378.41 (Dafydd Y Coed).

as 'Llety'r glêr', 'Cell y glêr', and 'trysorer clêr' ('treasurer of *clêr*', of Dafydd ap Gwilym) (*GIG* III.48; VI.68; XXI.31) surely refer to poets in general; and when Owain Glyndŵr is described as one who knows how to love *clêr* (*GIG* IX.23–4), or when it is said that, before his death, Tudur Fychan of Penmynydd used to reward musicians (*cerddorion*) and *clerwyr* with fine garments (*GIG* VI.15–20), it must have been his fellow qualified poets who were foremost in Iolo's mind. But these terms may well embrace the various kinds of minstrels who entertained the noble patrons, and the four bedrooms where the *clêr* sleep in Owain Glyndŵr's new home at Sycharth (*GIG* X.43–4) surely were not reserved for the qualified bards alone. Iolo's dialogue between the body and soul (*GIG* XIV) is significant in that it is the earliest surviving description of a bardic circuit ('taith glera'), a circuit which takes the poet to various secular and religious houses in different parts of Wales. Johnston remarks that the use of the verb 'clera' in this poem (l. 22) and in *GIG* XXXII.5 suggests that Iolo considered himself to be one of the *clêr*.[75] However, the internal evidence of fourteenth-century verse shows the great majority of poets to be itinerant to some extent by this period, so that Iolo's use of 'clera' is no reason to identify him with the inferior type of performers known as *Clêr*.

The verb is used in the same sense by Dafydd ap Gwilym when he describes Newborough in Anglesey as a rewarding place to go on a circuit—'Lle diofer i glera' (*GDG* 134.17)—and when he reminds the Grey Friar that he has as much right to sing for reward as has the friar to beg—'A chyn iawned ym glera | Ag i tithau gardota'(*GDG* 137.55–6). As one might expect, *clêr* is used in the general sense, as when Dafydd describes Ifor Hael as 'Caeth y glêr', 'captive of the *clêr*', or in the phrase 'Dy fedd glas difaddau i glêr', 'your ceaseless fresh mead for *clêr*', of Ieuan ap Gruffudd ap Llywelyn, father of Dyddgu (*GDG* 7.14; 45.11). The only clearly derogatory reference to the *Clêr* in Dafydd's work, apart from the satire of Rhys Meigen (*GDG* 21.74), is the use of the adjective 'clerŵraidd' in the following lines:

> Nid un claer araith dyn clerŵraidd
> Â llwybr gŵr ewybr yn garuaidd
> (*GDG* 15.33–4)

---

[75] *GIG* 195.

(The loud pronouncement of one who has the attributes of an inferior *clerwr* is not comparable with the affectionate manner of a quick-witted man.)

He goes on to contrast the song of the rhymester Bleddyn with the verse of the great *gogynfardd* Cynddelw. It is noteworthy too that *clêr* as a collective term for inferior poets seems to occur at least once in the bardic contention. Gruffudd Gryg declares that their dispute has been caused by the lies of a slanderer which Dafydd has believed to be true, concluding: 'Crediad yw a glyw y glêr', 'it is a gullible man who listens to the *Clêr*' (GDG 151.6).[76]

The instances of *clêr* (and 'clerẃraidd') which can be said to apply to inferior poets in Dafydd's work, few as they are, demonstrate his antipathy towards these poets. It is therefore somewhat surprising to find the term used in rather ambiguous contexts, which is not the case in the work of Iolo Goch, and if the meaning of a certain class of minstrels is to be accepted in these instances, then we should perhaps admit a certain ambivalence towards these minstrels on Dafydd's part. Indeed, the question arises as to whether Dafydd considered himself to be one of the *Clêr*, as was suggested long ago by Ifor Williams.[77] His verse shows him to be particularly responsive to sub-literary influences. But given the dual meaning of *clêr* in the fourteenth century, it must be admitted that such an ambivalence towards these entertainers is not proven beyond question by the internal evidence of his poems. The lines which present the strongest case for identifying Dafydd with the *Clêr*, especially as falsity and vanity have been seen to be inseparable from condemnations of these minstrels in both religious and secular sources, are the Grey Friar's reproachful words:

> Nid oes o'ch cerdd chwi, y glêr,
> Ond truth a lleisiau ofer
>   (GDG 137.29–30)

(Your verse, the *clêr*, contains nothing but falsity and vain noises.)

---

[76] Alternatively, 'it is a belief which will become known to the *Clêr*/poets.' (see GPC s.v. *crediad*).

[77] 'Dafydd ap Gwilym a'r Glêr', 143. That Dafydd was a thoroughly trained, qualified bard is, of course, beyond question. He describes himself as 'prydydd' and 'prifardd' (GDG 6.14; 9.51), and is referred to by Gruffudd Gryg as 'penceirddwalch', 'prifardd' and 'Fardd penceirddradd', and by Madog Benfras as 'Pennaeth penceirddiaeth' (GDG, pp. 427, 424).

However, it is clear that the Friar's indignation is incurred above all
by 'physical praise' ('moliant corfforawl') which 'incites men and
women to sin and untruth' and 'causes the loss of the soul to the
devil'. These words applied just as well to the love-poetry of the
Cywyddwyr as they did (presumably) to the lost verse of the Clêr,
so that it is preferable to interpret clêr in this instance as embracing
poets in general. Or it may be that the Friar did not distinguish
between the immoral verse of different grades of poets, choosing to
identify them all with the lowest and most despicable among them.
The sense of 'poets in general', and particularly love-poets, is equally
appropriate when Dafydd refers to his request to a watchman at a
convent for a willing nun as 'claim diwyd y glêr', 'the insistent claim
of the clêr', and when he describes his melody on the harp as 'cwlm
y glêr', 'the tune of the clêr' (GDG 113.13; 142.18).

In one of Gruffudd Gryg's irreverent remarks:

> Mawr eisiau cerdd ar glerddyn
> Mal Dafydd, awenydd wŷn.
> (GDG 153.37–8)

(A minstrel such as Dafydd, poet of wrath (/lust/passion), has great need of
poetry.)

the word 'clerddyn' ('clêr' + 'dyn', 'man') has an unmistakably con-
temptuous flavour. But if the sense of an inferior minstrel is intended
this would be hardly surprising considering the satirical tone of the
contention as a whole. In the following passage it is Dafydd who
insults his rival:

> Dianc rhag clêr yn eres
> Ydd wyd, dew leufwyd di-les.
> Rhyw elyn beirdd rhy olud,
> Rhywola dy draha drud.
> (GDG 152.7–10)

(You escape wondrously from clêr, you fat, no-good lice-food. Most stubborn enemy of poets, restrain your foolish boasting.)

One's immediate reaction is that the comparatively conservative
Gwynedd poet, who chastises his South-Walian rival for his 'geuwawd
o gywydd' (worthless or empty cywydd), avoids the Clêr at every
opportunity, arrogantly believing them to be unworthy of a bard's
attention, while Dafydd does not. But in the light of the words
'Gwahawdd nawdd', 'welcome support (or aid)', and 'Gwahardd . . .

dy fost', 'restrain your boasting' (*GDG* 152.13–14), it would appear that what Dafydd is actually implying is that Gruffudd's arrogance causes him to refuse instruction from other qualified bards, particularly Dafydd himself, so that the meaning of *clêr* as poets in general is again perfectly acceptable. This is also the case in the personification of birds as 'Clerwyr coed' and of the nightingale as 'Clerwraig nant' (*GDG* 121.18; 122.29), poets of woodland and valley, although, of course, the metaphor of wandering minstrels is equally appropriate here. In the second instance the religious connotations of *clêr* may well be present since it occurs in the context of a woodland mass.

Lastly, consideration must be given to an intriguing passage from a *cywydd* in which Dafydd expresses his bitter disappointment at Morfudd's becoming pregnant by another man, in spite of all his praise and all the expense incurred in seeking her devotion:

> Treuliais wrth ofer glêr glân
> Fodrwyau; gwae fi druan! . . .
> Treiglais, gweais yn gywir,
> Defyrn gwin, Duw a farn gwir.
> Treiglais hefyd, bywyd bas,
> Defyrn meddgyrn gormoddgas.
> Perais o iawngais angerdd
> Prydu a chanu ei cherdd
> I'r glêr hyd eithaf Ceri,
> Eiry mân hoen, er ei mwyn hi.
> (*GDG* 85.11–24)

(I have lavished fine rings on frivolous *clêr*; woe is me, wretched one! I have travelled—and faithfully have I composed (*lit.* woven)—from one wine-tavern to another, God be my witness. I have frequented also—sordid life—most despicable mead-horn-taverns. Through passion's true quest I have had the *clêr* compose and sing her song as far as furthest Ceri, for her sake, [she of] the colour of fine snow.)

The first couplet implies that Dafydd has rewarded frivolous *clêr* for composing or declaiming verse in praise of Morfudd. The following lines speak of the sordid world of the common taverns, and if the poets concerned are to be associated with this world, we would indeed seem to be dealing here with *Clêr* as popular entertainers. However, Dafydd's 'ofer glêr' is not necessarily synonymous with the common abusive epithet 'y glêr ofer' (indeed, 'ofer glêr glân' is a more natural reading than 'glân fodrwyau'). The *Cywyddwyr*, no doubt ironically, often refer to themselves and each other as 'ofer-feirdd' and the like, particularly in relation to love-poetry, and 'ofer-gerdd' is in fact used for love-poetry, not unlike Dafydd's famous 'geuwawd o gywydd' (a *cywydd* of false praise). Thus Dafydd, in the *cywydd* which likens Morfudd to the sun's deceptive radiance, is himself an 'oferfardd' who laments his fate as a rejected lover (*GDG* 42.11–14).[78] In the last two couplets of the passage he explicitly states that he has made the *clêr* compose and sing Morfudd's praise as far as the commote of Ceri in Powys, close to the English bor-der—to sing, therefore, throughout the length and breadth of Wales. It is tempting to regard these poets as belonging to a numerous and inferior class of minstrels known as the *Clêr*, whose repertoire would have included love-poetry. Such an interpretation would confirm Dafydd's possible ambivalence towards them. This seems to me a valid interpretation in this case, but given the ambiguity of the term neither this passage, nor the various other references considered here, can be regarded as irrefutable evidence of the kind of love–hate rela-tionship which may well have existed between Dafydd ap Gwilym and the *Clêr*.

It has been suggested in relation to this passage that Dafydd would occasionally undertake a circuit from his native Cardiganshire or from the court of Ifor Hael in Glamorgan, with a host containing other itinerant performers, including inferior poets and minstrels, and even performers of physical feats.[79] While such a colourful ret-inue may appear somewhat fanciful, it is probable that Dafydd would occasionally have been accompanied by bardic pupils,[80] and also, perhaps, by professional reciters (*datgeiniaid*), of whom it is said in 'Statud Gruffudd ap Cynan' that they must not go on a cir-cuit except in the company of a *prydydd*. It is thus possible to inter-pret Dafydd's assertion that he ensured that Morfudd's praise was on the lips of the *clêr* as a reference to his own love-poems declaimed

---

[78] Cf. 'Gwynvyt clerwyr ac overwyr' from an incomplete *awdl* (*RP* 1,225.5), com-posed in the last quarter of the 14th cent. On *oferfardd* in a non-pejorative sense see Eurys Rowlands, *LlC* 6 (1960), 232. However, *oferfardd* is clearly pejorative in *CIGE* XLIII.42 (Gruffudd Llwyd), and *Gwaith Tudur Aled*, vol. 2, CXLI.25, as is *ofergerdd* in *GP* 133.23; 136.15; 148.12; 151.35.

[79] D. J. Bowen, 'Dafydd ap Gwilym a Cheredigion', *LlC* 14 (1983–4), 179.

[80] He is referred to as a teacher of poets in *DGG* LXX.41; LXXXII.13; *GIG* XXI.26, 37; cf. also the bardic dispute, *GDG* 149.7–12. As an *uchelwr* he is accom-panied in *GDG* 124 by a page or squire ('gwreangyn'), and in *GDG* 128 by a servant. Gruffudd Gryg refers to his own pupils in Anglesey; see Gruffydd Aled Williams, 'Cywydd Gruffudd Gryg i Dir Môn', *YB* 13 (1985), 150.

by professional reciters, *clêr* being understood in this case as denoting poets in general.[81] One is reminded of Iolo Goch's elegy to Llywelyn Goch Amheurig Hen, where it is said that it was customary in the noble courts to demand of the musicians that they perform first of all 'Rhieingerdd y gŵr hengoch', 'the love-poem of the red-haired old man' (*GIG* XXII.21–6). While it is unlikely that Dafydd ap Gwilym would actually have been followed on his circuits by a motley band of *clerwyr* and various other lowly entertainers, he and his fellow *Cywyddwyr* would no doubt have been familiar with their repertoires from their visits to the noble homes during the festive periods. A little-known contemporary poet, Dafydd Bach ap Madog Wladaidd, paints a lively picture of the merriment seen each Christmas at a noble hall, where musicians and poets provide 'great mirth above a slippery floor.' The festivities are open to *pencerdd* and *clerwr* alike, and doubtless to all manner of medieval entertainers:

> Pa ddyn bynnag fych, pa gerdd a fetrych,
> Gydag a nodych yn enwedig,
> Dyred pan fynnych, croeso pan ddelych,
> A gwedi delych tra fynnych trig.[82]

(Whoever you may be, whichever craft you profess, as long as you declare your name come when you wish, a welcome awaits you, and having come, stay as long as you like.)

Another fourteenth-century poet, Gruffudd Fychan fab Gruffudd fab Ednyfed, gives a vivid description of a hall brimming over with people as the entertainment comes to an end, a hundred rhymesters ('gofeirdd') in their midst (*RP* 1,293.14–18).

The kind of diversity of entertainment which, it has been suggested, resounded in many a medieval Welsh court and noble hall from an early time is glimpsed in a striking passage from a *cywydd* by Rhys Goch Eryri to Robert ap Maredudd of Eifionydd, composed around 1436. This patron welcomes not only the bards ('Beirdd a

---

[81] References to the *datgeiniad* in the 'Statute' are summarized by T. Gwynn Jones in *Gwaith Tudur Aled*, vol. i, p. xxxii (see also *GP* p. ciii; 17.45–6; 36.31–5; 37.8–10). Since their duties are said to include 'gwneuthur englyn', it is possible that they performed their own simple compositions as well as the *pencerdd*'s more elaborate verse (cf. 'Prydu a chanu ei cherdd' (*GDG* 85.22)).

[82] *BBBGDd* 63.53–6. On Dafydd Bach (*c*.1350–1400), also known as Sypyn Cyfeiliog, see *CIGE* pp. lxxx–lxxxii. Two *cywyddau serch* attributed to him (*CIGE* LXXI, LXXII) are discussed in Ch. 6 below, pp. 210–11

phrydyddion'), but also all manner of humble entertainers—'Pob amryw ofer glerwr' . . .

> Pob crythor ddihepgor ddyn
> Dilys a phob cerdd delyn;
> Pob trwmpls propr hirgorn copr cau,
> Pob sôn pobl, pob sŵn pibau;[83]
> Pob hudol, anfoddol fydd,
> Llwm hadl, a phob llamhidydd;
> Pob ffidler law draw y dring,
> Pob swtr tabwrdd, pob sawtring . . .
> (*CIGE* C.47–54)

(Every crowder—indispensable, faultless man—and every air on the harp; every seemly trumpet with its long, hollow copper horn, every chatter from people, every sound from pipes; every conjurer—unseemly is he—and every tumbler; every fiddler's hand climbs up yonder, every adversary(?) with a drum, every psaltery . . .)

The mention of magicians and acrobats is particularly striking, since they are all too rarely referred to, as court entertainers at least, in the formal eulogies of the period.[84] Such a wealth of musical instruments, however—some, such as the harp and *crwth*, more highly regarded than others—is attested throughout the *cywydd* period,[85] and there are several allusions to dancing to the accompaniment of music.[86] It is clear that the *Clêr* enjoyed the hospitality of the less conservative

[83] Cf. Tudur Penllyn's satire of a certain Wiliam Bibydd whose performance, as he grapples buffoon-like with his bagpipes 'fal tin y glêr', is preferred to the proud poet's more dignified *awdl* at an Englishman's wedding-feast in the town of Fflint (*Gwaith Tudur Penllyn . . .*, 30).

[84] The *hudolion* in *Ffordd y Brawd Odrig*, 53.27–31, practise feats of illusion, and the term corresponds, as does *clêr*, to Latin *histriones*; cf. also the triad cited earlier, which combines the *hudol*, *clerwr*, and *bardd y blawd* as disreputable entertainers.

[85] Early references, from the law tracts onwards, to the traditional triad of instruments—harp, *crwth*, and pipes, are discussed by Jarman, 'Telyn a Chrwth', 157–8. For a list of instruments attested in 14th- and 15th-cent. Welsh poetry see Mair Jones, 'Byd y Beirdd, sef Ymchwiliad i Amgylchfyd a Diddordebau Beirdd Yr Uchelwyr yn y Bedwaredd Ganrif ar Ddeg a'r Bymthegfed Ganrif', unpublished MA thesis, University of Wales (1983), 152–5. See also D. J. Bowen, 'Beirdd a Noddwyr y Bedwaredd Ganrif ar Ddeg', 89–90, and cf. the Peniarth 20 version of the Bardic Grammar (*GP* 57.20–3):

> Teir prifgerd tant ysyd, nyt amgen: kerd grwth,
> kerd delyn, a cherd timpan.
> Teir prifgerd megin ysyd, nyt amgen: organ, a
> phibeu, a cherd y got.

[86] See *GIG* II.13; XII.12; XVI.56. In the 15th cent. cf., for instance, *CIGE* CIII.40; *Gwaith Lewis Glyn Cothi* (1953), 50.25; *Gwaith Guto'r Glyn*, LIII.1–4.

uchelwyr, probably in return for eulogy as well as lighter forms of verse, and the use of *clêr* in the sense of inferior minstrels persists in the poems of the *Cywyddwyr* throughout the fifteenth and sixteenth centuries. In some instances it is clearly implied that both poets (*beirdd*) and *clêr*, therefore presumably the inferior *Clêr* as distinct from the qualified bards, enjoyed a nobleman's patronage, as when Gutun Owain speaks of 'beirdd a chlêr', which is translated by his editor as '(des) bardes et (des) ménéstrels'.[87] It is often difficult to judge whether *clêr* is used in this sense, which is clearly not pejorative, or as a term for poets in general; but it may be said that, in the vast majority of cases, when the context is not clearly derogatory, it is the second meaning which is to be understood.

Despite the references to the *Clêr* in a 'neutral' sense as entertainers at the homes of noblemen in this period, there is no mistaking the fact that they were still regarded by the qualified bards with some contempt, an attitude which has been seen to colour the first recorded instances of the word in the early fourteenth century. This attitude is best exemplified in the fifteenth century by Lewis Glyn Cothi in his eulogy to Wiliam ap Morgan, obviously one of the more conservative patrons of his day:

> Penkerdieit ai kar lle. m. gymharant.
> Hait o dinkerieit uyth nis karant.
> Teuluwyr ai kar darpar kerd dant.
> Erestyn nis kar ef ai grastant.
> Kler y dom erom heb warant. amlwc.
> J guwch ai olwc a ochelant.[88]

(Chief poets love him where they compete with each other; a flock of tinkers will never love him; *teuluwyr* love him, providers of harp-music; a minstrel with his coarse string loves him not; the *Clêr* of the dung-heap, who are upon us without a warrant for all to see, avoid his frown and his regard.)

The official bards, whose authority and status was based on rigorous training and approved grading by means of poetic contests, are

---

[87] *Œuvre poétique*, XLVIII.40; p. 256. Cf. E. Stanton Roberts (ed.), *Peniarth MS. 67* (Cardiff, 1918), LXXIII.29; W. Leslie Richards (ed.), *Gwaith Dafydd Llwyd o Fathafarn* (Cardiff, 1964), 58.7–8.

[88] *Gwaith Lewis Glyn Cothi* (1953), 25.33–8; cf. the same poet in *Gwaith . . .* (1837), p. 313.53–4. GPC translates *erestyn* as 'minstrel; juggler, buffoon' (1,231). In *The Text of the Bruts from the Red Book of Hergest*, ed. J. Rhŷs and J. Gwenogvryn Evans (Clarendon Press, Oxford, 1890), 186, *erestyn* corresponds to Latin *ioculator*. Cf. also *GDG* 130.21, and DG's personification of the wind as 'Gŵr eres . . . garw ei sain', 'Drud byd', 'Drythyllfab', and 'hudol' (*GDG* 117.3–4,34–5).

set against the 'tincer', 'erestyn', and 'clêr y dom', the minor minstrels who did not possess a bardic licence, and were therefore excluded from the élite hierarchy. One of the purposes of the so-called eisteddfodau, the first of which was held at Carmarthen in 1451, was to regulate the grading and practices of the bards, a function largely motivated by the desire to protect the dignity of the bardic order from the encroaching pretenders, the Clêr. Thus 'Statud Gruffudd ap Cynan', which was drawn up in preparation for the first Caerwys eisteddfod, held in 1523, speaks of the 'worthless weeds' ('gorweigion chwynn') which must be rooted out by the regular and orderly grading of poets.[89]

Throughout the cywydd period, then, there is ample evidence to suggest that the official bards, whilst retaining their privileged status and the lavish attention of their uchelwyr patrons, were never allowed to lose sight of the activities of those anonymous clerwyr who must have enlivened many a noble hall and swarming marketplace in medieval Wales. Since the twelfth century, at least, these popular minstrels were generally regarded by the bardic establishment with deep contempt. However, particularly during the turbulent and necessarily innovative years of the fourteenth century, it is an attitude which surely belies a considerable degree of interaction between the various grades of poets. The precise nature of this interaction remains unknown, but it is hoped that the following chapters will serve to cast some light on the ways in which the new kind of poetry developed by Dafydd ap Gwilym and his fellow Cywyddwyr may have been influenced by the submerged popular verse tradition which the Clêr represent.

---

[89] J. H. Davies, 'The Roll of the Caerwys Eisteddfod of 1523', Transactions of the Liverpool Welsh National Society (1904/5–1908/9), 94. The commission for the second Caerwys eisteddfod states that 'vagraunt and idle persons naming theim selfes mynstrelles Rithmers and Barthes, are lately growen into such an intollerable multitude within the principalitee of north wales, that . . . thexpert mynstrelles and musicions in tonge and Coñyng [are] therby much discouraged to travail in thexercise and practize of theire knowledges, and also not a litle hyndred in theire Lyvinges and prefermentes' ('The Commission of the Caerwys Eistedvod 1568', in J. Gwenogvryn Evans, Report on Manuscripts in the Welsh Language, vol. I (1898), 291); cf. also 'A Petition for Another Eistedvod 1594' (ibid. 293–5). These declarations, supported by the gentry and the English Crown alike, must be regarded in the same light as the numerous royal ordinations intended to regulate the activities of poets and minstrels, such as those which followed the Glyndŵr rebellion; see D. J. Bowen, 'Agweddau ar Ganu'r Bedwaredd Ganrif ar Ddeg a'r Bymthegfed', LlC 9 (1966–7), 69–72; id., 'Dafydd ap Gwilym a Datblygiad y Cywydd', LlC 8 (1964), 2.

2

Satirical Verse

In view of the, albeit prejudiced, evidence of the Bardic Grammar and of the bards themselves, there can be little doubt that the *Clêr* were notorious for their satire and vituperative verse. It must not be thought that the repertoires of all these minstrels were necessarily confined to this particular type of entertainment, but satirical verse is clearly one of the more likely areas of sub-literary influence on those poets who were active in the early part of the fourteenth century, and on their immediate successors—Dafydd ap Gwilym and his contemporaries. We are fortunate to have in the Red Book of Hergest, alongside the familiar compositions of panegyric and piety, a substantial collection of satirical poetry which represents an important aspect of bardic activity in this period. Most of these pieces are hardly to be counted among the century's most inspired or artistically commendable productions, and they are certainly not the most edifying. But as their general technical accomplishment indicates, they are the work of trained poets, many, if not all, of whom were also adept at composing traditional eulogy in the *awdl* metres. They have, it will be seen, much in common with the early *cywyddau*, and they not only belong in part to a crucial period of transition for the bardic hierarchy, but afford a valuable insight into the world of the *Clêr* themselves, who are often the subjects of the satire. It is, therefore, somewhat surprising that this corpus, which reflects the other, equally valid side of the bardic coin, should until recently have been largely neglected by editors and critics alike.

Thomas Parry, whose textual notes in his edition of the work of Dafydd ap Gwilym refer frequently to the Red Book satires, chooses to ignore this body of verse in his brief survey of the post-Conquest period in his Sir John Rhŷs Memorial Lecture delivered to the British Academy in 1961. Whilst maintaining that: 'In the closing years of the thirteenth century and the opening years of the fourteenth interest in bardism was at an ebb', he speaks of 'the scarcity of the usual eulogistic poetry, which seems to have been supplanted by sophisticated poems to women and poems on religious

subjects'.[1] There is no mention of satire. Indeed, very little has been
written on the subject of satire in medieval Welsh poetry, as opposed
to formal eulogy. It was an integral part of Celtic society from an
early time, deriving, it seems, from age-old (possibly druidic) customs of composing curses and spells. Diodorus Siculus' account of
the fighting habits of the ancient Gauls is well-known: 'And when
some one accepts their challenge to battle, they loudly recite the
deeds of valour of their ancestors and proclaim their own valorous
quality, at the same time abusing and making little of their opponent
and generally attempting to rob him beforehand of his fighting
spirit.'[2] He testifies too that their lyric poets, or 'bards', 'sing to the
accompaniment of instruments resembling lyres, sometimes a eulogy
and sometimes a satire'.[3] The psychological and social significance
of satire in a heroic society which valued praise and the fame it
engendered above all else cannot be over-emphasized:

The kind of society which sets a high value on individual sense of honour,
the 'shame society', readily finds a use for satire as an integrated counter-
balance to the overweening claims of heroes in its warrior class. In ancient
Ireland, satirists were feared by the ruling class and achieved a species of
backhanded domination which itself was oppressive.[4]

The malignant power of satire is well attested in both the Welsh and
Irish traditions.[5] The hero of *Culhwch ac Olwen*, having been
refused entry into Arthur's court, threatens the porter, the aptly
named Glewlwyd Gafaelfawr (Glewlwyd Mighty-grasp), with the

[1] 'The Welsh Metrical Treatise Attributed to Einion Offeiriad', *Proceedings of the British Academy*, 47 (1961), 190. On the paucity of purely satirical verse preserved from the pre-Conquest period, see J. E. Caerwyn Williams, 'Beirdd y Tywysogion: Arolwg', *LlC* 11 (1970), 62.
[2] J. J. Tierney, 'The Celtic Ethnography of Posidonius', *Proceedings of the Royal Irish Academy*, Section C, 60 (1960), 250.
[3] Ibid. 251.
[4] H. D. Rankin, *Celts and the Classical World* (London and New York, 1987), 162. On the subject of honour and shame as motivating forces see also M. W. Bloomfield and C. W. Dunn, *The Role of the Poet in Early Societies* (D. S. Brewer, Cambridge, 1989), 6–8, 37–41.
[5] The Irish satirical tradition has received a great deal more attention than its Welsh counterpart. See in particular F. N. Robinson, 'Satirists and Enchanters in Early Irish Literature', in D. G. Lyon and G. F. Moore (eds.), *Studies in the History of Religions Presented to Crawford Howell Joy* (New York, 1912), 95–130; Howard Meroney, 'Studies in Early Irish Satire', *Journal of Celtic Studies*, 1 (1950), 199–226; 2 (1953), 59–130; Kim McCone, 'A Tale of Two Ditties: Poet and Satirist in *Cath Maige Tuired*' in D. Ó Corráin et al. (eds.), *Sages, Saints and Storytellers: Celtic Studies in Honour of Professor James Carney* (An Sagart, Maynooth, 1989), 122–43; id., *Pagan Past and Christian Present* (An Sagart, Maynooth, 1990), 220 ff.

following words: 'Ot agory y porth, da yw. Onys agory, mi a dygaf
anglot y'th arglwyd a drygeir y titheu.'[6] ('If you open the gates all
is well. If you do not I shall bring dishonour to your lord and
defamation to you.') He then threatens to utter three mighty cries,
making all pregnant women inside infertile for ever more by causing their wombs to become inverted. The motif of inducing infertil-
ity through satire occurs in Irish in the tale of the *fili* Laidcenn, who
is said to have satirized the men of Leinster for a whole year after
they had killed his son. Tradition has it that many of them died and
that neither wheat, grass, nor leaves were seen in Leinster during
that year.[7] Satire was also reputed to cause actual injury to the victim's face, thus emphasizing the loss of personal dignity. In the
Welsh law tracts, *wynebwerth* has the meaning of an imposition for
insulting a person's honour, and the well-known phrase 'colli
wyneb', 'to lose face', may also be compared.[8] It is said that when
the *fili* Nede mac Adnai cursed Cáier, king of Connacht, three blis-
ters appeared on his face, and he was forced to flee in shame. The
poet later repented and sought out the king, whom he found hiding
in the crevice of a rock. But when he approached him the king died
of a guilty conscience.[9]

Death through satire was not uncommon, or so we are led to
believe. In 1414 the death of Sir John Stanley, lord-lieutenant of
Ireland, was thought to have been brought about by the vicious
invective of the family of Niall Ó hUiginn, and even as late as the
Elizabethan period we hear that: 'The Irishmen will not sticke to
affirm that they can rime either man or beast to death.'[10] The most
famous example in Welsh is the tradition surrounding Dafydd ap
Gwilym's satire of Rhys Meigen (*GDG* 21), who is said to have
dropped dead on hearing the poem. He may, of course, have been a
figment of the poet's imagination, but it is noteworthy that both

---

[6] Rachel Bromwich and D. Simon Evans (eds.), *Culhwch and Olwen: An Edition
and Study of the Oldest Arthurian Tale* (Cardiff, 1992), 4.

[7] J. E. Caerwyn Williams, *Traddodiad Llenyddol Iwerddon* (Cardiff, 1958), 46.
Cf., for instance, in one of the Red Book satires, the lines: 'nycheir drwy serch
nacharyat | nac epil na hil nahat' (*RP* 1,358.3–4).

[8] See T. M. Charles-Edwards, 'The Date of the Four Branches of the Mabinogi',
THSC (1970–1), 277–8. Cf. a 15th-cent. poet's threat (*BDG* CCXXV.17–20):

> Os er ysgorn, neu fènair.(*sic*) | Y gwnant â mi, gwae fi, Fair!
> Dialedd, drwy fy ngweddi, | A ddel, Gwen, i'th dalcen di!

[9] J. E. Caerwyn Williams, *Traddodiad Llenyddol Iwerddon*, 47.

[10] Ibid. 147; see also Tomás Ó Cathasaigh, 'Curse and Satire', *Éigse*, 21 (1986), 10-
15.

Dafydd and Gruffudd Gryg refer to the incident in their bardic dispute,[11] which is, at times, almost equally biting in its satire. An
intriguing explanatory note to one of the Red Book satires reads as
follows:

Trahaearn brydyd mawr ae cant y gadwgawn vicar ae daw ac y llosges y dy
y kalan nessaf wedy y dychanu nos natolic ac y llas y daw. (*RP* 1,357.1)

(Composed by Trahaearn Brydydd Mawr to Cadwgawn the Vicar and his
son-in-law, whose house burnt down on New Year's Day after he had been
satirized on Christmas night, and whose son-in-law was killed.)

Whether or not these words are meant to be taken literally, we are
obviously dealing here with the same tradition.[12] Dafydd Y Coed's
satire of another cleric expresses the same convention:

> Gwnaf drwy not agglot am eglyn—yn varw
> daer agarw darogyn
> (*RP* 1,359.40–1)

(Through the mark of dishonour, with my *englyn* I shall cause the death of
a rough, persistent scoundrel.)

Wishing or presaging the victim's death is common practice in verse
of this kind—in the words of Rhys ap Dafydd ab Einion to a certain
'Willi':

> Dachwedyl yr genedyl bei othgennyat—gleu
> oed glywet dy uarwnat
> (*RP* 1,357.39–40)

(To hear your death-song—were you to allow it without delay—would be
good news for the whole nation.)

Similarly, Y Prydydd Breuan opens his satire of the harpist Darre by
stating his intention of 'singing his undying death-song'—'kanu
marw nat diymadaw' (*RP* 1,355.33)—and proceeds to pervert the
terms of formal lament in most unvenerable fashion. It seems likely,
however, that he is merely following here one of the established conventions of the satirical genre, since the effect of the invective would
be lost on its recipient were he actually dead. If this is so, the poem
may be compared with the early *Cywyddwyr*'s custom of composing
fictitious elegies to living persons.[13]

[11] *GDG* 151.70; 152.53–60. On this tradition see ibid., pp. xl–xli.
[12] The motif persists in the later *cywydd* tradition in satires of Eiddig, the jealous
husband, as for instance in the 'apocryphal' *BDG* CCXVIII: 'Lladd y taeog, a'i
grogi, | A cherdd gan farwed a chi!' (ll. 33–4).
[13] These poems are discussed by Bromwich, *APDG* 159–61.

As was suggested in the opening chapter, the treatment of satire in the Bardic Grammar does not reflect contemporary practice. Although it does recognize the validity of a particular kind of bardic satire as part of the *teuluwr*'s art, its sparse examples of satirical verse (representing metre rather than genre) are in stark contrast to the numerous illustrations of the topos of vituperation in medieval Latin grammars such as those of Matthew of Vendôme and Geoffrey of Vinsauf.[14] The very fact that the compiler distinguishes so insistently between praise and satire suggests that the qualified bards of the early fourteenth century had been over-indulging in satire, thereby lowering themselves, as he saw it, to the level of the popular poets, to whose influence they were more susceptible than ever before. Vituperative verse—'goganu, ac agloduori, a gwneuthur kewilid a gwaradwyd' (*GP* 35.11), 'satire, defamation, and causing shame and dishonour'—was clearly an important part of the *clerwr*'s repertoire, whatever else it may have included. The early *Cywyddwyr* continued to contradict the grammarian's all-too-dogmatic precepts, even to the extent of combining praise and satire within the same poem, although it is clearly stated that they are incompatible (*GP* 16.30–1; 36.3–4). This is not to say that satirical or vituperative verse was regarded by the bards as being equal in value to formal eulogy. The point is well illustrated in Hywel Ystorm's satire of Casnodyn,[15] where it is stated that 'a traitor who sings a song of mockery is not comparable to a quick-witted, lordly *prydydd*':

> . . . Mal nat un penn cun kynnar—o brydyd
> a bratwr kerd wattwar.
>
> (*RP* 1,341.1–2)

---

[14] See Edmond Faral, *Les arts poétiques du XIIe et du XIIIe siècle* (Paris, 1958); on the scholastic tradition of satire and invective in medieval Latin verse see F. J. E. Raby, *A History of Secular Latin Poetry in the Middle Ages* (2nd edn., Clarendon Press, Oxford, 1957), ii. 45–54. A. T. E. Matonis, 'Medieval Topics and Rhetoric in the Work of the Cywyddwyr', unpublished Ph.D thesis, Edinburgh University (1973), 215–48, discusses 14th-cent. Welsh satirical verse in the context of the European vituperative tradition.

[15] G. J. Williams, *Traddodiad Llenyddol Morgannwg* (Cardiff, 1948), 6–7, considers it to be the work of Hywel Ystorm, as does D. J. Bowen (*YB* 11, 78). In fact, the only Red Book poem attributed to 'Howel Ystorym' is a satire of 'Addaf Eurych' (*RP* 1,337–8), and the anonymous satires which follow (cols. 1,338–48) are not known to be attributed to Hywel elsewhere. However, this body of imaginatively scurrilous verse may well be his work, and will be considered as such.

From the time of Taliesin in the sixth century formal panegyric was esteemed above all other verse, and throughout the *cywydd* period the *cywydd gûr*, or *cywydd* of praise to a noble patron, was considered far superior to love-poetry, even after the heyday of Dafydd ap Gwilym. The Red Book satirists, as well as the *Cywyddwyr*, often refer pompously to their bardic status, and feel it necessary to justify their attacks by stressing the unworthiness of their victims. Gruffudd Gryg warns a proud girl:

> 'Mogel dy farnu megis
> Chwerwedd dwyll, chwarëydd dîs
> (*DGG* LXXII.43–4)

(Beware of being judged as a dice-player, bitter deceit),

and in a similar vein Dafydd ap Gwilym, with characteristic frankness, warns a certain Efa not to give him reason to satirize her like the ungenerous—'Na haedd ogan fal anhael' (*GDG* 97.17)—typically transposing the values of noble patronage to the context of love-poetry. As one might expect, lack of generosity is a common cause of censure in the Welsh, as in the Irish, poetic tradition, and is one of the elements in the perversion of conventional panegyric which forms the essence of satirical verse. This verse replaces generosity with avarice, nobility with rusticity, bravery with cowardice, and so forth, so that its subjects are generally despicable, the very antithesis of the paragon of the noble patron. Thus, in Hywel Ystorm's *awdl* to 'Adam the tinker' a modest dwelling is ironically described in the rhetorical style of courtly panegyric:

> lle anard lle an amyl selsic.
> lle anoew lle anosgeidic . . .
> lle di vennwant plant plennic-lluciffer.
>   llys uffern wennwynic.
> lle y bryssir bressych wyl badric . . .
> lle berwir baryf y wwch kerric . . .
> (*RP* 1,337.42–1,338.6)

(An ugly place where sausages are scarce; a sorrowful, inelegant place where the radiant children of Lucifer pour their scorn—court of venomous hell—where cabbage is rushed on the feast of Patrick; where they boil a wild goat's beard ...)

A fine example of the use of this particular *cymeriad* device, in which the word 'Lle' recurs at the beginning of several lines, is Dafydd ap

Gwilym's homage to Newborough in Anglesey (*GDG* 134), where abundance and generosity prevail.

In Hywel Ystorm's stinging satire, Addaf is depicted as a lowly minstrel whose efforts are dismissed as 'ureith gerd drewyedic' (*RP* 1,338.33–4), 'motley, pungent verse'. If Hywel is indeed the author of the satires of Casnodyn and Trahaearn (Brydydd Mawr)[16] (*RP* 1,340–5), then he must have been composing in the early part of the fourteenth century, and his numerous assaults on inferior minstrels are certainly consistent with the general derision of the *Clêr* in this period. For instance, a crowder is ridiculed as 'athro cler' (*RP* 1,345.35) ('teacher of *Clêr*'), and the term sometimes appears in compound forms, such as the pejorative 'car clergrwth' ('companion of the *Clêr's crwth*'), and 'crwydyrgler' ('wandering *Clêr*') (*RP* 1,345.16; 1,346.42). Hywel Ystorm's attitude towards these minstrels is typical of the Red Book satire as a whole, and is reminiscent of their depiction in the Bardic Grammar. They are vilified above all for their indiscriminate mockery and defamation—which are forever emphasized in order to justify the bards' attacks—and, of course, for the poor quality of their verse. Thus Hywel speaks of 'bratwr kerd wattwar' ('a traitor singing mocking verse'), 'Gogan ymadrawd' ('pronouncement of satire'), 'kynnhenngerd' ('bickering verse'), and 'man odleu eneu anurd' ('the petty rhymes of an undignified mouth') (*RP* 1,341.2; 1,340.22; 1,346.13, 10). Y Prydydd Breuan says of the harpist Darre: 'Kymmudyr y amkan. kymu agogan' (*RP* 1,355.40–1)—'loathsome is his intention; he has made a pact with satire'; and the proud *prydydd* is at his most arrogant in Hywel Ystorm's humorous lampoon of Trahaearn, in the words: 'dinkyr tawl dibennkerd taw' (*RP* 1,344.10)—'mean tinker, devoid of sublime song, be silent!' If the poets are to be believed, the *Clêr's* boastful ranting also makes them worthy objects of satire. According to Hywel he satirizes Addaf, the tinker-poet, 'since [his] bruised mind has no intention of forsaking its vaunting'—'Kany mynn emennyd yssic. | ymadaw ae ffrost . . .' (*RP* 1,338.35–6). Rhys Meigen used to boast from the River Teifi to the

---

[16] Among the poems attributed to Trahaearn is a satire of a cleric (*RP* 1,357). A certain Trahaearn is satirized in a faulty *englyn* in the Peniarth 20 version of the Bardic Grammar (*GP* 53.14–17; cf. ibid. 62.41–4). The resemblance between the lines 'Ys amlach am dy semlgerd | O'r byt a chwyt noc a chward', and lines from the satire of Casnodyn—'ys amlach . . . a chwyt am dy gerd chwidach | noc achward wrthlys bard bach' (*RP* 1,342.2–4)—suggests that this *englyn* may also be the work of Hywel Ystorm. Alternatively, the satires of Casnodyn and Trahaearn in *RP* may have been composed by these two poets to each other.

Menai Straits (*GDG* 21.9–10), and he would 'sing abuse to everyone, without knowing what it might be'—

> Gwaith o ymgeiniaith a ganai—i bawb
> Heb wybod beth fyddai
>
> (ll. 61–2)

He is a flatterer—'truthain' (l. 18)—and this accusation of insincerity is also levelled by the Red Book poets. Again, Hywel Ystorm mocks the accomplished Glamorgan poet Casnodyn's 'trutheingerd' (*RP* 1,341.14) and (once more, presumably, in jest) belittles Trahaearn's 'ffol oergeu | ffilor gerd aghywir' (*RP* 1,344.41–2), 'an incorrect (or untruthful) poem of nonsense, foolish, cold, and false.'

Reference has been made to satires of a harpist and a crowder. It was the harpist Darre who 'made a pact with satire', and the crowder's mouth is described by Hywel Ystorm as 'a pit of mocking verse'—'ryw bydew kerd wattwar' (*RP* 1,345.42–3), which indicates that his repertoire, too, included verse as well as music, probably performed to the accompaniment of the *crwth*. His instrument, which is said to produce a coarse tune—'garwglwm' (*RP* 1,345.12)— may well be the kind of foreign introduction so despised by Iorwerth Beli in his complaint to the bishop of Bangor. Hywel's satire also refers to 'dwrd dyfwn dabwrd dan dabar' (*RP* 1,345.43), 'the din of a deep drum under a cloak', another of the instruments ridiculed by Iorwerth Beli; and Rhys ap Dafydd ab Einion's portrayal of the 'thief' Willi as having the form of an ugly leather string—'Hagyrdant lledyr dyuyant' (*RP* 1,357.42)—again recalls Iorwerth's derision of the willow *crwth* with its strings of gut. The mention of bells in relation to the *Clêr* in this verse and elsewhere suggests that they may have been used by these minstrels to draw attention to their performance in public places.[17] Hywel Ystorm's 'bloed hengloch blwm' (*RP* 1,345.14–15), 'the cry of an old lead bell', Gruffudd ap Maredudd's 'llef cloch' (*RP* 1,336.9), and Dafydd ap Gwilym's description of Rhys Meigen as 'gloch y glêr' (*GDG* 21.74), are echoed in similar contexts in the fifteenth and sixteenth centuries. Tudur Penllyn, in a series of *englynion* which belongs to the *cyff clêr* convention, depicts his fellow *cywyddwr* Hywel Cilan as a lowly

---

[17] I am indebted to Helen Fulton for this suggestion, who believes that this characteristic links the *Clêr* to the Latin *praeco* (public crier) as part of a diverse group of wandering entertainers. Cf. the picture of a minstrel holding a bell in each hand, in Bodleian Library MS 264, fo. 188v., reproduced by J. Southworth in *The English Medieval Minstrel* (Woodbridge, 1989), 136.

minstrel, stretching his jaws and calling out loudly under tin bells -
'Hywel, galw uchel dan glochau—ystaen | Ac estyn ei weflau . . .'.[18]
The figurative meaning of 'cloch', 'one who praises or proclaims', as,
for instance, in Llywelyn Goch's description of himself as the praise-
poet of Lleucu Llwyd—'Llywelyn Goch, gloch dy glod' (DGG
LXXXVII.18)—is clearly inappropriate in a satirical context. The
word may have been used in some instances by the satirical poets in
another metaphorical sense, to convey the loudness of the Clêr's public declamations,[19] but literal reference to bells does seem particularly
appropriate when applied to popular entertainers.

It will be remembered that Iolo Goch, in his satire of Gwyddelyn,
speaks disparagingly of 'beirdd y blawd' and of 'clêr . . . llawr tref'
(GIG XXXVII.52–3), the minstrels who plied their trade in public
places alongside other itinerant entertainers. Some, at least, of these
minstrels would no doubt have provided entertainment at the homes
of the less conservative noblemen, along with the qualified bards. But
as one might expect, they are again depicted in the Red Book satires
as disreputable performers who solicited at the market-place and at
the homes of peasants.[20] Hywel Ystorm's Einion would beg for
gruel—'Gruel a archei' (RP 1,339.11)—while the long-suffering
Casnodyn is caricatured as 'a beast whose sustenance is meagre from
the cottages of Cilfai, fatted sow of peasants' dwellings':

> Pryf waeth waeth y uaeth o vytheu—kiluei
> pasgwch tei taeogeu.
>
> (RP 1,342.23–4)

Trahaearn, who is similarly depicted as an inferior minstrel, is seen
as 'a fat lad who wanders across many a merry land, very wrathful
calf (pej.) of summer dwellings':

> Daramretwas bras broyd.—llawenffraeth.
> llo Jawnffrom havodyd.
>
> (RP 1,344.20–1)

[18] Gwaith Tudur Penllyn . . . , p. 65 ll. 5–6; cf., for instance, a 16th-cent. cywydd of
uncertain authorship: 'Melltith clêr, lle clywer clych, | Sydd enbyd i Swydd Ddinbych'
(BBCS 29, 475).
[19] Cf. Madog Benfras's caricature of a Black Friar as 'Tafod cloch bres yn crefu'
(BDG CCXVII.43), and see GPC, s.v. cloch.
[20] The 15th- and 16th-cent. clerwyr Y Nant and Robin Clidro both depict themselves as soliciting among the common folk as well as the nobility; see BBCS 17, 83;
CRhC 46 ('Taith Glera').

The subject of one of Madog Dwygraig's so-called 'Chwedleu Chwytlyt' (Sickly Tales), who travels around composing satire in return for meat during Shrovetide—'krwydyrwr goganwr am gic ynyt' (RP 1,273.18)—is described as 'krwydyrffeir' (ll. 19–20), one who wanders from one fair to another, probably performing for material reward. But this minstrel is referred to primarily as a weaver, 'gwehyd' (l. 36), a 'tinker-craftsman'—'Tingkyr greffdyn' (l. 13)—and it would appear therefore that he only occasionally composed satirical verse, 'in return for meat'. Although such overtly hyperbolic verse should not be read too literally—note, for instance, Hywel Ystorm's description of the bard Trahaearn as being in charge of his father's flock, 'Swynnyat preid y dat'[21] (RP 1,344.35)—it is reasonable to assume that, as well as experienced minstrels, the Clêr included those who turned to verse and minstrelsy only when the need arose, or when time allowed. This type of performer would doubtless have been regarded as especially odious by the thoroughly trained qualified bards.

Since his surviving work consists entirely of satire Hywel Ystorm has inevitably been referred to as one of the Clêr. He may not have been a poet of the highest rank, but the quality and complexity of his verse-craft identify him as a trained bard of considerable merit, who, like several of the other Red Book satirists, such as Madog Dwygraig and Dafydd Y Coed, is likely to have been versed in formal eulogy and religious poetry. It has been seen that he depicts both Casnodyn and Trahaearn Brydydd Mawr as inferior minstrels for the purpose of humour (although, in view of the theory proposed in the opening chapter concerning the semantic evolution of the term clêr during the course of the fourteenth century, it is perhaps significant that the word is not used in these satires of accomplished bards, whereas it does occur in all but one of Hywel's other satires). These two poems would seem to belong to the cyff clêr convention, and the outright hyperbole of this genre, allied to the fact that the names and works of many bards have been lost to posterity, makes it extremely difficult to distinguish between verse of this type and the genuine attacks on the Clêr themselves. The genre is certainly well attested in the following centuries. In the fifteenth century Tudur Penllyn composed englyn sequences which satirize a number of poets, several of them well known, who made him the butt of their humour, and

---

[21] This is a conventional motif of 14th-cent. satire; cf., for instance, RP 1,273.38–9, and RP 1,291.32–3 (Iolo Goch's satire of the cleric Madog ap Hywel, GIG XXXVIII).

some of these names also occur in similar satires by Gutun Owain and Tudur Aled.[22] Some of the *testunau* or ridiculous slurs which provided the themes for the satire of the respected *pencerdd* have been preserved in the manuscripts.[23] According to 'Statud Gruffudd ap Cynan', which associates the practice with the 'testunio' attributed to the *teuluwr* in the Bardic Grammar, these often ribald subjects should be patently untrue so as not to bring shame upon the bard.[24] A more detailed account of this bizarre custom is given in Siôn Dafydd Rhys's late sixteenth-century Grammar:

Neithior Brenhinawl, a bhydh pann briôder vn o waed y Tywyssawc . . . ac ynn honno, y gweir Cyph Clêr, a hwnnw bhydh Pencerdh o'r goreu: ac yno y rhoir testyn dhigribh dhiwladâidh arr y Pencerdh i'r Prydydhion erailh i ganu idho ebh, i lawenhau'r Orsedh. A'r Prydydhion hynny a dhôn a'i Cerdh idho ebh, ac a'i canant arr ostec. A thrannoeth y daw ynteu a'i atteb idhynt hwytheu; a dyblu eu rhodhion a gânt hwytheu yno. A hynn olh a notaynt ei wneuthur wedy ciniaw, er mwyn didhânwch i'r Gynnulheidbha . . . [25]

(A royal wedding feast is held when a descendant of the Prince is married . . . and there a *Cyff Clêr* is appointed, who is a Chief Poet of the highest rank: and a slur of a humorous and urbane nature is put upon the Chief Poet as a subject on which the other poets may compose to him, for the merriment of the throne. And these poets bring their poem to him, and declaim it for all to hear. The next day he himself comes to answer the slur in their presence; and their reward is doubled there. And it was their custom to do all this after dinner, to entertain the assembled audience.)

It would appear, then, that the convention was chiefly related to the merriment of the wedding feast, and it may be, as J. E. Caerwyn Williams has suggested in a discussion of the epithalamic genre,[26] that it reflects the ancient custom of inviting satire and vituperation in order to bring good luck. It is worth noting that the Red Book

---

[22] *Gwaith Tudur Penllyn . . .*, pp. 61–5 (the *cyff clêr englynion* of 15th- and 16th-cent. poets are discussed by T. Roberts, ibid. 131); *L'Œuvre poétique de Gutun Owain*, LXIV; *Gwaith Tudur Aled*, vol. 2, CXLII.

[23] Examples are cited by T. Gwynn Jones, *Gwaith Tudur Aled*, vol. 2, 535, 651–2; vol. 1, p. xxv; G. J. Williams, *Traddodiad Llenyddol Morgannwg*, 56–7. A possible example of such a *testun* from the first half of the 14th cent. is found in the Hendregadredd MS, following a ribald *englyn* to Ieuan (probably none other than Ieuan Llwyd of Glyn Aeron): 'gwir yni koryf yr argylwd aberythwd i chyrychu hyd yr ysdafell yn yr aryd ac ynno iewann hyd y dwygeill.' (Daniel Huws, 'Llawysgrif Hendregadredd', *NLWJ* 22 (1981–2), 25).

[24] *BBCS* 5, 27.

[25] Cited by J. E. C. Williams, 'Cerddi'r Gogynfeirdd . . .' *LlC* 13 (1974–81), 92, from *Cambrobrytannicæ Cymræcæve Linguæ Institutiones &c.* (1592), 304.

[26] 'Cerddi'r Gogynfeirdd . . .', 91 ff.

corpus includes at least a couple of references to wedding feasts ('neithiorau') in relation to the *Clêr* (*RP* 1,339.41; 1,355.36), and many a mocking *clerwr* may have diverted a festive audience at an *uchelwr*'s hall with his satire of an established bard. As far as we know there are no existing examples of such verse by inferior minstrels.[27] However, the term *cyff clêr* does imply that the *pencerdd* might originally have been satirized by the *Clêr* themselves, and it may well be that some of the Red Book satires were composed in response to lampoons of this kind. As in the verse of the early *Cywyddwyr*, we are sometimes afforded glimpses of an ongoing dispute between bard and minstrel. Madog Dwygraig's claim that the weaver-poet refuses his alliance or friendship—'Cas bryf ywrthyf awrthyt kyngreir' (*RP* 1,273.19)—is possibly a tantalizing reference to a poetic dispute, and in Rhys ap Dafydd ab Einion's satire of Willi, the lines

> hynn o orneir hen ywr nat
> hwde etto hyt attat.
> (*RP* 1,357.43–4)

(This song is the same old insult. Here it is, hurled at you yet again.)

suggest a long-standing enmity between the two men.

The kind of interaction between the various grades of poets which is suggested by this body of verse would seem largely to have been a direct consequence of the loosening of the bardic hierarchy in the late thirteenth century. Indeed, the evident popularity of satirical verse in the fourteenth century would seem to reflect this state of affairs. Since the *Clêr*, we know, specialized in the dubious art of vituperation, it is quite likely that their compositions had some impact on the satirical modes of their more accomplished counterparts, although they may themselves have been influenced, particularly in this period, by a long tradition of bardic satire in which the *prydyddion* were no doubt well-versed. One likely sign of sub-bardic influence is the preponderance in the Red Book satires of English loan-words which had clearly become part of everyday speech, a feature which, one presumes, would also have characterized the more colloquial verse of the *Clêr*.[28] A later example of the kind of verse which may have been

---

[27] The scurrilous *englyn* attributed to Rhys Meigen (see *GDG*, p. xl), which is said to have caused DG's satire of the minstrel, is of doubtful authenticity, as is another *englyn* which bears his name (*GDG*, p. 419).

[28] T. H. Parry-Williams remarks that the prominence of loan-words in 14th-cent. satire 'suggests that English words and expressions were mainly used by the lower order of bards, whose works were restricted, according to the Codes, to lampoon and

composed by these minstrels is found among the rather crudely fashioned poems of the *clerwr* known as 'Y Nant', who was active
mainly in Glamorgan in the last quarter of the fifteenth century. It is
a rare example of a cursing-poem,[29] in which the wretched poet vents
all his spleen on the men of Llandysul who robbed him of his belong-
ings, including his five gowns, six doublets, two hats, four books,
and even his two pairs of glasses! In a chillingly graphic passage he
wishes them dead, 'a thousand nooses around their necks', 'the bones
of their skulls pounded by swords' . . .

> . . . ay hywinedd bytron
> ay micyrnedd tuon
> a cwaet y calon
> ar hyt bob celfi . . .

(and their filthy nails and black knuckles and the blood of their hearts splat-
tered everywhere . . .)

They shall have no honourable burial . . .

> . . . nac yfeiriat na chylochudd
> na tim or elorwydd
> nac amto na betydd
> ont uffern bytew.[30]

(neither priest nor sacrist, neither bier nor shroud nor baptism, but the pit
of hell.)

Y Nant prays that his assailants may have no rest in paradise, and
his curse becomes a formulaic, almost incantatory spell, in which he
wishes them destitute, poisoned, burnt, and hanged:

> mi a cana ddews lawten
> ar y llatron hen
> hynny cafon yr wten
> am y cyddce rytec . . .

---

caricature. It also implies that English words were finding their way to the colloquial
language and were being assimilated in considerable numbers' (*The English Element
in Welsh* (London, 1923), 5).

[29] The poem has been edited by T. Gwynn Jones, 'Ein Kymrisches Fluchgedicht',
ZCP 17 (1928), 167–76; see also his remarks in 'Bardism and Romance', *THSC*
(1913–14), 298–9, and J. E. Caerwyn Williams, 'Beirdd y Tywysogion: Arolwg', 63.
Cf. the opening lines of one of Y Nant's request poems, in which he curses English
thieves (G. J. Williams, 'Cerddi'r Nant', *BBCS* 17, 80), and his cumulative maledic-
tion in Peniarth MS 54, i. 410–11.

[30] Cf. Iolo Goch's satire of Hersdin Hogl (*GIG* XXXVI), esp. ll. 75–7.

ac na bon tair wyddnos
ac na bon byddhewnos
ac na bon wyddnos
  heb newyn a noeddi . . .
ac na bon teirawr   .
ac na bon ddwyawr
ac na bon unawr
  heb y cwenwyno

(I shall sing a *dews lawden* (= hymn of praise to God?) to the rotten old thieves, until they feel the noose round their pretty little necks . . . and let them not be three weeks, nor two, nor even a single week without famine and nakedness . . . and let them not be three hours, nor two, nor even a single hour without being poisoned.)

While malevolent spells of this type may well have been one aspect of the 'goganu, a gwarthrudaw', and perhaps also of the 'Swynogleu, a dewindabaeth' condemned in the Bardic Grammar (*GP* 17.7–8; 35.19), there is nothing in the Red Book satires which can be called a spell, or a curse in the shape of a formal prayer. However, the rhetorically repetitive style of much of this verse, especially in Madog Dwygraig's vicious satire of a hag in which the word 'gwrach' recurs in almost every clause (*RP* 1,274),[31] is not all that far removed from the sinister composition of the fifteenth-century *clerwr*. And it has been seen that many of these poems contain a strong element of cursing, most notably in the wishing or presaging of the victim's death.

   Y Nant may in fact have been following an established convention of Welsh satirical verse. Thieves are often vilified in the Red Book satires. The author of one of these poems, Y Mab Cryg,[32] relates in pathetic detail how his house was plundered one dark night and, like Y Nant, lists the things which he has lost and wishes to see the thief hanged,[33] ravens hovering vengefully 'above his rump' (*RP* 1,362). Another Red Book poet of whom little is known, Yr Ustus Llwyd,

[31] See Twm Morys's edition and discussion, 'Canu Dychan y Llyfr Coch: 1. Gwrach', *Barddas*, 200–1 (Dec./Jan. 1993–4), 24–5.

[32] It is noteworthy that he speaks of the area 'rwng gwy a hafren' (*RP* 1,362.36; cf. 1,363.30), since Y Nant is believed to have been a native of Breconshire which, along with Glamorgan, was his main hunting-ground; see G. J. Williams, *Traddodiad Llenyddol Morgannwg*, 113–14; id., 'Cerddi'r Nant', 78.

[33] From the 15th cent. cf. also *Gwaith Tudur Penllyn . . .*, 29; *Gwaith Deio ab Ieuan Du a Gwilym ab Ieuan Hen*, ed. A. Eleri Davies (Cardiff, 1992), 17. The tradition survives in free-metre verse, as for instance in a vindictive cursing-poem by a poet who claims to have suffered a fate similar to that of Yr Ustus Llwyd, recorded in an early 18th-cent. MS (*LlRMG* 40–2).

adopts an equally lively narrative style in his crude satire of Gruffudd Iarll Mawddwy (*BBBGDd* 71), which in its account of the poet's mal-treatment at the court of a tight-fisted patron is very similar to the poem by Iocyn Ddu discussed in the opening chapter.[34] With its diverting, often scurrilous subject-matter and its leisurely and rela-tively uncomplicated expression, the work of all three poets, Iocyn Ddu, Yr Ustus Llwyd, and Y Mab Cryg, surely had much in com-mon with the unrecorded verse of the contemporary *Clêr*. (However, although these poets probably did not belong to the higher echelons of the bardic profession, it is, I think, unlikely that the work of an inferior *clerwr* (in the restricted sense) is recorded in the Red Book of Hergest, alongside the elaborate creations of the qualified bards.)[35] A further likely resemblance between Yr Ustus Llwyd's satire of the earl of Mawddwy and the verse of the *Clêr* is its metre, which is a syllabically regular version of that used by Y Nant in his cursing-poem, and in almost all his other extant verse.[36] It is a loose form of the bardic metre *cyhydedd hir*,[37] the alliterative correspondence (which in Y Nant's hands is not always in correct *cynghanedd*) being confined to the end of each 'verse'. It later came to be known as 'mesur Clidro', after the sixteenth-century *clerwr* Robin Clidro from the Clwyd Valley, who used the metre for his own distinctive brand of humorous, often self-mocking narrative poems, which include, sig-nificantly, a fair smattering of caricature and satire.[38] In view of the

[34] The poem is discussed by Twm Morys, 'Lle Anaml Selsig', *Barddas*, 202 (Feb. 1994), 8–10. An elegy in the *englyn* metre to an unknown poet is attributed to him in the Hendregadredd MS; see Huws, 'Llawysgrif Hendregadredd', 17, 23 n. 49, who shows that he was probably active before 1350.

[35] Although both Y Mab Cryg and Yr Ustus Llwyd ignore the conventional bardic practice of sustaining the end-rhyme, both poets show a mastery of *cynghanedd*, and the latter in particular makes considerable use of *cymeriad cynganeddol* and *cymeriad llythrennol*.

[36] His work includes a *gosteg* of *englynion* (including two *englynion proest*) (Peniarth 54, i. 375–6), which shows that he was able to compose in *cynghanedd*, although this is not always complete or correct. There follows in the MS an *englyn* whose irregular final couplet, rhyming two unstressed syllables, resembles the popu-lar *traethodl* metre (a metrical fault condemned in the Bardic Grammar, *GP* 14, 33, 54).

[37] It is noteworthy that the *cyhydedd hir* (with the end-rhyme sustained through-out) is commonly used for satire in the 14th cent. (e.g. *RP* 1,355–6, *GIG* XXXVIII). The syllabically identical *toddaid* metre (5, 5, 5, 4) is also very common (e.g. *RP* 1,353–4, and the satire of Rhys Meigen, *GDG* 21.65–88); in the 15th cent. cf. *Gwaith Deio ab Ieuan Du* . . ., 17.

[38] For some typical examples see *CRhC*, nos. 44–7. His work has been edited by Cennard Davies, 'Robin Clidro a'i Ganlynwyr', unpublished MA thesis, University of Wales (1964).

evidence, we would seem to be dealing here, as G. J. Williams has
suggested, with one of the *Clêr*'s favourite metres,[39] and from the
fourteenth century at least, it may well have been used by the popular poets for verse of a narrative character as well as for satire and
defamation.

The other poem attributed to Yr Ustus Llwyd in the Red Book (*RP*
1,364–5) is yet another satire of a miserly patron, a priest who is
referred to as 'Madawc corunawc', 'tonsured Madog'.[40] This priest
had promised him a fine surcoat more than a year ago, and with a
scurrilous wit of which any *clerwr* would have been proud the poet
assures us that he will not keep his promise to any man until the day
'a black bishop comes from an otter's arse'—'. . . yny del escob du
odin dyfyrgi.'[41] This cleric is also satirized for his lechery: he is a
rhymer who sings to whores, the lover of a certain Gweirful—
'weiruul gont gul'—and what is more, he 'sings matins on a thrust-
ing arse'—'. . . agan denebras ar din ebrwyd.' This most irreverent
image is strongly reminiscent of an anonymous *englyn proest* in the
Peniarth 20 version of the Bardic Grammar, which illustrates one of
the forbidden faults:

> Klermwnt abat di-Ladin,
> Klorya pla, ply[gw?]eith ganon,
> A dyrr aruer efferenn,
> Ar dorr merch y korr y kan.
> (*GP* 53.7–10)

(A beggar of an abbot with no Latin [and] a pestilent arse [or/and 'pestilent
hymn'], who distorts the canon and breaks the custom of mass—it is on a
girl's belly that the dwarf sings.)

---

[39] 'Cerddi'r Nant', 78; cf. id., *Traddodiad Llenyddol Morgannwg*, 139. Cennard
Davies, 'Robin Clidro . . .', pp. xx ff., suggests some possible origins, and discusses
also Clidro's other favourite metre, a four-beat line with end-rhyme, suggesting that
this too may have had a long sub-literary history in the verse of the *Clêr*. On these
metres see further R. M. Jones's survey in 'Mesurau'r Canu Rhydd Cynnar', *BBCS* 28
(1979), 422 ff.

[40] See Dafydd H. Evans's discussion and edition, 'Yr Ustus Llwyd a'r Swrcod', *YB*
17 (1990), 63–92, and Twm Morys, 'Canu Dychan y Llyfr Coch: Nid Rhydderch
Gampau', *Barddas*, 205 (May 1994), 9–11. This is another form of satire which survives in the *canu rhydd*; cf., for instance, Robin Clidro's 'Owdl dychan rhyw Berson
caled' (*CRhC*, no. 48), who 'hates the sight of poets and beggars'.

[41] Y Nant also has several informal and often self-mocking poems asking for a
cloak or a doublet (G. J. Williams, 'Cerddi'r Nant', 81–3, 84–6; Peniarth 54, i. 422–3,
440–4, 444–5); he too, like Yr Ustus Llwyd—'noeth vy ysgwydeu anosgeidic' (*RP*
1,365.36)—complains of his nakedness to gain the patron's sympathy.

Although the fact that the *englyn* is technically faulty indicates that
it is unlikely to be the work of a poet of the highest rank, it is once
more doubtful whether this is an actual example of the verse of the
Clêr. But as Meirion Pennar has remarked: 'Mae'n damaid hynod
bwysig o dystiolaeth i'r canu hwnt-eglwysig a oedd yn brigo i'r
wyneb ar union adeg ymddangosiad y cywydd newydd o faswedd'
('It is an extremely important piece of evidence for the Church-
defying verse which was surfacing at precisely the same time as the
appearance of the new type of love poetry'), and it clearly reflects the
heretical impulse which attracted the *Clêr*.[42] These poems, and other
satires of clerics and friars in the Red Book of Hergest which may
be termed *clerŵraidd* in content and spirit, surely had their cruder
counterparts in the subversive pronouncements of the *Clêr* themselves.

The satirical verse of the early *Cywyddwyr* draws on many of the
conventions of theme and language which characterize the Red Book
corpus, and they were, needless to say, equally accessible to the influence of the popular poets. The lecherous clerics of Yr Ustus Llwyd
and the Bardic Grammar find a kindred spirit in one of Iolo Goch's
Grey Friars, whom he wishes were caught in the act 'with his grey
hood in the burning crotch of a sour, lustful Englishwoman'—

> A'i gwfl llwyd mewn gafl llodur
> Cynhaig o Seisnigwraig sur.
> (*GIG* XXXIV.51–2)

There are no full-scale attacks on lechery in the work of the other
Cywyddwyr of the period, although Dafydd ap Gwilym is not averse
to playful sexual innuendo and *double entendres*. A fine example is
the *dyfalu* description in *GDG* 125 ('Y Rhugl Groen') of a herds-
man's rattle consisting of a skin bag filled with stones and gravel on
the end of a stick, which is described, for instance, as 'Cloch ddiawl,
a phawl yn ei ffwrch' (l. 38)—'the devil's bell with a pole in its
crotch'.[43] Some of the Red Book poets, it will have been noted, go
beyond innuendo, and men and women alike are satirized for their

---

[42] 'Dryll o Dystiolaeth am y Glêr', *BBCS* 28 (1979), 411. This 'heretical impulse' is,
indeed, central to the (clerical?) critique of the *Clêr* in the poem 'Bustl y Beirdd'
(*c.*1350–1400): cf. 'Yr Eglwys a gashânt, Gwiliau na suliau nis addolant', and espe-
cially 'sawl syn arfer o gam arfaeth | Am watwar Iesu ai wasanaeth' (*MA* 29). It is
conceivable, as Meirion Pennar believes, that the stanzas illustrating the forbidden
faults are drawn from the work of the *Clêr* themselves.
[43] See Gilbert Ruddock, 'Rhagor o Eiriau Mwys?', *LlC* 11 (1970–1), 125–6.

promiscuity. In Y Prydydd Breuan's unusually nauseating attack on Siwan Morgan of Cardigan, who has obviously deceived the poet in some way, the girl's wide buttocks are 'gymmar kalyeu' (*RP* 1,356.24–5), 'companion of penises', and Madog Dwygraig's hag is open to all without exception—'gwrach egoret gyffredin' (*RP* 1,274.10–11). The same poet treats the 'apple thief' Mald Ferch Dafydd as a common prostitute—'putein din angkrein nyt a ynangkres' (*RP* 1,274.37–8), 'a whore with sprawling buttocks—she will not become a nun'. 'The main sustenance of the unmarried girl', he maintains, 'was drunken men; their penises would become limp [or 'she would bend their penises'] around the hour of dawn'—

> Prif vuched merch wedw oed wyr medweint.
> plygei eu kalyeu amgylch plygeint.
> (*RP* 1,275.30–2)

Lechery is, of course, among the Seven Deadly Sins which pervade medieval literature, and which are referred to in the Bardic Grammar as being unworthy of the *prydydd*'s art—'balchder' (pride), 'cyghorueint trahaus' (arrogant jealousy), 'cybydyaeth' (avarice), 'godineb' (adultery or lechery), 'glythineb' (gluttony), 'llid' (wrath), and 'llesged' (idleness) (*GP* 35.29–33). These are all gleefully exploited by the Welsh poets, as they are in medieval satire in general, in which lechery and gluttony are extremely prominent. In both Iolo Goch's attacks on the Grey Friars, the Franciscans, who have angered him with their insistence that young women should not have an intimate relationship with an ordained clerk, both these sins are combined with devastating effect, as they are in much of the Continental literature directed against monks and clerics. Iolo, who is more vindictive and less subtle than both Dafydd ap Gwilym and Madog Benfras in their critiques of the friars,[44] satirizes the wanton friar whom we have already met as 'Mawr o was bras', 'a big fat lad', and 'Rhyw does dŵr', 'watery dough' (*GIG* XXXIV.43, 82); and the final line of his other satire—'Moes moch, mwy a ŷs no march!' (*GIG* XXXV.72) ('[he of the] pig-like manners, he eats more than a horse')—must have raised many a mocking laugh from a contemporary audience. Dafydd's *awdl* to Rhys Meigen has a sickening account of the *clerwr*'s eating habits, which contains the following jibe:

---

[44] *GDG* 136–9, *BDG* CCXVII (on this poem's ascription to Madog Benfras see *GDG¹*, p. clxxiv).

Rhuthrud wêr a mêr mawr esgyrn—ceudawd,
Rhythgnawd cyn diawd, myn Cyndëyrn.

(GDG 21.71–2)

(You would attack the fat and marrow of great big ribs; gaping flesh before
drink, by [Saint] Cyndëyrn.)

This word 'gwêr', which also refers to the fat used to make candles,
is used by Gruffudd Gryg, who describes the *clerwr* Tudur Goch as
'foly babwyrwer' (GDG 153.18), 'having a belly of candle-wax'. The
noun, and the adjective 'gwerawc', is common too in the Red Book
satires, as, for instance, in a satire by Llywelyn Ddu Fab y Pastard,[45]
who in another poem shows us a certain Madog devouring nuts and
plums with crooked beak, and adds scornfully: 'ryued yw di vouoned
[*sic*] vin.' (RP 1,355.13), 'an ill-bred mouth is a wondrous thing.' In
Prydydd Breuan's 'elegy' the harpist Darre is also satirized for his
gluttony, as in this humorous tableau:

llwyrdrwc y dysgwyt. lloryeu cwm cawlwyt.
llawer oed y vwyt kynnoe lwydaw.
llawvronn hen uegin. llofryd dryll mehin.
lloneit kaer vyrdin oed yginyaw.

(RP 1,356.11–14)

(His education was wretched [on the] floors of Cwm Cawlwyd; plentiful was
his food before he perished [*lit.* became grey/mouldy]. Old bellows his chest,
murderer of a lump of fat; his dinner would fill Carmarthen Castle.)

In his concluding lines the poet could hardly have imagined a more
fitting outcome for his enemy:

Ynllawr uffernblas. ynllyngcu kic bras.
mae gan was sudas swydeu idaw.

(RP 1,356.16–17)

(On the floor of hell's palace, gulping fatty meat, the servant of Judas has
plenty to keep him occupied.)

Insincerity and arrogance, it has been seen, are common features
of the moral depravity which comes under attack in the verse of this
period, especially in satires of inferior entertainers. As an extension
of the topos of insincerity the poets' victims are often portrayed as
rogues and robbers, and in the work of the early *Cywyddwyr* such
motifs are not confined to the purely satirical verse. Dafydd ap

---

[45] RP 1,353.28. As well as two satires (RP 1,353–5) he has an elegy in the
Hendregadredd MS (H 229–30; BBBGDd 68). He appears to have been a Ceredigion
poet who was active before 1350 (Huws, 'Llawysgrif Hendregadredd', 23 n. 48).

Gwilym's owl, creature of ill-omen, sings at night for thieves (*GDG* 26.41), and its song is described as 'ffals gywyddiaeth' (l. 16), 'false verse'. The woodcock which disturbs a love-tryst is cursed as 'frychleidr anghyfrwys' ('a speckled, unrefined thief') and 'bribiwr' ('a briber') (*GDG* 61.27, 56). Even his beloved Morfudd becomes 'Hudoles ladrones lwyd' (*GDG* 139.44), 'grey-haired enchantress and thief', her beauty having been ravaged by the passage of time. In a more vulgar vein, one of Iolo Goch's friars is 'a tonsured thief with a crazed penis'—'leidr gwylltgal gwalltgylch' (*GIG* XXXIV.49). Similarly, in the Red Book satires various rascals are branded as cheese-thieves (*RP* 1,356.1), sheep-raiders (*RP* 1,357.42–3), and there is even a robber of silver chalices from parish churches (*RP* 1,338.38–9). These victims, often itinerant minstrels, are also reduced to the status of beggars. Madog Dwygraig, in his moralizing tale of Deykyn who fell from riches to rags through his sins, describes him wandering aimlessly begging for cheese—'cawssa' (*RP* 1,272.38)— and the terms 'yttei' (*RP* 1,342.9), 'beggar of wheat', and 'blottei' (*RP* 1,274.23), 'beggar of flour', are used by Dafydd ap Gwilym, most notably in his satire of Rhys Meigen, where we also find similar forms such as 'cawlai' and 'cicai', beggars of broth and meat (*GDG* 21.27–47). In Iolo Goch's satire of Hersdin Hogl the verbs 'blota', 'cawsa', 'cica', as well as 'gwlana' and 'gwera' (to beg for wool and fat) are all comically juxtaposed in the space of two lines (*GIG* XXXVI.50–1). The *Cywyddwyr* commonly associate the sins of insincerity, wrath and, of course, jealousy with the figure of Eiddig, the jealous husband. He is typically depicted as an unrefined oaf, sly, fearful, and over-protective, often impotent and always despicable. In one of Dafydd's more humorous poems we learn that Eiddig, whom he calls 'mab gogan' (*GDG* 75.9), 'son of satire'—probably the historical figure known as 'Y Bwa Bach', husband of Morfudd— has departed on a military expedition to France, and the poet wishes with all his heart that he may be drowned on the way.[46] Here he is characterized as 'an eye—bequeather of distress—and an ear on a hundred hedges (or 'walls'); a sounding-horn, deceitful, lying, and dull-natured, the girl's punisher and her catchpole'—

---

[46] In the later *cywydd* tradition the wish for Eiddig's death, sometimes expressed in the form of a prayer, becomes an established motif: cf. *DGG* IV; *BDG* LXVI, XC, CCXVIII; *The Cefn Coch MSS.*, ed. J. Fisher (Liverpool, 1899), 24, 103–4, 108–11 (Thomas Prys).

Un llygad, cymyniad cawdd,
Ac unclust yw ar ganclawdd;
A chorn celwydd-dwyll pwyll pŵl,
A chosbwr bun, a'i cheisbwl.
(*GDG* 75.13–16)

Gruffudd Llwyd, who belongs to the next generation of *Cywyddwyr*, portrays his Eiddig as 'an idiot, wrathful, vicious and foolish'—'bril erddig ffyrnig ffôl'—and as 'a cold, filthy lad, a fierce and hateful fool'—'Brwnt oerwas ffyrnicas ffŵl' (*CIGE* XLVI.8, 13), with 'oer' here probably signifying impotence, as it sometimes does in the poetry of Dafydd ap Gwilym. In his *cywydd* to Eiddig and his wife (*CIGE* XLV) the husband is again portrayed as being obsessively watchful and unrefined. Although most of these traits are recognizable in the Red Book satires, these lampoons do not include a single caricature of the jealous husband. Indeed, as shall become clear in subsequent chapters, the few references to *eiddig* ('a jealous person') attested before the *cywydd* period hardly constitute an established poetic convention, and it appears that this particular type of satire is largely influenced by the fabliaux and the *chansons de mal mariée* of the Northern French bourgeois and semi-popular literary tradition, elements of which became absorbed into the pre-existing native tradition of satire and vituperation.

Dafydd's Eiddig is cowardly, in stark contrast to the unflinching warrior of the heroic tradition. Similarly, Rhys Meigen is described as 'anaergryf', 'feeble in combat', and as one who would shy away from any dispute or heated battle—'Cyfranc nac aer daer nid. âi' (*GDG* 21.58, 32). Turning again to the Red Book of Hergest we find that the subject of one satire 'will not stand in battle' (or 'in an army')—'ny seif ofywn cat' (*RP* 1,357.30–1), and Dafydd Y Coed's cleric seems positively terrified as he 'trembles in fear with quivering lips'—'vin cryd rac yf [*sic*] ovyn y cryn' (*RP* 1,360.4). As in medieval literature in general, rustic boorishness is ridiculed as the antithesis of nobility and refinement. Terms such as 'bilain' (villein), 'taeog' (peasant), 'aillt' and 'caeth' (bondsman), and 'costog' (churl) are widespread in the early *cywyddau*, and it comes as no surprise to find them applied to the loutish Eiddig. The following passage is from *GDG* 145 ('Caru Yn Y Gaeaf'), in which Dafydd returns drunk from the tavern on a frozen winter night and has the misfortune of waking his rival:

Cyfodes y delff celffaint
O'i wâl ei hun, awel haint.
Llwfr fu ddigwas anrasol,
Llefain o'r milain i'm ôl.
(*GDG* 145.39-42)

(The scoundrel, resembling a withered stump, rose from his own bed, [and there was] a waft of pestilence. Cowardly was the angry, graceless lad—the villein cried out after me.)

One of Iolo Goch's friars is 'a sullen, sour-natured peasant'—'Taeog anserchog surchwibl', and an 'awkward grey-gowned English friar'—'Y Brawd Sais, llwytpais lletpai' (*GIG* XXXV.8,6). This uncourtly clumsiness is extended to the abstract and inanimate. For instance, the ship so imaginatively vilified by Iolo is 'crooked as an old churn'—'Lletpai fal hen fuddai fydd' (*GIG* XXXIII.26), and both the month of January and the thick mist which prevents Dafydd from meeting his beloved are cursed for their 'gwladeiddrwydd' (*GDG* 69.44; 68.53), the literal meaning of which is 'rusticity', corresponding to the concept of 'vilenie' which pervades European literature in this period. With the striking exception of Iolo Goch's praise of the ploughman (*GIG* XXVIII), which reflects contemporary sermon literature, the peasantry itself is generally regarded with contempt by these poets. The most obvious instance in Dafydd's work is his invitation to Dyddgu to join him in an idealized woodland tryst:

Nid gwahodd glwth i fwth fydd.
Nid gorchwy elw medelwas,
Nid o ŷd, gloyw amyd glas.
Nid tam o ginio amaeth,[47]
Nid fal ynyd ciglyd caeth.
(*GDG* 119.6-10)

(It shall not be a glutton's invitation to a cottage; or a harvester's reward—no feast of wheat, bright, green crop; it shall not be a ploughman's meagre dinner, neither shall it resemble a peasant's meaty spread at Shrovetide.)

In Madog Benfras's 'Cywydd yr Halaenwr', which recounts his successful attempt to foil the girl's husband by disguising himself as a

---

[47] Meirion Pennar, 'Dryll o Dystiolaeth . . .', 408–9, compares this and other references in Dafydd's poetry with the learned poet's derision of the 'bilein aradyrgaeth' ('villein bound to the plough') in the *awdl-gywydd* preserved in the Bardic Grammar (*GP* 12.46). On *rusticus* as a term of abuse see G. G. Coulton, *The Medieval Village* (Cambridge, 1925), 91–2.

salt merchant, the servants who mock the poet are described as
'anwreangwaith' ('churlish'), and the girl, up above in her bedroom,
tells her maid that the commotion seems to her like 'rhyfel bugelydd',
'strife among shepherds' (DGG LXIX.32, 41).

In the Red Book corpus such caricaturing of the rustic peasant
underscores the satire in almost every instance. The apple-thief Mald
is 'aghwrteis' (uncourtly, unrefined) (RP 1,276.29–30); Hywel
Ystorm's Bleddyn is 'a gluttonous, most boorish wolf'—'glwth dra
gwladeid vleid' (RP 1,340.29)—and he refers insultingly to Trahaearn
as 'wyr y kaeth warthegyd' (RP 1,344.26–7), 'grandson of the peasant cowherd'. The adjective 'lletpai' ('crooked', and by extension
'clumsy, unrefined') is common, as in the cywyddau, and once more
the characteristics of boorishness are applied to the non-human, as
in Dafydd Y Coed's lampoon of the waterfall on the River Wye as
'a servile waterfall of unlordly nature, a brazen leprous woman, a
peasant full of deceit'—

> kaeth raeadyr di waladyrbwyll.
> clafres bres taeoges twyll.
> (RP 1,360.21–2)

The victim's lack of breeding is emphasized by recurring motifs.
When Madog Dwygraig sees a minstrel one Christmas 'on a floor
between two of his cows, flea-like, deprived of sweet beverage'—

> ar barth rwng dwy oe warthec
> dyat chwein heb diawt chwec.
> (RP 1,273.38–9)

he is merely repeating a familiar concept, namely that the churl does
not deserve to drink wine or mead, an essential part of a noble
upbringing. Thus, Madog's hag is 'heb wirawt heb win' (RP
1,274.25), 'without liquor or wine', and the home of Adam the tinker is 'lle heb win . . . na med' (RP 1,338.13), 'a place without wine
or mead'. The motif is central to the satire of Rhys Meigen who,
according to Dafydd, is fit only to drink dregs. The awdl's closing
line, 'Rhed, gwedd yt yfed gwaddod tefyrn' (GDG 21.88)—'Away
with you, it becomes you to drink the dregs of alehouses'—may be
compared with the 'gwadawt wirodeu' of Hywel Ystorm's satire of
Bleddyn (RP 1,339.41), and with the countless other references to
sediment and left-overs in the Red Book of Hergest. A similar motif
which is again present in both bodies of verse is the unworthiness of

the subject to wear expensive clothing, as, for instance, when the same poet says of Einion that 'neither fur nor sendal [silk] became him'—'Ny wedei idaw . . . gra na syndal' (*RP* 1,339.2–3).[48] There are also a few instances of the use of 'Iddew' (Jew) as a term of abuse, in keeping with the anti-Semitic content of much medieval Latin and vernacular literature.[49]

The boorish Eiddig finds a feminine counterpart in the conventional figure of the *gwrach*, or hag, who is frequently satirized in medieval literature, often, as, for instance, in the thirteenth-century French poem *Le Roman de la Rose*, as a redoubtable guardian who thwarts the lover's attempts to see his beloved.[50] Dafydd's comic caricature of the hag in *GDG* 80 ('Tri Phorthor Eiddig'), who, along with a fierce dog and creaking door, proves the poet's undoing, is well within this tradition:

> Gwrach heinus ddolurus ddig,
> Daw ei dydd, diwyd Eiddig.
> Pei cyd y nos, pei caid nef,
> Â dengnos, wrach ddidangnef,
> Unawr, mewn gwâl chweinial chwyrn,
> Ni chwsg, am nad iach esgyrn.
> Cynnar nychled yn cwynaw
> Ei chlun, drwg ei llun, a'i llaw,
> A dolur o'i dwy elin,
> A'i phalfais yn glais, a'i glin.[51]
>
> (*GDG* 80.13–22)

(A sick hag, sore and wrathful—her day will come!—servant of Eiddig. Were the night—if only she would reach heaven!—as long as ten nights—ever-restless hag—she would not sleep a single hour in a turbulent, flea-ridden bed, so infirm are her bones. Ailing [hag], quick to moan about her thigh (which is in a pitiful condition) and her hand, and the pain from both her elbows, and her bruised shoulder and knee.)

---

[48] Cf. *GDG* 21.29–30, 40; 116.42.

[49] *GDG* 76.4; *BDG* LXXXIV.42 (Madog Benfras?); *RP* 1,360.38 (Dafydd Y Coed). See Jacob Katz, *Exclusiveness and Tolerance: Studies in Jewish–Gentile Relations in Medieval and Modern Times* (Oxford University Press, 1961), 67 ff.

[50] See Ch. 6 below, p. 217. On the figure of the hag in Classical and medieval literature see *Recherches*, 251–8.

[51] The 'apocryphal' *cywydd BDG* CLVIII contains a similar portrayal. Compare Ovid's gruesome description of Envy in *Metamorphoses*, Book II, especially ll. 778–9: 'risus abest . . . | nec fruitur somno, uigilacibus excita curis . . .' ('She has no smile . . . and she never enjoys sleep, roused as she is by wakeful cares') (*Ovid: Metamorphoses I–IV*, ed. and trans. D. E. Hill (Warminster, 1985), 85–6).

These physical, as opposed to moral, shortcomings—infirmity, defor-
mity, uncleanliness, often enhanced with references to lice and mag-
gots and the like—are an essential part of the stock-in-trade of the
medieval satirist. Iolo Goch's ship is personified as 'Ffriwuchel wrach,
fingrach fort' (GIG XXXIII.23), 'a hag with upturned nose and
scabby-edged side'.[52] Like Eiddig's sleepless servant, Madog
Dwygraig's hag, who is also described as a 'guardian hag'—'gwrach
achadw'—has infirm limbs—'gwrach oeraf lawn anaf lin'—she is
lousy ('horawc'), filthy ('lychwin'), and furthermore she is toothless
and wrinkled—'gwrach vantach gwrach groenach grin' (RP
1,274.6–28). Phrases such as 'carr cramennawc' (RP 1,353.17), 'scabby
jaw', and 'brych wegil' (RP 1,347.5), 'leprous nape of the neck', are
an extremely common form of vituperation.[53] Hywel Ystorm's Ieuan
is 'a sick man, slimy and scabby-limbed'—'lleidyawc clafyrconawc
clafwr' (RP 1,346.32), and Einion 'a custodian of pest-houses'—
'greawr clafdyeu' (RP 1,339.12), just as Rhys Meigen is described by
Dafydd as 'Clafaf anllataf llatai—clafesau' (GDG 21.25), 'most sick,
most debauched love-messenger for sick women', or Gruffudd Gryg
as 'Gwas i gleifion Uwch-Conwy' (GDG 154.45), 'a servant to the sick
of Uwch-Conwy'. In both bodies of verse the scatological element is
strong, references to excrement and anuses being commonplace. For
instance, Rhys Meigen is vilified as 'ci sietwn' (GDG 21.27), 'a dog
defiled with excrement', and Dafydd's own shadow is cursed as
'Drum corff wedi'i droi mewn carth' (GDG 141.37), 'the form of a
body rolled in dung'. Dafydd Y Coed wishes one of his victims,
whom he depicts as a goat excreting leeks, 'beich o vaw diawl' (RP
1,360.41), 'a heap of devil's dung'. This colourful phrase, which
occurs elsewhere in the Red Book satires, is also found in the early
cywyddau, as for instance when Dafydd curses the jealous husband:

> Bid iddaw yn ei law lwyth
> O faw diawl, ef a'i dylwyth.[54]
>   (GDG 75.21–2)

[52] Cf. 'Crimog henwrach yn crymu', of the gut-stringed harp (GIG XXXII.62), and
'gwrach gronglwydwan grin', of an old mill (GIG XIII.58).

[53] Certain birds which incur Dafydd's wrath, such as the owl, the woodcock, and
the magpie, are similarly described as unclean or speckled (cf. GDG 26.23–8; 61.39–58;
63.49–60).

[54] Cf. GIG XXXVII.92; RP 1,357.21; 1,360.41; GP 60.10. GPC gives 'baw diawl:
devil's dung, asafoetida' [= a pungent plant gum] (p. 265). External parallels for the
scatological content of Welsh satire, mainly from Chaucer, are cited by Matonis,
'Medieval Topics . . .', 236.

(That his hand were filled with a heap of devil's dung, he and his family.)

A striking feature of Dafydd's poetry is his association of natural phenomena which frustrate him in some way, such as the mist, the peat-bog, and the owl (GDG 68, 127, 26), with Annwfn, the Celtic Otherworld, and its legendary prince, Gwyn ap Nudd.[55] Though this is not among the conventions of the Red Book satires, it is worth noting that, as in the cywyddau, the words 'ellyll' and 'ŵyll' (fiend, ghost, goblin) are sometimes used by these poets in a satirical context.[56]

Another of the conventions of fourteenth-century Welsh satire is the association of both the animate and inanimate with banal, everyday objects derived mainly from the world of the peasantry. A fine example of this is Dafydd ap Gwilym's cywydd to the mist (GDG 68), and his humorous dyfalu of the briar in GDG 65 and of icicles in GDG 91 and 145 may also be compared. Terms such as 'cerbyd' (carriage), 'llestr' (vessel), 'cryw' and 'cawell' ('basket' or 'cage'), are constantly used by these poets to suggest the hollowness, the ungainliness, and often also the corpulence of their victims. Vegetal metaphors are also widespread, a source of imagery which is best exemplified in the cywyddau by Iolo Goch and Llywelyn Goch cursing their beards for impeding their amorous advances (GIG XXV, DGG LXXXIV). Yet more common is the reducing of humans to bestial levels by comparing them with various animals which, unlike the eagle, the lion, or the stag, do not form the traditional epithets of panegyric. Thus, Dafydd turns a Black Friar into a crow, a kite, and a ram (GDG 139.2–12); his own shadow becomes a goat, and a heron nibbling at reeds in a marsh (GDG 141.23, 32); and Eiddig is variously described as a drone, a piglet, and a beaver's anus (GDG 75.9,23, 31). The goat, traditionally a symbol of lechery, appears frequently, most notably in Gruffudd Llwyd's satire of Eiddig (CIGE XLVI).[57] Again, the non-human is not excluded from these comparisons, as, for instance, when Dafydd comically curses the din of a clock which wakes him from a pleasant dream as 'Cenau ci yn cnöi cawg' (GDG 66.32), 'a whelp gnawing at a basin', or the sound of the echo stone which frightens a hitherto responsive maiden as

[55] See E. I. Rowlands, 'Cyfeiriadau Dafydd ap Gwilym at Annwn', LlC 5 (1958–9), 122–35.
[56] e.g. RP 1,273.23; 1,354.42; 1,363.42; 1,354.41.
[57] For external parallels see Matonis, 'Medieval Topics . . .', 235.

'Goslef gast gref dan gist grom' (*GDG* 130.38), 'the cry of a strong
bitch under a humped chest'. Equally expressive is Iolo Goch's
description of an old mill which he fears will frighten his horse, 'its
clapper like a limp sow devouring beans down below the road'—

> A'i chlap megis hwch lipa
> . Is y ffordd yn ysu ffa . . .
> (*GIG* XIII.59–60)

Animal imagery is central to Iolo's satires of the ship and of the gut-
stringed harp, whose sound is likened, among other things, to 'the
wild neighing of a yellow mare after horses'—'Gweryrad gwyllt . . .
Gwilff felen am geffylau', and to 'geese bickering over territory'—
'Gwyddau yn dadlau am dir' (*GIG* XXXII.45–6, 54). With vivid
imagination Hywel Ystorm sees Adam the tinker as 'Medw grwp ban
lloppan lleipyrvric' (*RP* 1,338.17–18), 'a drunken tortoise (or, possibly, 'crab' or 'lobster'), a limp old rag boot', and in other Red Book
satires one minstrel is turned within a single stanza into a frog, a
bear, and a goat (*RP* 1,346.5–7), while another becomes a serpent, a
boar, a wolf, a heron, and a drone (*RP* 1,345.13–21). Willi is as
worthless as 'waelawt nyth crach hwyat' (*RP* 1,357.23), 'the floor of
a teal's nest', and the somewhat grotesque image of a cockerel's
scrawny leg—'coes keilyawc' (*RP* 1,355.24)—is echoed in Dafydd ap
Gwilym's 'coes gwylan craig' in his satire of Rhys Meigen (*GDG*
21.28), a poem which is full of images of this type.

Animal imagery is also used to good effect by Hywel Ystorm to
assert his superiority as a poet. When he claims in his satire of
Casnodyn that 'a young chicken and an eagle, fearless king of birds,
are not of equal worth'—

> Nyt unwerth kywerth kyw iar—ac eryr
> gwrawl vrenhin adar.
> (*RP* 1,340.42–3)

he seems to be drawing on another of the stock motifs of the satirical genre. These lines are possibly echoed in Gruffudd Gryg's words
to Dafydd ap Gwilym—

> Llew ydwyf rhwysg, llo ydwyd,
> Cyw'r eryr wyf, cyw'r iâr wyd.
> (*GDG* 151.55–6)

(I am a splendid lion, you a calf; I am a young eagle, you a young chicken.)

In Iolo Goch's satire of Gwyddelyn the same formula is extended to form part of a particularly biting rhetorical passage (*GIG* XXXVII.57–64), and the convention survives in the satirical poetry of the following centuries.[58] But for sheer originality in the Red Book corpus we must turn, finally, not to the work of Hywel Ystorm, but to a poem by another of the century's foremost satirists, Madog Dwygraig. In a diverting cartoon of a poem (*RP* 1,277–9) he tells the tale of a calf he received as a gift, but which is so sick and bony and utterly useless that it is not even worth the pains of a cattle thief, and all attempts to sell it at the fairs of North Wales are in vain. The poet expresses his contempt largely through a series of comparisons with other, equally ridiculous creatures. The calf becomes a ferret, a bald polecat, a water-hen, it has the heart of a cockerel, and it is even compared to 'a lifeless old lobster, about the size of a soap-holder'— 'gwyw gimwch | gogymeint corn sebon' (*RP* 1,278.43–4). In fact it is no bigger than a flea on a bedside—'nyt mwy nor chwannen ar erchwynnawc' (*RP* 1,277.29–30)—and the luckless Madog likens his tireless search for a buyer to searching for whelks in seaweed.[59]

Enough has been said to show that these poets were all clearly drawing on a common tradition of satirical verse, which, with its distinctive motifs and its own richly varied vocabulary, was as well established and conventional in nature as that of formal panegyric. In their verbal exuberance, graphic description, occasional narrative style, and flashes of humour the Red Book satires have a certain affinity with the verse of the early *Cywyddwyr*, not only with their purely satirical poems but with their occasional verse in general. The earliest pieces, such as the satires believed to be the work of Hywel Ystorm, can be said in this respect to foreshadow the poetry of Dafydd ap Gwilym and his fellow *Cywyddwyr*. The colour and

[58] Cf. *Gwaith Guto'r Glyn*, LXXI.23–4; *Gwaith Tudur Aled*, vol. 2, CXLII.41–4; *Gwaith Gruffudd Hiraethog*, ed. D. J. Bowen (Cardiff, 1990), 10.56.

[59] The poem may be compared with Iolo Goch's humorous *cywyddau* asking and thanking for the gift of a horse (*GIG* XII, XIII). Feeble old horses are similarly ridiculed in request poems by Thomas Prys (*The Cefn Coch MSS.*, 67–70) and his younger contemporary, the *clerwr* Robin Clidro (Cennard Davies, 'Robin Clidro . . .', no. IX). Y Nant also has an informal poem requesting a mare (Peniarth MS 54, i. 377–82), and another, rather indecent, request for a bull (G. J. Williams, 'Cerddi'r Nant', 88–9). The satirizing of animals is not, of course, confined to Wales. The 14th-cent. French poet Guillaume de Machaut has a request poem which bears a striking resemblance to the work of Iolo Goch in its mockery both of the ageing poet and the horse itself. In another lampoon he complains, not unlike Madog Dwygraig, that no one will buy his horse, cursing the person who gave it to him. (V. Chichmaref (ed.), *Poésies lyriques de Guillaume de Machaut* (Paris, 1909), i. 262–5).

vitality of fourteenth-century satire, it has been argued, are in part
due to the impact on the pre-existing bardic satirical tradition of a
vigorous native sub-literary culture, at a period when *prydydd* and
clerwr were brought closer together than ever before. Verse of a similar character to Y Nant's fifteenth-century cursing-poem, with its
colloquial tone and popular metre, may well have been familiar to
Hywel Ystorm and Dafydd ap Gwilym alike, and it may be that these
and other accomplished poets were subjected to the abuse of many
a lowly minstrel in accordance with the *cyff clêr* convention. But the
Clêr surely did not live on satire alone. Indeed, the likely influence
of the elusive popular substratum is discernible in quite different
poetic genres even before Dafydd ap Gwilym's time.

3

Popular Elements in Pre-*Cywydd* Poetry

It has been established that, while the *Clêr* were generally regarded by the official poets, at least on the face of it, with a kind of professional disdain, it would certainly have been possible in medieval Wales for poets of all orders to come into contact with each other, and therefore to become familiar with each other's repertoires. This would have been particularly true in post-Conquest Wales, in the wake of the collapse of the legally defined bardic hierarchy of the Poets of the Princes; but it is reasonable to assume that there had already been limited interaction for many centuries. Even the most accomplished and aloof court poet, though he may consciously have confined himself to the time-honoured conventions of his profession, is unlikely to have remained entirely oblivious of—or, for that matter, entirely impervious to—the popular fashions and diversions of his age. In the absence of a significant body of hard evidence the popular verse tradition of medieval Wales, no more than that of the rest of Europe, cannot be defined or discussed with any degree of certainty. However, it will be helpful to enquire whether the submerged tradition can be said to reveal itself at any points in the mainstream of bardic verse, not only in the years which immediately preceded the emergence of the *cywydd* poets, but also in the poetry of the earlier *Gogynfeirdd* and in other poetic vestiges which have survived from the pre-Conquest period.

From the *hengerdd* period (*c*.550–1100), the stray verse 'Peis Dinogat' ('Dinogad's Shirt') immediately springs to mind as a possible early instance of a 'folk-song' preserved by chance. Although it is commonly considered as such, I prefer to accept Jenny Rowland's description of the poem as an 'artistic nursery rhyme' composed by a qualified poet in a non-bardic capacity,[1] an explanation which

---

[1] Jenny Rowland, 'Genres', in *Early Welsh Poetry: Studies in the Book of Aneirin*, ed. Brynley F. Roberts (Aberystwyth, 1988), 185. For differing views see e.g. Bromwich, *APDG* 92, and R. M. Jones, 'Mesurau'r Canu Rhydd Cynnar', *BBCS* 28 (1978–80), 413. For a text and translation see A. O. H. Jarman (ed. and trans.), *Aneirin: Y Gododdin*, 'Welsh Classics' series (Llandysul, 1988), 68–9.

would at least partly account for its preservation. Whatever its provenance, it has no special relevance for the poetry of medieval Wales. The brief but well-observed evocations of natural phenomena in anonymous early gnomic verse such as the 'Eiry mynydd' and 'Kalan gaeaf' *englyn* sequences (*EWGP* III, V), which probably represent a tradition which is considerably older than the earliest written records in the thirteenth century, provide a striking native precursor for the *Cywyddwyr*'s fondness of natural description, as does the 'nature' element in some so-called 'saga poetry' such as the 'Llywarch Hen' cycle. Several scholars have advocated a popular or, at least, a semi-popular origin for verse of this type: Kenneth Jackson describes the gnomic sequences as 'a kind of folk-philosophy adapted by poets in touch with folk-ideas and given a literary cast and setting',[2] and the early *englyn*-poetry in general as 'a semi-popular genre' not composed by 'the bards of high rank'.[3] The precise status of these poets remains an open question, but Jenny Rowland has recently argued, convincingly in my view, for the essentially bardic character of what she terms 'non-eulogistic *hengerdd*', stressing that prior to the *Gogynfeirdd* period qualified poets of high rank are likely to have composed in other genres as well as the formal eulogy and religious verse prescribed by the greater ceremony of the royal courts from the time of Gruffudd ap Cynan. But this later development, she suggests, 'may have given a chance for lower bards and others to take over previously bardic entertainment functions.'[4] It is generally accepted that the three-line *englyn* metre favoured by the gnomic poets, termed in the fourteenth-century Bardic Grammar 'englyn o'r hen ganiad', and known also in subsequent treatises as 'englyn milwr', survived during the *Gogynfeirdd* period 'under-

[2] *Studies in Early Celtic Nature Poetry* (Cambridge, 1935), 138. This, he believes, is equally true of the analogous Anglo-Saxon, Irish, and Norse gnomic collections. T. J. Morgan argues that the Welsh gnomic poems are not the work of the professional bardic order, and that they were intended for a non-courtly audience ('Canu Gwirebol', *YB* 8 (1974), 17–18). Morfydd E. Owen, however, suggests that these, along with gnomic triads and proverb collections, may have been the product of bardic exercises ('"Trioedd Hefut Yw Yrei Hynn"', *YB* 14 (1988), 98).

[3] 'Incremental Repetition in the Early Welsh *Englyn*', *Speculum*, 16 (1941), 317. Cf. N. J. A. Williams, who remarks that: 'The popular nature of *Canu Llywarch* needs no underlining', and goes so far as to suggest that 'the originator, or rather, originators, of the englynion may well not have been far removed from peasants themselves' ('*Canu Llywarch Hen* and the Finn Cycle', in R. Bromwich and R. Brinley Jones (eds.), *Astudiaethau ar yr Hengerdd: Studies in Old Welsh Poetry* (Cardiff, 1978), 249).

[4] 'Genres', 188 ff; cf. id., *Early Welsh Saga Poetry* (Cambridge, 1990), 355 ff.

ground', as it were, in the unrecorded verse of the *Clêr*.[5] And it may be noted here that it resurfaces—as do several other archaic metres such as the *awdl-gywydd* and *cywydd deuair fyrion*, which were either rejected by the strict-metre poets or upgraded through the introduction of *cynghanedd*—in the sixteenth- and early seventeenth-century *canu rhydd* or free-metre poetry, a body of verse which, it will be seen, may have preserved many of the characteristics of an earlier popular verse tradition. The *englyn* quoted in the Grammar reads as follows:

> Chwerdit mwyalch mywn kelli;
> Nyt ard, nyt erdir idi;
> Nyt llawenach neb no hi.
>
> (GP 9)

(The blackbird laughs in the grove; she does not plough, nor does anyone plough for her; yet none is happier than she.)

Its language is unadorned, and in its content—a simple description of the blackbird in its natural habitat which serves as a proverbial exemplum—it is in direct descent from the earlier gnomic poetry. Unless it be as archaic as that poetry, which is improbable, as the compiler of the Grammar was drawing almost exclusively on contemporary or closely contemporary material, it seems likely to be of popular or, at least, sub-bardic provenance. The fact that the stanza is closely paraphrased by Dafydd ap Gwilym gives it added significance, since it indicates that he may well have been familiar with similar nature poetry of a sub-bardic character current in the fourteenth century.[6] It is surprising to find stanzas which echo closely the early gnomic poems, each having the opening formula 'eira mynydd', incorporated rather incongruously, it appears, into an anonymous wassail song preserved in a manuscript as recent as the eighteenth century.[7] As Meredydd Evans has shown, the original model has been mutilated in such a way as to suggest oral contamination over

[5] Cf., for instance, Bromwich, *APDG* 109; R. M. Jones, 'Mesurau'r Canu Rhydd Cynnar', 418; John Morris-Jones, *Cerdd Dafod* (Oxford, 1925), 319–20.

[6] See Chotzen, *Recherches*, 86–7; Bromwich, *APDG* 92, 108–9. She notes that two closely similar descriptions of the carefree blackbird are found in 'poems of popular origin and of uncertain age which have been traditionally associated with the *clêr*' (a *traethodl* and *englyn cyrch*). The popularity of the stanza is also suggested by a slightly variant version in *GP* 218.

[7] *LlRMG* 108–9. The possibility that wassail songs were composed in medieval Wales and are reflected in the verse of the strict-metre poets is considered in Ch. 5 below.

a long period of time. His remarks are pertinent to the present discussion:

Os traddodiad llafar a ddaeth â'r penillion hyn i lawr i ddechrau'r ddeunawfed ganrif, a naturiol yw tybio mai dyna a ddigwyddodd, y mae'n ffaith ryfeddol. At ba haen bynnag o gymdeithas yr anelwyd y Canu Gwirebol hwn yn y lle cyntaf, ymddengys i beth ohono ddod yn eiddo gwerin gwlad ac i'r werin gyffredin honno, efallai, o'r Oesoedd Canol ymlaen, ddefnyddio'r penillion hyn yn eu canu gwyliol, a'u canu amser hamdden, fel y defnyddiwyd yr hyn a alwn ni heddiw yn benillion telyn gan eu disgynyddion yn ddiweddarach.[8]

(If it was oral transmission which brought these stanzas down to the beginning of the eighteenth century, and it is natural to assume that that was the case, it is an amazing fact. Whichever level of society this Gnomic Verse was originally intended for, it appears that some of it became the property of the people, and that perhaps these common folk, from the Middle Ages onwards, made use of these stanzas in their festive and recreational singing, just as 'harp stanzas', as they are now known, were used by their descendants in a later period.)

Verse of this kind, then, perhaps, as Dr Evans suggests, in the context of seasonal festivities, may already have been part of the popular culture of medieval Wales before the emergence of free-metre verse in sixteenth-century manuscripts.

It must not, however, be thought that such verse is characteristic of the free-metre poetic tradition as it is preserved in the manuscripts. In fact, it may be said that although the early *canu rhydd* poets drew readily on the external world for their comparisons and for common motifs such as the bird-messenger and the woodland tryst, they were not, with a few notable exceptions, given to the observance of nature for its own sake. But it is reasonable to infer that simple songs such as that to the blackbird, not dissimilar in content and spirit to the early gnomic poetry, would have formed part of the repertoire of many a nameless *clerwr* throughout the medieval

---

[8] 'Y Canu Gwasael yn *Llawysgrif Richard Morris o Gerddi*', *LlC* 13 (1974–81), 223–4. This may also apply to the 'Englynion y Misoedd' sequence (*EWGP* IX), first attested in 16th-cent. MSS but believed to have been written in its present form in the 15th cent. That it was parodied by Siôn Tudur in the 16th cent. (see *CRhC*, no. 66 and the editor's notes) suggests that it represented by that time a popular, widely known convention and, once more, some rare forms unfamiliar to copiers point to a long period of transmission; see Kenneth Jackson's remarks in *EWGP* 12–17, and Morfydd E. Owen, 'Hwn yw e Gododin. Aneirin ae cant', in *Astudiaethau ar yr Hengerdd*, 143–4.

period. The significance of the early *englyn* poetry for our understanding of the *cywyddau* of Dafydd ap Gwilym and his contemporaries lies not only in its general affinity with nature and its attention to detail, but also in its actual subject-matter. Perhaps the most striking precedent which it provides for *cywydd* poetry lies in the early poets' depiction of bird-life. Bird-song forms part of the idyllic description of the summer season—

> Gorwin blaen pertheu. keingywrev adar.
> hir dit bann cogev.[9]

(Resplendent are the tips of the bushes; sweet bird-song; long is the day, loud are the cuckoos.)

and there are simple descriptions of specific birds, such as the thrush, the cuckoo, and the blackbird:

> Marchwyeil dryssi a mwyar erni;
> a mwyalch ar y nyth . . .[10]
> (*EWGP* II.7)

(Briar shoots laden with berries, and a blackbird on its nest . . .)

Apart from its characteristically proverbial final line, which has no apparent relevance to the rest of the stanza, the *englyn*

> Kyt boet bychan, ys keluyd
> ⟨yd⟩ adeil adar yg gorwyd coet;
> kyuoet vyd da a detwyd.
> (*EWGP* IV. 11)

(Though they are small, skilfully do birds build [their nests] on a woodland's edge; the good and the fortunate will forever be companions.)

is somewhat reminiscent of the *englyn* to the blackbird known to Dafydd ap Gwilym. Some of the so-called early Irish hermit verse is closely analogous with the Welsh gnomic poetry, and this verse in particular has in common with the *cywyddau*, as Rachel Bromwich

---

[9] *LIDC* 26.43–4; cf. *EWGP* V.6; VI.31.

[10] Cf., for instance, the simple couplet 'Bronureith breith bron. | Breith bron bronureith' inserted into the Mechydd ap Llywarch *englynion* in *LIDC* 30.61–2; also the descriptions of the cuckoo in another poem from the Llywarch Hen cycle, 'Claf Abercuawg', especially the *englyn*:

> Kethlyd kathyl uodawc hiraethawc y llef,
> Teith odef, tuth hebawc.
> Coc vreuer yn Aber Cuawc.

(Ifor Williams (ed.), *Canu Llywarch Hen* (Cardiff, 1935), VI, st. 10).

has observed, 'a similar vision of community with nature, and one which is expressed with a comparable clarity and directness'.[11] Here, bird-life is more minutely observed than in the *englynion*, as is amply illustrated in the following ninth-century verse:

> Int én gaires asin tsail
> álainn guilbnén as glan gair:
> rinn binn buide fir duib druin:
> cas cor cuirther, guth ind luin.

(The bird which calls from the willow: beautiful beaklet of clear note: musical yellow bill of a firm black lad: lively the tune that is played, the blackbird's voice.)[12]

Elsewhere the blackbird is a hermit who rings no bell,[13] the cuckoo sings 'in a grey cloak from bush fortresses',[14] and a common motif is that of birds as poets or musicians who praise God with their joyful singing.[15] To anyone who is familiar with the early *Cywyddwyr* this type of personification is strongly suggestive, and calls to mind the *dyfalu* passages which are so characteristic of their work, and of Dafydd ap Gwilym in particular.[16] The *Cywyddwyr's* more consciously artistic treatment of these elements, especially the religious imagery which informs their nature poetry, may be related to the same characteristically Celtic affinity with the natural world. One is, therefore, tempted to postulate that birds were portrayed in similar fashion in early Welsh nature poetry which has not survived, and that the tradition may well have been transmitted to the fourteenth-century *Cywyddwyr* through popular or, at least, sub-bardic channels.

---

[11] *APDG* 80. On the Irish poems see Kenneth Jackson, *Studies in Early Celtic Nature Poetry*, 93–109. The general belief that they were actually composed by hermits, a product of the anchorite movement of the eighth to tenth centuries, has recently been challenged by D. Ó Corráin, 'Early Irish Hermit Poetry?', in *Sages, Saints and Storytellers: Celtic Studies in Honour of Professor James Carney*, 251–67.

[12] Text and translation from Gerard Murphy (ed.), *Early Irish Lyrics* (Clarendon Press, Oxford, 1956), no. 6.

[13] Thomas Kinsella (ed. and trans.), *The New Oxford Book of Irish Verse* (Oxford, 1986), no. 46.

[14] Murphy, *Early Irish Lyrics*, no. 2.

[15] e.g. ibid., nos. 2, 44; Kinsella, *New Oxford Book of Irish Verse*, no. 46.

[16] For examples of DG's personification of birds as poets (and vice versa) see R. M. Jones, 'Dafydd ap Gwilym ac R. Williams Parry', *YB* 4 (1969), 40 ff. The image is not explicit in the extant early Welsh nature and gnomic poetry, but it may be implied in the words 'keingywrev adar' from the *englyn* cited above; and cf. *Canu Llywarch Hen*, no. VI, st. 4 ('Claf Abercuawg'). *Cyfrau*, which *GPC* defines as 'words, conversation; song' (p. 712), is commonly used for poetry (e.g. *LlDC* 5.75).

One motif found in *cywydd* poetry which is apparently attested in what survives of the early native verse tradition is that of the cuckoo as a bird of love. In the elegiac 'Claf Abercuawg' *englyn* sequence from the 'Llywarch Hen' cycle the bird's song fills the sick man with longing for his past, and the words 'Coc uann, cof gan bawp a gar', 'loud cuckoo, everyone remembers that which he loves', are particularly suggestive of this motif, which is prominent in Celtic literature.[17] The gnomic stanzas known as the 'Gorwynion' (*EWGP* VI) contain several instances of the word 'serchawc', 'lover', and these, as well as other cryptic allusions to the matters of love, are significant in that they reflect a preoccupation with the subject from an early period. These stanzas in particular contain many proverbial statements pertaining to love, such as 'medwl serchawc syberw vyd', 'a lover's mind is ever proud', and 'a wyl a gar, gwynn y uyt',[18] 'blessed is he who sees the person he loves'. There are also two references to 'eidic', 'a jealous person', although it seems unlikely that these represent an early native precedent for the stock figure of the jealous husband who plays such a prominent part in the early *cywyddau*, heavily influenced by the Continental *Jaloux*. The possibility, however, should not be discounted that in the stanza

> Gorwyn blaen kawn; gwythlawn eidic;
> ys odit ae digawn—
> gweithret call yw caru yn iawn.

(Resplendent are the tips of the reeds; angry is the jealous one; rare are the things that satisfy him—it is a wise deed to love truly.)

the reference is to a conventional type of the jealous husband, the talk of faithful love being therefore ironic, or, alternatively, a reflection of the kind of idealized adulterous love which came to be identified with the *amour courtois* of the Provençal and French

---

[17] *Canu Llywarch Hen*, no. VI, st. 9. See Chotzen, *Recherches*, 183–6, and Ch. 4 below, pp. 112–14. The motif of the cuckoo as a bird of love or love-longing, be it the merry cuckoo of the spring awakening or the nostalgic cuckoo of elegiac literature, is not, of course, by any means confined to the Celtic countries. For a useful survey of the bird's significance in various traditions see A. T. Hatto (ed.), *Eos: An Enquiry into the Theme of Lovers' Meetings and Partings at Dawn in Poetry* (The Hague, 1965), 800–8.

[18] Cf. also 'bit anniweir deueiryawc' in *EWGP* VII, st. 7. Similar statements are found in early proverb lists, for instance, 'Y kar kywir yn yr yg y gwelir', 'Chverdit bryt urth a garer' (*Y Cymmrodor*, 7, 142; *BBCS* 4, 6), and in the 12th- or 13th-cent. 'Englynion y Clywaid', e.g. 'gnawt rygas gwedy ryserch' (*BBCS* 3, 22).

love-poets.[19] The 'Gorwynion' also speak of the longing ('hiraeth') and sickness ('heint') caused, it seems, by love, and there is an intriguing allusion to the 'arrow' of pain (or sadness) which pierces the lover—'gwnelit aeth saeth y syberw'.[20] Here, then, is an early precedent for an image which is central to the love-poetry of the early *Cywyddwyr*, although it will become apparent that their use of the 'weapons of love' motif does show clear signs of Continental influence. The attitude expressed in the 'Gorwynion' no doubt reflects the Celtic convention of love as a wasting sickness, and as an overwhelming power which may drive its victims to distraction. The convention is well attested in the early prose tales of Wales and Ireland and in Irish saga-poetry—compare, for instance, Culhwch's love for Olwen, Maxen and Elen, Cuirithir and Líadan.[21] It is essentially the same native conception of love, in a more courtly guise, which informs the lyrics of Hywel ab Owain Gwynedd in the twelfth century, and these, it will be seen, need by no means be explained in terms of external influence, be it Provençal or Latin.

The phrase 'kynnadyl y serchawc' from the 'Gorwynion' stanzas is important as an early instance in verse of the 'oed', or lovers' tryst, and if these words are to be connected with the 'Gorwyn blaen banadyl', 'resplendent are the tips of the broom', which precedes them, then they are doubly significant as a precedent for the theme of the woodland tryst which was so dear to Dafydd ap Gwilym. Equally suggestive are the early verse fragments reflecting the 'Myrddin Wyllt' legend, which have acquired much unrelated vaticinatory material from the Norman period. The following passage from the 'Afallennau' sequence in the Black Book of Carmarthen

---

[19] It is not inconceivable that this and the other reference—'Gorwyn blaen meillyon; digallon llyfwr; | lludedic eidigyon' (st. 5)—foreshadow the convention of Eiddig's antipathy for summer in the *cywydd* tradition (see pp. 77–8 below). Again, cf. the early proverbs: 'Ny chret eidic yr a deker', 'Dewin pob eidic' (*Y Cymmrodor*, 7, 143; *BBCS* 4, 7). It could be argued that this native motif later merged with the more specific figure of the 'jealous husband' under external influence. On Eiddig in the *cywydd* tradition see also Ch. 7 below, pp. 271–5.

[20] *Syberw*—'proud', sometimes 'courtly, well-mannered'—is commonly used for the lover, as for instance in st. 27 of the same poem: 'medwl serchawc syberw vyd', and *LlDC* 17.137.

[21] See Chotzen, *Recherches*, 321–4; J. E. Caerwyn Williams, 'Cerddi'r Gogynfeirdd i Wragedd a Merched . . .', *LlC* 13 (1974–81), 20 ff. See also H. J. T. O'Sullivan's section on 'Early Irish Concepts of Beauty and Lovesickness', in 'Developments in Love Poetry in Irish, Welsh and Scottish Gaelic before 1650', unpublished M.Litt. thesis, Glasgow University (1976), 20–6, and the references cited by T. P. Cross in *Motif-Index of Early Irish Literature* (Bloomington, Ind., 1952), 480.

speaks of the invisible apple-tree in the Caledonian forest which after the Battle of Arfderydd conceals Myrddin from the soldiers of Rhydderch Hael, and the madman looks back to happier days when he entertained a maiden at the foot of the tree:

> Afallen peren a tiff ar lan. afon.
> In y llurv. ny lluit maer. ar y chlaer aeron.
> Tra fuvm puyll. wastad. am buiad in i bon.
> a. bun wen warius. vn weinus vanon.[22]

(Sweet apple-tree that grows on the river bank, on its trail no steward is able to reach its glistening fruit. While I was in my right mind there was for me at its foot a fair, playful maiden, a slender darling.)

This or similar aspects of the legend, as is shown in the next chapter, were known to the *Cywyddwyr*, and they may well have been echoed many times across the centuries by the popular *Clêr* in verse which spoke of love in a background of wild nature. In one of the early Irish poems (*c.*800) which belongs to the cognate Irish legend of Suibhne Geilt, the madman describes his woodland refuge:

> M'airiuclán hi Túaim Inbir:
> nī lántechdais bes sēstu—
> cona rētglannaib a réir,
> cona gréin, cona ēscu.
>
> Gobbān du-rigni in sin
> (co n-ēcestar dūib a stoir);
> mu chridecān, Dīa du nim,
> is hé tugatōir rod-toig.

(My little oratory in Túaim Inbir: a full mansion could not be more delightful (?)—with its stars in due order with its sun and its moon.

It is Gobbán who has made it (that its tale may be told you); my beloved God from Heaven is the thatcher who has roofed it.)[23]

In its religious imagery (obviously a result of the Christianization of the original tale), in its implied contrast of the natural dwelling with

---

[22] *LlDC* 16.54–7. The 'maiden' may be Myrddin's sister Gwenddydd, who is named earlier in the poem, but the description is clearly redolent of love-poetry. Concerning the early verse material see A. O. H. Jarman's chapters on 'The Welsh Myrddin Poems' in R. S. Loomis (ed.), *Arthurian Literature in the Middle Ages* (Clarendon Press, Oxford, 1959), 20-30, and 'The Merlin Legend and the Welsh Tradition of Prophesy', in Bromwich, Jarman, and Roberts (eds.), *The Arthur of the Welsh* (Cardiff, 1991), 117–45. On the development of the Myrddin legend see id., *The Legend of Merlin* (Cardiff, 1960).

[23] Text and translation from Murphy, *Early Irish Lyrics*, no. 43.

those of man's creation, and in the concept of God as architect, the poem provides a striking parallel for the depiction of the *deildy* (*lit.* 'house of leaves') in *cywydd* poetry, which is most fully developed in (and, no doubt, in part imitated from) the work of Dafydd ap Gwilym.[24] In an Irish poem dating from the ninth century a hermit describes to a king his simple woodland dwelling which is known only to God: it is made of trees and has two heather doorposts for support, and 'a woman in blackbird-coloured cloak sings a pleasant song from its gable'. The hermit then describes the woodland in terms reminiscent of the Celtic paradise Tír nan-Óg, with its wells, its tree bearing 'huge apples such as grow in fairy dwellings', and 'an excellent clustered crop from small-nutted branching green hazels'.[25] It is conceivable that this conception of the Celtic Otherworld, combined with Christian values, bears some relation to the *Cywyddwyr*'s depiction of the *deildy* as an idealized *locus amoenus*,[26] and again, one can only guess at the part which the popular poets may have played in developing such themes before their time.

No doubt of more significance than the Myrddin legend as regards the convention of the woodland tryst are the elopement tales (*Aithid*) common in Celtic literature, where adulterous love and a wild woodland setting go hand in hand. Brynley Roberts has drawn attention to the theme in an article on Gwyn ap Nudd, legendary king of the Celtic Otherworld, who, judging by a reference in *Culhwch ac Olwen*, seems to have been part of an elopement tale which has not survived, a tale similar to those of Drystan, March, and Esyllt, or Melwas, Arthur, and Gwenhwyfar. He observes that in tales of this type the lovers flee to the woods, where they spend an idyllic time together before being discovered by the king. Trystan and Esyllt take refuge in the Caledonian Forest ('Coed Celyddon'), where they pre-

---

[24] See in particular *GDG* 121 ('Y Deildy'); *DGG* XLIII, for instance, is clearly for the most part an imitation of this poem. The motif is common in many of the other *cywyddau* falsely attributed to DG: cf. *DGG* XXI, XLV; *BDG* LII, LXXXIII, LXXXVII, CXII, CLXXIX, CCXVIII, CCXXII. In the *canu rhydd* cf. *CRhC* 3.55; 101; 103; *CLlC*, vol. III, no. II; vol. V–VI, no.I; *LlC* 17 (1992), 146.

[25] Murphy, *Early Irish Lyrics*, no. 8.

[26] The concept of the earthly paradise is very often implicit, but in *GDG* 119 the woodland retreat is actually described as 'lle nef yma', and its clover as 'ymellin nef', 'manna of heaven' (ll.36, 28). This is, of course, a literary commonplace. The famous garden of the 13th-cent. French allegorical poem *Le Roman de la Rose*, for instance, has been described as an embodiment of 'the "other world", not of religion, but of imagination; the land of longing, the Earthly Paradise. . .' (C. S. Lewis, *The Allegory of Love* (Oxford, 1936), 75).

pare 'a bed of leaves'.[27] This type of legend almost certainly reflects the ancient theme of the battle between the young and the old god for the young goddess, which, it is thought, embodies the struggle for supremacy between summer and winter in Celtic mythology. As Eurys Rowlands has so perceptively shown, this kind of mythological background is of the greatest relevance for the seasonal poetry of Dafydd ap Gwilym.[28] It must have formed part of the general folklore of medieval Wales, and again the question arises to what extent it may have received a popular poetic form in the verse of the Clêr.[29] Interestingly, Chotzen has suggested Esyllt's husband, March ap Meirchion, as a native prototype for the figure of Eiddig in cywydd poetry.[30] While it seems fanciful to consider this character as the actual progenitor of the conventional figure of the jealous husband, there are indeed several indications in the cywydd tradition that the poets did come to identify the convention with the Trystan legend.[31] Eiddig is typically identified with winter, as in Dafydd ap Gwilym's

> Rhoed i'w gyfoed y gaeaf,
> A rhan serchogion yw'r haf.
> (GDG 24.33–4)

(Winter was given to those of his age, and summer belongs to lovers.)

---

[27] 'Gwyn ap Nudd', LlC 13 (1974–81), 287. The Irish and Welsh tales of this type are discussed by Alwyn and Brinley Rees in their chapter on 'Elopements' in Celtic Heritage (London, 1961), 279–96.

[28] 'Cywydd Dafydd ap Gwilym i Fis Mai', LlC 5 (1958–9), 1–25; see also Alwyn and Brinley Rees, Celtic Heritage, 286 ff. There is no doubt a degree of truth in T. Gwynn Jones's remark that 'the poems attributed to Dafydd, and many others, derive much of their "natural magic" from legends, and what often passes for imagination on the part of the bards is basically the symbolism of early nature cult' (Welsh Folklore and Folk-Custom (London, 1930), 154).

[29] Eurys Rowlands suggests that poems of the same type as Dafydd's cywydd to May (GDG 23), and related customs, were common throughout Wales, and may have been particularly popular in certain areas, including Morgannwg, in his time (note on 'Cywyddau Mai', LlC 5 (1958–9), 143). He argues here for the importance of Glamorgan with regard to the influence of native popular verse, as well as Continental influence, on Dafydd's poetry.

[30] Recherches, 244. On March see J. J. Jones, 'March ap Meirchion: A Study in Celtic Folk-lore', Aberystwyth Studies, 12 (1932), 21–33.

[31] To the references cited by Chotzen, Recherches, 244 n. 1, should perhaps be added the lines 'A gwr Esyllt dan groesau, | Ny ffos gau ... | A gwernen felen yn farch [leg. i Farch?]', from the 'apocryphal' DGG IV.38–40. The girl is often compared to Esyllt; cf. Alwyn and Brinley Rees, Celtic Heritage, 288, and see ibid. 290 for possible echoes of the 'March' tradition in folklore.

The couplet may contain a veiled allusion to the tale,[32] where the husband, March, given the choice by Arthur of possessing Esyllt either when there are leaves on the trees or when there are none, chooses the latter, since the nights are longer in winter. One version of the story proceeds:

Ac y managawdd Arthur i Esyllt hynny Ac y dywawdd hitheu bendi[gedic] vo'r varn ar neb ai rhoddes, ac y canai Esyllt yr englyn hwnn

> Celyn ac yw ac eiddie
> a ddeilia ei dail yd ange
> celyn ac eiddie ac yw
> a ddeilia y dail yn y byw

Ac yn y modd hwnnw y colles March am Eirchion ei wraic yn dragwyddol.[33]

(And Arthur told Esyllt this. And she said: 'Blessed be the judgement and he that passed it,' and Esyllt sang this *englyn* [*sic*]: 'The holly, yew and ivy | Grow leaves until they die; | The holly, ivy and yew | Grow leaves as long as they live.' And it was thus that March ap Meirchion lost his wife forever more.)

While this simple free-metre stanza may not itself be old, a long tradition of similar verse may well have contributed to the theme of a poem such as Dafydd ap Gwilym's praise of the holly bush which serves as a *deildy* during the winter months—

> Pwy mewn gaeaf a gafas
> Mis Mai yn dwyn lifrai las?[34]
> (*GDG* 29.11–12)

(Who ever found in winter the month of May wearing a livery of green?)

---

[32] Cf. D. J. Bowen, 'Nodiadau ar Waith y Cywyddwyr', *BBCS* 25 (1972), 21–2. However, the explicit association of the jealous husband with winter is not unknown outside Wales. Cf. the medieval dance-songs of Continental Europe, related to the *fêtes de mai*, such as the Provençal song 'A l'entrada del tems clar' (see Ch. 7 below, p. 271). Also relevant is the late-12th-cent. Anglo-Norman poem 'Le Donnei des Amants', which fancifully derives *gelus* from *geler*, 'to freeze', since the ice 'binds the running water' as surely as the husband his wife (ed. Gaston Paris, *Romania*, 25 (1896), pp. 497–541, ll. 543 ff.).

[33] Jenny Rowland and Graham Thomas, 'Additional Versions of the Trystan Englynion and Prose', *NLWJ* 22 (1981–2), 247; for other redactions of the tale see Ifor Williams, 'Trystan ac Esyllt', *BBCS* 5 (1930), 115–29. No Welsh version is earlier than the 16th cent. Eiddig's destruction of the *deildy* and leafy woodland in the *cywyddau serch*, a motif noted by Chotzen (*Recherches*, 250–1), is an extension of his antipathy towards summer and nature in general, and a uniquely Welsh version of the ultimately Ovidian motif of the watchful husband. Cf. *BDG* LXXXIII, LXXXVII, XCIV, CCXVIII, CCXXII; *Gwaith Tudur Aled*, vol. 2, CXXXIV; *The Cefn Coch MSS.*, 101, 103–4 (Thomas Prys).

[34] Cf. 'Afraid yt ddala trymfryd | Am bren na bedwen o'r byd, | Tra atai Dduw y

The 'evergreen' motif continues in the early *canu rhydd*, as, for instance, in the well-known 'Carol i'r Gelynen', and here the 'green holly' is once more described as a meeting-place for lovers.[35]

The influence of a submerged current of popular verse on the court-poetry of the *Gogynfeirdd* has recently been advocated by Helen Fulton, who draws an analogy with the contemporary poets of Provence:

An aristocratic poetic tradition, embodying specific social values and intended for a limited and exclusive audience, is aware of its courtly func-tion, and makes use of only a minimum of themes from the wider body of popular material, selecting and transforming these to comply with the pur-pose and expectations of the courtly poetry. Thus the troubadours apply their technical skills and poetic wit to the *pastorela*, the *alba*, and the *reverdie*, raising these popular forms up to the level of accomplishment of the *cansos* in order to define further their interpretations of *fin' amors*. Similarly, the *gogynfeirdd* select and transmit native popular themes through the system of bardic poetry, enriching the range of poetic conventions avail-able to them.[36]

In the work of the Poets of the Princes this process is apparent in two poems in particular, the *gorhoffeddau* or boasting poems com-posed by the twelfth-century poets Hywel ab Owain Gwynedd (*fl.* 1140–70) and Gwalchmai ap Meilyr (*fl.* 1130–80). While these poems may be related to a widespread literary genre, represented in France by the *gab* and common too in other warrior and courtly tradi-tions,[37] and although they were no doubt intended as artistic amuse-ments at royal feasts, behind the convention there lies a truly personal note which sets them apart from the mainstream of pre-dominantly eulogistic verse. In both poems the poets' delight in bat-tle, in nature, and in love forms a curious patchwork of description and sentiment. The martial element is, of course, commonplace in *Gogynfeirdd* eulogy; it is the other two elements, and the association of the one with the other, which are suggestive of popular influence. Reference was made in the opening chapter to Chotzen's suggestion

---

celyn . . .' (*GDG* 25.15–17). In the 'apocryphal' *DGG* XLV it is the broom bush which serves as the winter *deildy*, replacing the birch.

[35] *CRhC* 103.21–4. Note the conventional contrast in ll. 33–6 between the evergreen holly and the birch, of all trees that most symbolic of summer in the Welsh verse tra-dition.

[36] *DGEC* 79–80.

[37] See *Recherches*, 156 ff; Jeanroy, *Origines*, 17; J. E. Caerwyn Williams, 'Cerddi'r Gogynfeirdd i Wragedd a Merched . . .', 98–9.

that the princes, having listened with pride and patience to the intricate and often lengthy *awdlau* sung in their honour, might have called on the *clerwyr* and the *croesaniaid* to divert them with their satire and their 'vulgar farces'. He goes on to suggest that, when spirits had been raised by mead and wine, these entertainers would indulge in boasting contests, and might, at the request of their noble audience, have performed poems of this type.[38] This is, of course, pure speculation, but it is not altogether improbable. At the festive periods in particular the courts were no doubt open to all manner of entertainers, and the dispute between Phylip Brydydd and certain inferior poets in the early part of the thirteenth century is one instance of the kind of interaction which must have taken place.

If boasting poems were indeed part of the repertoire of popular poets, these might have included accounts of the poets' amorous exploits, most typically, perhaps, in a natural setting; and it is quite possible that both Hywel ab Owain and Gwalchmai were inspired in part by the same sub-bardic verse tradition. Gwalchmai proclaims his love in the harmonious context of the early summer season:

> Pellynnig fy nghof yng nghyntefin
> Yn ethryb caru caerwys febin . . .
>
> (ll. 11–12)

> Gorwyn blaen afall, blodau fagwy,
> Balch caen coed, bryd pawb parth yd garwy;
> Caraf gaerwys fun, fenediw deithi,
> Cas gennyf ganddi ni gynhelwy . . .
>
> (ll. 25–8)[39]

---

[38] *Recherches*, 156–7. The triad 'Tri pheth annweddvs ar gerddor: ffrost, a gogangerdd, a chroessanaeth' (*GP* 135) implies that boasting poems were perhaps primarily associated with poets of inferior status. The poem by Iocyn Ddu discussed in Ch. 1 above (*BBBGDd* 70), which cannot be far removed from the work of a 14th-cent. *clerwr*, opens with a shameless bout of sexual boasting, followed by an entertaining account of a personal misfortune, a theme much loved by DG himself. Both boasting and self-mockery are prominent in the poems of the 16th-cent. *clerwr* Robin Clidro, cf., for instance, *CRhC* 46 ('Taith Glera') and 45 ('"Awdl" Taith Clidro i Lwdlo'); cf. also Y Nant's poems (G. J. Williams, 'Cerddi'r Nant'), esp. 82–3, 85.

[39] Text edited by Kathleen Anne Evans, 'Cerddi'r Gogynfeirdd i Rianedd a Gwragedd', unpublished MA thesis, University of Wales (1972), 120–5. (Since going to press, an edition of Gwalchmai's work has appeared in J. E. Caerwyn Williams and Peredur I. Lynch (eds.), *Gwaith Meilyr Brydydd a'i Ddisgynyddion* (Cardiff, 1994).) Cf. Prydydd y Moch's *awdl* to Gwenllian ferch Hywel, ll. 21–4 (*GLlLl* 14). Both this poem and Cynddelw's 'Rhieingerdd Efa' (*GCBM* 5) have much in common with the two *gorhoffeddau*; see J. E. Caerwyn Williams, 'Cerddi'r Gogynfeirdd i Wragedd a Merched . . .', 86 ff.

(My mind wanders far in the May season because of my love for a fair maid . . .

Resplendent are the tips of the apple trees, flower-clustered; the trees are proudly clad, everyone's thoughts turn to their loved-ones; I love a beautiful girl of noble character, and despise those who will not stand by her.)

The obvious echo of the 'Gorwynion' stanzas[40] is suggestive, since it is in this sequence that the love theme is most prominent in the early period, where it seems to be implicitly identified with the nature element. Whether or not the nominal phrases which characterize Gwalchmai's nature poetry are a conscious echo of the early gnomic verse, they clearly reflect the same distinctly native conventions, whose ultimate origins may well owe something to popular tradition. Thus, the origins of the *reverdie* theme in the poetry of Dafydd ap Gwilym and his contemporaries, where love is celebrated in harmony with its seasonal setting, need not be looked for in Continental sources, be they French or Latin, although, of course, one may argue for later external influence in points of detail and in the *Cywyddwyr*'s conception of love in general. The 'nature openings' common in *Gogynfeirdd* eulogy, elegy, and religious verse, as well as in poems to women, are probably best regarded as a natural development of the same tradition, and need not be perceived as deriving from the *Natureingang* convention in Latin or Provençal love-poetry.[41] Kathleen Anne Evans, following the example of those scholars who have advocated the popular celebration of the *fêtes de mai* as the ultimate source of the Continental *Natureingang*, suggests a comparable native origin for the *Gogynfeirdd*'s practice.[42] Despite the fact that May-time carols are not attested until well into the *canu rhydd* period, it is difficult to believe that such songs did not circulate orally in medieval Wales. Dafydd ap Gwilym's famous *cywydd*

---

[40] *EWGP* VI, esp. stanzas 13–14. With Gwalchmai's 'Bid ewynnog ton . . . | Bid swysog serchog' (ll. 91–2) cf. 'Englynion y Bidiau' (*EWGP* VII–VIII). For further echoes of early *englyn* poetry in the work of the *Gogynfeirdd* see Jenny Rowland, 'Genres', 205; Gwyn Thomas, *Y Traddodiad Barddol* (Cardiff, 1976), 119–22.

[41] For a discussion of the device in *Gogynfeirdd* and Continental poetry, which contains a useful survey of scholarship on the subject, see J. E. Caerwyn Williams, 'The Nature Prologue in Welsh Court Poetry', *SC* 24/25 (1989–90), 70–90.

[42] 'Cerddi'r Gogynfeirdd i Rianedd a Gwragedd . . .', 83–100. J. E. Caerwyn Williams also suggests an ultimate origin in native popular seasonal verse, but his conclusions are more guarded: 'By [the *Gogynfeirdd*'s] time so many genres of poetry and prose contained references to nature in their exordia that it is no wonder that some of them thought it desirable to introduce their poems with such references' ('The Nature Prologue in Welsh Court Poetry', 87).

to the month of May (*GDG* 23) may be related to such a tradition; indeed, it has been suggested that the gnomic sequence 'Calan gaeaf . . .', 'First day of winter . . .', and the early religious poem which begins 'Cyntefin ceinaf amser . . .', 'Month of May, loveliest season . . .', may reflect an old tradition of seasonal verse related to the two most important periods in the Celtic calendar.[43] However we choose to explain the origin and function of the nature introduction, it has been seen that the early nature poetry is semi-popular in content if not in provenance, and that similar seasonal verse may well have been composed at a sub-bardic level from the time of the *Gogynfeirdd* onwards, if not earlier.

Hywel ab Owain's praise of his beloved Gwynedd appears less conventional than Gwalchmai's more general nature descriptions, and love and nature are not as closely intertwined. However, the occurrence in Hywel's *gorhoffedd* of the love-tryst motif in a natural setting does indicate the possible influence of a sub-bardic tradition:

> Caraf y morfa ym Meirionnydd,
> Man y'm bu fraich wen yn obennydd.
> Caraf yr eaws ar wyriaws wŷdd,
> Yng Nghymer Deuddyfr, dyffryn iolydd.[44]
>
> (ll. 30–3)

(I love the sea-marsh in Meirionnydd, where a white arm was my pillow. I love the nightingale in a drooping tree, at Cymer Deuddyfr, pleasant vale.)

Hywel's reference to the nightingale may owe something to Latin secular verse and in particular, perhaps, to Ovid, especially as the bird is not thought to have ventured much further west than the English border.[45] The much-imitated Latin poet is in fact mentioned, in the line 'Ced bwyf-i cariadog cerdded Ofydd' (l. 40), 'though I be a lover after Ovid's manner(?)', an early instance, it appears, of the

---

[43] R. Geraint Gruffydd, 'Cyntefin Ceinaf Amser o Lyfr Du Caerfyrddin', *YB* 4 (1969), 17–18.

[44] Kathleen Anne Bramley (*née* Kathleen Anne Evans), 'Canu Hywel ab Owain Gwynedd', *SC* 20/1 (1985–6), 167–91, no. 1. Subsequent citations from the work of Hywel ab Owain are taken from this edition of his love-poetry. (Since going to press, an edition of his work has appeared in Kathleen Anne Bramley *et al.* (eds.), *Gwaith Llywelyn Fardd, I, ac Eraill a Feirdd y Ddeuddegfed Ganrif* (Cardiff, 1994).) Gwalchmai, in his *gorhoffedd*, speaks of 'a secluded meeting-place' ('Eilwyddle didrif') where a bird sings, a 'dwelling' ('addod') which soothes his pain (ll. 115–8). There is no mention here of love, but it is worth noting that in later poetry *eilwydd* is often synonymous with *oed*, 'a love-tryst' (cf. *GDG* 56.14, 22; 146.5).

[45] See W. M. Condry, *The Natural History of Wales* (London, 1991), 120 ff.

convention according to which, as in the *cywydd* tradition, the name is synonymous with 'lover' or 'love-poet'.[46] The nightingale also plays a part in Gwalchmai's poem, and in the words 'Caraf-i eos Fai, forehun ludd' (l. 57), 'I love a May nightingale who hinders morning sleep', it is more obviously the bird of love. It is possible that the motif had already been assimilated into the native sub-bardic tradition of love-poetry; but whatever its ultimate origin, its appearance in the early *cywyddau* need not be explained as a direct borrowing from French or Latin verse, though it will be seen in the next chapter that later external influence may account in part for its prominence there. Another reference by Gwalchmai to the nightingale—'Gorddyar eos awdl gynefin' (l. 8), 'loud nightingale, familiar ode'—may be compared with the line 'Cathl oar adar, awdl osymwy' (l. 22), 'melodious bird-song, languid ode', where birds are apparently depicted as poets in a manner reminiscent of Irish hermit poetry and the Welsh *cywyddau*. However, I am aware of no other comparable instances from this period, and it is difficult to judge whether or not Gwalchmai was consciously following an established native tradition.

The humorous section of Hywel ab Owain's *gorhoffedd*, where he sings the praises of eight or nine women, married and unmarried, who have a right to his poetic muse, and declares his love for them, is one of the most 'uncourtly' in tone of all the works of the Poets of the Princes. Even though the poem is more than likely tongue-in-cheek, and the women mentioned no doubt familiar to Hywel's noble audience and perhaps present themselves in the hall, the emphasis on physical love is striking. Words such a 'Ni orpo hi ddi-weirdawd', 'may she not retain her chastity', 'berfedd fy mhechawd', 'the very heart of my sin', and the use of the verb 'cael', 'to have', with its sexual connotation (ll.72, 70, 55–6, 75–82), reveal a shamelessly light-hearted attitude to love and physical desire which anticipates the poetry of Dafydd ap Gwilym some 200 years later. In the lines:

---

[46] Cf. 'boen ouyt gennad' (*H* 314.5), clearly another early reference to the Latin poet. On the apparent ambiguity of these and similar forms, such as 'cad ofydd', see G 385; *BBCS* 15, 198–200. The Welsh glosses on the first book of the *Ars Amatoria* in Bodleian MS. Auctor. F. 4.32 prove that Ovid's poetry was known in Wales at least as early as the 9th cent. (see *BBCS* 5, 1–8; 6, 112–15; cf. *APDG* 71). On the numerous references to Ovid in the early *cywyddau* see Ch. 5 below, n. 15.

Moch gwelwyf, a'm nwyf yn eddëin iwrthaw,
Ac i'm llaw fy lläin.
Lleucu glaer, fy chwaer, yn chwerthin,
Ac ni chwardd ei gŵr hi rhag gorddin.

(ll. 63–6)

(With my passion remarkable compared to him, and my spear in my hand, may I soon see my 'sister', fair Lleucu, laughing, and her husband shall not laugh because of oppression.)

Hywel's audience may conceivably have recognized a native convention which pre-dates the influence of the Continental *Jaloux*.[47] His *gorhoffedd* may be understood as a humorous reflection of the extreme form of sexual licence which is known to have characterized the lives of the Welsh princes and nobility in this period,[48] and it is possible that love-songs of a similar directness circulated also at a more popular level. Meirion Pennar, in his stimulating article 'Syniad "Y Caredd Digerydd" ym Marddoniaeth Gymraeg yr Oesoedd Canol', makes the interesting suggestion that this attitude to love which, as will be shown, is reflected also in a poem by the *Cywyddwyr*'s important predecessor, Gruffudd ap Dafydd ap Tudur, may have been discouraged or, at least, modified under Norman influence. With regard to Gruffudd's poem, 'Gwyl vun a dry hun . . .' (*RP* 1,264–5), which speaks of mutual love free of blame under the leaves of May, he remarks:

Mae'r gerdd yn un bwysig o safbwynt deall datblygiad y syniadaeth rydd am rywioldeb hyd at Ddafydd ap Gwilym. Yn wir, yn nhraddodiad Hywel ab Owain a Gruffudd ap Dafydd mae'r athrylith gloyw hwnnw yn ei holl ymorfoleddu yn y cnawd. Heblaw'r un 'gorhoffi' yng ngwaith y Gogynfeirdd eu hunain mae'n amlwg eu bod oll ac un yn tynnu ar yr un 'anadl' deinamig â'r glêr ddienw.[49]

---

[47] In a review of *GCBM* in *LlC* 18 (1994), 136–40, Dafydd Johnston suggests that the short *awdl* ascribed to Cynddelw (*fl.* 1155–1200) which ends: 'Ni mad gyrchawdd gwen gwely Eiddig!' (*GCBM* 4)—'it was not fortunately that the girl made for Eiddig's bed'—actually belongs to a later period. With regard to this poem Helen Fulton remarks: 'The very concept of the "jealous husband" suggests contact with French popular poetry, but may also refer to a native tradition. Since women were regarded as, and equated with, material property in both French and Welsh society and literature, the related idea of the "owner" jealous of his "property" may easily have arisen independently in both cultures' (*DGEC* 93).

[48] Concubinage and the offspring of such relationships were legally recognized in both Wales and Ireland. Hywel's father, Owain Gwynedd, himself had nineteen sons by thirteen wives; see P. C. Bartrum (ed.), *Early Welsh Genealogical Tracts* (Cardiff, 1966), 96–7.   [49] *YB* 9 (1976), 37.

(The poem is important for our understanding of the development of the liberal concept of sexuality up to the time of Dafydd ap Gwilym. Indeed, through all his celebration of the flesh that brilliant genius lies within the tradition of Hywel ab Owain and Gruffudd ap Dafydd. If we consider the same exultation ('gorhoffi') in the work of the *Gogynfeirdd* themselves, it is clear that they were all drawing on the same dynamic 'breath' as the nameless *clêr*.)

It is reasonable to assume that these 'nameless' poets and minstrels had always existed alongside the main bardic tradition, contributing to it and no doubt also borrowing from it across the centuries. But— in large measure, it would appear, as a result of the loosening of the bardic hierarchy in the fourteenth century—it is in the *cywyddau* of Dafydd ap Gwilym that their contribution to that tradition is most remarkable and most profound.

It might be thought that, with all its conventional language of love-suffering, *Gogynfeirdd* poetry to women—which may bear some relation to the tradition regarding the *bardd teulu* discussed in the opening chapter, namely that he should entertain the queen in her own room—came under the influence of the Provençal poetry of *fin' amors*, since poets such as Hywel ab Owain, Gwalchmai, and Cynddelw all composed during the great flourishing of the troubadour lyric movement. The 'Continental' theory is eloquently supported by J. Lloyd-Jones in his lecture on 'The Court Poets of the Welsh Princes':

There can be little doubt that these love-lyrics, and the other poems addressed to women, were mainly the product of the pervasive and permeating spirit of that literary movement of which the poetry of the wandering scholar, the troubadour, and the trouvère were the outstanding expression on the Continent.[50]

Several channels have been suggested through which Provençal influence may have reached these poets by the middle of the twelfth century, not the least of which is the intermarriage of the Welsh and Anglo-Norman nobility and royal families.[51] However, such speculation is

---

[50] *Proceedings of the British Academy*, 34 (1948), 192; cf. T. Gwynn Jones, *Rhieingerddi'r Gogynfeirdd* (Denbigh, 1915), 40–3.

[51] See *Recherches*, chs. 7–9; Kathleen Anne Evans, 'Cerddi'r Gogynfeirdd i Rianedd a Gwragedd', ch. 1; see also Constance Bullock-Davies, *Professional Interpreters and the Matter of Britain* (Cardiff, 1966), esp. 16–18. Bromwich speaks of 'the possibility of some kind of two-way traffic between Wales and the south of France, by the early years of the twelfth century', and asks whether troubadour

largely undermined by the simple argument that it seems highly
unlikely that troubadour influence would have reached Wales, and
independent Gwynedd in particular, a decade or so before its earliest manifestation in Northern French literature, in the romances of
Chrétien de Troyes.[52] It is noteworthy too that the scant poetry to
women preserved from the first half of the thirteenth century[53] shows
no development from earlier *Gogynfeirdd* verse, so that both
Provençal and French influence at this period, at least in the 'official'
poetry which has survived, is also unlikely. A more feasible explanation of the so-called 'courtly love' elements in early *Gogynfeirdd*
poetry has been developed at some length by Caerwyn Williams,
Kathleen Anne Evans, and more recently, by Helen Fulton, who per-
ceive these poets' highly stylized attitude towards love as emanating
from a sophisticated courtly society in which the position of the
noblewoman as patron was of paramount importance. Fulton argues
that the *Gogynfeirdd*'s poems to women make use of a closed set of
conventions arising out of their original function as praise poems. In
this respect she considers what she terms the idealized 'bardic love'
of a court-centred society to be analogous with the Provençal ideal
of *fin' amors*, while stressing, however, the uniqueness of the latter
as 'a complete courtly love ethic based on feudal service and spiritual fulfilment',[54] whose social and philosophic implications could be
explored for their own sake. These scholars draw attention to the
significance of Peter Dronke's concept of a 'universal courtly love',
according to which some of the spirit and several of the conventions
which are commonly identified with the particular form of· *amour
courtois* which arose in eleventh-century Provence may be reflected
in various cultures at various times, predominantly, though not
exclusively, in literature produced by courtly societies.[55]

  The short poem containing the Eiddig motif, dubiously attributed

influences could not have reached Wales directly, perhaps via trade-channels. 'Two
quite separate streams of influence', she suggests, 'could well be involved, so that there
is no reason to suppose that Dafydd ap Gwilym's love-poetry was directly indebted
to the same external influences as those which may have affected Hywel ab Owain
Gwynedd' (*APDG* 103–4). On the possibility that the wine and wool trades served as
channels of direct Provençal influence on the medieval English lyric see H. J. Chaytor,
The Troubadours and England (Cambridge, 1923), 24–33.

  [52] Cf. Anthony Conran (trans.), *The Penguin Book of Welsh Verse*
(Harmondsworth, 1967), 57; Fulton, *DGEC* 76. J. E. Caerwyn Williams, 'Cerddi'r
Gogynfeirdd i Wragedd a Merched . . .', 40.

  [53] *H* 40–1 (Einion ap Gwalchmai, *fl.* 1203–23); *H* 64 (Goronwy Foel, *fl. c.*1225).

  [54] *DGEC* 85.   [55] Dronke, *MLRELL*, i. *passim*.

to Cynddelw, and five lyrical *awdlau* by Hywel ab Owain Gwynedd
are generally regarded as the only poems to women from the pre-
Conquest period which were not composed primarily as praise
poems. The feelings expressed in them are not necessarily sincere;
their debt to literary convention is no doubt as great as that of the
Provençal and French poets of courtly love. But unlike the other
poems which have come down they do not readily betray an underlying eulogistic function, for instance, through more or less overt
allusions to payment or to spreading the subject's fame by means of
poetry. In the praise poems the poet's stance as suitor to an unat-
tainable noblewoman serves as a conventional metaphor for the
essentially formal relationship between them. As a male patron
should inspire admiration, a female patron should inspire love. All
the poets, therefore, make use of a familiar language of love-suffering, and since they are clearly drawing on a common set of established conventions it will not be necessary to attempt to distinguish
between their various expressions of love, whether figurative or literal. It has been seen that the 'Celtic' attitude towards love as it
appears in Welsh and Irish prose tales depicts it as a wasting sickness and a force which overwhelms its victims, causing longing and
even madness. Although the register of the court poetry is on the
whole deliberately exalted, much of the imagery through which the
Gogynfeirdd's declarations of love is expressed need not be looked
for outside this convention. Thus Hywel ab Owain, in his poems to
unnamed women, complains:

> Ad(d)wyf-i yn anfedr o ynfydrwydd caru
> > (2.19)
> Ethyw â'm enaid-i, athwyf yn wan.
> > (4.13)
> Hiraethog fy nghof yng nghyweithas,
> Hoed erddi, a mi ganddi yn gas . . .
> Ton o galon hon, hoed a gafas
> > (6.7–11)

(I have become incapable through the madness of loving.
  She has taken my life; I have become weak.
  In company my mind is filled with longing; I pine for her, and am despised
by her . . . Mine is a broken heart, sorrow has befallen it.)

Another manifestation of these poets' suffering is sleeplessness,
which has already been seen to be an effect of Gwalchmai's

infatuation with his 'eos Fai'. One of Hywel ab Owain's *awdlau* begins with the striking lines:

> Caraf-i gaer falchwaith o'r Gyfylchi,
> 'Ny bylcha balchlun fy hun ynddi.
>
> (5.1–2)

(I love a magnificently constructed fortress at Gyfylchi, in which a proud graceful one disrupts my sleep.)

These motifs can be multiplied from those poems to women which are primarily eulogistic. Cynddelw, in his *rhieingerdd* (maiden's song) to Efa, complains: 'Ym mhwyllad newid, neud ydwyf—am fun | Yn anhun anhedd . . .' (*GCBM* 5.25–6), 'with unstable mind, I am in a restless state of sleeplessness on account of a girl'. Since the extent of his suffering is in direct proportion to his 'beloved''s merit, he ensures his listeners that no one ever suffered even a 'ninth' of his pain, or anything like it! (ll. 47–8). In the *awdl* to Gwenllian by Prydydd y Moch (*fl.* 1173–1220), the outward display of suffering is even more ostentatious than that of Cynddelw.[56] Hywel ab Owain sighs the lover's sigh, but discreetly—'Achenaf uchenaid gyfrin' (1.61)—whereas Prydydd y Moch's passion causes his sighs to rise higher than the sky itself, and his broken heart burns as fiercely as any bonfire (*GLlLl* 14.19–20, 33–4).

It has been necessary to survey the love-poetry of the earlier *Gogynfeirdd* at some length in order to show the full scope of an essentially native tradition, which Dafydd ap Gwilym and his contemporaries inevitably inherited. The set of motifs which make up this body of verse has obvious analogues in the Continental love-lyrics, and while the impact of these lyrics on *cywydd* poetry is undisputed, it is clear that any such influence is likely to have acted upon a pre-existing native 'language of love', and must not be over-emphasized. It would be surprising if the joys and trials of love did not also concern poets at a more popular level from an early time,[57]

[56] J. E. Caerwyn Williams, 'Cerddi'r Gogynfeirdd i Wragedd a Merched . . .', 90–7, detects here an element of parody, and compares both this poem and 'Rhieingerdd Efa' with the *gorhoffeddau*, in that they may have been intended in part as courtly entertainment. Hywel ab Owain's conventional portrait of the suffering lover in the humorous section of his *gorhoffedd* should no doubt be read as a deliberate parody of an already well-established native literary tradition. Cynddelw's poem is discussed more fully by Ann Parry Owen, 'Rhieingerdd Efa ferch Madog ap Maredudd. Cynddelw Brydydd Mawr a'i cant', *YB* 14 (1988), 56–86.

[57] Jenny Rowland, 'Genres', 185–6, notes the absence of Welsh love-poetry before the 12th cent., in contrast to Western Europe in general and the early pieces which

and it has been seen that the woodland *oed* is a likely element in the sub-bardic verse tradition. It is difficult to judge to what extent the vision of love in early popular verse is likely to have corresponded to that of the Welsh court poets. While the *Clêr* may have idealized the emotion to some degree, it is hardly conceivable that they would have treated the theme with that particular aura of sophisticated gentility which pervades the largely eulogistic court poetry, elevating the beloved almost as a figure of worship. In the prose tales, although Maxen's love for Elen, for instance, has the effect of elevating her in the reader's mind, and though suitors must sometimes undergo various tests or difficulties before winning the beloved's hand in marriage—the most obvious example being Culhwch's quest for Olwen—love is commonly depicted as mutual. The relationship of Blodeuwedd and Gronw Pebr is a case in point:

Sef a wnaeth Blodeued, edrych arnaw ef, ac yr awr yr edrych, nit oed gyueir arnei hi ny bei yn llawn o'e garyat ef. Ac ynteu a synywys arnei hitheu; a'r un medwl a doeth yndaw ef ac a doeth yndi hitheu . . .[58]

(Blodeuwedd looked at him, and from the moment she looked there was no part of her that was not filled with love for him. And he too gazed at her; and the same thought came to him as had come to her.)

But it is pertinent here to recall Dronke's remarks in his important chapter on 'The Unity of Popular and Courtly Love-Lyric', where he maintains that the feelings and conceptions of *amour courtois* may occur 'in popular as well as in learned or aristocratic love-poetry', and that 'we can, if we wish, postulate archaic courtly traditions behind all popular poetry; on the other hand, we can equally well postulate simple, primordial popular traditions behind all courtly poetry . . . in times when high and low ate together in the same hall, perhaps popular and courtly poetry were seldom far apart'.[59] Those motifs in *Gogynfeirdd* poetry which may be identified with this

---

survive in Irish. With regard to the *Gogynfeirdd* poems she remarks that: 'The more courtly poems seem to have originated from the extention of praise poetry to women patrons, while the earthy pieces may have a popular origin. Love poetry may be an example of a genre treated both by the bards and popular poets. It may have arisen as an interaction between the groups in the twelfth century, but the lack of early poems may also be an accident of survival.' J. E. Caerwyn Williams postulates the existence of popular love-poetry in the *Cynfeirdd* period on the basis of various inferences from other early societies ('Cerddi'r Gogynfeirdd i Wragedd a Merched. . .', 43–5).

[58] Ifor Williams (ed.), *Pedeir Keinc y Mabinogi* (Cardiff, 1930), 85.

[59] *MLRELL* i. 2–3.

notion of a 'universal courtly love', such as sleeplessness, longing, and sighing, and particularly those which are most characteristic of Celtic tradition—sickness, languishing, pallor, madness—may well have been drawn upon simultaneously by poets of a less exalted status. The references in the 'Gorwynion' gnomic stanzas to *hiraeth* and *heint* may be significant in this respect.

The elusive popular vein continues to be tapped by the poets of the post-Conquest period, the immediate predecessors of the early *Cywyddwyr*. Indeed, some of the love-poetry of this period, both in its lighter tone and in its manipulation of elements of a likely popular provenance, prefigures the astonishing freshness and vitality of the early *cywyddau*. The development seems to be indicative of increased interaction in this period between poets and minstrels in general, as a direct result of the disruption of the old bardic structure of independent Gwynedd, or, at least, of a greater readiness on the part of the established 'poets of the gentry' to draw on the popular-verse tradition for their subject-matter. It has been suggested that the inevitable blurring of the functions of *pencerdd* and *bardd teulu* is partly responsible for the increasing number of love-poems from the late thirteenth century onwards.[60] But we must bear in mind also that, even allowing for the probable disappearance of much of the poetry composed to women in the earlier period, especially in the thirteenth century, the tastes of many of the new *uchelwyr* patrons, no doubt affected by the pervasive spirit of the European courtly love movement—whose influence begins to become apparent in the work of a handful of Dafydd ap Gwilym's forerunners—would have created a considerably greater demand for such poetry at this time. It is not unlikely, as Rachel Bromwich has argued,[61] that these influences may, at least in part, have reached the later *Gogynfeirdd* indirectly, through the verse of the *Clêr*, where some of the characteristic features of Northern French poetry may have been assimilated with the native vision of love during the course of the thirteenth century. The theory is given more guarded expres-

---

[60] Kathleen Anne Evans, 'Cerddi'r Gogynfeirdd i Rianedd a Gwragedd', 62–3. Meirion Pennar remarks that, following the fall of Gwynedd, 'Yn lle bod galw'n bennaf am foliant ar awdl yn y dull mwyaf astrus ac urddasol, y dull "penceirddaidd", llunnid ar gyfer llysoedd yr uchelwyr gerddi yn y dull canolig symlach, y dull "teuluaidd" ar englyn.' ('Teuluaeth a Maswedd', *YB* 16 (1990), 52).

[61] See her articles 'Tradition and Innovation in the Poetry of Dafydd ap Gwilym', 'Dafydd ap Gwilym and the Bardic Grammar', and in particular 'The Sub-literary Tradition', in *APDG* 57–131.

sion by Helen Fulton, who remarks that 'the apparent borrowings even in the later *gogynfeirdd* poetry may in fact represent a distinctively native tradition, either entirely independent from the French, or influenced by it at a much earlier stage through oral transmission'.[62] Fulton does, in fact (correctly, in my view), argue for some external influence on the work of these poets, while at the same time stressing the importance of the pre-existing 'distinctively native tradition' which is reflected in the poetry of the earlier *Gogynfeirdd*. Whereas she considers the Welsh court poetry to be analogous in many respects with troubadour poetry, she draws a comparison between the later *Gogynfeirdd* and the 'later courtly love poets' of the Continent. The typically *jongleresque* lyrics of some of these poets, in a manner which foreshadows the emergence of French popular verse (as shall become apparent in the final chapter), embodies what she terms 'extended courtly love', whereby the conventions of the idealized form of *amour courtois* associated with the trouvères are set in a less exclusive context, characterized by the depiction of mutual love as an attainable goal which often goes hand in hand with the joys of the natural world. In the poems to women composed by the later *Gogynfeirdd* the emphasis on love-poetry as opposed to formal eulogy becomes more widespread, a change of poetic stance which was noted long ago by T. Gwynn Jones in his pioneering study *Rhieingerddi'r Gogynfeirdd*.[63] This is in itself, of course, no proof of foreign influence, but the development may have been facilitated by such influence, perhaps in part through the intermediacy of native popular verse. It should be stressed that alongside the more lyrical love-poetry the custom of composing formal eulogies to noblewomen continues to thrive, and as in the earlier court poetry, these poems often make use of the conventional language of love-suffering. Thus, Llywelyn Brydydd Hoddnant (*fl. c.*1300–50) describes Ellylw, for instance, as 'llu diurawd', 'a host's ruin', and 'clwyf cant', 'wound for a hundred men' (*H* 329.19; 330.24);[64] and Casnodyn (*fl. c.*1320–40), in his *awdl* to Gwenlliant, daughter of Cynan, confines the convention to only two epithets, both expressing the 'sleeplessness' motif (*BBBGDd* 5.11,30). These poems, and others like them by

---

[62] *DGEC* 80.   [63] See esp. 16–17.

[64] D. J. Bowen contrasts this 'sober' poem to Ellylw with DG's *cywydd* to her daughter-in-law Angharad (*GDG* 140), which he believes reflects the interest in the European fashion of courtly love during the innovatory second quarter of the 14th cent. ('Dafydd ap Gwilym a Datblygiad y Cywydd', *LlC* 8 (1964), 14–15).

the next generation of so-called *Gogynfeirdd*,[65] the contemporaries of the early *Cywyddwyr*, are clearly a continuation of the native verse tradition discussed above. This also applies to a considerable extent to the love-poems, in which the frequency of motifs such as sickness, longing, sleeplessness, and the like need not be explained in terms of external borrowing.

Among the earliest love-poems from this period are the two *awdlau* by Iorwerth Fychan ap Iorwerth ap Rhobert (*fl. c.*1300?), 'Medwl a dodeis . . .' and 'Neut wyf digeryd . . .' (*H* 324–7).[66] While both perhaps betray an underlying eulogistic function, for instance, in a reference to the dispensing of green garments, these poems, and particularly the second, consist for the most part of the lover-poet's subjective outpourings, so that the tone is less formal than that of the courtly praise-poet. The expression is more deliberately lyrical than that of the earlier *Gogynfeirdd*, as in this stanza from 'Medwl a dodeis':

> Mi awyf yrdi ardelw ermid.
> mwyuwy ym tramwy tramawr edlid.
> a meinoeth ym doeth o detholid nep
> lliw ar wy wynep ny llwyr edid.
> (*H* 324.9–12)

(I resemble a hermit on her account; an ever-increasing sorrow overwhelms me; and at midnight it came to me—if ever anyone was separated [from his love]—my face was left with hardly any colour at all.)

Although the comparison of the ailing lover with a hermit[67] may be new, the basic theme here is familiar enough, as are the other descriptions of the poet's suffering in this poem, with the exception of the phrase 'medwid wy kofein' (*H* 324.1), 'my thoughts were intoxicated'. The metaphor of love as a form of drunkenness prefigures the imagery of Dafydd ap Gwilym, as does the enchantment

---

[65] To Caerwyn Williams's list of later *Gogynfeirdd* poems to women in *LlC* 13, 73 should be added 'Mi a baraf y dyn araf . . .' (*RP* 1,286–7) by Iorwerth ab y Cyriog (*fl. c.*1350–70), a poem composed mostly in the lyrical *rhupunt* metre. This and Gruffudd ap Maredudd's 'Meu dogyngur arthur . . .' (*RP* 1,326–7) are fine examples of subjective love-poetry in *awdl* and *englyn* metres contemporary with the flourishing of the *cywydd serch*.

[66] Daniel Huws argues that although the style of the two poems to women by Iorwerth Fychan suggests that they might belong to the early 14th cent., he may in fact have been a nobleman composing in the mid-13th cent. ('Llawysgrif Hendregadredd', 9, 20 n. 20).

[67] For analogues in later Welsh love-poetry and in French see Ch. 7 below, p. 247.

image in Iorwerth's other poem,[68] in which he declares his love for
a girl who had promised him nothing but 'hoet a hut' (*H* 325.25),
'longing and enchantment'. Both images could have been derived
ultimately from Northern French love-poetry,[69] but since they are
comparatively minor conventions in the Continental lyric tradition it
is equally likely that they evolved quite naturally in the work of the
Welsh poets. They are used by the poets of the post-Conquest period
to convey love's overwhelming power, and it will be seen that the
second in particular occurs in contexts which imply criticism of the
beloved. The appearance in some of the love-poetry of the period of
this theme of the 'two-sided nature of the beloved', as Fulton has
observed, 'marks the change of stance from all-admiring praise-poet
to manipulative love-poet'.[70] It is a theme which is universally
attested,[71] but it may well reflect here, directly or indirectly, the influence of the French lyric tradition, where, particularly in the songs of
the *jongleurs* and bourgeois poets, the conventional 'love-worship' is
tempered by complaints of the lady's cruelty and intransigence.
Iorwerth's other poem, 'Neut wyf digeryd', contains other motifs
which tend to support the argument for Continental influence on his
work. The idea of the poet as the beloved's captive or bondsman,
expressed in the line 'gwenlliant am gwnaeth rygaeth o ryd.' (*H*
326.30), 'Gwenlliant has turned me from a free man into a captive',
is perhaps not unexpected in love-poetry;[72] but it is, of course, central to the feudal imagery of the Provençal and French poets, and its
absence from the extant Welsh court-poetry to women, allied to its
appearance in thirteenth- and early fourteenth-century English love-
lyrics almost certainly as a result of Continental influence,[73] is

---

[68] See John Rowlands, 'Delweddau Serch Dafydd ap Gwilym', *YB* 2 (1966), 58–76,
and also his unpublished MA thesis, 'Delweddau Dafydd ap Gwilym', University of
Wales (1961), 91, 213, where he argues that the images of enchantment and intoxication are the key to understanding Dafydd's attitude towards love.

[69] Cf., for instance, *Roman*, ll. 4,615–6, 13,691, 13,810. Some of the other conventions of French love-lyric referred to here and their likely influence on the early *cywyddau serch* will be discussed in Ch. 6 below.   [70] *DGEC* 100.

[71] See Dronke's motif index, under 'bitter-sweet nature of love' (*MLRELL* ii. 599).

[72] Dronke speaks of 'the universal range of metaphors of the lover "serving" his
lady and becoming her "own man"', which 'may well in some circumstances have
come to carry feudal connotations as well as erotic ones' (*MLRELL* i. 55n.).

[73] 'icham in hire baundoun' (under her power/control) (G. L. Brook (ed.), *The
Harley Lyrics* (4th edn., Manchester, 1968), 4.8). Continental influence on these poems
is discussed by Brook in his introduction; see also Elinor Rees, 'Provençal Elements in
the English Vernacular Lyrics of MS. Harley 2253', *Stanford Studies in Language and
Literature* (1941), 81–95. For some parallels with early *cywydd* poetry see Ch. 7 below.

strongly suggestive of foreign provenance. This may also be true in
the case of the motif of the imminent death of the rejected lover
expressed in the epithet 'llofrud wy neurud' (*H* 325.18), (*lit.* 'murderer of my two cheeks'), and in his complaint that the girl shall not
smile until his death is accomplished (*H* 326.1–2). A similar idea is
expressed by Hywel ab Owain—'Cyn addef goddef, gwae fi na'm
llas' (6.16), 'alas that I was not killed before having to admit to suffering', and possibly in Gwalchmai's *gorhoffedd*—'Genilles a'm llif
ced, a'm lladdwy ar air'[74] (l.29), 'Genilles, who showers me with
gifts, who may kill me with a single word'. Again, it is a motif which
one might expect to arise spontaneously as an extension of the
lover's conventional sufferings. But its frequency in the poems of the
later *Gogynfeirdd* and especially in the *cywydd serch* may once more
indicate external contact.

A similar blending of native and foreign elements is found in the
poetry of Gruffudd ap Dafydd ap Tudur (*fl. c.*1300), although here
the debt to popular tradition—despite the poet's apparent disdain for
the *Clêr* glimpsed in the opening chapter—and in particular to
Continental verse, is more readily apparent. His five extant poems
fall outside the mainstream of official eulogy, and inasmuch as they
may be described as occasional verse they are potentially related to
a thriving sub-bardic tradition which, in pre-Conquest Wales, may
possibly have been reflected in the repertoire of the *bardd teulu* as
well as the more popular poets. His request poem (for the gift of a
bow) (*RP* 1,253–4) represents a genre which was to become common
especially among the fifteenth-century *Cywyddwyr*.[75] The poem is
typically informal in tone, and even contains a section more in keeping with the conventional language of love-poetry. His *englynion*
sequence which tells the lost tale of how Rhun was freed from
imprisonment by Cedig (*RP* 1,265–6) also has a certain freshness in
its simple narrative style. But it is his three remaining poems which
are most revealing with regard to the background to the poetry of
Dafydd ap Gwilym and his contemporaries. He has indeed been

[74] It is possible to understand 'lladd' here (as in Hywel ab Owain's 'Er fy lladd-i â
llafnau deufin' ('Canu', 1.57)) in its original sense, 'to strike', rather than 'to kill'. It
is noteworthy that both Iorwerth's poem (*H* 327.8,11) and Hywel's *gorhoffedd*
('Canu', 1.40, 46) refer to Ovid (synonymous with lover), and to Myrddin as poet.

[75] The only earlier request poem which has come down is an incomplete *englyn*
series by Llywarch Llaety (*fl. c.*1150) (*H* 294–6), a poem which, on metrical grounds,
Lloyd-Jones ('The Court Poets of the Welsh Princes', 175) believed to be the work of
a *bardd teulu*.

called the 'most significant of Dafydd's predecessors as regards his subject-matter',[76] and the fact that Dafydd repeats a couplet from one of Gruffudd's love-poems[77] suggests that he was familiar with his work. The *englynion* thanking a woman for the gift of a *cae* (*RP* 1,266), apparently a belt made of silk and gold and precious stones, call to mind the love-tokens received by Dafydd ap Gwilym and others, usually humbler garlands of twigs and leaves.[78] Since similar tokens are common in the lyrics of the Continental love-poets, we cannot discard the possibility of external influence.[79] But it is the two love-poems which are most strongly suggestive of the introduction into the pre-existing verse tradition of conventions of ultimately foreign origin. Both poems are to unnamed women, and in any case there is no question of any eulogistic function whatsoever. In the *awdl* which begins 'Gwyl vun adry hun drwy hut . . .' (*RP* 1,264–5), the poet's affected criticism of his beloved's intransigence is unambiguous, and her 'two-sidedness' is expressed, for instance, in the striking paradox 'gwedeid elyneid wyl lun' (*RP* 1,264.33), 'gentle form, graceful [yet] hostile'. This concept of the lady as her lover's enemy,[80] and also that of treachery—'brat goleu' (*RP* 1,264.21)—are characteristic of French love-poetry, both courtly and popular, and are the kind of salient motifs one might expect already to have penetrated the native popular verse tradition. The 'sorcery' or 'enchantment' motif introduced in the opening line is here more fully developed than in the lyrics of Iorwerth Fychan. It is connected with the beloved's deceitfulness ('twyll') which has driven the poet to distraction—'amllithrawd ym gorffwyll' (*RP* 1,265.10)—and his infatuation is again likened to intoxication, the girl's deceit having robbed

[76] Bromwich, *APDG* 69n.

[77] 'nyt diboen nam attebut | nyt hawd ymadrawd a mut.' (*RP* 1,264.3–4). In DG's elegy to his uncle, Llywelyn ap Gwilym, the words are given an ironic twist (*GDG* 13.23–4), and the second line is also used by Iolo Goch (*GIG* XIV.26).

[78] Cf. *GDG* 31, 38, 84; *BBBGDd* 47 (Iorwerth ab y Cyriog), and see Johnston's note in *GIG* 314–15. The fact that Gruffudd's *englynion* are remarkably paralleled by an *englyn proest* in the Bardic Grammar suggests that such poems were not uncommon before Dafydd's time (see *GP* 8.25–8; *APDG* 119). As D. Myrddin Lloyd has remarked, Gruffudd's 'Delight in detailed description of an artefact is a new feature' ('The Later Gogynfeirdd', in Jarman and Hughes (eds.), *A Guide to Welsh Literature*, vol. 2 (1979), 41), and it clearly foreshadows the *Cywyddwyr*'s more elaborate *dyfalu* passages.

[79] See G. L. Marsh, 'The Sources and Analogues of "The Flower and the Leaf"', *Modern Philology*, 4 (1906–7), 121–67, 281–327, esp. 153 ff.

[80] Cf. also 'gwiw elyn' (*RP* 1,264.28), which is reminiscent of the French poets' 'douce anemie'. Cf., for instance, Chichmaref (ed.), *Poésies lyriques de Guillaume de Machaut* (Paris, 1909), ii. 302, 540, 585, 653. See also Ch. 6, p. 209.

him of his sanity as if he were a drunken wreck—'mal dyn medw
diawtryd' (*RP* 1,265.12–13). The 'captivity' motif is reflected, in the
line 'dyn aryd geuyn argof' (*RP* 1,264.12), 'a girl who shackles the
mind' (and also, more unexpectedly, in the 'narrative' *englyn*
sequence already mentioned, in which the poet wishes to be relieved
of his love-passion ('nwyf') just as Rhun was freed from prison (*RP*
1,265.39)). The motif of the lover's death is also present, where
Gruffudd rebukes the girl for not sending a messenger to greet him
while he is still in the land of the living—'hyt tra geit eneit ynof' (*RP*
1,264.41–2). While several of these elements are probably of external
origin, whatever the channels of transmission, it should be borne in
mind that the essential image of the suffering lover is also central to
the native verse tradition, and Gruffudd's underlying theme of the
silent, unresponsive maiden has antecedents in the earlier Welsh
court poetry, such as Cynddelw's 'Rhieingerdd Efa' (*GCBM* 5.27–8).
His poem may be regarded as a happy fusion of two complementary
traditions rather than as a wholly new departure. When Meirion
Pennar referred to Gruffudd's fusing of the native tradition of 'free
love' in a natural setting with the European 'courtly love' ideal,
adding that he, like Hywel ab Owain and Dafydd ap Gwilym, was
no doubt 'drawing on the same dynamic "breath" as the nameless
clêr', he had in mind in particular the following passage:

> Ynol adaf naf nwyfrad
> kynnkyfreith pab nae drablud
> y goruc pawb y gared.
> ae gares yndigeryd.
>
> Digeryd uyd ryd rwydgael.
> da y gwnaeth mei dei or deil.
> deuoet dan goet y dan g[o]el.
> y minneu ui am annwyl.[81]
>
> (*RP* 1,265.20–4)

(After Adam, passionate lord, before the Pope's law or his trouble, everyone
fulfilled his lust with his lover without rebuke.

Free and easy loving is beyond blame. Well has May fashioned houses
from the leaves; a tryst for two with mutual trust beneath the trees—for me,
me and my beloved.)

[81] Iolo Goch may have had this passage in mind when he composed his satire of
the Grey Friar who had chastized a group of clerics for taking lovers. Compare the
lines (*GIG* XXXIV.27–30):

> Pan na bai rydd, seythydd serch, | I urddol wraig neu ordderch,
> Rhoed cennad, rhad a'i cynnail, | Rhydd, myn y dydd, mewn y dail.

The theme of the woodland tryst (*oed*), it has been seen, is prefigured in earlier Welsh verse and story, so that Gruffudd is probably
drawing on a familiar popular tradition. While this is the earliest
specific reference to the *deildy*, it may even be that this motif, particularly in view of the analogous elements in Irish 'hermit verse' discussed above, had already been developed by poets at a sub-bardic
level.

In the remaining poem (*BBBGDd* 1), Gruffudd makes use of the
technical language of the court of law[82] to accuse his beloved, whom
he has apparently angered by revealing her name, of causing his
death 'without weapons'—'a'm lladd heb arfau' (l. 11). She gives the
lightly mocking reply:

> Dy gŵyn fu gynnau dy ladd heb arfau
> Â llafnau geiriau gwyron llednais;
> A'm llw, bei'th leddid â gair, llesmair llid,
> Yn fyw na'th welid, edlid adlais;
> A byw y'th welaf, i bawb y tystaf,
> A brawd a archaf ac a erchais.
>
> (ll.39–44)

(Your complaint just now was that you had been killed without weapons,
by the blades of deceptive, courteous words. Forsooth, were you killed with
a word—with passion swooning—you would not be seen alive (cry of sorrow); and I see you alive, to which I testify to you all, and demand judgement as before.)

The poem is unprecedented, in theme and structure, in the native
lyric tradition. I am not aware either of any significant parallels in
Northern French love-poetry for the distinctive mock-legal framework which gives it a kind of poetic wit unique in this period.[83] The

---

[82] Iorwerth ab y Cyriog similarly makes use of legal terminology in accusing his
beloved of having fatally wounded him (*RP* 1,286–7). (The metrical similarity may be
more than coincidence: Iorwerth's poem is composed of *rhupunt* followed by a single
englyn, whereas Gruffudd has *cyhydedd hir + englyn*). Cf. also DG's use of legal
imagery in his love poetry, most notably in his elaborate personification of the mistle
thrush in *GDG* 123; for further examples see John Rowlands, 'Delweddau Dafydd ap
Gwilym', 185.

[83] The closest parallel is an early free-metre dialogue poem in which a youth fears
that he might be killed by the 'arrows' of his beloved's eyes. Her replies are similarly
mocking, and she finally gives him 'acwitans' with the words 'Dôs yn Holliach'
(H. Meurig Evans, 'Iaith a Ieithwedd y Cerddi Rhydd Cynnar', unpublished MA thesis, University of Wales (1937), ii. 203–4). There is also a medieval Latin poetical
account of a lawsuit between husband and wife (Raby, *A History of Secular Latin
Poetry in the Middle Ages*, ii. 289).

idea of the lover's death 'without weapons', however, is strongly reminiscent of the French love-poets: the fourteenth-century poet-musician Guillaume de Machaut, for instance, claims to have been wounded 'sans lance' and 'sans plaie' (without spear or wound), and the lady is able to kill her supplicant without striking a single blow— 'Sans cop ferir'—and such conventional phrases as these echo the lyrics of earlier French poets.[84] The motif of 'love's weapons' which pierce the heart of the unsuspecting lover is inseparable from the Continental lyric tradition, both in its courtly and popular forms, deriving ultimately from the classical image of Cupid's arrow.[85] There are only a couple of seemingly analogous references in earlier Welsh verse—the arrow which causes 'longing' referred to in the 'Gorwynion' gnomic stanzas, and the 'two-edged blades' ('llafnau deufin') of Hywel ab Owain's love for Gweirfyl in his *gorhoffedd* (l. 57). It may be that these isolated early instances of the motif, if they did not arise spontaneously, are due to the influence of Ovid, who, it has been seen, was known, at least by name, to the court poets of the twelfth century. However, the fact that Gruffudd ap Dafydd is here making use of this motif as the central image of his poem, thereby significantly anticipating the poetry of Dafydd ap Gwilym in particular, suggests that it does indeed represent another aspect of external borrowing, which had been assimilated at least by the early fourteenth century. Gruffudd Gryg's celebrated denouncement of the convention in the poetry of Dafydd ap Gwilym in their famous poetic dispute (*GDG* 147) implies that he regarded such obvious insincerity as being incompatible with the native bardic tradition. However, Gruffudd ap Dafydd's poem shows that it was not new, and his satirical treatment of the motif—which may be compared with Dafydd's often ironic attitude towards the excesses of courtly love in general— suggests that it would have been immediately familiar to a Welsh audience by his time. Gruffudd's humorous, light-hearted attitude to the conventional sufferings of the lover may have had much in com-

[84] *Poésies lyriques de Guillaume de Machaut*, vol. ii. pp. 605–6; cf. ibid. 288, 328, 581; i. 99, 173, 193. Earlier instances include G. Raynaud (ed.), *Recueil de Motets Français des XIIe et XIIIe siècles* (Paris, 1881), vol. i. p.93; vol. ii. p.1; S. N. Rosenberg and H. Tischler (eds.), *Chanter m'estuet: Songs of the Trouvères* (London, 1981), nos. 141.19–20; 211.8. In a 14th-cent. *cywydd serch* (see Ch. 6 below, p. 211) Sypyn Cyfeiliog claims to have been injured 'Heb friw gan arf' (*CIGE* LXXI.27), and Llywelyn ab y Moel (*fl. c.*1430) complains: 'Nychais heb glais a heb glwyf', smitten by 'gwewyr serch' (*CIGE* LXIV.36–7).

[85] Cf. John A. Barsby (ed. and trans.), *Ovid's Amores, Book One* (Clarendon Press, Oxford, 1973), 1.21–6, and see Ch. 6 below.

mon with an unrecorded popular-verse tradition, which may already
have absorbed such motifs as the 'weapons of love' and others discussed above which are essentially alien to the earlier Welsh court
poetry. It is unlikely that the poem is modelled solely on 'native folk
literature' as Meirion Pennar has suggested.[86] But the opposite view,
T. Gwynn Jones's belief that it is an imitation of the Continental
poetic convention of the 'court of love', is equally untenable, since
the resemblance, as Helen Fulton has remarked, is extremely superficial.[87] The truth surely lies somewhere between the two. Gruffudd
was clearly aware of some of the European fashions of love-poetry,
but he may well have been drawing on an established blend of native
and foreign modes developed in the verse of the *Clêr*.

Of the three love-poems attributed to Casnodyn (*fl. c.*1320-40)
two betray elements of formal eulogy. In these the poet employs the
stock motifs which are familiar from earlier *Gogynfeirdd* poems to
women, and the only departure from earlier tradition in the first
poem, 'Kynn bwyf gwas grudlas . . .' (*RP* 1,243–4), is the intoxication motif in the phrase 'medw gofyon' (*RP* 1,243.34), 'drunken
thoughts'. The second poem, 'Synhwyrus deus duw goruchaf' (*RP*
1,244), contains a stanza describing the summer season which, as in
the *gorhoffeddau*, is intended to set the mood for the poet's love:

> Saethuarch keindrafnidyr dinidyr da naf.
> seri eglur vrynn kynnkynnhayaf.
> Syw dymawr rwyfwawr yr haf arbennic.
> sorredic eidic elwic alaf.
>
> (*RP* 1,244.16–19)

(A swift, finely exchanged, arrow-like steed beneath me; a prominent hill is
[as if it were] a [mere] causeway before the harvest; a splendid, lordly season is peerless summer; the jealous are sullen, wealth is precious.)

---

[86] 'Syniad "Y Caredd Digerydd" . . .', *YB* 9 (1976), 37 n. 20. Cf. Fulton, *DGEC*
104: 'Far from being suggestive of foreign influence . . . this poem testifies to a rich
native tradition of popular love-song which was increasingly accessible to the court-
poets.'

[87] 'A "Court of Love" Poem in Welsh', *Aberystwyth Studies*, 4 (1922), 85–96. As
Fulton has rightly observed: 'While this poem clearly foreshadows the kind of
extended metaphor and elaborate wit often employed by Dafydd ap Gwilym, it bears
little relationship to medieval "court of love" poems. In these, a topic connected with
love is debated by a number of speakers, often represented by birds, and a final ver-
dict is delivered by a prominent figure presiding over the debate. Gruffudd's poem is
not consciously following this genre but merely utilizing legal jargon as a source of
metaphor' (*DGEC* 104). The 'court of love' convention is discussed in Ch. 7 below.

In style and content—including the reference to *eiddig*—these lines echo the early gnomic poetry, as does Gwalchmai's *gorhoffedd*. And, as in the gnomic stanzas, *eiddig* need not be identified with the stock character of the jealous husband, although the adjective 'soredig' is suggestive of the husband's antipathy towards spring and summer as it appears in the *cywydd serch*. In the lines

> Hy boen yw vy hoen ny hunaf—obleit.
> hebogeid lygeit eureit araf.
>
> (*RP* 1,244.27–9)

(My passion (/joy) is excruciating; I cannot sleep on account of gentle, golden hawk-like eyes.)

the importance attached to the girl's eyes is somewhat reminiscent of the trouvères, whose hearts are often pierced by the lady's 'regard'.[88] These words may be entirely unrelated to the Continental convention, but it is noteworthy that they are not paralleled in earlier Welsh poetry. It might perhaps be expected that a poet as traditionally minded as Casnodyn would have regarded all signs of foreign influence, and certainly all popular elements, in bardic verse with utter disdain. However, the remaining love-poem attributed to him, the poem to Awd (*BBBGDd* 6), tends to confirm that this was not entirely true in relation to love-poetry. It is unambiguously a love-poem, and its most striking feature is another occurrence in this period of the 'woodland tryst' motif. Since the poet cannot have her for himself (or in marriage)—'yn briawd'—he has no choice but to meet her beneath the branches—'Dan frig y goedwig ag Awd' (l. 44). The 'two-sidedness' of the beloved is less prominent than in the poems of Gruffudd ap Dafydd, but it is implied by the sorcery motif in the description of Awd as one who causes grief and is quick to enchant—'Hoed beri hud barawd' (l. 50)—and also by the words 'Treisig yw fy nifrawd' (l. 18), 'my devastation is violent', which are preceded by yet another instance in this period of the image of love as a form of intoxication—'o fedd-dawd—traserch' (l. 17). In the words 'Ys braidd ym fyw' (l. 27), 'I am scarcely alive', and the complaint that death is all that is left for him because of Awd (ll. 39–40), Casnodyn, like his contemporaries, foresees his imminent demise if his wish is not granted. The same motif is found in a short *awdl* by

---

[88] See Ch. 6 below, pp. 209–10. The importance of the eyes is stressed in Andreas Capellanus' 12th-cent. treatise on courtly love, *De amore*; see P. G. Walsh (ed.), *Andreas Capellanus on Love* (London, 1982), 35.

Goronwy Ddu (*fl. c.*1330–70) to an unnamed woman (*MA* 337), whose radiant beauty is fatal, and who is 'able to cause the dire death of a host'—'gwyr dygnllaith llu' (l. 14). As this phrase implies the poem is basically a eulogy to a noble patron, but once more the tone is lighter than that of the earlier poetry to women; and despite the display of bardic word-craft, most evident in the extensive use of *cymeriad*, the poem's lyrical quality is greatly enhanced by the metre, a curious adaptation of the *rhupunt hir*. In the *awdl* by Hywel ab Einion Llygliw (*fl. c.*1330–70) to Myfanwy Fechan of Dinas Brân (*BBBGDd* 46), the poet's eulogistic function is equally apparent, but the central theme is the extreme suffering of the rejected lover. Like some of his immediate predecessors, Hywel rebukes the lady for her intransigence, and again the image of enchantment is explicitly introduced in the opening *englyn*. In the same stanza, the words 'rhwym gwyd rhwy' (l. 3), 'a bond of excessive passion', reflect the captivity motif, and 'dy facwy' (l. 6), 'your squire', recalls the feudal imagery of the Continental courtly love poets who figuratively become their lady's 'man'. There is also reference to treachery ('brad', l. 37), and in the paradoxical 'Mau glwyf a mawrnwyf' (l. 39), 'my wound and great joy/passion', the 'bitter-sweet' quality of love is concisely expressed. By this period such protestations as 'Gofyn ni allaf . . . fyw'n hwy' (ll. 9–12), 'I cannot ask to live longer', and the claim that dying would be no more difficult than living (ll. 67–8), are familiar enough. Although the poet's attitude, on the surface at least, seems to be appropriately earnest, the almost ridiculous hyperbole of statements such as 'anawdd i ynad—eglur | Adrodd fy nolur . . .' (ll. 73–4)—'it would be difficult even for an eloquent judge to give an account of my pain'—does raise the question whether the lover's extreme self-abasement is not once more intended as an ironic reflection of a literary convention. It is noteworthy that Hywel too draws attention to the eyes, complaining of their constant sleeplessness—'Maint anhun . . . fy nau lygad' (ll. 47–8); there is no direct reference to the effect of the beloved's eyes, but simply setting eyes upon her has been fatal (ll. 49–50).

The fusion of native and Continental traditions, then, is clearly reflected in love-poetry before the time of Dafydd ap Gwilym and the early *Cywyddwyr*, and their debt to popular verse is in some respects prefigured by the poets of this period. Further evidence of the pervasion of these trends in the love-poetry of post-Conquest Wales is provided by the metrical examples of the early versions of the Bardic

Grammar attributed to Einion Offeiriad. Rachel Bromwich has discussed in some detail the relevance of the subject-matter of this verse to the poetry of Dafydd ap Gwilym, and has drawn attention to a number of more or less significant verbal similarities which point to Dafydd's familiarity with the Grammar.[89] Furthermore, she has rightly stressed the importance of the likely date and location of the compilation of the tract—sometime around 1330 in Dafydd's native Ceredigion—only a few years, therefore, before the supposed beginning of his poetic career. Taking as her text the Red Book of Hergest version, which she believes to be closest to the archetype, Bromwich remarks that: 'The source of the *englynion* and *cywyddau* are (*sic*) almost entirely unknown', and that 'the occasional differences in wording between the four versions suggests that they are excerpts from poems transmitted orally' (p. 110). Several of the *awdl* stanzas, however, are known to have been taken from the work of poets who composed towards the end of the thirteenth and the beginning of the fourteenth century, including Iorwerth Fychan, Casnodyn, and Einion Offeiriad himself. Indeed, she points out that in contrast to the other manuscripts, particularly Peniarth 20, with one doubtful exception there is no evidence that the examples of the Red Book version were composed later than the middle of the fourteenth century.[90] Some two-thirds of these stanzas—twenty-three out of a total of thirty-eight—are addressed to women, a striking reflection of the compiler's personal tastes and, no doubt, of the general interest in love-poetry in the early part of the fourteenth century. It might be thought that Einion Offeiriad, although clearly well-versed in bardic eulogy, was here consciously turning towards the European tradition of love-poetry. It would perhaps be more correct to say that, while Einion would no doubt have been conscious of the proliferation of European conventions, his selection of exemplary material in fact

[89] 'Dafydd ap Gwilym and the Bardic Grammar', *APDG* 105–31 (an expanded version of 'Gwaith Einion Offeiriad a Barddoniaeth Dafydd ap Gwilym', *YB* 10 (1977), 157–80). This is the source of several of the translations below.

[90] *APDG* 113. G. J. Williams believed that the *englyn* to Lleucu Llwyd (*GP* 8), which may be an example of the verse composed to a woman of that name by Llywelyn Goch, was probably included in the second half of the 14th century (see *GP*, p. xxviii). Bromwich, however, accepts Saunders Lewis's suggestion in 'Y Cywyddwyr Cyntaf' (*LlC* 8 (1965), 191–6) that the beginning of Llywelyn's career slightly predated that of DG, in which case his work could have been included in the Grammar around 1330. The theory is strengthened by the evidence of the Hendregadredd MS; see Daniel Huws, 'Llawysgrif Hendregadredd', *NLWJ* 22 (1981), 18.

represents an attempt to raise the status of such verse[91] which, as in a number of poems already discussed, reflects a blending of external elements with a well-established native tradition of love-poetry. This process of assimilation, it has been suggested, may already have begun at a more popular level before Einion's time.

As in much of the poetry composed to women in this period, the posture assumed by the authors of many of these poems is unequivocally that of 'lover' rather than formal 'eulogist'. Thus, in the well-known *awdl-gywydd* 'O gwrthody, liw ewyn . . .' (GP 12.42–7)[92] the poet adopts a forthright, almost threatening attitude which prefigures the poetry of Dafydd ap Gwilym, and elsewhere the subject, as in Northern French love-poetry, may be accused of deceit, enchantment, and even treachery. The following *englyn* is a fine example:

> Un dwyll wyt o bwyl[l], o ball dramwy—hoet,
>   A hut mab Mathonwy;
> Vnwed y'th wneir a Chreirwy,
> Ennwir vryt, ryhir vrat rwy.
>
> (GP 7.15–18)

(Of like deceitful thought are you, from failure of excessive longing, to the enchantment of the son of Mathonwy; you are formed in a like shape to Creirwy, of cruel disposition, too long, too great betrayal.)

A certain Angharad, quite possibly the wife of Ieuan Llwyd of Glyn Aeron to whom Dafydd ap Gwilym composed a love-poem and an elegy (GDG 140, 16), is described as follows:

> Dy garu, gorhoen eglur,
> Agharat, gwenwynvrat gwyr,
> Hoyw gangen, hy a gyngor,
> Hawl eneit y direitwr.
>
> (GP 8.12–15)

---

[91] As Bromwich points out, *APDG* 123, Einion's choice of stanzas from love poetry is all the more remarkable since so many of the metres are exemplified in his own *awdl* to Syr Rhys ap Gruffudd. See Ifor Williams, 'Awdl i Rys ap Gruffudd gan Einion Offeiriad', *Y Cymmrodor*, 26 (1916), 115–46.

[92] Peniarth 20 gives four additional lines (GP 52). It is the most striking reflection in Welsh of 'a theme which was popular among the *clerici vagantes* or "wandering scholars" in European countries during the Middle Ages . . . the scholar's (or clerk's) superiority to the labourer or "villein captive to the plough"' (*APDG* 126). See Ifor Williams, 'Dafydd ap Gwilym a'r Glêr', *THSC* (1913–14), 174; Meirion Pennar, 'Dryll o Dystiolaeth am y Glêr', *BBCS* 28 (1979), 407–9. Gruffudd ap Dafydd's plea—'Na ddilynwch dlawd ni ddilynwy wawd . . .' (*BBBGDd* 1.45)—is in the same spirit, as is his emphasis on learning in another of his love-poems (*RP* 1,265.26).

(To love you, a bright joy, Angharad, venomous betrayal of men. Lively branch, bold her counsel, claiming the soul of a wretched man.)

The last line seems to reflect the 'dying of love' motif, as do the words 'Lletryt, nyt bywyt, a'm byd' (*GP* 13.10), 'sorrow, not life, shall be my lot', from a verse addressed to Goleuddydd,[93] and 'Llwyr y gwnaeth . . . lleas gwas' (*GP* 11.40), 'she has completely slain the youth', from another of the *awdl* exempla, the *cyrch a chwta* to Angharad. The *hir-a-thoddaid* addressed to a woman of the same name is an excellent example of a conventional love-poem which need not necessarily be explained in terms of any external influence:

> Gwynuyt gwyr y byt oed uot Agharat,
> Gwenvun, yn gyuun a'e gwiwuawr garyat;
> Gwannllun a'm llud hun, hoendwc barablat;
> Gwynlliw eiry divriw, divris[c] ymdeithyat;
> Gwenn dan eur wiwlenn, ledyf edrychyat—gwyl,
> Yw pann wyl yn y hwyl, heul gymeryat.
>
> (*GP* 11.27–32)

(The joy of the world's men was Angharad's being, the fair maid, of one accord in their great love; her slight form prevents my sleeping, her speech inspires passion [*or* takes away my colour]; fair hue of unbroken snow, a journey untrodden, fair beneath her golden head-dress, of gentle aspect; my darling is of gentle nature, the Sun's peer.)

This graceful description of a modest noblewoman, with its conventional images of brightness so reminiscent of earlier *Gogynfeirdd* poetry, is entirely consonant with the Welsh bardic tradition, as is the account of the lady's effect on her poet—sleeplessness and pining. The inherent duality, the joy and the sorrow of love, which has been seen to be a characteristic feature of the love-poetry of this period, perhaps reflecting in part the influence of the Continental poets, is most explicitly illustrated in the Grammar in an *englyn* to a girl called Generys (*GP* 7.40–3): although the poet's thoughts may bring him joy, his countenance betrays the sorrow of a broken heart—'Lletryt kallon donn ef a'e dengys—grud.' In another *englyn*

[93] Cf. the grammatical example 'Rys ac Einawn a garant Oleudyd' (*GP* 6.8–9). Goleuddydd was the girl loved by Gruffudd Gryg (cf. *GDG* 20.20; *DGG* LXXI.36, LXXIII.38), and if the stanza is indeed his work it should not necessarily be regarded as a late addition. On the poet's dating see E. D. Jones, 'Cartre Gruffudd Gryg', *NLWJ* 10 (1957), 230–1. It is significant that *englynion* are attributed to him in the third 'layer' of the Hendregadredd MS (Daniel Huws, 'Llawysgrif Hendregadredd', 17, 24). See also *APDG* 159, 123n.

the phrase 'glwyfgat glew' (GP 8.20), 'wounding-battle of the brave', may be understood as another instance of the 'weapons of love' motif before the time of Dafydd ap Gwilym, and possibly also the words 'erwan brat' (GP 14.15), which translate literally as 'a stab (or 'sting') of treachery'.[94] The references by Gruffudd ap Dafydd and Casnodyn to the woodland tryst are paralleled in three of the metrical exempla. The first alludes specifically to the lovers' tryst:

> Kathleu eos nos yn oet—y kigleu,
> [M]eu gofeu gofalhoet,
> Koethlef, herwodef hiroet,
> Kethlyd, kein awenyd koet.
> (GP 7.34–7)

(At [lovers'] tryst by night I heard a nightingale's song—mine are sad memories of longing—a pure voice, suffering the long grief of exile, sweet singer, inspired poet of the forest.)

The fairly detailed description of the nightingale in this *englyn* is reminiscent of the early gnomic verse and of the three-line *englyn* to the blackbird discussed earlier, and particularly in the metaphor of the bird as poet it provides a significant parallel for the love and nature poetry of Dafydd ap Gwilym.[95] In the second instance, the example of the *awdl* metre *gwawdodyn hir*, the poet complains of the wound of love ('clwyf') which has made him weak, expressing his longing ('hiraeth') and declaring that his passionate heart shall break 'because she whom I love, on whom my mind dwells, will not come to me beside the grove—[that would indeed be] a pleasant reply'—

> Am na daw y law y lwyn—a bwyllaf
> A garaf attaf, atteb addfwyn.
> (GP 10.47–8)

In one of the *englynion proest* (GP 8.39–42), although there is no specific mention of the *oed* or the woodland retreat, the poet's love is expressed in harmony with the natural world. Though he may be

[94] The word 'gwaywawr' does occur in a faulty *englyn* to a woman in Peniarth 20 (GP 47), but probably in the common figurative sense of 'pangs' rather than 'spears'.
[95] Bromwich draws attention to possible verbal echoes of the stanza by DG, and suggests that the reference to the nightingale's longing and exile stems ultimately from the tale of the nightingale Philomela in Ovid's *Metamorphoses* (ADPG 117–18). It is noteworthy, however, that the description in the Grammar bears a striking resemblance to that of the cuckoo in the older 'Claf Abercuawg' *englyn* sequence (cited above, n. 10), which is likewise 'hiraethawc y llef'.

frowned upon, he wishes that he might have his beloved for his own ('Meu dy gael') in a glen, 'in the saddle of Mwg', his horse(?) ('ygo-bell mwc'),[96] in the hope of bright sunshine and also, it is implied, in the hope of a bright future for their love; and in this context, as in the love-poetry of Dafydd ap Gwilym and others, the verb *cael* would no doubt have possessed a playful erotic connotation for a contemporary audience.

While it is, indeed, more than likely that such themes were treated by Welsh poets at a popular, sub-literary level, I believe that Rachel Bromwich's opinion that Einion Offeiriad actually 'chose examples of the different kinds of *englynion* and *cywyddau* almost entirely from the work of popular poets, orally current and rarely, if ever, previously committed to writing . . .'[97] should be regarded with some reservation. The theory is given its most persuasive expression in the following passage:

Taken as a whole, then, the *exempla* in the Bardic Grammar represent the fullest collection of excerpts that has come down to us of the verse of the so-called *clêr* . . . which were in oral circulation throughout Wales during the 13th and 14th centuries. Very little, apart from the excerpts fortuitously preserved in the Grammar, has come down to illustrate the nature of the sub-literary productions of this period. But it seems certain that it was in verse of this kind that there lay the *matrix* or deepest source of inspiration for Dafydd's love-poetry: in their content, in their native metrical techniques and in their inherited poetic vocabulary and stylistic devices. And these fragments show that the themes of continental *amour courtois* were already securely established in Welsh poetry at the time when Dafydd's career began . . . (p. 129)

That Dafydd and, to a lesser degree, the other early *Cywyddwyr* were largely inspired by the sub-bardic verse tradition is beyond question. However, to interpret Einion Offeiriad's collection of metrical examples as containing a considerable body of verse actually composed by the popular *Clêr* is perhaps to overstate their importance. It has been seen that the *englyn milwr* to the blackbird may indeed be of popular origin, and, significantly, the stanza is virtually free of the adornments of bardic word-craft.[98] It is among the metres

[96] Alternatively, 'Gobell Mwg' might be a place-name, cf. *GPC* s.v. *gobell*: 'Digwydd yn enw'r mynydd *Rhobell Fawr*, sef *Yr Obell*, ym mhlwyf Llanfachreth, Meir.'

[97] *APDG* 128. This is accepted by Fulton, *DGEC* 146, 246 n. 20.

[98] An example from a later grammar also lacks full *cynghanedd* (*GP* 179). From the 15th cent. onwards the *englyn milwr* is named among the worthless or frivolous

which resurface in the sixteenth-century *canu rhydd*—quite possibly after a long sub-literary existence; so too is the *awdl-gywydd*, which, in the Grammar, is also virtually untouched by *cynghanedd* (although this, as is shown by Dafydd ap Gwilym's celebrated *traethodl* (*GDG* 137), is not a priori a sign of sub-bardic authorship). The *traethodl* is itself prominent in the *canu rhydd*, but the lines cited in the Grammar (*GP* 12.29–30; 31.20–5) (i.e. as an illustration of the *cywydd deuair hirion*), though devoid of *cynghanedd* are characterized by some very involved alliteration, compound word-forms, and the device of *cymeriad cynganeddol*, so that they should probably be regarded as an example of the 'upgrading' of the popular *traethodl* which preceded the introduction of full *cynghanedd* into the *cywydd* metre.[99] The example of the *cywydd deuair fyrion* (*GP* 12.34–9), which was to become extremely popular with the free-metre poets but was hardly ever used by the qualified bards, although entirely free of *cynghanedd* does have *cymeriad llythrennol* in every line, so that this too may represent an attempt to bring some degree of bardic respectability to a predominantly popular metre.[100] The only four-line *englyn* included by Einion Offeiriad which does not have *cynghanedd* is the *englyn cyrch* (*GP* 7.48–51), yet another metre which was to resurface in the verse of the free-metre poets.[101] However, it does contain a degree of alliteration, and although linguistically simpler, it is in the same mould as the other poems to metres (*ofer fesurau*) which are inferior to the twenty-four recognized bardic metres (cf. *GP* 113).

[99] The *traethodl*, from which the *cywydd* is now generally accepted to be derived, is discussed by R. M. Jones, *Seiliau Beirniadaeth*, vol. 2 (Aberystwyth, 1986), 170–88. The excerpt from the Grammar is also discussed in Ch. 4 below, in relation to *dyfalu*. For a detailed survey of the nature and origins of the various metres used by the early free-metre poets see id., 'Mesurau'r Canu Rhydd Cynnar', *BBCS* 28 (1979), 413–41 and the references cited there (416 n. 2).

[100] Meirion Pennar makes a similar remark with regard to the *cywydd* metres exemplified in the Grammar (with the exception of the *cywydd llosgyrnog*): 'Ond odid taw mesurau'r glêr oeddent yn wreiddiol a'u bod wedi'u dal megis ar ganol cam, o fod yn ddi-gynghanedd i fod yn llwyr gynganeddol' ('Dryll o Dystiolaeth am y Glêr', *BBCS* 28 (1979), 407). They may all, he suggests, be examples of the type of verse defined as *teuluaidd*, less formal than that which is said to befit a *prydydd*. It is likely that the line between verse of this type and that of the popular *Clêr* became gradually thinner in the post-Conquest period, as the prescriptive character of the Bardic Grammar suggests.

[101] In Peniarth 20 the stanza is followed by the revealing remark : 'A'r mod hwnnw ar ynglynn ny perthyn ar brydyd y ganu namyn ar deuluwr diwladeid, rac y hawsset a'y vyrret' (*GP* 48.42–3). In a late grammar (*c*.1600) an example of the *englyn cyrch* 'o'r hen vath' (as opposed to the 'new type' in *cynghanedd*) is drawn from contemporary free-metre verse (*GP* 214).

women, so that once more it is doubtful, in my view, whether this particular stanza should be considered as an early example of 'popular' verse. It may be that this, as well as some other *englyn* and *cywydd* stanzas, including the *englynion* illustrating the 'forbidden faults', are taken not from the verse of inferior *clerwyr* who were conversant with some of the simpler 'bardic' metres, but from the work of apprentice-poets who had reached various stages of accomplishment in the traditional bardic training. But as for the four-line *englynion* in general, adorned as they are with *cynghanedd* and other bardic devices, although their expression is by and large less complicated than the more stately *awdlau*, they do not differ substantially, in style or content, from the *awdl* stanzas, as is evident from the examples cited above.

It is clear also that the poetry addressed to women fortuitously preserved in the Bardic Grammar corresponds closely to the love-poetry of the later *Gogynfeirdd*. As Bromwich herself points out, 'before Dafydd ap Gwilym the *englyn* was the poetic form most frequently chosen for love-poems' (p. 128). It seems likely that the *englyn* poetry with which we are concerned was drawn for the most part not from popular sources but from the work of trained poets composing in the late thirteenth and early fourteenth century, poets such as Gruffudd ap Dafydd ap Tudur, who would have been particularly susceptible to popular influence in the post-Conquest period. As in the poems of Gruffudd ap Dafydd love is occasionally celebrated in a natural setting, and with the native conventions of love-poetry are combined motifs likely to be Continental in origin which, it has been argued, may have penetrated bardic poetry partly through the intermediacy of the *Clêr*. The overriding importance of Einion Offeiriad's remarkable anthology of contemporary love-poetry is that it provides further evidence of the pervasion of European literary fashions and of the increasing influence of native popular verse on those poets who immediately preceded, and in many ways made possible, the great flowering of the *cywydd serch*. In the following chapters it will be seen to what extent this submerged native tradition can be said to have affected the *Cywyddwyr* themselves, and the poetry of Dafydd ap Gwilym in particular.

4

The Early *Cywyddwyr* and the
Sub-Literary Verse Tradition: I

It has long been suggested that the considerable body of early free-metre verse which first appears in sixteenth-century manuscripts is in part a late manifestation of an older tradition of *Clêr* poetry. These poets composed in non-bardic metres with very little or no use of *cynghanedd*, and, as Thomas Parry has observed, their conventional style and distinctive language are suggestive of a gradual development which pre-dates the manuscript tradition.[1] That is not to say that the poems are considerably older than the manuscripts in which they are preserved, although this may possibly apply in the case of a few of the anonymous poems,[2] or that they are all composed by the kind of wandering versifiers evoked by the term *Clêr*. Indeed, much of the free-metre verse preserved from the sixteenth and the first half of the seventeenth century is the work of accomplished strict-metre poets, such as Siôn Tudur, *uchelwyr* such as Richard Hughes, and learned priests such as Edmwnd Prys.[3] However, as a body of verse the early *canu rhydd* is certainly popular in the sense that it was not reliant on bardic learning and was accessible to a wider audience than was strict-metre verse; and also in that it may reasonably be assumed to have retained much of the spirit and subject-matter as well as the metrical apparatus of the submerged sub-bardic verse tradition of medieval Wales.

One of the first to appreciate fully the implications of this later verse for the study of the poetry of Dafydd ap Gwilym and his

---

[1] *Hanes Llenyddiaeth Gymraeg* (3rd edn. Cardiff, 1953), 134. (On this aspect of the poetry see H. Meurig Evans, 'Iaith a Ieithwedd y Cerddi Rhydd Cynnar', unpublished MA thesis, University of Wales (1937)). Cf. for instance, T. H. Parry-Williams, *CRhC* pp. xi ff; G. J. Williams, *Traddodiad Llenyddol Morgannwg*, 134–42. For a more tentative view see Brinley Rees's remarks in *DCRh* 12 ff., and especially H. J. T. O'Sullivan, 'Developments in Love Poetry in Irish, Welsh, and Scottish Gaelic Before 1650', unpublished M.Litt. thesis, Glasgow University (1976), 210 ff.

[2] On the possible existence of some kind of free-metre poetry in the 15th cent. see *Traddodiad Llenyddol Morgannwg*, 117, 134 ff.

[3] Some poems are, however, ascribed to poets of humbler status, such as 'Edward y gwŷdd' and 'Dafydd ap Huw'r Go o Fodedern'; see *DCRh* 12–13.

contemporaries was Chotzen.[4] But as he himself admitted, his acquaintance with early free-metre poetry was rather limited, and as a result his conclusions in this field are of no great importance. More recently Rachel Bromwich has stressed the relevance of this verse to Dafydd's *cywyddau*, particularly so in relation to the bird-messenger motif and to dialogues between bird and poet. With regard to the early free-metre bird-dialogue poems she suggests that

if their prototypes go back as far as the time of Dafydd ap Gwilym . . . then it would seem reasonable to conclude that Dafydd ap Gwilym derived these and many other themes in his poetry from a popular tradition which had already before his time absorbed many elements from outside sources, and that this tradition continued to exist 'underground' and un-recorded (as did the parallel tradition in Ireland) until it re-emerged when drawn upon again in the sixteenth and seventeenth centuries by the poets of the *canu rhydd*.[5]

It has been seen that signs of the kind of external influence suggested here are already apparent in the love-poetry of Dafydd's immediate predecessors, and the final chapters will examine the effect of European literary fashions on the *Cywyddwyr* themselves, whether these are likely to have reached them through native popular channels or by other means of transmission. Our immediate concern is to identify those elements in early *cywydd* poetry which may owe something to the peculiarly native character of the pre-existing verse tradition. Needless to say, the literary substratum of medieval Wales can never be reconstructed with any great confidence or clarity. But by means of a comparative study of the early *cywyddau*, the *canu rhydd*, and also a number of 'apocryphal' *cywyddau*—some fourteenth- but mostly fifteenth-century poems attributed to Dafydd ap Gwilym but rejected from the canon by Thomas Parry[6]—it is hoped that some light will be cast on the likely popular origins of several of the innovations which Dafydd and his contemporaries introduced into the predominantly 'aristocratic' poetic tradition.

Among the striking similarities which exist between strict- and free-metre poetry is the prevalence of bird-life and bird-lore, and the

[4] *Recherches*, 85 ff.

[5] *APDG* 101. See in particular 'Tradition and Innovation in the Poetry of Dafydd ap Gwilym'; 'The Sub-literary Tradition', ibid. 57–104. The theory is accepted by Thomas Parry in his review of the former in *LlC* 10 (1968–9), 125–6. On the analogous Irish development to which Bromwich refers, a tradition similarly affected by Continental influence, see Seán Ó Tuama, *An Grá in Amhráin na nDaoine* (Dublin, 1960); id., 'Serch Cwrtais mewn Llenyddiaeth Wyddeleg' in *DGChSOC* 18–42.

[6] See *GDG*[1], pp. lxxiii ff. A total of 177 spurious poems are listed (pp. clxxi–cxc), most of which (in more or less corrupt form) are included in *BDG*.

importance of man's 'feathered friends' as the lover's confidants and spiritual companions. These poets are all evidently drawing on a common native tradition. While recognizing the inevitable, though largely superficial, influence of the *cywyddau* on the free-metre poets, we may suppose that the latter were in this respect drawing on various folk-beliefs and customs which were probably common in the work of their popular predecessors, on which the *Cywyddwyr* may also have drawn. We may reiterate here the significance of the apparently popular verse to the blackbird quoted in the Bardic Grammar, which is so closely echoed by Dafydd ap Gwilym (*GDG* 76.23–30). Though Dafydd may here have been paraphrasing directly from the Grammar, it has been seen that he and his contemporaries would almost certainly have had access to a current of comparable floating, sub-literary material. Apart from the lark, which (it will be shown in Chapter 6) was conventionally described by medieval poets as singing God's praise, the only bird whose portrayal in *cywydd* poetry seems possibly to have been influenced by external traditions is the nightingale. We must, however, bear in mind that the bird, as has been seen, is associated in Welsh poetry with love and the joys of spring at least as early as the twelfth century, perhaps due to early Latin influence. It is noteworthy too that for the poets and writers of medieval Europe there existed several disparate strands of traditions relating to the nightingale: it may be the tragic Philomela of Ovid's *Metamorphoses*; it may represent Christian love or the suffering of the Passion; or its song may even be depicted as a war-cry in a fairly common military metaphor.[7] But as in the songs of countless medieval Latin, Provençal, and Northern French lyric poets, the nightingale is for the early *Cywyddwyr* the bird of love and the rebirth of spring. Dafydd ap Gwilym has Madog Benfras describe the bird as the 'sacring-bell of lovers'—'Cloch aberth y serchogion' (*GDG* 25.35). In the poem believed to be the work of Madog Benfras which seems to have inspired this *cywydd* the nightingale is 'laswyr-wraig y cariad' (*BDG* LXXXIV.23), 'psalmist of love', and, perhaps significantly, it is said that its memory is dear to Ovid—'Prid yw ei chof gan Ofydd' (l. 15). The convention is well represented in the *canu rhydd*, with the difference that in some poems learned allusions

---

[7] On the depiction of the nightingale in Classical and medieval literature see J. L. Baird and J. R. Kane, *Rossignol: An Edition and Translation* (Kent University State Press, 1978), 1–53; T. A. Shippey, 'Listening to the Nightingale', *Comparative Literature*, 22 (1970), 46–60.

to the legend of Philomela betray a late classical influence, no doubt via contemporary English verse.[8] Not surprisingly, Eiddig, the jealous husband, is represented as the nightingale's foe—in GDG 25, for instance, it appears that it is he, or possibly some unnamed slanderers, who have 'indicted' the poet's messenger, causing its exile from the land of Gwynedd. This forms part of a larger, apparently native convention,[9] of rivalry between Eiddig and the creatures which are the poets' servants in love, a motif which, it will be seen, is commonly reflected in the *llatai* or love-messenger poems where the messenger is warned of the husband's fatal snares and crossbow bolts.

Other, more characteristically native birds are also portrayed in the Welsh poetic tradition as 'birds of love'. Among those specifically associated with love are the blackbird, described in *BDG* CXXX.34 as 'Edn y Serch', 'bird of love', the pheasant-cock, which is portrayed as a love-poet in *DGG* XXXIV.29-30 (both poems probably belong to the fifteenth century), and the lark, which again is compared by Dafydd ap Gwilym to a love-poet—'Modd awdur serch' (*GDG* 114.23). Dafydd is especially fond of the cock-thrush, which in one poem is 'the poet of Ovid's faultless song'—'Prydydd cerdd Ofydd ddifai' (*GDG* 28.21), and in another the fosterson of May—'mab maeth Mai' (*GDG* 122.14). Similarly, in free-metre poems the thrush is greeted as 'ceiliog . . . serchog' and 'bronfraith serchogfwyn',[10] and particularly in the *canu rhydd* these birds are found together in evocations of the twin joys of spring and love.[11] It was seen in the previous chapter that there are indications that the cuckoo was associated with human love from an early time, and the affection in which it is held by the Welsh poets is matched only by the more familiar convention of the nightingale. In *GDG* 121 it is the cuckoo

[8] Cf. Evans, 'Iaith a Ieithwedd . . .', ii. 335–8; *CRhC* I, VI, and see *DCRh* 73; cf. also a contemporary *cywydd* by Thomas Prys (*The Cefn Coch MSS.*, 422–5).

[9] Cf., however, the 'Lai de Laüstic' by the 12th-cent. poet Marie de France, where the jealous husband kills the nightingale since his wife claimed to be listening to its melodious song at her window while in fact she entertained her lover (K. Warnke (ed.), *Die Lais der Marie de France* (Halle, 1900), 146–51). The tale is reflected in a 15th-cent. popular French poem (Gaston Paris (ed.), *Chansons du XVᵉ siècle* (Paris, 1875), CIX), and in a (probably faked) Breton poem claimed to have been recorded in the last century (H. de la Villemarqué (ed.), *Barzaz Breiz: Chants populaires de la Bretagne* (6th edn., Paris, 1867), XX).

[10] Evans, 'Iaith a Ieithwedd . . .', ii. 258; *CRhC* 35.9. The description of the bird in the former is unusually extended, clearly due to the influence of the *cywydd* tradition.

[11] For instance, *CRhC* 12, 105; *CLlC*, vol. III, p. 24. In *CRhC* 21 the cuckoo, cock-thrush, and blackbird all promise to help a girl seek out her departed lover. Cf. also *GDG* 119 and 122 where the thrush and nightingale are found together.

and the nightingale which assist May in the building of the *deildy*, and in *GDG* 24, 'Y gog serchog' (l. 21), along with the thrush and the nightingale, are part of Dafydd's celebration of summer. He also personifies the cuckoo, in a manner so typical of the early *Cywyddwyr*, as 'morwyn gyflog Mai' (*GDG* 34.32), 'May's hired servant-woman', and an unnamed girl is described as 'nith y gog' (*GDG* 41.38), 'the cuckoo's niece'. Elsewhere, as, for instance, in *BDG* C, the cuckoo is the lovers' most faithful ally, the archetypal enemy of Eiddig, a theme which is reflected in a poem by the Elizabethan poet Richard Hughes, in which the nightingale refuses to act as *llatai* for fear that the jealous husband might mistake it for the cuckoo (*CRhC* 1, VI). In two other sixteenth-century poems, probably the work of the gifted and enigmatic Llywelyn ap Hwlcyn,[12] the cuckoo's advice is entirely to the poet's own mind. It makes clear its loyalty—'Kas gan eiddig ddig yn i, | Os dy di ydiw llelo' (*ClIC*, vol. III, no. XIII), 'angry Eiddig hates us, if you are indeed Llelo'—and if Eiddig's wife shall come under the birch-trees, the cuckoo urges the poet to conspire with it in poisoning his food. In the second poem the bird's advice regarding the jealous husband is no less extreme:

> Kymer afel intho fo,
> A dyrro segfa iddo,
> A lladd unwaith hwnw yn siwr,
> A dos di yn wr i Weno.
> (ClIC, vol. III, no. XIV)

(Take hold of him and give him a good shaking; make sure you kill that man once and for all, and then become Gwenno's husband.)

A similar pact between bird and lovers is apparent in another free-metre dialogue poem, composed in a form of the old *awdl-gywydd* metre. No matter how much the three of them are despised by their enemies, the poet assures the cuckoo that he shall accompany it to the woods when the time comes, to which the bird replies:

> 'Dvw a mair ach katwo yn wych
> rhag hirnych a chlyfyde
> pan ddel dail ar goed y knav
> mi ach dyga chwi ych dav r vnlle.'
> (CRhC 34.21–4)

---

[12] On this poet, a native of Anglesey who probably flourished *c*.1540–70, see R. M. Jones, 'Ow! Ow!', *Barddas*, 149 (Sept. 1989), 8–9, where he is described as the best of the early free-metre poets. See also *ClIC*, vol. III, 17–20; Ifor Williams, 'Rhys Goch ap Rhiccert', *Y Beirniad*, 3 (1913), 230–44.

('May God and Mary protect you well from pining and ill health; when leaves appear on the hazel-trees I shall bring you both together in the same place.')

And these lines call to mind the final couplet of an 'apocryphal' *cywydd* which may belong to the fourteenth century,[13] in which the cuckoo is again sent as the poet's love-messenger:

> Drwy dy nerth di a'r Rhiain
> Dwgwn y ferch deg wen fain.
> (*BDG* CCX.67–8)

(Through your strength and that of the Virgin, we shall steal away the fair, slender girl.)

The woodcock to which the cuckoo of this *cywydd* entrusts its errand with the coming of winter is killed by a man's bolt,[14] and it may be said that the two birds are the very antitheses of each other in popular tradition. Indeed, the contrast is underlined in this poem: the cuckoo is 'serchogfwyn', the woodcock the exact opposite— 'anserchog-fwyn' (*BDG* CCX.1, 35). In a delightful *carol deuair* (the free-metre version of the *cywydd deuair fyrion*) which is strangely analogous with, though probably uninfluenced by, the closing scene of a *cywydd* by Dafydd ap Gwilym, the poet falls asleep to the sound of bird-song on the eve of St John, and on awakening is terrified to find that the trees have shed their leaves and that the ground lies under ice and snow. Instead of the two cuckoos whose song he had heard there are now two woodcocks—'Yn lle r ddwu gog, ddau gyffylog' (*CLlC*, vol. III, no. IX).[15] As in the 'apocryphal' *cywydd* and in Dafydd's dialogue poem in which the woodcock refuses to perform its errand for fear of the winter cold (*GDG* 115), the bird is depicted as a creature of winter, just as in the same tradition Eiddig is associated with winter and mocked for his antipathy towards springtime and all it implies. Dafydd has another humorous poem to

[13] Cf. Parry's note in *GDG*[1], pp. clxxvi–clxxvii: '. . . Y mae'r arddull ar y cyfan yn ddigon tebyg i eiddo'r 14 g., ond bychan yw rhif y cynganeddion Sain, ac y mae'r awdur yn sillafu enw'r ferch, sef Annes, peth na wneir mohono yn yr un o gerddi dilys DG, heblaw fod enw'r ferch yn ddieithr.' On the use of acrostics for a girl's name in 14th-cent. poetry see p. 149 below.

[14] Compare *GDG* 61.57–8; 115.19–24, and cf. *GPC* s.v. *cyffylog*(a): 'fe'i cyfrifid yn aderyn ehud a ffôl am ei fod yn hawdd ei rwydo.'

[15] The seasonal symbolism of the poem is discussed by Rhiannon Ifans, 'Y Canu Gwaseila a'r Gyfundrefn Farddol', *YB* 15 (1988), 173. In *GDG* 145 ('Caru yn y Gaeaf'), a slightly drunk Dafydd takes refuge from Eiddig in his beloved birch grove, only to find it denuded of its summer splendour and of all signs of the joys of love.

the woodcock (*GDG* 61), in which the bird's flapping wings disturb
a winter love-tryst, while the poet would in any case rather await his
beloved on a warm summer evening to the sound of the cuckoo's
song. It is once more one of the birds of winter (ll. 31–2), and its
connection with Eiddig [16] is implicit in the fact that Dafydd mistakes
its commotion for the arrival of the girl's husband (ll. 39–44). The
amusing satire of the bird's lack of fine song and general boorishness
is reminiscent of the portrayal of Eiddig not only in Dafydd's poetry
but across the whole of the Welsh verse tradition. In Madog
Benfras's *BDG* LXXXIV it is the crow that frightens away the
nightingale which is described as 'Edn Eiddig' (l. 49), 'Eiddig's bird',
and it is perhaps no coincidence that Dafydd ap Gwilym mocks
Morfudd's husband as 'Gŵr yn gweiddi | . . . Ar gân fal brân am ei
brawd' (*GDG* 79.43–4), 'a man yelling as if he were a crow calling
for its companion'.

Other, more familiar birds of ill-omen, the magpie and the owl,
are associated by the poets with hell and the Celtic Otherworld. This
is implicit in Dafydd's description of the magpie as 'Uffernol edn tra
ffyrnig' (*GDG* 63.50), 'extremely vicious, infernal bird', and also in
the '[g]wrach' ('witch') and 'gwyneb [ŵ]yll' ('ghost's face') of the
imitative *cywydd BDG* CXLV (ll. 27, 8). A free-metre poet who
sends the magpie to his beloved crosses himself on hearing the bird:

> ag yno/i/klown/i//r/ bioden
> yn inion wch y mhen
> yn rhoddi anfed grechwen
> ai ffig yn pigo/r/ pren
> Mi ymgroesis rhag gwrthweb [*sic*]
> a garwed oedd i llais . . .
> (*DCRh* 234)[17]

(And there I could hear the magpie just above my head, with her sinister,
mocking laugh, and her beak pecking at the tree. I crossed myself in case of
ill fortune; so harsh was her voice . . .)

And in the long poem known as 'Prognosticasiwn Twm Hwsmon',
one of the many 'prognostication' poems current in the sixteenth
and seventeenth centuries, the sound of the magpies' voices at the

---

[16] This was clearly a well-established tradition. Cf. the versified 'love-triad' *CRhC*
12.45–8, and the similar triadic material discussed in Ch. 5 below.

[17] Despite the immense popularity of *GDG* 63 (see *GDG*[1], p. cxvii) this poem shows
no obvious signs of imitation. In *Yr Areithiau Pros*, ed. D. Gwenallt Jones (Cardiff,
1934), 60 'crechwen pioc' is named among 'Casbethau Ieuan Brydydd Hir'.

beginning of winter is a portent that the year shall see many wid-
ows—'ond tybio wrth lais y piod | y kair digon o wydwod.' (CRhC
62.150–1) (although, of course, such folk-beliefs are by no means
peculiarly Welsh or, for that matter, Celtic).[18] For Dafydd ap
Gwilym the owl is the 'fiend of birds'—'ellylles adar' (GDG 26.32)—
and he assures us that he has not been bewitched by it—'bychan
rhaib ynof' (l. 9). It is the bird of Gwyn ap Nudd, king of Annwfn,
which sets on the 'hounds of night', more commonly known as the
'cŵn Annwn' which survived in Welsh folklore long after the close
of the Middle Ages.[19] A similar superstition is expressed in the long
moralistic dialogue poem 'Ymddiddan rhwng yr Wtreswr a'r
Dylluan', where the carouser tells the owl: 'duw Jessu or nef am
katwo | rhag ofn y ty fy witchio' (CRhC 111.302–3),[20] 'God and
Christ from heaven protect me, lest you bewitch me'. Although this
poem belongs essentially to a verse tradition which goes back as far
as the twelfth-century English debate poem 'The Owl and the
Nightingale',[21] it does reflect some of the native popular beliefs
which are also found in the cywydd tradition. When the owl complains that the birds of the whole world are cruel (l. 30), it is echoing a belief whose origins are at least as ancient as the Fourth Branch
of the Mabinogi. In the 'apocryphal' cywydd BDG CLXXXIII (which
may perhaps belong to the fourteenth century)[22] the owl answers the
mocking poet: 'gad fi'n llonydd | I ddwyn poen . . . A bar holl adar
y byd!' (ll. 10–12), 'leave me alone to suffer the torment and wrath
of all the world's birds', and it goes on to relate how the magician
Gwydion transformed Blodeuwedd into an owl as punishment for

[18] It is, however, noteworthy that in Breton folklore the sight of a magpie is a bad
omen before a marriage, and that in a popular poem the same bird denounces
women's fickleness, just as in DCRh 234–6 (see de la Villemarqué, Barzaz Breiz, 411,
237 ff.).

[19] Cf. GDG 68.43–4; 129.32, and see Eurys Rowlands, 'Cyfeiriadau Dafydd ap
Gwilym at Annwn', LlC 5 (1958–9), 122–35; Brynley F. Roberts, 'Gwyn ap Nudd',
LlC 13 (1974–81), 283–9; T. Gwynn Jones, Welsh Folklore and Folk-Custom, 203.

[20] It is no coincidence that in the well-known free-metre poem 'Coed Glyn Cynon'
the owl is to act as hangman for those responsible for cutting down the forest (CRhC
102.45–8). In the old folk-tale known as 'The Oldest Animals' the owl—'Tylluan
Cwm Cawlwyd'—is described as 'hên wrach, yn canv Twhwhw ac yn dychrynnv
plant ai llais. . .' (BBCS 24, p. 464).

[21] Cf. DCRh 73, and see J. W. H. Atkins (ed.), The Owl and the Nightingale
(Cambridge, 1922), esp. pp. lv–lxxiii.

[22] Thomas Parry simply notes: 'Nid yw hwn yn yr un o'r casgliadau mawr, ac y
mae gan DG gywydd arall i'r Dylluan . . .' (GDG¹, p. clxxxiv). See also W. J.
Gruffydd's discussion in Math Vab Mathonwy (Cardiff, 1928), 253–5.

her love of Gronw Pebr (ll.19–32). Thus Dafydd ap Gwilym's owl, just as the ill-fated Blodeuwedd after her transformation, is despised by other birds—

> Pob edn syfudr alltudryw
> A'i baedd; pond rhyfedd ei byw?
>   (GDG 26.33–4)[23]

(Each filthy bird of alien nature harasses her; isn't it a wonder that she lives?)

and in another *cywydd* to the owl by the fifteenth-century poet Robin Leiaf we find the epithet 'cas yr adar' (*BDG* CLIX.63), 'birds' foe'.[24] The free-metre poet also refers to the owl as 'eiddiges' (*CRhC* 111.17), 'jealous one', and although I am aware of no overt association of the bird with Eiddig in *cywydd* poetry, it is associated with ivy, a plant which is commonly symbolic of jealousy, and by extension the jealous husband. In his poem to the owl Dafydd, perhaps to exorcise evil spirits, threatens to set fire to every ivy-covered tree in sight (*GDG* 26.43–6); Robin Leiaf's owl is 'Câr eiddiorwg' (*BDG* CLIX.38), 'companion of ivy'; and in yet another *cywydd* to the owl by the sixteenth-century poet Siôn Tudur, it is described as having 'a cold beak from amongst the ivy'—'oer ddvryn or eiddiorwg' (NLW MS. 5269.311b). It is noteworthy too that in the carol 'Ymrafael Holyn ac Ifin' ('The Contention of Holly and Ivy'), while the personified ivy is satirized in the manner of the fifteenth-century English carols with which it is closely analogous, it· is also specifically described as Eiddig's companion:

> digon afiach ydiwr kimach
> bwbach kilfach koedwig
> nid da genyf ddim oi ryw
> kydymaith yw fo i eiddig[25]
>   (CRhC 106.17–20)

---

[23] Cf. also 'Tebyg iawn wyt i'r dylluan; | O bren i bren bydd honno'i hunan | A phob 'deryn yn ei phigo . . .' (*HB* 254.17–20). It should be noted, however, that this seems to reflect a trait of nature: in a popular French poem the screech-owl claims to fly by night 'Car tous oyseaux le guerroyent' (F. Ferrand (ed.), *Chansons des XVᵉ et XVIᵉ siècles* (Paris, 1986), CXII.8).

[24] In this largely imitative *cywydd* the owl is also 'cyw'r ddera' (the devil's imp) and 'Gwrach y Rhuglgroen' (witch of the skin-rattle) (ll. 38, 44), an epithet which echoes DG's humorous poem to that object (*GDG* 125).

[25] On this poem and related folk customs see *DCRh* 28–31; Rhiannon Ifans, *Sêrs a Rybana* (Llandysul, 1983), 42–3, 63. As she remarks, 'Yn y carolau Saesneg fe gynrychiola Holyn y rhyw wrywaidd ac Ifin yn cynrychioli'r merched . . . Ond yn y traddodiad Cymraeg ystyrir Holyn fel "ior o ras yn kadw/r/ plas yn benna" tra ystyrid

(Quite sickly is the surly one(?), bogeyman who lurks in the woods; I do not care for any of his kind—he is a companion of Eiddig.)

There are several other suggestions of apparently native and, no doubt, widespread popular beliefs and legends concerning birds in the Welsh verse tradition, which are often difficult to decipher for the modern reader. Both of Dafydd ap Gwilym's poems to the cock-thrush suggest a folk-tradition which connects the bird with the 'birds of paradise' of Celtic Otherworld mythology, which are best represented in Welsh by those well-known 'Adar Rhiannon' whose tuneful song lulls humans to sleep and awakens the dead.[26] In GDG 28 it is said of the thrush:

> Odid ydoedd i adar
> Paradwys cyfrwys a'i câr . . .
> Adrodd a ganodd o gerdd.
>   (ll. 29–32)

(It were a wonder if the skilful birds of Paradise, who love him, could declaim all the songs that he sang.)

In GDG 123 the bird is described as 'Brydydd serch o Baradwys'[27] (l. 48), 'a love-poet from Paradise', and Dafydd asks that God may allow it to return where it belongs[28] (ll. 43–50). Eurys Rowlands, in two perceptive articles, has drawn attention to the significance of word-play and ambiguity in Dafydd's poetry, in relation to seasonal

---

Ifin, nid fel benyw ond fel gŵr salw yn ceisio mynediad i'r plas. Yn y ddau achos y mae gofyn sefydlu'r oruchafiaeth' (p. 42).

[26] See Bromwich's note in SP 92. An intriguing analogue is provided by a 15th-century French poem which speaks of the thrush and the nightingale (Chansons du XVe siècle, LXX.14–22):

> J'ouy chanter ung si doulx chant
> Qu'il n'est homme si près de mort,
> S'il l'escoutoit, bien je m'en vant,
> Qui n'y pransist moult grant confort.

> C'estoynt les oysillons du bois,
> Le doulx rousigneul et la troye,
> Qui demenoyent si tres grant joye
> Qu'avis me fut en bonne foy,
> Que paradis fust près de moy.

[27] Cf. the description of two cock-thrushes as 'Dau bencerdd y loywgerdd lwys, | Pur, o adar paradwys.' (BDG CLXXIX.21–2); also 'Trefn adar gwlad Baradwys' (GDG 29.29).

[28] The same idea is expressed in the closing couplets of DG's elegy to Gruffudd Gryg—'Edn glwys ei baradwyslef . . .' (GDG 20.61–6). Cf. Gruffudd Llwyd's elegy to Rhys Goch Eryri (CIGE LIII.13–14), and see note (p. 360).

mythology and Otherworld beliefs,[29] and this *cywydd* seems to me
to contain several allusions suggestive of the thrush's otherworldly
associations which place it in the same poetic tradition. The description of the thrush as 'Cantor hydr ar gaer wydr gyll' (*GDG* 123.3),
'a mighty singer on a fortress of shining hazel', surely contains a reference to the 'caer wydyr', the 'glass fortress' which occurs in early
poetry of the Middle Welsh period as an epithet for the Celtic
Otherworld.[30] In these words, as in the similar phrase 'o'i dŷ
glaswydr' (l. 32), 'gwydr' may be understood both as a noun with
the primary meaning 'glass', which forms part of the familiar
imagery of the *deildy* as a house or castle (Gruffudd Gryg's 'dan
fedw laswydr' (*GDG* 153.47) may be compared), and as an adjective,
'lustrous'. The 'Tŷ Gwydrin', with its supernatural properties, is
connected in the Triads with the legend of Myrddin,[31] and a similar
tradition is reflected in a *cywydd* which is ascribed to Dafydd ap
Gwilym but is probably the work of the fifteenth-century poet Robin
Ddu. Here, the poet fashions the broom bush into a secret lair for
his love-trysts just as Myrddin made a 'house of glass' for his beloved
(*DGG* XLV.17–20). According to the legend the magic properties of
the 'house' ensured that Myrddin and his companion remained invisible to their enemies. In light of this the words 'Saith ugeiniaith a
ganai', 'he sang in seven-score tongues', 'ieithydd', 'linguist', and
'dewiniaeth', 'divination', in Dafydd's *cywydd* to the thrush (*GDG*
123.10, 14, 22) all assume an added significance,[32] since, according
to the legend, Myrddin is said to have become mad after the Battle
of Arfderydd, fleeing to the Caledonian forest where he led the life
of a hermit, hence his great powers of prophecy and poetry in later
tradition.[33] The poem contains another, even more intriguing

[29] 'Cywydd Dafydd ap Gwilym i Fis Mai', *LlC* 5 (1958–9), 1–25; 'Cyfeiriadau Dafydd ap Gwilym at Annwn', 122–35. He is no doubt right in relating this aspect of DG's art to the 'gorderchgerd o gywydeu teulueid *drwy eireu amwys*' of the Bardic Grammar (*GP* 6.38–9)—see *LlC* 5, 1–3.

[30] See Marged Haycock, ' "Preiddeu Annwn" and the Figure of Taliesin', *SC* 18/19 (1983–4), 73; Rachel Bromwich, *TYP* 474.

[31] See *TYP* pp. cxxxii–iii, 474, and Ifor Williams's note in *DGG* 210. For further references by the *Cywyddwyr* see Eurys Rowlands, 'Y Tri Thlws ar Ddeg', *LlC* 5 (1958–9), 52; *GPC* s.v. *gwydrin*.

[32] Cf. 'keliogg bronfraith da J gwyr bob iaith' (*CRhC* 2, IV.5); also 'Proffwyd rhiw' (*GDG* 28.11).

[33] See A. O. H. Jarman, *The Legend of Myrddin* (Cardiff, 1960). Another example of potential ambiguity in this poem is the line 'A gynnull pwyll ac anian' (*GDG* 123.18) which calls to mind the hero of the first branch of the *Mabinogi*, Pwyll Pendefig Dyfed; cf. the personification 'Pendefig' (l. 8). It may be significant that he

allusion which seems to associate the thrush with Otherworld mythology. It follows the reference to 'caer wydr':

> Cantor hydr ar gaer wydr gyll,
> Esgud dan wyrddion esgyll . . .
> (GDG 123.3–4)

(A mighty singer on a fortress of shining hazel, agile beneath wings of grey.)

Eurys Rowlands has drawn attention to the significance of a similar phrase—'esgyll dail mentyll Mai', 'the leafy wings of the mantles of May'—in the celebrated *cywydd* to May (*GDG* 23.16), and to Dafydd's image of May as a green-winged peacock—'Paun asgellas dinastai'—in the same poem (l. 37). In the same article he makes the following remarks with reference to the reflections of May-day mythology and folklore in Dafydd's seasonal poetry:

Da fyddai gwybod beth sy'n cyfrif am y pwyslais ar gyll a beth yn hollol yw ystyr y sôn am fantell (neu 'fentyll') yma fel mewn cywyddau eraill gan Ddafydd. Da hefyd fyddai gwybod a oes arwyddocâd arbennig i'r sôn am asgell (neu 'esgyll') a diddorol yw sylwi (*GDG*, rhif 32) i Ddafydd gael ger-lant o blu paun yn lle cae bedw ar un achlysur. Sylwer hefyd ar y cyfeiriad at 'weddeiddblu gwŷdd', *GDG*, 101.[34]

(It would be good to know what accounts for the emphasis on hazel-trees, and what exactly is meant by the reference to a mantle (or 'mantles') here as in some of Dafydd's other poems. It would also be good to know whether the mention of a wing (or 'wings') has any special significance, and it is inter-esting to note (*GDG* no. 32) that on one occasion Dafydd received a garland of peacock-feathers instead of a birch-garland. Note also the reference to 'fair tree-plumage', *GDG* 101.)

---

becomes known as 'Pwyll Penn Annwuyn', having changed places for a year with an Otherworld king (Ifor Williams (ed.), *Pedeir Keinc y Mabinogi* (Cardiff, 1930), 8). The story is echoed in DG's reference to his uncle Llywelyn ap Gwilym as 'Pendefig, gwledig gwlad yr hud—is dwfn' (*GDG* 13.17). Also relevant is his description of the cock-thrush as 'Pellennig, pwyll ei annwyd' (*GDG* 122.7), which R. Geraint Gruffydd interprets as a comparison with the legendary prince of Dyfed (see 'Sylwadau ar Gywydd "Offeren Y Llwyn" Dafydd ap Gwilym', *YB* 10 (1977), 182). For further echoes of the *Mabinogi* and other prose tales in *GDG* see Rachel Bromwich, 'Allusions to Tales and Romances' in *APDG* 132–51.

[34] 'Cywydd Dafydd ap Gwilym i Fis Mai', 23. Similar folk-customs are perhaps reflected in a free-metre verse (*HB* 503):

> Plannaf esgyll dan fy mron,   Mi a' i Bumlumon fynydd;
> Cadwaf lwyn i'm cadw'r haf,   Ac yno mi gaf lonydd.
> Brysia dithau i gneua ar des   Dan loches mynwes manwydd.

This is all highly suggestive, and Eurys Rowlands goes on to draw attention to the relevance of an evocative passage from an Irish tale which recounts a journey to the Otherworld:

Ocus is amhlaid do bí an t-oilen sin cona abhlaibh caemha cubhraighe 7 lán do tibradaibh fíráille fina 7 coill caem-edrocht ar na comhecar do challaib crimhann um na tibradaibh. . . . Confacaidh a n-imfocus dó (i)arsin an mbruidhin cumdaighi arna thuighi do eitibh én find 7 bhuighi 7 ngorm.

(And it is thus the island was, having fair fragrant apple-trees, and many wells of wine most beautiful, and a fair bright wood adorned with clustering hazel trees surrounding those wells. . . . Then he saw near by a shapely hostel thatched with birds' wings, white, and yellow, and blue.)[35]

As well as the significance of the otherworldly associations of birds' wings apparent here, it may be noted that the conventional reference to hazel trees makes the phrase 'gaer wydr gyll' even more pregnant with meaning. While the primary meaning of Dafydd's 'wyrddion esgyll' is the thrush's grey wings, the secondary, figurative meaning of the green 'wings' of the hazel-branches 'beneath' which the bird is perched is almost certainly present.

In Dafydd ap Gwilym's other *cywydd* to the thrush the mention of angel-wings—'angel esgyll' (*GDG* 28.28)—would also seem to reflect the thrush's supernatural associations. The description 'Plu yw ei gasul' (l. 8), 'his chasuble is made of feathers', may or may not have any symbolic significance beyond its apparent religious imagery. These words are, however, somewhat reminiscent of an allusion in the 'apocryphal' dialogue with the cuckoo already referred to, and here we are certainly dealing with some form of Otherworld mythology. Having greeted the cuckoo the poet asks:

'P'le buost edn diwedn-lais,
Pa wlad bell? Plu yw dy bais!'

('Where have you been, clear-voiced bird, which distant land? Feathers are your coat!')

The bird replies:

---

[35] Text and translation from R. I. Best, 'The Adventures of Art Son of Conn . . .', *Ériu*, 3 (1907), 156–7. For a closely similar description see Alwyn and Brinley Rees, *Celtic Heritage*, 310–11; cf. also Kenneth Jackson, *A Celtic Miscellany* (revised edn., Harmondsworth, 1971), 172–6. See further Patrick Sims-Williams's remarks in 'Riddling Treatment of the "Watchman Device" in *Branwen* and *Togail Bruidne Da Derga*', *SC* 12/13 (1977–8), 114–15, and the references cited there.

'Bum y'nglyn, megis dyn dall,
Bedeir-oes mewn byd arall . . .'
(*BDG* CCX.3–6)

('I have been stuck, like a blind man, four ages [*or* lifetimes] in another world.')

Whatever the precise meaning of 'Bedeir-oes', it seems that the 'other world' in which the bird was imprisoned signifies winter,[36] and the passage may be compared with the words spoken by Dafydd ap Gwilym's summer prince, who after three months of fertility returns to Annwfn to escape the winter cold (*GDG* 27.39–40).[37] The otherwise rather prosaic reference to the cuckoo's feathers—'Plu yw dy bais'—gains in poetic meaning when related to the 'distant land' which comes before it, which should probably be related to Celtic Otherworld beliefs. In another *cywydd* of uncertain authorship which has been attributed to Dafydd ap Gwilym the leaves of the *deildy* are again, apparently, described as feathers, in the line 'Cysgu dan blu dien blas' (*BDG* LXXXVII.26),[38] 'sleeping under the feathers of a fair mansion'. But the idea of *sleeping* beneath the feathers, especially in the context of a somewhat obscure but charming free-metre poem, suggests the presence of yet another folk-belief which is not readily intelligible to the modern reader. The poem in question is the anonymous *carol deuair* known as 'Carol Claddu'r Bardd'

---

[36] On the association of Annwfn with winter see Eurys Rowlands, 'Cyfeiriadau Dafydd ap Gwilym at Annwn'. The more explicit connection of the cuckoo with Annwfn in another 'apocryphal' *cywydd*, probably 15th-cent. (see *GDG*¹, p. clxxxix), again reflects a lost folk legend:

> Y goc las ar gogail ir
> Yn bwrrw adwyth in brodir
> Yn anwn ith wenwynwyd
> Gwin gorn wenwinic wyd
> Nith dynid oth adanudd
> Oni bai yn wrn gwyn ab nudd.

(G. J. Williams, *Iolo Morganwg a Chywyddau'r Ychwanegiad* (London, 1926), 10).

[37] On the seasonal mythology implicit in this poem ('Mawl i'r Haf') see T. Gwynn Jones, *Welsh Folklore and Folk-Custom*, 154. For a more imaginative interpretation see Eurys Rowlands, 'Cyfeiriadau Dafydd ap Gwilym at Annwn', 125 ff.

[38] Cf. also 'A than dy ben gobennydd | O fanblu, gweddeiddblu gwŷdd' (*GDG* 36.13–14). The 'coat of feathers' brings to mind the bardic tradition of early Ireland: 'Such priestly functions as divination and prophecy also came within the province of these early Irish poets who . . . wore cloaks of bird-feathers as do the shamans of Siberia when, through ritual and trance, they conduct their audiences on journeys to another world' (A. and B. Rees, *Celtic Heritage*, 17). It is noteworthy too that in some Irish versions of the Myrddin legend, the madman Suibhne grows feathers and gains the power of levitation (see Jarman, *The Legend of Merlin*, 13–15).

('The Carol of the Poet's Burial'), which may well be older or, at least, may represent a prototype which is considerably older than the late-sixteenth-century manuscript in which it is preserved. The relevant passage reads as follows:

> koge ssy imi: dan goed kelli
> a phe kawn gysgv: yn i man blu
> tra vo düw hyd i gwn hyfryd vyddwn
> ag oni cha marw a vydda . . .[39]
>
> (CRhC 30.1–4)

(I have cuckoos under hazel-trees, and if I could sleep in their downy plumage, I know, by God, that I would be happy; and if not I shall die.)

Although the precise significance of these enigmatic lines is not immediately apparent, as in Dafydd ap Gwilym's poem to the thrush the combination of the hazels and birds' feathers is highly suggestive; and it seems reasonable to infer that remnants of a half-forgotten mythology, and popular beliefs such as those reflected here, would have pervaded much of the free- as well as the strict-metre verse tradition throughout the medieval period.

An equally intriguing tradition regarding the cuckoo is hinted at in GDG 34 ('Talu Dyled'), in which Morfudd is described as 'Chwaer . . . | I ferch Wgon farchoges' (ll. 29–30), 'sister of the daughter of Gwgon, horse-woman'. The couplet which follows reads:

> Unllais wyf, yn lle y safai,
> Â'r gog, morwyn gyflog Mai.
>
> (ll. 31–2)

(I am of one voice, where she stood, with the cuckoo, May's hired servant-woman.)

There would be no reason to believe that the two couplets are essentially related were it not for the obscure allusion 'A chogau fal merch Wgon', 'and cuckoos like the daughter of Gwgon', in another of the poems spuriously attributed to Dafydd ap Gwilym (BDG CI.34).[40]

---

[39] The poet was clearly following a well-established literary convention. In lines which recall the important early 'apocryphal' cywydd 'Claddu Y Bardd o Gariad' (DGG XIX), he goes on to state that upon his death he wishes to be buried covered with various flowers, a birch growing on either side of his head. On the likely Continental origin of this theme see Ch. 7 below, n. 65.

[40] The cywydd is probably the work of the 15th-cent. poet Bedo Aeddren (CSTB XXXV).

Nothing is known of the 'daughter of Gwgon', apart from her implied association with the cuckoo, and Dafydd's description of an unnamed girl as 'nith y gog', 'the cuckoo's niece', in another poem (*GDG* 41.38) may perhaps echo the same tradition. But the fact that this Gwgon (referred to elsewhere by Dafydd as 'Gwgon Gleddyfrudd',[41] *lit.* 'of the red sword') should probably be identified with a historical ninth-century king of Ceredigion suggests that Dafydd is here alluding to a local legend, which would have been familiar to a local audience if not throughout fourteenth-century Wales. Furthermore, when Dafydd portrays himself in this *cywydd* as being 'of one voice with the cuckoo', whose single, incessant note is compared to the poet's love-songs to Morfudd (*GDG* 34.31–42), he seems to be elaborating in typically rhetorical fashion a conventional motif whose proverbial nature may well be indicative of popular provenance. The couplet

> Ni chân gywydd, lonydd lw,
> Nag acen onid 'Gwcw'.[42]
>
> (ll. 37–8)

(He sings no *cywydd*—gentle oath—or note except 'Cuckoo'.)

finds a verbal analogue in an 'apocryphal' (probably fifteenth-century) *cywydd* where the poet describes his verse as 'gwaith acen y gog' (*BDG* CXCIX.17), *lit.* 'the work of the cuckoo's song'. And another, similar couplet by Dafydd ap Gwilym, in which he compares himself to the nightingale—

> Ni thawaf, od af heb dâl,
> Mwy nog eos mewn gwial.
>
> (*GDG* 101.9–10)

(I am not silent, [even] if I remain unrewarded, more than a nightingale amongst the twigs.)

[41] *GDG* 46.67–8. See Parry's note, ibid., p. 483; Bromwich, *TYP* 389–90, *APDG* 145; 'Mab Gwgon/Gwgan' appear as variant readings of 'Mab gogan', an epithet for Eiddig (*GDG* 75.9).

[42] Compare this striking, though no doubt coincidental, analogue in a French poem, from a 15th-cent. MS:

> . . . Ne point tarre ne se voloit
> Maiz toudis plus fort cantoit
> De dens bois
> Cocu cocu cococu cocu
> Et non dissoit autre canson.

(Giulio Bertoni, 'Poesie musicali francesi nel cod. estense lat. nº 568', *Archivum Romanicum*, 1 (1917), 36).

is closely paralleled in the *canu rhydd*:

> Mwy na'r eos ar frig pren,
> Ni thaw fy mhen amdani.[43]

(No more than the nightingale on a branch do my lips stop praising her.)

The possible influence of the *cywyddau* on the free-metre poets must here, as elsewhere, be taken into account. But while this poem clearly cannot be much older than the free-metre manuscript tradition, in its use of this motif it may echo earlier verse composed in the 'popular' metres.

One of the characteristic elements of Welsh love-poetry from the time of Dafydd ap Gwilym down to the early and, indeed, the later free-metre verse tradition is the *llatai* or love-messenger motif. The messenger may be an animal, a person,[44] or even a natural phenomenon as in Dafydd's *cywydd* to the wind (*GDG* 117), or Gruffudd Gryg's commission to the wave[45] on his return from Santiago de Compostela (*DGG* LXXIII). But throughout the poetic tradition the *llatai* is most typically a bird, and particularly in the *canu rhydd* the theme forms part of the more widespread convention of the dialogue between bird and poet. The term *llatai* is not attested earlier than the time of Gruffudd ap Dafydd ap Tudur, who speaks of 'llatteion' in a section of his asking-poem composed in the style of *Gogynfeirdd* poetry to women,[46] but it may be that the word was common in earlier love-poetry which has not been preserved. Several scholars have drawn attention to the significance in the earlier poetry to women of the part played by the poet's horse, a motif which is used by Hywel ab Owain, Cynddelw, and Prydydd y Moch,[47] and which survives

---

[43] *Cerddi Rhydd Cynnar*, ed. D. L. Jenkins (Llandysul, 1931), no. 45. Cf. 'Mwy no rhegen mewn rhagnyth, | Am nith Fair, ni thewi fyth, | . . . | Yn sôn am ferch dynion da' (*CIGE* LXX.11–14).

[44] These, however, are comparatively rare; see *GDG* 113 ('Cyrchu Lleian'), 94 ('Galw ar Ddwynwen'), a witty parody of invocations to saints, typically combining piety and provocative frivolity; and cf. also *GDG* 128 ('Athrodi ei Was'). Human love-messengers also feature in the 'trioedd serch' (see Ch. 5 below), possibly reflecting actual contemporary practice.

[45] Cf. DG's description of the River Dyfi as 'lateiwraig aig' (*GDG* 71.38); a river is again addressed as a love-messenger in *CRhC* 2, IV, and by Siôn Tudur (Enid Roberts (ed.), *Gwaith Siôn Tudur* (Cardiff, 1980), no. 276). For some isolated Continental parallels see *Recherches*, 199.

[46] *RP* 1,254.1; cf. *RP* 1,342.12 (the satire of Casnodyn—early 14th cent.).

[47] Bramley, 'Canu Hywel ab Owain Gwynedd', no. 6; *GCBM* 5; *GLlLl* 14. The convention may be reflected in the 'Gorwynion' gnomic sequence, in which a horse, love and a messenger are mentioned together, though in the usual disjointed manner:

well into the fourteenth century in poems by Casnodyn, Hywel ab Einion Llygliw, and Gruffudd ap Maredudd.[48] All these poets are evidently drawing on a common tradition which is apparently reflected in the triadic lists of the names of heroes' horses preserved in 'Trioedd y Meirch', where the 'Tri Gordderchfarch Ynys Prydain', the 'three lovers' steeds of the Isle of Britain', are particularly suggestive with regard to love-poetry.[49] The poet commonly addresses his horse, expressing his love and asking it to travel to the beloved's home. But it appears that it is only Cynddelw, in his *rhieingerdd* to Efa, who does not himself ride to the girl's court, and in this respect the horse is comparable to the love-messengers of the *Cywyddwyr*. This poem has been described as the earliest *llatai* poem,[50] and the affinity with the *cywyddau llatai* is indeed striking. Cynddelw addresses directly the 'Gorfynawg drythyll', the 'eager, lively horse', expressing his suffering, asking it to seek out the girl and to convey to her his message, and beseeching it to return with a favourable answer (*GCBM* 5.39–52). The *Cywyddwyr* may well have been familiar with 'Rhieingerdd Efa', but despite the similarities it is difficult to believe that it is this poem and others which draw on the same tradition that gave rise to the many and various love-messengers which enliven the *cywyddau serch*. Not only are horses almost completely absent from the love-poetry of Dafydd ap Gwilym and the other early *Cywyddwyr*,[51] but these poems contain no significant echoes of this well-defined convention of the earlier poetry to women. The traditions recorded in the triads reflect the heroic ideals of a noble society in which the horse played a central role;[52] and in the *Gogynfeirdd* love-poetry which has come down there is nothing

'Gorwyn blaen yspydat; hydyr hwylyat gorwyd; | gnawt serchawc erlynnyat; | gwnelit da diwyt gennat' (*EWGP* VI.28).

[48] H 331–2; *BBBGDd* 46; *RP* 1,329.

[49] See *TYP* 97–116, pp. xxix–xxx, xcviii–cvii.

[50] Ann Parry Owen, 'Rhieingerdd Efa . . .', 65. In the contemporary 'Eglynyon a gant teulu ywein kyueilyawc y gylchyaw kymry' the mounted messenger is described in one *englyn* as 'boen ouyt gennad' (*lit*. 'messenger of Ovid's pain'), and in another is entreated to greet the poet's beloved: 'Dos was y gennyf ac nac annerch nep | ony byt uyg gorterch' (*H* 314.5, 25–6).

[51] Dafydd mentions his horse only in *GDG* 127, where it is unceremoniously trapped in a peat-bog. Even Iolo Goch's poems asking and thanking for a horse (*GIG* XII, XIII) contain no obvious echoes of the *Gogynfeirdd*.

[52] Cf. J. E. Caerwyn Williams, 'Cerddi'r Gogynfeirdd i Wragedd a Merched. . .', 88. He also suggests here that the horse's function in the *Gogynfeirdd* poems to women may have derived from the animal's possible erotic connotations, as exemplified in Classical Greece.

which prefigures the essentially popular convention of birds as love-messengers.

Given the lack of any significant antecedents, at least in the poetry which has been preserved in the manuscripts, it is not inconceivable that the *llatai* genre was in fact invented by the remarkable creative genius of Dafydd ap Gwilym himself, and developed by him in a highly stylized form, to be imitated by succeeding generations of poets. But while Dafydd would probably have been capable of such an innovation, he did not compose in a vacuum, and there are indications that his treatment of this motif is yet another instance of his lending a more artistic form to a convention which may already by his time have thrived at a sub-literary level, in the unrecorded verse of the *Clêr*. Chotzen drew attention long ago to the relevance for the love-messenger motif of the part played by 'obedient' or helpful animals in Celtic folklore.[53] He refers to the starling which in the Third Branch of the *Mabinogi* is nurtured by Branwen to carry a message across the Irish Sea to her brother Bendigeidfran, and to the version of the internationally known tale of the 'Oldest Animals' which forms part of Culhwch's quest for Olwen. Here, five animals known for their great age and wisdom—the blackbird of Cilgwri, the deer of Rhedynfre, the owl of Cwm Cawlwyd, the eagle of Gwernabwy, and the salmon of Llyn Lliw—are all consulted by the men of Arthur in their search for Mabon fab Modron. *Culhwch* is believed to have been written down in the eleventh century, but this particular story is well attested also in manuscripts of the later Middle Ages as an independent folk-tale.[54] Although the *cywyddau llatai*, even those which have as their subjects the very animals mentioned here, show no overt affinity with the folk-tale, the *Cywyddwyr*'s numerous allusions certainly display their familiarity with the 'Oldest Animals'.[55] It is noteworthy too that in an anonymous early free-metre poem the nightingale, cuckoo, thrush, and blackbird all promise to help a girl find her lover, and to act as love-messengers on her behalf.[56] Another

[53] *Recherches*, 197–8.

[54] Texts have been edited by Thomas Jones, 'Chwedl yr Anifeiliaid Hynaf', *NLWJ* 7 (1951–2), 62–6, and Dafydd Ifans, 'Chwedl yr Anifeiliaid Hynaf', *BBCS* 24 (1971–2), 461–4.

[55] See Rachel Bromwich and D. Simon Evans (eds.), *Culhwch and Olwen*, pp. lxii–lxiii.

[56] *CRhC* 21 ('Ffeind i Law a'i Lygad'). Cf. also a Scots Gaelic poem in which a maid asks a trout for tidings of her absent lover, the trout being renowned in the Isles for its wisdom and piety (Alexander Carmichael (ed.), *Carmina Gadelica, Hymns and Incantations*, vol. 4 (Edinburgh, 1941), 366–7).

free-metre poet has the blackbird pronounce that he has wandered
the fields for 600 years and has seen all there is to see—'Rwi/n/
chwechant o flwyddau yn rhodio coed cauau' (DCRh 65)—clearly an
allusion to the 'mwyalch Cilgwri' of the ancient folk-tale.

While popular traditions such as these did not necessarily play a
formative part in the poetic convention of birds and animals as the
love-poet's accomplices and confidants, its development may well
have been facilitated by the poets' familiarity with such traditions.
And as Chotzen has suggested, it may have been the 'poets of inferior status', having on the whole a closer affinity with popular culture than the court poets, who were the first to give the llatai
convention a poetic form. The essentially popular nature of the motif
is attested in other literatures, including French, where in countless
songs from the fifteenth century onwards it is typically the nightingale, the 'rossignolet du vert bocage', which is sent to greet the lover,
often by a young girl.[57] The motif is also used by a few of the
Provençal and earlier French poets, and also by the medieval Latin
love-poets,[58] who all seem to have been drawing on contemporary
popular-verse traditions,[59] deriving, it has been suggested, from an
unrecorded tradition of women's love-songs which pre-dates the
courtly love poems of the troubadours and trouvères.[60] Although
medieval Welsh and Continental love-poetry are clearly analogous in
their use of the love-messenger motif, there is no need to suppose
that the one is influenced by the other. While the Continental poets
commonly introduce the motif over a few lines in highly conventional language, often as a convenient conclusion to a poem, the
cywydd llatai is in itself a specific and well-defined genre, in which
the creature or natural phenomenon which acts as messenger is likely
to be the poet's true subject. It is significant too that although the
Middle English love-poets may depict birds as confidants and spiri-

---

[57] For examples see Chansons du XVᵉ siècle, V, XVIII, LXXII, LXXVII, CIV,
CXXIII, CXXXIX; J. Tiersot, Histoire de la chanson populaire en France (Paris, 1889),
87–9.
[58] See DGG, p. xxxvii; Recherches, 196–7. Chotzen also draws attention to the tor-
nadas of the troubadours, the envois of the trouvères, a device also used by Ovid, whereby
the poem itself is sent as a 'messenger' to the beloved in the final stanza (ibid. 190).
[59] See Dronke, The Medieval Lyric, 145–6, and cf. MLRELL, ii. 361. The bird-messenger is included in Pierre Bec's 'Index des motifs popularisants' (La Lyrique française
au moyen âge (XIIᵉ–XIIIᵉ siècles), vol. 2 (Paris, 1978), 183).
[60] Jeanroy, Origines, 132 ff.

tual companions,[61] they seem to be little influenced by the French and Provençal poets' use of the *llatai* convention; even in the popular verse contemporary with the early *canu rhydd* the portrayal of birds as love-messengers is extremely rare.[62] We should also bear in mind that birds are already prominent in the early Welsh gnomic and 'saga' poetry, as well as the *gorhoffeddau*, and that bird-dialogues, which especially in the *canu rhydd* are an important part of the *llatai* convention, are also attested in the earlier native literary tradition. The religious poem composed in the form of a dialogue between Arthur and the Eagle is dated by its editor in the mid-twelfth century,[63] and other dialogue-poems of this type may have been lost to posterity. Rachel Bromwich has remarked that in Wales, as in Ireland, 'the foreign literary influences when they came in, encountered and reacted upon a long-established and highly developed native poetic tradition', and that such an assimilation would, in the case of the bird-dialogue convention, have been facilitated by 'a pre-existing and essentially Celtic awareness of birds and animals as sentient fellow-beings'.[64] I believe, however, that Bromwich's suggestion that the popular prototypes of the free-metre bird-dialogue poems may already by the fourteenth century have been heavily influenced by the French bird-debate poems should not be over-emphasized. This genre which flourished in thirteenth-century France, in which (as shall be seen in the final chapter) a number of birds engage in a mock-scholastic debate on the questions of courtly love within the conventional framework of the 'court of love', has no specific parallels in the Welsh verse tradition. There is no reason why 'the angelic power of knowledge which is traditionally attributed to birds'[65] should not have given rise to dialogues between birds and humans in the verse of the popular poets independently of any formative external influence, so that again the French poems may more properly be regarded as analogous rather than as 'one of the ultimate models for these dialogues in the *canu rhydd*'.[66]

---

[61] Cf., for instance, R. M. Wilson, *The Lost Literature of Medieval England*, 181. Birds are commonly endowed with the power of speech by Chaucer—see Charles Muscatine, *Chaucer and the French Tradition* (Berkeley, Calif., 1957), 115 ff.

[62] See Brinley Rees's remarks in *DCRh* 66–7.

[63] Ifor Williams, 'Ymddiddan Arthur a'r Eryr', *BBCS* 2 (1923–5), 269–86. Cf. the *englynion* addressed by Gwydion to his nephew Lleu in *Pedeir Keinc y Mabinogi*, 89–90, the latter, like Arthur's nephew, Eliwlad, having been transformed into an eagle.

[64] *APDG* 102.   [65] Dronke, *MLRELL*, i. 5.   [66] *APDG* 80.

However one chooses to explain the prominence of personified birds and of bird-dialogues in the poetry of Dafydd ap Gwilym, there is no doubt that his distinctive handling of the *llatai* motif has little to do with the Continental literary tradition. In GDG 112 ('Yr Annerch'), a little-discussed and possibly incomplete *cywydd* of only eight couplets, he provides a humorous parody of the convention as it is presented in his own poems.[67] As in the genuine *cywyddau llatai*, the usual set of instructions are duly laid out, with the difference that here they have no substance whatsoever. Dafydd entreats his messenger to address a married woman, although he claims not to know her identity. Neither does he know what the messenger should tell her, or the place or time of their tryst. If she asks who sent him he is simply to answer 'I do not know', and then to remain silent. Such a mannered satire[68] seems to presuppose an established and, perhaps, a somewhat tired convention with which the poet's audience would have been wholly familiar, suggesting the existence of an antecedent verse tradition. Rather than satirizing a type of poetry which he himself invented, it seems more probable that Dafydd is here exploiting one of the many themes which he and his fellow *Cywyddwyr* are most likely to have drawn from the verse of the popular poets. The extant poems of Dafydd's contemporaries provide but two, possibly three, instances of the *llatai* convention. These are Llywelyn Goch's *cywydd* in which he sends the titmouse to implore Lleucu Llwyd to await his return from Deheubarth (*DGG* XXXIII), the *cywydd* to the wave by Gruffudd Gryg (*DGG* LXXIII), and an 'apocryphal' *cywydd* to the trout (*BDG* CCVI) which may also be the work of the Anglesey poet.[69] Although, in view of the early *Cywyddwyr*'s well-known liking for borrowing each other's themes and expressions, we might expect some degree of imitation in these cases, it seems likely that the ultimate source of this particular theme in the work of all three poets lay in the sub-bardic verse tradition current in fourteenth-

[67] A rather more irreverent parody has recently been edited by Dafydd Johnston, *CMOC* 3, where the poet sends his own genitals as messengers. See Johnston's introduction, p. 24, and his discussion in 'The Erotic Poetry of the *Cywyddwyr*', *CMCS* 22 (Winter 1991), 86–7. His suggestion that, judging by the style of the poem, its ascription to DG in the sole surviving manuscript copy could be genuine, seems reasonable.

[68] The poem may also be read as a satire of the secrecy of courtly love; for analogues in French and Provençal 'nonsense poetry' see Ch. 7 below, pp. 278–9.

[69] Cf. *GDG*[1], p. clxxxii: 'Cywydd yn union yn null y 14g. . . . Tybed ai GGr biau'r cywydd?' Gruffydd Aled Williams has suggested to me that the words '*croyw* awdr o Fôn' (l. 19) may contain an ironic allusion to Gruffudd's speech impediment.

century Wales. But given the prominence and stylized treatment of the theme in the poetry of Dafydd ap Gwilym, allied to his flair for innovation and adaptation apparent in his handling of other popular as well as courtly models, there is reason to believe that it was he who was mainly responsible for moulding the *cywydd llatai* into the distinctive form it was to assume in the work of succeeding generations of poets. (This, I believe, would still hold true even if a greater proportion of his contemporaries' work had been preserved.) The most finished and aesthetically pleasing of Dafydd's *llatai* poems, those to the lark (*GDG* 114), the wind [70] (*GDG* 117), and the seagull (*GDG* 118), follow more or less closely the structure of the short parody, with two major differences. First, the opening sections of these poems are devoted to a detailed description of the subject mainly by means of *dyfalu*—these descriptions constitute well over half of the first two poems mentioned; and secondly, with varying degrees of detail directions are given concerning the journey to greet the beloved. In these and other *cywyddau llatai* the messenger is charged to avoid the wrath of the jealous husband or of any other pursuers, and these poems typically end with a commendation or blessing before the messenger performs his errand. Although Dafydd's three most formalized and consciously artistic *llatai* poems may be considered as forming the 'classic' model for the genre in the *cywydd* tradition, the commonly held view that 'the poet's chief interest is in elaborating the *dyfalu* or descriptive address to a bird or an animal'[71] is a partly misleading generalization. In the *cywydd* to the woodcock (*GDG* 115) the descriptive element is confined to essentially parenthetical epithets which alternate ironically between flattery and insult, and the interest lies rather in the humorous and animated dialogue between bird and poet. Similarly, in Dafydd's address to the deer (*GDG* 116) the most sustained description of the animal extends over no more than two couplets (ll. 9–12), the main focus of attention being the poet's message, and in particular the detailed directions for the journey to Dyddgu's home. The striking narrative quality of this poem, and especially the dialogue structure of the *cywydd* to the woodcock, which is unique among Dafydd's

---

[70] The motif of the wind as messenger is widespread—see *Recherches*, 199–200; J. M. d'Heur, 'Le motif du vent venu du pays de l'être aimé . . .', *Zeitschrift für romanische Philologie*, 88 (1972), 69–104. According to Dronke it derives ultimately from the 'Song of Songs' (*The Medieval Lyric*, 175); see also *MLRELL*, i. 20–1.

[71] *APDG* 66.

cywyddau llatai, suggest that it is these poems which had most in common with the likely popular prototypes of the *llatai* convention.

Gruffudd Gryg's *cywydd* to the wave consists of a sustained *dyfalu* passage followed by an even lengthier dialogue, while the comparatively short poem to the trout follows closely Dafydd ap Gwilym's 'classic' model. Llywelyn Goch's *llatai* poem also contains a descriptive passage which, untypically, is not introduced until the sixth line, and is confined to six couplets, the main interest being in the poet's message to the bird. The 'apocryphal' *cywyddau llatai* display a similar variety in structure and content. At least four (probably fifteenth-century) poems—to the swan (*DGG* XXVI), the eagle (*DGG* XXVII), the salmon (*DGG* XXIX), and the pheasant-cock (*DGG* XXXIV)—are by and large faithful to the 'classic' model, which is no doubt one of the reasons for their inclusion in *DGG* as Dafydd's work. However, the stock descriptions of the eagle and the salmon are comparatively brief, allowing for considerable elaboration, particularly in the second instance, in the poet's message and directions. The structure of *BDG* CLXIV is unique in that it begins with a short description of the beloved (ll. 1–6), and the lovelorn poet's lengthy complaint (ll. 1–26). Then comes a cursory description of the swallow (ll. 27–30), and the customary directions as to how the girl may be reached and how the bird should address her (ll. 31–66). The most interesting of the 'apocryphal' poems is the dialogue between the poet and the cuckoo discussed above (*BDG* CCX). Here, the bird fails to return with a sign ('arwydd')[72] from the girl due to the coming of winter, and since the woodcock to which it delegated the task has been killed by a crossbow bolt, the cuckoo is asked by the poet to return once more to greet his beloved and to present her with a letter. Again only two couplets (ll. 55–8) are devoted to describing the bird. The *cywydd*, which in the oldest manuscript version is unfortunately anonymous, is, with its lively, humorous dialogue, its lack of descriptive detail, and relative simplicity of style and language,[73] the most popular in tone of all the *cywyddau llatai* with which we have been concerned, and its affinity with their supposed sub-literary antecedents may be more than superficial.

---

[72] Cf. *BDG* CCVI.28 (Gruffudd Gryg?), *DGG* XXVII.21; *CRhC* 34.3 ('Ymddiddan Rhwng y Bardd a'r Gog'). DG twice asks that his messenger return with a kiss (or two) from the girl (*GDG* 114.47–8; 116.37); cf. *BDG* CLXIV.37, *DGG* XXVII.21.

[73] The slick-sounding 'Gwyl y Grog i gil y gwrych' and 'Gwr a bolld dan gŵr y berth' (ll. 40, 44) are reminiscent of passages of incremental repetition found in both strict- and free-metre poetry; see Ch. 5, pp. 182–3 below.

In favour of the thesis that the free-metre poets were composing within an older popular-verse tradition is the fact that their treatment of the love-messenger theme seems to owe surprisingly little to the *cywyddau* of the previous 200 years. These poets would therefore appear to be drawing, at least in part, on a separate, less consciously artistic expression of the convention. The difference is apparent mainly in the lack of any sustained description of the messenger, as one might expect in a popularly orientated body of verse, and in the frequency of dialogues. The bird is usually qualified by a token adjective or epithet, as in the following examples: 'Od eid troso fi/r heden heini' (*CRhC* 1, VI.37), 'if you will go on my behalf, lively bird'; 'keliogg bronfraith da J gwvr bob iaith' (*CRhC* 2, IV.5), 'cock-thrush, well does he know every language'; 'Kroeso adre yr gog fwyn | iarlles llwyn llywenydd' (*CRhC* 34.5–6), 'welcome home to the pleasant cuckoo, countess of the grove of joy'; and in the traditional four-line *penillion* of uncertain date such tags as 'Y deryn du pigfelyn',[74] 'yellow-beaked blackbird', and 'Ceiliog du'r fwyalchen',[75] 'dark male blackbird', are common. In the *carol deuair* which begins 'Dowch i wrando arna i yn kwvno/am fy llatai erbvn kalamai' (*CRhC* 2, II) ('Come listen to my complaint about my love-messenger on the eve of May'), possibly the work of Llewelyn ap Hwlcyn, even such minimal padding as this is done away with. In another poem (*CRhC* 2, IV) Llewelyn asks the thrush to travel to Shrewsbury where it should seek out the bailiff's house at dusk and greet the beloved in a whisper, asking her whether she will return to Wales. But it is noteworthy that this is the only instance which I have come across in the *canu rhydd* of the *Cywyddwyr*'s convention of explaining directions for the journey. Moreover, none of the free-metre *llatai* poems which I have read contain advice for avoiding the clutches of Eiddig, although in one instance, as has been seen, the nightingale refuses to oblige the poet for fear that Eiddig might mistake it for the cuckoo (*CRhC* 1, VI.41–4), and elsewhere Eiddig's hatred of the cuckoo as the bird of love is proverbial. It may be added that the cuckoo's report by means of direct speech of its dialogue with the beloved in *CRhC* 34 is unparalleled in *cywydd* poetry.

[74] Cadrawd, 'The Folklore of Glamorgan', *Cofnodion a Chyfansoddiadau Buddugol Eisteddfod Aberdâr* (1885), 205; cf. the charming penultimate couplet of the 'apocryphal' *DGG* XLIII: 'Yr eos fain adeinllwyd, | Llatai ddechrau Mai im wyd!'

[75] *HB* 493.1. As noted by Brinley Rees, *DCRh* 65, the more unusual description of the lark as being 'heb vn pren ymgynal' (*CRhC* 33.6) is almost certainly indebted to *GDG* 114.

Equally striking is the fact that, with the exception of the stock phrases 'ffarwel a duw ich kadw' (DCRh 236), 'farewell, and may God protect you', and 'Dvw a dalo yt' (CRhC 33.49), 'may God reward you', the familiar motif of the poet's blessing plays no significant part in the free-metre bird-poems.

If the lost verse tradition associated with the Clêr is indeed the most significant source of inspiration for the cywydd llatai, there is another minor detail which is worth considering here. Dafydd ap Gwilym addresses the messenger by name in the opening line of his poems, with the sole exception of the woodcock which is, however, named in the opening couplet; likewise Gruffudd Gryg in his poems to the wave and the trout (assuming that he is the author of this cywydd). Llywelyn Goch's titmouse is duly named in the second line of DGG XXXIII. With just the one exception, the uniquely structured BDG CLXIV, the 'apocryphal' poems referred to above all follow the same pattern. Since this is also seen in the canu rhydd, particularly in the penillion telyn,[76] it may be tentatively suggested that Dafydd and his contemporaries derived the convention from early prototypes of such lyrics, while in most cases developing the familiar descriptive epithet into an elaborate dyfalu passage in keeping with their delight in the natural world, and with the refined artistic tastes of a fourteenth-century noble audience. It may be that it is those cywyddau llatai which lack such elaboration, and the dialogue poems in particular, which come closest to reproducing the popular model. Rachel Bromwich is not the only scholar to have postulated a link between the free-metre bird-poems and an earlier verse tradition which remained submerged until the sixteenth century. In his comparative study of the early canu rhydd and contemporary English verse Brinley Rees, while arguing for the probability of late English influence, particularly on those areithiau or ymddiddanion (dialogue poems) in which the bird's advice is of a strictly religious or moral nature, suggests that these poets were on the whole following an essentially native convention, derived from the work of Dafydd ap Gwilym or from the tradition which manifests itself there, if it existed.[77] He makes the highly significant point that the use of birds

[76] Cf. Cadrawd, 'Folklore of Glamorgan', 205, 208, 210; HB 493. Examples from early free-metre verse (i.e. bird-poems which lack a narrative introduction) are noted in DCRh·69, n. 5; cf. also LlRMG 118.

[77] DCRh 65–73. Helen O'Sullivan also argues for English influence, referring, for instance, to Richard Hughes's dialogue with the nightingale (CRhC, 1, VI) in which the speech of bird and poet is divided into alternate stanzas in the manner of English

as love-messengers is, as has been seen, virtually unknown in the English poetry of the period.

Some of the free-metre *llatai* poems do show signs of imitating the *cywyddau* in certain minor points of detail.[78] But it is at least as likely that some of the more general similarities which exist between the two bodies of verse derive from a common popular tradition as from direct imitation on the part of the free-metre poets. In *CRhC* 2, II, as in *BDG* CCX, the poet awaits the bird's return after the winter months, and there are some striking analogues with Dafydd ap Gwilym's dialogue with the woodcock. In *CRhC* 1, VI, the nightingale bluntly refuses to carry out the poet's request, and Dafydd's woodcock, equally bluntly, admits its fear of the winter cold, and in any case, it declares, a rival suitor has captured the girl's heart— 'Aeth arall hoywgall â hi' (*GDG* 115.48). Similarly, the magpie in *DCRh* 234–6 informs the poet that slanderers have led the girl into the arms of a new lover, and warns: 'Mae rwan gyfall arall | yn emyl Mynd a hi', 'another friend is now about to take her away'. In a poem by 'llelo llwyd', who should probably be identified with Llywelyn ap Hwlcyn, the cuckoo is even more outspoken, rebuking the poet for wishing to have Eiddig hanged without first having an inquest by the birds and flowers:[79]

> Taw ath braitio, llelo llwud,
> Ai fellu ir wut ti ym erbun,
> Kilia om golwg dos di ymhell,
> Nid wut ti well nar gelun.
> (*CLlC*, vol. III, no. XIII)

(Leave your babbling, Llelo Llwyd, is this the welcome you give me? Get out of my sight, go far away—you are no better than the enemy.)

The birds' practical, often cynical, advice in these and other free-metre poems[80] is strongly reminiscent of the attitude of Dafydd ap

dialogue poems of the 16th century. She remarks, however, that: 'If, as I suspect, there was a continuing Welsh folk tradition of asking birds for advice, birds in this tradition may have been as sparely described as in the *canu rhydd* . . .' ('Developments in Love Poetry . . .', 231).

[78] Cf. *DCRh* 65.
[79] Another 16th-cent. poet, Thomas Prys, has a *cywydd* on the same theme (*The Cefn Coch MSS.* 96–9). It is possible that it is ultimately related to the medieval French bird-debate convention, although there is no reason why the conceit should not have arisen independently in Welsh; compare DG's personification of the thrush as 'Siryf', 'Ustus', and 'Ystiwart llys' in *GDG* 123.
[80] Cf. *CRhC* 33, 36; *CLlC*, vol. III, no. XIV; Evans, 'Iaith a Ieithwedd . . .', ii. 209–11, 231–3, 258–60.

Gwilym's woodcock and magpie (*GDG* 63), and an ultimate popular origin for such dialogues seems likely. In the 'apocryphal' *cywydd BDG* CXLV, as in *GDG* 63 of which it is largely an imitation, the magpie mocks the poet for awaiting in vain the arrival of his beloved, and the poem diverges from its model only where the bird advises the poet to say his prayers rather than compose frivolous love-songs. The magpie is here more obviously symbolic of a monk or priest than in Dafydd's poem, and this is also the case in another 'apocryphal' *cywydd*, where the kite's advice to the poet is that he should no longer make trysts with 'merched y gwledydd', but believe and follow him—'Coelia a thyr'd i'm canlyn' (*BDG* CXV.26). That the poet here chooses to ask the bird's advice is more reminiscent of the *canu rhydd* than of the *Cywyddwyr*'s bird-poems, and the theme of the poet's fruitless wait in the woods as well as the bird's frank cynicism are common elements in the *cywyddau* and *canu rhydd* alike. In fact, the words of comfort spoken by the thrush in *GDG* 36 (which is not strictly a dialogue poem), urging the poet to spend the month of May in the idyllic environment of the *deildy*, is fairly untypical of the nature of birds' advice in the Welsh poetic tradition in general.

These birds' lack of compassion often arouses the anger of the ailing poets so that they sometimes, with rather comic effect, resort to threats. When Dafydd ap Gwilym is flatly advised by the magpie to forsake love and become a hermit (*GDG* 63), he satirizes the bird and warns that if ever he happens to find a nest of his there will remain in it neither egg nor bird. Similarly, *GDG* 61 ('Y Cyffylog') ends with a heartfelt death-wish, and the final couplet of the 'apocryphal' *BDG* CXLV is a curse upon the magpie. Dafydd's threats call to mind his equally humorous satire of the owl which disturbed his sleep in *GDG* 26, where he promises to set fire to every ivy-covered tree in sight in order to get rid of the unwelcome bird. In a free-metre poem the wren, in a typical tirade on the vanity of womankind, declares:

> o d[o]yda fi ywch gelwydd vyth
> kymerwch fy nyth a llosgwch

(If ever I lie to you, take my nest and burn it.)

and the poet threatens:

> mi a rof vaglav ar y ddayar
> ith ddal ag ith roi yngharchar[81]
> (*CRhC* 36.95–6, 113–14)

[81] The underlying popular tradition of bird-dialogues is perhaps reflected in

(I shall place snares on the ground to capture and imprison you.)

However, as one might expect, the *Cywyddwyr*'s sustained satire of critical or unobliging birds is unparalleled in the *canu rhydd*. In the 'apocryphal' poems both the preaching magpie and the kite are vilified for their pains, and in *BDG* LXXXIV, the *cywydd* to the nightingale believed to be the work of Madog Benfras, the vehemence of the satire is comparable with Dafydd ap Gwilym's poems to the owl, the magpie, and the woodcock which disturbs a love-tryst (*GDG* 61). The crow which frightened away the nightingale as the poet listened to it singing mass in a leafy chapel is lampooned, as in Dafydd's poems, by means of cumulative *dyfalu*, which, as in the following extract, achieves a comic effect through its verbal intensity:

> Euryches yn oer ochain,
> Blowman du (*sic*) a'i blu mewn drain.
> Hug dorllaes mudwraig daerllyd,
> A dyn bob oen a boen byd . . .
> (*BDG* LXXXIV.53–6)

(A tinker-woman groaning chillingly, a black negro with feathers in briars; the long cloak of a querulous beggarwoman, which plucks every lamb from the world's pain.)

Here, as in the more laudatory descriptive passages common in the *cywyddau llatai*, it appears that the early *Cywyddwyr* have lent all their artistry, in this case reflecting the language of bardic satire and vituperation, to an essentially popular tradition, which resurfaces in simpler form in the free-metre bird-poems of the sixteenth century.

As well as being a common element in bird-poems, particularly so in the *cywyddau llatai*, the device known as *dyfalu* is also especially characteristic of the *cywydd gofyn* or asking poem. Several scholars have commented on the formal resemblance between the two genres, and bearing in mind that Dafydd ap Gwilym, as far as we know, did not compose a single asking poem—a fact which is perhaps explained by his *uchelwr* status—there may be some truth in Saunders Lewis's suggestion that his *llatai* poems were composed in direct opposition to the *cywyddau gofyn*, or as a parody of them.[82]

another, comparatively minor detail. Dafydd's initial reaction to the magpie's mockery—'Taw â'th sôn, gad fi'n llonydd | Ennyd awr oni fo dydd' (*GDG* 63.41–2)—may be compared with the equally abrupt responses of some free-metre poets, two of whom use a similar turn of phrase: 'ffi taw son ath siarad' (*DCRh* 234); 'Ist taw son rhag ofn dy glowed' (*CRhC* 1, VI.77); cf. also *CRhC* 36.89.

[82] *Braslun o Hanes Llenyddiaeth Gymraeg*, 90–1.

The resemblance of the rhetorical *dyfalu* passage—which in the more formalized asking poems is devoted to the object being solicited—is obvious. (It should, however, be borne in mind that in the earliest *cywyddau* of request and thanks, including Dafydd's poem thanking Ifor Hael for a pair of gloves (*GDG* 9),[83] there is little extended description, although this may, of course, be an accident of preservation.) The *cywydd llatai* also contains an element of petition, since the messenger is asked to perform an errand on the poet's behalf, and is sometimes asked to return with a kiss or some other token of the girl's affection.[84] It may well be, therefore, that the *llatai* poems reflect Dafydd's liking for composing in terms of, or even in opposition to, the mainstream of the 'official' bardic tradition. It is one of the salient features of his work, apparent, for instance, in his portrayals of May and Summer as noble patrons, in his fusion of love-poetry with the venerable art of heraldry in *GDG* 92 ('Achau Hiraeth'), and most notably in his depiction of the *deildy* as a noble court.

The question of the origins of *dyfalu*, whereby the subject of a poem is described by means of cumulative and often fanciful comparison with various other objects, is a complicated one. But it may be that the early *Cywyddwyr*'s accomplished and highly imaginative use of the device, like the *llatai* convention with which it is so often combined, has its roots in popular tradition. In the opening chapter it was seen that in the Bardic Grammar 'ymdaualu geir tra geir' is associated with 'clerwryaeth', and a similar practice, 'ymdyualu gwers tra gwers', with 'teulwryaeth', and it was suggested that the term denotes satirical or vituperative verse of some kind, perhaps in the form of reciprocal abuse in alternate stanzas and of poetic contentions. It is noteworthy that the few examples of the verb *dyfalu* which survive from the time of the early *cywyddau* are clearly related to satire and vituperation, which implies that the original meaning of 'likening' or 'comparison' suggested by the root seen in 'fal',

---

[83] As early as the 12th cent. Cynddelw has three poems composed in the *englyn* metres thanking for a hunting horn, a bull, and a sword (*GCBM* 6, 22, 23).

[84] The likely literal meaning of 'llatai' is 'one who requests a gift' (*llad* + agent suffix *-ai/-hai*); see *Recherches*, 188–9; *GPC* 2,099. It is noteworthy that the word, as mentioned above, is first attested in Gruffudd ap Dafydd ap Tudur's poem requesting a bow (*RP* 1,254.1). In his closing *englyn*—which calls to mind *Gogynfeirdd* poems to women—he addresses a messenger ('cennad'), as does Llywarch Llaety (*c.*1160) in the earliest surviving request poem (*H* 294–6); cf. also *GIG* XII.85–94 ('I Ofyn March').

'hafal', and so on (GPC 1,122) had acquired a strong negative con-notation, at least in certain contexts. It will be recalled that 'dyfalu', along with 'tesdiniaw', describes the abuse which Madog Benfras endured from his beloved's household in 'Cywydd yr Halaenwr'[85] (DGG LXIX.33 ff.), and a fine example occurs in a satire by Madog Dwygraig:

> Canaf dy valaf du vawlyt—gidwm
> kerd y ystilwm hirllwm horllyt.
> Ki aeth arol brein kythreulbryt—satan.
> kwthyr bran gal y garan agel gwryt.
>
> (RP 1,273.24–8)

(I shall sing—lampooning a black, filthy rogue—a song to a miserable, lousy stillion(?); a hound that stole away the spear-wort, [with] Satan's fiendish appearance (?);[86] raven's anus, heron's penis, who conceals his valour!)

It is striking that the verb is used here in a poem which consists in the main of strings of the kind of metaphorical epithets exemplified in this stanza, in the characteristic style of fourteenth-century satiri-cal verse. The technique, which is attested in verse which pre-dates the earliest cywyddau, does have affinities with the Cywyddwyr's dyfalu passages, although these are generally more inspired, more intricately constructed, and achieve a higher level of artistic achieve-ment than the purely satirical poetry. The satire by Madog Dwygraig was no doubt the kind of verse which Rachel Bromwich had in mind when she remarked that

although it is sometimes suggested that dyfalu had its origin in riddle-making, such as is found in Latin and Anglo-Saxon poetry, it seems never-theless more probable that it is to be related to the richly figurative, vitu-perative, and elaborately-compounded language of bardic satire, as this is exemplified both in Welsh and in Irish, and hence is likely to have sprung

---

[85] 'Clau ddyfalu . . .' is given as a variant reading of Llywelyn Goch's 'Clau ddy-chanu llu lledffrom, | Clywir ei dwrf, cler y dom' (DGG LXXXV.49–50). Cf. also 'A gwirion ddynion a ddyfalant' in the vehement condemnation of the Clêr, 'Bustl y Beirdd' (MA 29) (c.1350–1400). The earliest examples in GPC of 'dyfalu' in a neutral or positive sense belong to the first part of the 15th cent.

[86] The meaning of this line is unclear. G 270 is undecided between 'â'r olbrain' (according to the unpublished slips of GPC, spearwort or swine-cress, a herb which was used by beggars to make their flesh raw) and '. . . ar ôl brain . . . cythraul bryd . . .', which may be rendered: 'a hound that went after Satan's fiendish ravens'. A pos-sible amendment is 'a rolbren' (â rholbren)—'a hound that stole away Satan's fiendish rolling-pin'; cf. DG of his penis: 'Casaf rholbren wyd gennyf' (CMOC 1.9).

from an ancient tradition common to the two branches of the Celtic peoples.[87]

As well as drawing attention to the possible significance of this stylistic resemblance, Bromwich also points out that *dyfalu* is generally used by the early *Cywyddwyr* for the purpose of satire. Dafydd ap Gwilym, she remarks,[88] unlike his contemporaries on the whole (as far as we can judge from their extant verse), uses *dyfalu* for praise as well as satire, although he too most commonly employs it pejoratively in *cywyddau rhwystr* such as GDG 65 ('Y Fiaren'), GDG 66 ('Y Cloc'), GDG 91 ('Y Rhew'), and GDG 127 ('Y Pwll Mawn'), poems which describe various impediments to the poet's love. The following passage describing a farmer's rattle ('Y Rhugl Groen') is a typical example:

> Cod ar ben ffon yn sonio,
> Cloch sain o grynfain a gro.
> Crwth cerrig Seisnig yn sôn
> Crynedig mewn croen eidion.
> Cawell teirmil o chwilod,
> Callor dygyfor, du god . . .
>   (GDG 125.29–34)

(A noisy bag at the end of a stick, a resounding bell of pebbles and gravel. A .trembling *crwth* of English stones in a bullock's skin. A basket of three thousand beetles, a cauldron in tumult, a black bag . . .)

Just as in much of the personal satire of the period, abuse is here heaped upon abuse in a cumulative sequence of quick-fire metaphors.

Dyfalu, then, is clearly closely associated in fourteenth-century Welsh poetry with satire and vituperation, and the theory adduced by Bromwich is certainly persuasive. However, it is impossible to ignore the obvious affinity which exists between the *Cywyddwyr*'s characteristic descriptive technique and the ancient art of riddling, and this line of inquiry does seem to me to be more suggestive with regard to the ultimate origins of the device. It has often been suggested, more or less tentatively, that *dyfalu* may indeed be derived from some form of riddling. D. Myrddin Lloyd seems more convinced than most when he remarks that, although *dyfalu* as a specific literary device belongs to the *cywydd* period, it has obvious affinities with the Latin writings of Symphosius and his imitators, and with the Old English riddle poems. He therefore supposes that the prac-

tice had survived and had somehow reached Wales, the very term
dyfalu as it was understood by the *Cywyddwyr* being an indication
of its origin in some kind of riddle.[89] The Latin riddles of the fifth-
century author Symphosius, which are thought to have been told in
the carnival atmosphere of the Saturnalia, provided the model for
riddle-makers down to the Renaissance. It was he, it appears, who
inspired the school of Anglo-Latin riddlers which flourished in the
early Middle Ages, influencing the author or authors of the important collection of Old English riddles preserved in the Exeter Book,
which are usually dated in the eighth century.[90] These are probably
the earliest extant vernacular riddles in Western Europe, but the literary riddle as a genre has a much longer history. It is believed to
have originated in the Near and Far East, the oldest recorded riddles
being Babylonian school texts; the oldest extant riddles in Sanskrit
date from around 1000 BC, and the first work to pay attention to riddling as a literary genre is a bibliography of Arabic riddles written
in the fourteenth century.[91] The only early example of a riddle-poem
in Welsh is the poem known as 'Canu y Gwynt' in the Book of
Taliesin.[92] The poem, which opens with the conventional challenge
'Dechymic pwy yw', 'Guess who it is', may be as old as the tenth
century, and its length—it is considerably longer than most Anglo-
Saxon and Latin riddles—in itself identifies it as a literary, rather
than a folk riddle. As John Morris-Jones showed long ago, it may
well have been influenced by Latin riddles on the same theme,[93]
which would probably have been known in Wales through the
religious houses; at least two collections of Latin riddles were in

---

[89] 'Estheteg Yr Oesoedd Canol', *LlC* 1 (1951), 164n. He discusses here the merging
which may have taken place on the eve of the Middle Ages between the ornate style
of the 'Asiatic' tradition, inherited from classical learning, and the Celts' well-known
love of intricacy which is so characteristic of their art. He suggests that this style has
left its mark on Irish court poetry and on the *awdlau* of the *Gogynfeirdd*. Note
Diodorus Siculus' testimony that the Celts 'use few words and speak in riddles' (J. J.
Tierney, 'The Celtic Ethnography of Posidonius', 251).

[90] Craig Williamson, *The Old English Riddles of the Exeter Book* (North Carolina,
1977), henceforth referred to as *Exeter Book*. On riddle literature in general see Archer
Taylor, *The Literary Riddle Before 1600* (Berkeley, Calif., 1948); id., *English Riddles
from Oral Tradition* (Berkeley, Calif., 1951); H. M. and N. K. Chadwick's chapter on
'Descriptive Poetry', in *The Growth of Literature*, vol. 1 (Cambridge, 1932), esp. 412 ff.

[91] D. G. Blauner, 'The Early Literary Riddle', *Folk-lore*, 78 (1967), 49–50.

[92] *BT* 36–7. The poem has been edited by Marged Haycock, 'Llyfr Taliesin: astudiaethau ar rai agweddau', unpublished Ph.D. thesis, University of Wales (1983),
507–11.

[93] 'Taliesin', *Y Cymmrodor*, 28 (1918), 255. The riddle on the wind which he cites
from [pseudo-] Bede's *Flores* is particularly relevant.

circulation in Ireland in the seventh century. But it is not unlikely that its author also drew on an indigenous oral tradition.

It is well known that Dafydd ap Gwilym's *cywydd llatai* to the wind (*GDG* 117) contains a number of overt echoes of 'Canu y Gwynt'. Iolo Goch's *awdl GIG* XXX ('Gweddi') also includes a long riddle-like section which is similarly indebted to the early poem, as Dafydd Johnston notes in his edition, and perhaps to other material of the same type. The lines:

> Ef ni hëed, ef ni aned,
> Ef ni weled yn iawn olau,
> Ar fôr na thir ef ni welir . . .
> (*GIG* XXX.7–9)

(He has not been sown, he has not been born, he has not been seen clearly, he is not seen either on sea or on land . . .)

seem to be a conscious elaboration of the Book of Taliesin's

> Ac ef ny anet. Ac ef ny welet. Ef ar vor
> ef ar tir ny wyl ny welir . . .

(And he has not been born, and he has not been seen; on sea or land he sees not nor is he seen . . .)

and Iolo's words 'nis gwn beth yw' (l. 29), 'I know not what it is', are particularly reminiscent of the riddling tradition. The *cywydd* to the trout discussed above, which may be the work of Gruffudd Gryg, provides further echoes, especially in the couplet:

> Di-ddwylaw ar nawf i'r nef,
> A didroed y doi adref.
> (*BDG* CCVI.33–4)

(Swimming towards heaven with no hands, and without feet you will return home.)

In 'Canu y Gwynt' the wind is 'heb law aheb troet', 'without hand or foot', and we may compare also the descriptions 'heb droed heb adain', 'without foot or wing', and 'heb untroed' in *GDG* 117.4, 6. The attributes of the trout are described by means of a series of negative statements, such as 'Dur ni'th ladd', 'steel will not kill you', 'Dwfr ni'th fawdd', 'water will not drown you', and 'Deifr ni'th feddwan'', 'the men of Deira (i.e. the English) will not make you drunk' (ll. 13–14), and there are strikingly analogous passages in the poems by Dafydd and Iolo Goch. In a comparably stylized passage which

extends over eight couplets (ll. 9–22) it is said of the wind, for
instance, 'Ni boddy', 'you will not drown', 'ni'th etail . . . llafn glas',
'no silver blade will hold you back', 'Ni'th lysg tân',[94] 'fire will not
burn you'; and analogous elements in Iolo's *awdl* include 'nis llysg
ufel', 'sparks cannot burn him', 'nis lladd arfau', 'weapons cannot
kill him', and 'Nis bawdd cleuddwfr', 'a flood cannot drown him'
(*GIG* XXX.23–6). A similar rhetorical device is used in 'Canu y
Gwynt', as for instance in the lines

> Ny byd hyn ny byd ieu. no get ydechreu. Ny daw
> oe odeu yr ofyn nac agheu . . .

(He will be neither older or younger than he was at the beginning. Neither
fear nor death cause him to move from his purpose . . .)

This strongly suggests that the *Cywyddwyr*, although no doubt in
typical fashion imitating each other to some degree, may also in these
poems have been consciously imitating the art of riddling. That those
analogous elements which have been singled out for comparison find
no significant antecedents in the older poem suggests that they may
well have been drawing on a broader tradition of medieval Welsh
riddle-poetry, of which 'Canu y Gwynt' is the sole surviving example.[95] It is striking that Dafydd ap Gwilym employs this distinctive
'negative' descriptive device in at least five other poems, in relation
to subjects as diverse as the roebuck (*GDG* 116.41–4), hazelnuts
(*GDG* 50.51–4), the spear of love (*GDG* 111.15–20), and the holly
bush (*GDG* 25.18–20; 29.35–40). Of the latter he says (in words
attributed to Madog Benfras):

> Nis llysg ac nis diysg dyn,
> Ac er a ddêl o ddrycin,
> Ni bydd llwm na chrwm na chrin.
> (*GDG* 25.18–20)

---

[94] These words addressed to the poet's *llatai* (cf. *GDG* 116.41–4), somewhat reminiscent of protective charms, find a suggestive parallel in the 12th-cent. request poem
by Llywarch Llaety, who addresses his envoy: 'Tremytyat mynyd manot tew nyth
lud | nyth losgo eiry na rew . . .' (*H* 296.9–10).

[95] Patrick Sims-Williams is not convinced that even DG did not draw independently
on the wind-riddle tradition, and cites an analogous Welsh example recorded in 1908:
'Beth sydd heb ddwylaw ac heb draed, heb erioed ben na chorff, er hyny [*sic*] gall
agor llidiart?' ('Riddling Treatment of the "Watchman Device" . . .', 101). In the same
article (p. 109) he suggests that riddling may have formed part of the repertory of
medieval story-tellers. The existence of an indigenous riddling tradition on which the
early *Cywyddwyr* may have drawn is also postulated by D. J. Bowen, 'Awduriaeth y
Cywyddau i'r Eira a'r Sêr', *LlC* 7 (1962–3), 196.

(Man will not burn it or lay it bare, and however stormy the weather it will not be naked or bent or withered.)

and in another *cywydd*:

> Ni chny gafr hyd yn Hafren
> Un baich o hwn, na bwch hen.
>
> (*GDG* 29.35–6)

(No goat from here to the Severn shall chew a single mouthful of this, nor an old buck.)

These lines are parodied, it appears, in Gruffudd Gryg's fictitious elegy to Dafydd, in the description of the yew-tree which grows above the poet's grave:

> Geifre ni'th lwgr nac afrad
> Dy dwf yng ngwedre dy dad.
> Ni'th lysg tan, anian annerch,
> Ni'th dyr saer, ni'th dyfriw serch. . .
>
> (*DGG* LXXXIII.29–32)

(No flock of goats shall defile you, do not waste your growth in your father's land. No fire shall burn you—it is Nature herself that I greet(?)—nor carpenter cut you down; love shall not shatter you.)

A final instance of the device is Iolo Goch's praise of the immortal art of poetry in *GIG* XII ('I Ofyn March'), which, among other things, has the conventional attribute of being immune to the danger of water — 'Ni lwgr ar ddŵr' (l.18).

There is nothing improbable in the inference that the early *Cywyddwyr* were familiar with a well-known body of traditional material of the kind represented by 'Canu y Gwynt'. Riddling is both very ancient and very widespread, and is likely to have been cultivated at a popular level from an early time. Frederick Tupper, discussing the poems in the Exeter Book, distinguished between *Volksträtsel*, folk riddles, and *Kunsträtsel*, artistic or literary riddles.[96] The two genres have been discussed more recently by D. G. Blauner, who remarks:

As do the tale and the ballad, the riddle also has popular and literary forms. The literary form is generally far longer, more vague and more diffuse than the folk-riddle . . . Also, literary riddles are more likely to employ abstract

---

[96] *The Riddles of the Exeter Book* (Boston, 1910), pp. xviff.

themes . . . A great many give evidence of being deliberate artistic elabora-
tions of folk-themes.[97]

This last remark would seem to apply to many of the Old English
riddles, not all of which can be explained as direct imitations of the
earlier Latin tradition; and some are more naïve and more simply
expressed than others. It has been suggested that: 'The variation of
Anglo-Saxon and Latin riddles is . . . convincingly accounted for by
supposing that in most instances they are developments of the same
common kernels taken from folk-material or the usual lore of the
time.'[98] With this in mind, and allowing for the obvious cultural differences which exist between Anglo-Saxon England and fourteenth-
century Wales, certain parallels may be suggested between the Exeter
Book riddles and the early cywyddau. In Iolo Goch's 'Cywydd y
Llafurwr' the plough is described, for instance, as

> Gŵr a'i anfodd ar grynfaen,
> Gwas a fling a'i goes o'i flaen;
> E fynn ei gyllell a'i fwyd
> A'i fwrdd dan fôn ei forddwyd . . .[99]
> (GIG XXVIII.51–4)

(A man who dislikes pebbles, a lad who flays with his leg outstretched; he
must have his knife, his food, and his table under the base of his thigh . . .)

The plough is similarly personified in one of the English riddles
(Exeter Book, no. 19), but as a warrior who carries cunningly shaped
weapons, waging war on the ground as he tears with his teeth, and
as a thegn who obeys his lord. This type of personification is the
usual mode of these riddles, in which everyday objects are commonly
portrayed in human terms. In GDG 143 ('Y Cleddyf') (though not in
the section which consists purely of dyfalu—ll. 23–32) Dafydd refers
to himself as his sword's master—'Meistr wyf' (l. 8)—and the sword

---

[97] 'The Early Literary Riddle', 49.

[98] G. A. Wood, 'The Anglo-Saxon Riddles', Aberystwyth Studies, 1 (1912), 39.

[99] Cf. DG's descriptions of the fox—'Gŵr yw ef a garai iâr', 'Gŵr ni ddilid gyrn
ddolef'—in GDG 22.23, 25, a cywydd which contains some inspired dyfalu; also 'Fy
ngwas gwych', 'hardd farwn hir', 'A'm bardd', of the roebuck (GDG 116.15–16, 30).
A riddle-like englyn to the deer is included in GDG (p. 421) among the pieces of uncertain authorship. See Dafydd Johnston's interpretation in 'The Erotic Poetry of the
Cywyddwyr', 79–80, and cf. Sims-Williams, 'Riddling Treatment of the "Watchman
Device" . . .', 105. Some closely similar dyfalu of the deer in a cywydd gofyn by
Thomas Prys (1564?–1634) (The Cefn Coch MSS., 142–4) suggests that such riddles
may have been commonplace in medieval Wales.

is addressed as if it were a servant who protects the poet from Eiddig:

> Ni ad dy lafn, hardd-drafn hy,
> Gywilydd i'w gywely.
> Cadwaf fi di i'm deau;
> Cedwid Duw y ceidwad tau.
>
> (*GDG* 143.3–6)

(Your blade—daring, handsome lord—will not allow shame to its bedfellow. I keep you to my right side; may God keep your keeper.)

The same metaphor, more overtly expressed, is also an element in one of the English riddles on the sword (no. 18). Indeed, as one writer has remarked, with regard to the common utensils which many of these riddles describe, 'all the service they yield to man is a part of their thegnhood . . .'[100] The obvious sexual undertone of the *cywydd* to the sword calls to mind the infamous 'Cywydd y Gal',[101] a poem which consists almost entirely of *dyfalu* that is among the most imaginative and technically accomplished in Dafydd's repertoire; and it is perhaps not without significance that the same subject is apparently riddled in several of the early English poems.[102] The subject of another of the Exeter Book riddles (no. 51), probably a battering-ram, had a joyous youth on a hillside, it suffered the blows of an axe, and then underwent the discipline of manufacture before beginning its new career. Gruffudd ab Adda ap Dafydd has a fine *cywydd* (*DGG* LXV) in which he bemoans the plight of a birch which used to serve as a shelter for lovers, but has now been made into a maypole in the town of Llanidloes. As in the English riddle, a sharp contrast is drawn between the tree's past joy and present sadness, and in phrases such as 'traetures llwyn', 'traitress of the grove', and 'Mal ar sud maelieres wyd', 'you resemble a merchantwoman' (ll. 4, 44), personification is used to great effect. The birch is directly addressed as a sentient being, and there is a pathetic irony in the final couplets in which the poet asks it to choose between one life or the other:

---

[100] Wood, 'Anglo-Saxon Riddles', 23. The master–servant metaphor is also found in a Latin riddle on the sword by Eusebius (ibid. 54).

[101] Edited by Dafydd Johnston, 'Cywydd y Gal by Dafydd ap Gwilym', *CMCS* 9 (Summer 1985), 71–89.

[102] e.g. *Exeter Book*, no. 23, which is representative of a particular type of riddle in that it is probably 'a verse elaboration of a folk-riddle . . . intended to have a coarse answer, and at the same time to admit of such moderately suitable and decorous answers as "onion" and "hemp"' (Wood, 'Anglo-Saxon Riddles', 57–8).

Dewis o'r ddau, ceinciau caeth,
Disyml yw dy fwrdeisiaeth,
Ai cyrchu'r ffrith gadr adref,
Ai crinaw draw yn y dref.

(ll. 61–4)

(Choose one of the two, captive branches—artless is your burgess-hood—
either to return home to the fine woodland, or to wither yonder in the town.)

Personification of this kind is characteristic of the poems of the
early *Cywyddwyr*, and it seems likely that this particular type of
imagery, while at the same time displaying an undoubted degree of
creative imagination, may have been inspired in part by a native oral
riddling tradition, just as much of Dafydd's seasonal imagery was
suggested by the folklore and actual folk-customs of his time. It has
been contentiously suggested that the epithetical style of *Gogynfeirdd*
eulogy is influenced by the Anglo-Saxon *kennings* or the
Scandinavian *heiti*,[103] but this would not explain the emergence of
dyfalu as a well-defined convention in *cywydd* poetry. The theory
has also been proposed that 'Canu Y Gwynt' may in fact be a rhetorical exercise, that similar riddle-poems may have been composed by
bardic disciples, and that the poets had become so familiar with the
art that by the time of the *Cywyddwyr* it had become an acknowledged part of their craft.[104] It is an interesting suggestion, and one
which cannot be rejected out of hand; but if this was the case, we
would expect that riddling would also have been practised by poets
of a lower order throughout the *Gogynfeirdd* period, and probably
earlier. W. J. Gruffydd suggested long ago that *dyfalu* may have been
a feature of the *cywydd* before the time of Dafydd ap Gwilym, and
a similar suggestion has been made, more tentatively, by Thomas
Parry in a discussion of the *cywydd deuair hirion* which serves as a
metrical example in the Bardic Grammar:

Rhy fentrus yn ddiau fuasai dywedyd mai cerdd gellweirus oedd traethodl,
ac mai cerdd ddyfalu, fel y llinellau o ramadeg Einion, oedd cywydd. Ond
cymerer yr awgrym am ei werth.[105]

[103] J. Vendryes, *La poésie galloise des XIIᵉ et XIIIᵉ siècles dans ses rapports avec la
langue* (Clarendon Press, Oxford, 1930), 18 ff.
[104] John Rowlands, 'Delweddau Dafydd ap Gwilym', unpublished MA thesis,
University of Wales (1961), 117–8.
[105] 'Datblygiad y Cywydd', *THSC* (1939), 216–7; cf. W. J. Gruffydd, *Dafydd ap
Gwilym* (Cardiff, 1935), 54.

(It would no doubt be too ambitious to claim that the *traethodl* was a light-hearted poem, and that the *cywydd* was a *dyfalu*-poem, like the lines from Einion's grammar. But take the suggestion for what it's worth.)

These important *cywydd* couplets, with their detailed description of a horse, are usually explained as being part of an asking poem,[106] which is quite probable (although it has also been suggested that they may come from a *llatai* poem, or even from a lost type of *cywydd rhieingerddol* in which a horse was addressed in the manner of the Gogynfeirdd).[107] The opening couplet—

> Breichfyrf, archgrwnn, byrr y vlew,
> Llyfn, llygatrwth, pedreindew
>
> (GP 52.16–7)

(Sturdy of foreleg, round-chested, short-haired, sleek, wide-eyed, thick-haunched)

is typical of the extract in its attention to detail and in its use of compound forms; and although there is only a single simile—the 'Kyfliw blodeu'r banadlvric' ('of the colour of the flowers of the broom-tips') of the final line—these features do seem to bear some relationship to the art of *dyfalu* as it came to be developed by the *Cywyddwyr*. This primitive *cywydd* is no doubt representative of the '[c]ywydeu kerdwryeid, anhawd eu kanyat a'e dechymic' (GP 6.40–1), 'intricate *cywyddau* of difficult composition and invention', which the Grammar specifies as being one of the three branches of *prydyddiaeth*, the other two being *englynion* and *awdlau*. 'Dychymyg'—'invention', 'imagination', or perhaps 'comparison'[108]—is certainly appropriate, and the fact that in the *prydydd*'s work this was required to be difficult or intricate perhaps suggests that a simpler, cruder descriptive technique, possibly more akin to riddling, was

---

[106] See e.g. Eurys Rowlands, 'Nodiadau ar y Traddodiad Moliant a'r Cywydd', *LlC* 7 (1962–3), where he remarks that this early form of *cywydd* and the 'eruyn da yn deulueid' attributed to the *teuluwr* (GP 17.10) both testify to an older tradition of descriptive request poems ('cywyddau dyfalu erchi'), though there is no evidence that the genre belonged to a specific class of poets (p. 226).

[107] D. J. Bowen, 'Y Cywyddwyr a'r Noddwyr Cynnar', *YB* 11 (1979), 93.

[108] Among the meanings given in *GPC* s.v. *dychymyg*[1], are 'imagination, fancy . . . invention; similarity . . .' From the 16th cent. (and no doubt earlier) it has the specific meaning of 'riddle, problem, enigma, conjecture'. On the importance of *dychymyg* in medieval Welsh poetics see A. T. E. Matonis, 'The Concept of Poetry in the Middle Ages: The Welsh Evidence from the Bardic Grammars', *BBCS* 36 (1989), 1–12.

employed by poets of less elevated pretensions.[109] And, while not
forgetting the lost verse of the shadowy figure of the *bardd teulu*, one
is tempted to ask whether such poems may not have been composed
by the *Clêr* in the *traethodl* metre, which is so closely related to the
cywydd. The Hendregadredd manuscript contains two pieces written
in the *cywydd* metre which are based on acrostics of girls' names,
and it has been shown that the poems in this section of the manuscript are closely contemporary with the metrical exempla of the
Bardic Grammar, and belong to the same social context.[110] The following is a not-easily translatable acrostic on the name of Lleucu
Llwyd:

> C a V yn selu seilym
> Ll V E a allei ym
> Ll ac W eilw olwc
> T ac Y tec yw y gwc[111]

The verse is followed by the challenge 'Dychymic pwy enw y verch',
'guess the girl's name'. This then, a genre which may be compared
with the Anglo-Saxon rune riddles and with the use of acrostics in
various verse traditions,[112] is another, albeit essentially learned, form
of riddling with which the *Cywyddwyr* were familiar. It is perhaps
not without significance that Madog Benfras (presuming that he is
the author of the *cywydd* to the nightingale, *BDG* LXXXIV), speaks
of 'Dychymyg bonheddig bwyll' (l. 45), 'imagination/invention of
noble nature', stressing, it appears, the nobility of the art of *dyfalu*
with which he proceeds to vilify an unwelcome crow. The implication may be, as in the Grammarian's 'anhawd eu kanyat a'e

---

[109] Given the probability that some form of *dyfalu* was cultivated before DG's time,
it is noteworthy that the densely vituperative style of an English poem preserved in a
late 13th-cent. hand in a MS associated with Shropshire has been attributed in part to
Welsh influence. (A. S. C. Ross, 'The Middle English Poem on the Names of a Hare',
Proceedings of the Leeds Philosophical and Literary Society, 3 (1935), 348). A similar
suggestion is made by Rachel Bromwich with regard to the 13th- and early 14th-cent.
'Harley Lyrics' (*APDG* 99).

[110] Daniel Huws, 'Llawysgrif Hendregadredd', *NLWJ* 22 (1981–2), 1–26.

[111] Ibid. 26. Acrostics are used for the same purpose in the 'apocryphal' *cywydd
llatai BDG* CCX.17–20 (14th cent.?) discussed earlier, and in *BDG* CLXVI. For further examples see Gilbert Ruddock, *Dafydd Nanmor*, 'Llên y Llenor' series
(Caernarfon, 1992), 53–4.

[112] Cf. *Exeter Book*, nos. 17, 22, 62, and see the editor's notes on these poems. For
a fine example in medieval Latin verse see Raby, *A History of Secular Latin Poetry in
the Middle Ages*, ii. 239.

dechymic', that there existed a more popular form of *canu dychymyg* from which the *prydyddion* wished to dissociate themselves.

If we turn to the *canu rhydd* we find that riddle-poetry is not particularly prominent in the manuscript tradition. Of the examples which have been preserved, such as the verse cited by Henri Perri in his handbook of rhetoric *Egluryn Ffraethineb* (1595) as an illustration of the style which he terms 'dhychymmic dammegawl',[113] ('allegorical invention'), it is difficult to judge whether these are a continuation of an indigenous tradition or rather a reflection of the new vogue for riddle literature which the Renaissance brought to much of Western Europe. The type of 'question-and-answer' riddles which characterize many of the wassail songs recorded by Richard Morris in the early eighteenth century may well have formed part of a considerably earlier wassailing tradition, if it existed.[114] Since these songs were collected in Anglesey, it is noteworthy that in the early part of the present century John Morris-Jones remarked that: 'In Anglesey, old riddles are still repeated, beginning with the words *Dychymig dychymig*', and he gave the example:

> Dychymig dychymig: mi gollais fy mhlant,
> Fesul chwech ugain a fesul chwe chant.

(Guess the riddle: I have lost my children, by the six score and by the six hundred.)[115]

The similarity between this riddle, on a tree which has shed its leaves, and that cited in *Egluryn Ffraethineb* more than 300 years earlier, gives some indication of the resilience of the oral tradition.

Finally, the asking poems of the fifteenth-century *clerwr* Dafydd Y Nant, although unrelated to the riddling convention as such, may provide some clues with regard to the kind of descriptive techniques favoured by the popular poets of medieval Wales. These poems are the less artistic, and often humorous, counterparts of the *cywydd gofyn* as it was cultivated by Y Nant's contemporaries in the fifteenth

---

[113] *Egluryn Ffraethineb, Sef Dosbarth Ar Retoreg*, facsimile edition of the copy in the National Library of Wales, 1595 (Cardiff, 1930), 41. In the same period Thomas Prys composed a 'question and answer' riddle in the form of a short *cywydd* (*The Cefn Coch MSS.*, 64).

[114] *LIRMG* 8–9, 12–16, 37–8, 101, 149–53. At least one of these seems to have been influenced by a type of riddle popular in English; cf. ibid., pp. lxxxvi–xc. For possible echoes of the wassailing tradition in medieval poetry see Ch. 5 below.

[115] 'Taliesin', 256. For similar riddles from the modern period see Vernam Hull and Archer Taylor, 'A Collection of Welsh Riddles', *University of California Publications in Modern Philology*, 26 (1942–50), 225–325; further sources are cited by Sims-Williams, 'Riddling Treatment of the "Watchman Device" . . .', 100.

century. The humour stems largely from exaggerated comparison, expressed in everyday language of the type one would expect to find in popular verse. The following lines describe an oak chest which the poet requests on behalf of a friend and patron:

> ma[e] hin cymeint y chroba a moel y widdfa . . .
> ny lanwei cant cwreacn y cist fawr catarn . . .
> mai hin dd[i]con vchel vwch no tev camel . . .
> bei cy[f]let y bola a ddyre citweli . . .[116]

> (Its hump is as large as Mount Snowdon . . .
> a hundred youths would not fill the great solid chest . . .
> it is high enough, higher than two camels . . .
> were its belly as wide as the towers of Cydweli . . .)

In one of his cruder poems the line 'ay lyceit a[y] froene fecis mecine', 'his eyes and nostrils like bellows', describes a rather over-active bull; the animal is personified as 'cwr yr aneir coch', 'husband of the red heifer', and as a rustic villein—'bilein', 'hen costoc ceill-trwm'. Even its mating is referred to in human terms—'. . . wrdd cylybot y ar[a]idd yn cordderchvr forwyn. . .', 'hearing his oration as he copulated with the maiden'.[117] The poems of Y Nant contain nothing which corresponds precisely to *dyfalu* as developed by the *Cywyddwyr*, but this simple instance of personification, as well as the colourful and extravagant comparisons, are not all that far removed from the more stylized artistic device which was so dear to the strict-metre poets.

If features such as these were known to Dafydd ap Gwilym and his contemporaries in the verse of the *Clêr*, they may have had some bearing on the descriptive techniques favoured by them. But we can be fairly certain that the art of *dyfalu* should be associated in some way with an old native riddling tradition, while at the same time admitting the probability that the dense, epithetical character of bardic satire also played an important part in determining the nature of the early *Cywyddwyr*'s distinctive descriptive style. There is a strong likelihood that riddle-poems circulated orally in medieval Wales at a popular level, and it may well be that some form of *dyfalu*—and perhaps even conventional riddles—were current before the early *Cywddwyr*'s time in the form of the primitive *cywydd* or

---

[116] G. J. Williams, 'Cerddi'r Nant', 80–1.

[117] Ibid. 88–9. Compare the similar, though more delicately expressed personification of these animals in a slightly earlier *cywydd diolch*, A. Eleri Davies (ed.), *Gwaith Deio ab Ieuan Du a Gwilym ab Ieuan Hen* (Cardiff, 1992), no. 15.

traethodl metres. But it was they—most notably, no doubt, the great innovative genius of Dafydd ap Gwilym—who in the second quarter of the fourteenth century elaborated the device as we know it, as an acknowledged convention in both praise and satire. It was, it appears, Dafydd and his contemporaries who were primarily responsible for elevating the tradition into a mode of composition worthy of poets of the highest order, combining all their technical expertise with the remarkable powers of imagination for which they are renowned.

The Early *Cywyddwyr* and the
Sub-Literary Verse Tradition: II

The colourful world of early *cywydd* love-poetry, with its astonishingly wide range of subject-matter, is nowhere more suggestively echoed in the *canu rhydd* than in the following series of 'love triads' from a sixteenth-century *carol merch*:

> Tri anglymiad kariad kain
> kowydd englyn im dyn fain
> llattai difai down ar rrain
> fo a bare yr hain// i hvdo.

> Tri chyfodiad kariad gwenn
> kvssan meinir dan frig pren
> kae ag arwydd i ferch wenn
> fo ddaw i ben// ai gwnelo.

> Tri afrwydddeb serchog saer
> noswaith fvdvr ferddv glaer
> gwrach neu gleiriach yn rroi haer
> a chostog taer// ar gyffro.

> a thri rrwydddeb serch y sydd
> noswaith dowyll dawel brydd
> dor dda ymagor gyngor gvdd
> ar tylwyth fydd// heb [*leg.* yn] hvno.

> Tri dilafar serchog mwyn
> hafddydd hir a dail ar lwyn
> keliog bronfraith ar gog fwyn
> ar rreini yn dwyn// argofion.

> Tri di lafar serchog gwiw
> kornant karw fry ar riw
> y kyffylog gwaetha i ryw
> ag eiddig friw// ddolvrion.
>
> (CR*h*C 12.25–48)

(Three unfastenings of noble love: a *cywydd*, an *englyn* to my slender girl, a faultless love-messenger—these shall we bring, these would be sure to entice her.

Three exaltings of a girl's love: a sweetheart's kiss under the branches, a garland, and a sign to a fair maiden—he who does this is sure to succeed.

Three hindrances to an architect of love: a filthy, short moonlit night, a hag or some old fellow hurling threats, and an excited, persistent mastiff.

And there are three expediencies of love: a dark, calm, quiet night, an easily opened door—secret counsel—and the household fast asleep.

Three pleasant things(?) for a gentle lover: a long summer's day and leaves on a grove, the cock-thrush and the merry cuckoo, both bringing back memories.

Three harsh things for a fine lover: a turbulent stream on a hillside yonder, the woodcock—most despicable of birds—and Eiddig, bruised and sore.)

Here, then, are the familiar motifs of the *oed* or woodland tryst, the love-messenger, the chaplet or garland, the birds which are the lovers' companions, and the general delight in the celebration of love in a natural setting which is so characteristic of Dafydd ap Gwilym's poetry. Here, too, is the lover's loathing for Eiddig and his association with the woodcock, bird of winter, and the moonlit night which frustrates the poet in *GDG* 70 ('Noson Olau'); and the rushing stream noted as one of the lover's enemies is reminiscent of the swollen River Dyfi (*GDG* 71) and the various other hindrances which impede the lover's journey in Dafydd's *cywyddau rhwystr*. Images of Dafydd's humorous narrative poems are also conjured up in these stanzas: the hag and fierce dog belong to the same tradition as *GDG* 80 ('Tri Phorthor Eiddig'), and the reference to the girl's family fast asleep recalls especially the poet's exploits in *GDG* 135 ('Lladrata Merch').

However, the free-metre poet, who is named as 'Llelo' (probably Llywelyn ap Hwlcyn of Anglesey), was not drawing directly on the *cywyddau serch* but on a traditional body of triadic love-lore which goes back as far as the fifteenth century, and probably earlier. This is the date of the earliest extant version of *trioedd serch*—which, incidentally, are attributed to '[Gr?] ap adaf ap dauyd', no doubt the *cywyddwr* who was a contemporary of Dafydd ap Gwilym—a series of twenty-four triads preserved in a fifteenth-century hand on empty pages at the beginning of the fourteenth-century religious manuscript Jesus Coll. MS.119, known as 'Llyfr Yr Ancr'.[1] The many variant

---

[1] As is suggested in the introduction to *The Elucidarium and Other Tracts in Welsh from Llyvyr Agkyr Llandewivrevi*, ed. John Morris-Jones and John Rhŷs (Oxford, 1894), p. xiii, it may be that 'an attempt has been made to erase them, probably by a pious owner of the MS. who considered their contents incongruous with the religious

readings in this and the later manuscript versions[2] indicate that the
material had a widespread oral circulation. No 'love triad' is actually quoted by the early *Cywyddwyr*, but there are various verbal as
well as thematic similarities. For instance, Dafydd ap Gwilym's couplet

> Neud glas gofron, llon llatai,
> Neud hir dydd mewn irwydd Mai.
> (*GDG* 23.27–8)

(Green is the hillside, joyous the love-messenger, long is the day in the leafy
woods of May.)

may be compared with the triad: 'Tri pheth y lawenhau serchawc
diwyd lattei a gorderch gywir a hirdyd tywyllgoe[t]',[3] 'three things
that gladden a lover: a loyal love-messenger, a faithful sweetheart,
and a long day, the woodland dark.' The following passage by
Gruffudd Gryg is especially reminiscent of the world of the *trioedd
serch*:

> Llawer cusan ac annerch,
> Llawer amnaid, falchblaid ferch,
> Llawer arwydd, lloer eurwallt,
> A llawer oed yn llawr allt,
> Llawer cae bedw dan fedwgoed,
> A llawer rhwym i'm llaw roed.
> (*DGG* LXXII.31–6)

(Many a kiss and greeting, many a nod of the head—girl of noble lineage,
many a sign—golden-haired moon, and many a tryst at the foot of a hill;
many a birch-garland beneath the branches, and many a girdle into my hand
was placed.)

But there is no way of knowing whether the *trioedd serch* are in
fact derived from the *cywyddau*, or whether the early *Cywyddwyr*

character of the book'. However, the assertion that only a few words are now legible
is misleading: some of the triads are all but complete, not one is wholly illegible, and
many of the lacunae can be filled by reference to later MSS. At least five of these triads do not appear in later versions.

[2] These 16th- and 17th-cent. texts are noted by R. Geraint Gruffydd in 'Cywyddau
Triawdaidd Dafydd ap Gwilym: Rhai Sylwadau', *YB* 13 (1985), 172. It is the series
printed in *MA* 834–5 which most closely resembles the versified triads of *CRhC* 12.

[3] Triad no. 10 in 'Llyfr Yr Ancr'. In *GDG* 61 ('Y Cyffylog') the words 'serchddyn
syw' and 'nid o'm porth oedd' (ll. 2, 38) are somewhat reminiscent of the love-triads
(cf. no. 15: 'Tri amhorth serchawc . . .'). With 'nid o serch da' and 'Calon serchog
syberw fydd' (*GDG* 143.48–52) compare 'Tri tywyssogaeth serch[awc] haelioni a
digrifwch a seberwyt' (no. 9).

themselves made use of an established tradition of native love-lore which may have been reflected in verse which has not survived. The prominence in several of these triads of colourful or 'poetic' adjectives and of compound forms, and especially the use of the 'Tri Phorthor Eiddig' triad in the rhetorical bardic texts known as the *areithiau pros*, suggests that as we have them they were possibly intended as part of the *Cywyddwyr*'s traditional learning.[4] But this does not preclude the view that the *trioedd serch* may draw on material, perhaps including triadic material, which was reflected in the sub-bardic verse of the medieval period, as well as in the *cywydd* tradition. Given their subject-matter, they are of a more intrinsically popular nature than that larger body of triadic material, the mass of historical and legendary lore known as *Trioedd Ynys Prydain*, in which the *Cywyddwyr* were so well versed. And it cannot be taken for granted that, for instance, those triads which speak of the hag, the hound, and the creaking door derive from the *cywydd* by Dafydd ap Gwilym, and not vice versa. In view of the use of variant forms of the same triad in the 'apocryphal' *cywyddau*,[5] such as that which complains of 'the three foes of the lover'—a creaking door, an iron lock, and the watchful Eiddig (*BDG* XCVI.45–50)—it is conceivable that the poets were drawing here on a well-known sub-literary tradition of incident and intrigue, which may have been reflected in the verse of the *Clêr*. As Chotzen has argued, the theme of the nocturnal visit to the home of a married woman, which is reflected in several of the *trioedd serch* as well as in *cywyddau* such as 'Tri Phorthor Eiddig', is no doubt influenced, with its familiar wife–husband–lover scenario, by the French fabliau tradition.[6] But this pervasive influence may already have had some impact on the native subculture of comic and scurrilous tales, and perhaps also on the popular poets them-

[4] *Yr Areithiau Pros*, ed. D. Gwenallt Jones (Cardiff, 1934), 33. Interestingly, the triad occurs in the text entitled 'Trwstaneiddiwch Gruffydd ab Adda ab Dafydd'. Morfydd E. Owen has argued that the 'gnomic triads', as well as the early gnomic verse and proverb collections, may be products of bardic exercises ('Trioedd Hefut Yw Yrei Hynn', *YB* 14 (1988), 87–114).

[5] See R. Geraint Gruffydd, 'Cywyddau Triawdaidd . . .', 173–4; L. C. Stern, 'Davydd ab Gwilym, ein walisischer Minnesänger', *ZCP* 7 (1910), 96–102.

[6] *Recherches*, 286–90. There is nothing in the recognized canon of DG's poems which bears a striking resemblance to any of the French fabliaux which have been preserved, but for some correspondences in popular French narrative verse see Ch. 7 below. The ruse of 'The Man Under the Tub' recounted in *CMOC* 19, a *traethodl* falsely attributed to DG, is closely paralleled in a fabliau (cf. *Recherches*, 245).

selves, as early as the thirteenth century, when the popularity of the literary *fabliau* was at its height.

There is nothing in the *trioedd serch* which specifically reflects the particular form of the theme of the nocturnal visit known as the *sérénade*, but *cywyddau* of this type may well have had antecedents both in the Continental lyric and in the indigenous popular verse tradition. It has long been recognized that the *sérénade* is among the many established medieval genres of which the *Cywyddwyr* made use. In its purest form the genre is represented in only one poem which can be dated with certainty to the fourteenth century, namely GDG 89 ('Dan y Bargod'), in which Dafydd ap Gwilym suffers the torments of rain and snow under the eaves of his sweetheart's house, bemoaning his plight and begging her for admittance. Dafydd's other humorous accounts of his nocturnal visits, poems such as GDG 64, 80, 91, and 145,[7] which are among those narrative poems that have a general affinity with the Continental fabliaux, do bear a certain resemblance to his *sérénade* and will be useful in determining the origin of the convention in the Welsh poetic tradition. With characteristic inventiveness Dafydd incorporated some of its familiar motifs into his *englynion* lamenting the death of his uncle and patron Llywelyn ap Gwilym c.1346. He implores the dead man to answer him, calling on him to open his house to the poet as was his custom (GDG 13.5–8),[8] and as in the love-poetry there are several references to the poet's tears (ll. 14, 21, 69). A similar conceit is more overtly

---

[7] These correspond to Chotzen's *sérénades narratives* (*Recherches*, 283), along with several other, mostly 15th-cent. poems which have since been rejected from the canon. *BDG* CLXV and CLXXII (a *traethodl* analogous with French fabliaux, see *Recherches*, 245) are humorous narrative poems in which the lover outwits the hag and the jealous husband. *BDG* XCVI (possibly 14th-cent.) consists of a conventional *sérénade* followed by a fabliau-type adventure, which appears to be an imitation of poems such as *GDG* 80 and *GDG* 145 (cf. *GDG*[1], p. clxxviii). *BDG* CXXXI (probably the work of Gruffudd Llwyd, *fl. c.*1380–1420) consists mainly of dialogue (the only instance in DG's *sérénade*-type poems is *GDG* 91.11–16), as does *BDG* CLII, a parody of courtly love in which the girl's excuses are countered by the persistent poet: in order not to wake her mother he advises her to wet the window-hinges with her spit! Dafydd Johnston has drawn attention to the fact that only in *BDG* CXXXI does the poet fail to gain admittance, perceptively remarking that: 'All these poems contain humour at the poet's expense, but the house itself as a restriction to the lover is of no particular importance in the work of Dafydd's imitators.' ('The Serenade and the Image of the House in the Poems of Dafydd ap Gwilym', *CMCS* 5 (Summer 1983), 18).

[8] Cf. ll. 83–4. The poem's affinity with the *sérénade* has been remarked upon by R. Geraint Gruffydd, who notes that the device of addressing the dead directly is extremely rare in *Gogynfeirdd* poetry ('Marwnad Lleucu Llwyd gan Llywelyn Goch Amheurig Hen', *YB* 1 (1965), 131).

apparent in another lament from this period, Llywelyn Goch's famous elegy to Lleucu Llwyd (*DGG* LXXXVII). As R. Geraint Gruffydd has argued, while there is no doubting Llywelyn's conscious application of the device to the traditional lament, too many of the *cywydd*'s features were long ago explained by W. J. Gruffydd in terms of the *sérénade* convention.[9] The latter drew attention, for instance, to Llywelyn Goch's accusation of breaking a promise in failing to keep an appointment, a detail which is not a common feature of the *sérénade*, but is, however, paralleled in Dafydd's 'Dan y Bargod'. The accusation of 'muteness', or of failing to answer, is common to both laments, and on the basis of these and other verbal correspondences, and bearing in mind the early date of Dafydd's lament, R. Geraint Gruffydd concludes that Llywelyn was probably influenced by his contemporary. Whatever may be the case, the early *Cywyddwyr*'s flair for innovation is once more in evidence here, and for a literary genre to have been so boldly improvised we can be fairly certain that its conventions were already familiar to a contemporary audience. It may be that Dafydd's 'Dan y Bargod' is the earliest of the three poems discussed here, and that it was he who introduced the genre to Welsh audiences, drawing directly from French (or English) popular verse, or from the influential thirteenth-century poem *Le Roman de la Rose*. It is not improbable, however, that similar poems were already familiar in fourteenth-century Wales by virtue of a thriving sub-literary tradition which is likely to have assimilated elements of foreign provenance during the course of the thirteenth century. A further possibility which must be considered is that this hidden popular tradition contained features closely analogous with the *sérénade* deriving from native folk-customs.

Rachel Bromwich has suggested in relation to 'Dan y Bargod' that 'it remains questionable whether the incident could not . . . have arisen spontaneously from the poet's predicament, whether this was real or imaginary'.[10] The *Cywyddwyr* were certainly fond of amusing their listeners by presenting themselves in the role of the self-sacrificial suitor, wooing the beloved 'under the eaves' on a winter evening. In one of his poems to the woodcock Dafydd imagines him-

[9] Ibid. 131; W. J. Gruffydd, 'Y Farwnad Gymraeg', I, *Y Llenor*, 18 (1939), 40–5. See also Gilbert Ruddock, 'Amwysedd ac Eironi ym Marwnad Lleucu Llwyd', *YB* 9 (1976), 61–79.
[10] *APDG* 97.

self wandering on a cold winter night 'Tan fargod to tŷ f'eurgun'[11]
(GDG 61.18), 'under the eaves of my fair love's house', and in GDG
54 ('Rhagoriaeth y Bardd ar Arall') the custom, real or imaginary, is
a sign of the poet's superiority over a rival suitor:

> Ni thrig allan, ledwan lif,
> Dan ddagrau to dyn ddigrif
> I mewn cof ac ym min cais,
> Mula' treigl, mal y trigais.
>
> (ll. 35–8)

(He does not linger outside—(trickling flow) under the tears of the pleasant
girl's roof, lost in memory and on the verge of an attempt (most foolish loi-
tering)—as I have lingered.)

But it seems to me that 'Dan y Bargod', and to a lesser extent some
of the 'narrative serenades' which resemble it, have too close an
affinity with literary convention to be considered as entirely spontaneous creations. We must bear in mind that the basic theme of the
locked-out lover was given literary expression long before the emergence of the sérénade as a more or less fixed medieval genre in thirteenth-century Europe.[12] The exclusus amator had by Ovid's time
become a traditional motif, the paraklausithyron or 'locked-door serenade' having passed from Classical Greek poetry into Latin. In a
poem from the first book of the Amores a slightly inebriated Ovid[13]
beseeches his beloved's doorkeeper-slave to 'open the stubborn
door', and the words 'Remove the bolt from the door', which recall
the pleas of Dafydd and other medieval serenaders, are repeated to

---

[11] From the 'apocryphal' cywyddau cf. 'Duw ni myn, dinam wyneb, | Dwyn brad
nos dan bared neb' (DGG XLV.7–8), and 'Ydoedd oer ar ros dyddyn, | Dan bar-
wydydd herwydd hyn . . .' (BDG XCVI.7–8). The stock phrases 'dan bared' and 'dann
vargod' are used in a 15th-cent. sérénade (Gwaith Dafydd ab Edmwnd, I. 8, 30).

[12] Chotzen observes that part of the 'Song of Songs', although spoken by a woman,
bears a formal resemblance to the narrative serenade (Recherches, 285). It is this passage which inspired the medieval Latin poem 'Quis est hic qui pulsat ad ostium' (Who
is it who knocks at the gate?), with its timeless plea 'rise quickly, open to me, sweetest one!' (cited by Dronke, MLRELL, i. 269–70; on the influence of the 'Song of Songs'
on the language of 'courtly love' in medieval Latin poetry in general see ibid. 264 ff.).
The same source is parodied by Chaucer in The Merchant's Tale, in the passage which
begins: ' "Rys up, my wyf, my love, my lady free!" ' (The Works of Geoffrey Chaucer,
ed. F. N. Robinson (2nd edn., Oxford, 1957), p. 124, ll. 2,138 ff.).

[13] In Classical poetry the locked-out lover is often the worse for drink, having pro-
ceeded to the girl's house from a party; cf. GDG 135 ('Caru yn y Gaeaf') which in
this respect is unique among the early cywyddau (Parry admits that it could be the
work of an imitator, GDG, p. 547).

no avail.[14] Like Dafydd too, Ovid is careful to draw attention to the tears with which he has wetted the oak door, another convention of the *paraklausithyron* , and he is as furtive as any medieval lover. In view of the early *Cywyddwyr*'s numerous references to the Latin poet, and Rachel Bromwich's belief that the *Amores* are among Dafydd's literary sources,[15] it is quite possible that it was his work which provided the inspiration for the development of the *sérénade* theme by Dafydd and his followers. Ovid's tone in the poem in question is typically detached and self-deprecating, not unlike Dafydd's rather pathetic and self-mocking portrayal in 'Dan y Bargod'. It is this resemblance which caused Dafydd Johnston to suggest that in this case: 'Dafydd may therefore be drawing directly upon Ovid rather than parodying the serious treatment of the serenade as found in *Le Roman de la Rose*.'[16] However, such a persona is frequently adopted by Dafydd, particularly in his narrative poems, and while he may perhaps have been aware of Ovid's poem, his work provides no significant parallels of the kind which might suggest direct imitation.

It seems more likely that Dafydd's models are to be found in the medieval *sérénade* than in classical sources, and comparison with a passage from *Le Roman de la Rose* does, in fact, prove rather more suggestive. The relevance of this passage, in which Guillaume de Lorris's Amors, God of Love, explains the code of conduct which the courtly lover should observe as he visits his beloved's home by night, was first pointed out by Chotzen,[17] although he makes no case for direct influence. As he remarks, it is peculiar that no *sérénades* have been preserved in French composed earlier than the fifteenth century,

[14] *Ovid's Amores, Book One*, ed. and trans. J. A. Barsby (Oxford, 1973), 6.2, 24 and *passim*). For further examples of the *exclusus amator* in Ovid see *Amores*, III, 8.23–4 (*Ovid's Amores*, ed. and trans. Guy Lee (London, 1968), 152–3); *Ars Amatoria*, III. 581–8 (*The Art of Love*, ed. and trans. B. P. Moore (London and Glasgow, 1935), 152–3). On the history of the motif see F. O. Copley, *Exclusus Amator* (Madison, 1956).

[15] *APDG* 72–3. Cf. her remarks in *SP* 100 : 'His refs. to Ovid are fairly frequent, but imprecise. They indicate that for Dafydd as for many other mediaeval poets Ovid was the paramount authority on all matters relating to love, since he was in fact the ultimate source for the mediaeval European conventions of "courtly love" . . .' The references are noted by Alan Llwyd in *50 o Gywyddau Dafydd ap Gwilym* (Swansea, 1980), 125–6; cf. also *DGG* LXXXVII.51 and *DGG*² LXXXIV.7 (Llywelyn Goch); *BDG* LXXXIV.15 (Madog Benfras); *BBBGDd* 77.55 (Gruffudd Fychan, *fl. c.*1370–90). On 'llyfr Ofydd' see Ch. 6, p. 217 below.

[16] 'The Serenade and the Image of the House . . .', 6. He also draws attention to Chaucer's humorous portrayal of the serenading Absalon in *The Miller's Tale*, who is shunned at his sweetheart's window (*Works*, p. 53, ll. 3,687 ff.).

[17] *Recherches*, 284.

when the genre is first attested in popular verse. In his inquiry into
the origins of the French love-lyric Jeanroy was able to find in the
poetry of the twelfth and thirteenth centuries only a single refrain
which bears any relationship to the *sérénade*—'Il est jors, s'amors
m'ocit, et je sui ki l'atendrai.'[18] To this may be added an anonymous
rondeau in which the lovelorn poet implores the girl, somewhat
ambiguously, to 'open the door to the little meadow', but is refused
entry owing to the presence of the jealous husband:

> Ovrez moi l'uis, bele tres douce amie,
> ovrez moi l'uis dou petit praëlet
> Si m'aïst Dieus, ce n'est pas cortoisie;
> Ovrez moi l'uis, bele tres douce amie
> Ralez vos en, vos n'i enterroiz mie,
> car mes mariz, li jalous couz, i est . . .[19]

('Open the door to me, fair sweetest love, open the door to the little
meadow, by God, this is not courtesy; open the door to me, fair sweetest
love.' 'Go away, you simply shall not enter, for my husband, the cuckolded
jealous one, is here . . .')

Despite the lack of textual evidence, it is difficult to disagree with
Jeanroy's conviction that the *sérénade* had a long sub-literary existence in medieval France. The evidence of the *Roman* adds weight to
the theory, and the passage by Guillaume de Lorris, although a
courtly adaptation of a no-doubt essentially popular theme, may provide some idea as to the nature of such poems in the thirteenth century:

> La nuit issi te contendras
> Et de repos petit prendras
> Se j'onques mal d'amors connui;
> Et quant tu ne porras l'ennui
> Soffrir en ton lit de veillier,
> Lors t'estovra appareillier,
> Vestir, chaucier et atorner,
> Ains que tu voies ajorner.
> Lors t'en iras a recelee,
> Soit par pluie ou par gelee,
> Tout droit vers la meson t'amie,
> Qui se sera bien endormie

---

[18] *Origines*, 146 n. 1.
[19] E. Baumgartner and F. Ferrand (eds.), *Poèmes d'amour des XIIe et XIIIe siècles*
(Paris, 1983), LXXVI.

Et a toi ne pensera guieres;
Une hore iras a l'uis derrieres
S'avoir s'il est remés desfers,
Et soucheras iluec defors,
Tous seus, a la pluie et au vent.
Aprés vendras a l'uis devent
Et se tu troves fendeüre,
Ne fenestre, ne serreüre,
Oreille et escoute par mi
S'il se sont leens endormi;
Et se la belle sans plus veille,
Ce te lo je bien et conseille
Qu'el t'oie plaindre et doloser,
Si qu'el sache que reposer
Ne pues en lit por s'amitié.
Bien doit fame aucune pitié
Avoir de celi qui endure
Tel mal por li, se trop n'est dure.
Si te dirai que tu dois faire
Por l'amor de la debonnaire
De quoi tu ne pues avoir aise:
Au departir la porte baise,
Et por ce que l'on ne te voie
Devant la maison n'en la voie,
Gar que tu soies repairiés
Ains que li jors soit esclairiés.
Icis venirs, icis alers,
Icis veilliers, icis parlers
Font as amans sous lor drapiaus
Maintes fois amegrir lor piaus,
Bien le savras par toi-meïmes.

(*Roman*, ll. 2,505–47)

(Thus, if I ever knew the sickness of love, you will carry on, with little sleep,
throughout the night. And when you can't bear your suffering lying awake
in your bed, you will have to dress, put on your shoes, and adorn yourself,
before you see the day dawning. Then, whether it is raining or freezing, you
will go in secret directly to the house of your sweetheart, who will be sound
asleep, with hardly a thought of you. One hour you will go to the back door
to see if it were left unclosed, and there you will perch all alone, outside in
the wind and rain. Afterward you will come to the front door, and if you
find a chink, a window or lock, put your ear to it to hear if they are lying
asleep. And if the fair one alone wakes up, I advise and counsel you to
lament and sigh so that she hears you and knows that for love of her you

cannot rest in your bed. A woman who is not hardhearted ought certainly to have pity on him who endures such pain for her sake.

Now I will tell you what you should do for the love of that high sanctuary whose comfort you cannot possess: on your return, kiss the door, and in order that no one sees you in front of the house or in the street, take care that you have left before the light of day. These comings and goings, these night watches and conversations make lovers waste away many times under their garments, as you will come to know very well from your own experience.)[20]

The fact that the lover here does not seek admittance or any form of physical fulfilment is in keeping with the attitude of awed humility which the *fin' amant* was expected to adopt towards his *dame*. Although Dafydd ap Gwilym addresses the girl directly in 'Dan y Bargod' and wishes to gain entry into the house, the lover's situation is essentially the same. Dafydd's comic exaggeration of his plight, as, for instance, in the words 'Aml yw rhëydr o'r bargawd . . . ar y mau gnawd' (*GDG* 89.19-20), 'many are the torrents [falling] on my flesh from the eaves', is not paralleled in the *Roman*, but the couplet

> Ni byddwn dan law ac ôd
> Ennyd awr onid erod.
>   (ll. 33–4)

(I would not be a single moment under rain and snow except for your sake.)

does call to mind Guillaume's 'Soit par pluie ou par gelee', and 'Tous seus, a la pluie et au vent' (ll. 2,514, 2,521). The words '[g]law na gwynt', 'rain or wind', which occur in a similar context in 'Rhagoriaeth y Bardd' (*GDG* 54.26) may also be compared, and the motif is even apparently reflected in Llywelyn Goch's elegy to Lleucu Llwyd, in the line 'Yn bwhwman rhag anwyd' (*DGG* LXXXVII.67), 'wandering aimlessly to and fro on account of the cold (*and/or* passion)'. In *GDG* 91 ('Y Rhew') these discomforts reach the level of burlesque as Dafydd falls into a frozen pond and is assaulted by the stalactites which hang from the eaves of the girl's house. The resemblance to the *Roman* may of course be fortuitous, particularly since such adverse weather conditions seem to be among the genre's

---

[20] This and all subsequent translations of the *Roman*, with some minor amendments mostly due to textual variants, are from Charles Dahlberg, *The Romance of the Rose by Guillaume de Lorris and Jean de Meun* (Princeton, NJ, 1971). Further parallels with the French poem are suggested in Ch. 6 below.

recognized conventions, common in French popular verse as in the later *cywydd* tradition.[21] Dafydd's protestations:

> Ni byddwn allan hyd nos,
> Ni thuchwn ond o'th achos.
> Ni ddown i oddef, od gwn,
> Beunoeth gur, bei na'th garwn.
> (*GDG* 89.29–32)

(I would not stay outside all night, nor would I groan, except for your sake. Assuredly, I would not come to suffer anguish each night if I did not love you.)

are reminiscent of Amors's advice that the lover should ensure that his beloved hears him 'plaindre et doloser' (l. 2,529) and realizes that his love for her deprives him of sleep. Similarly, in 'Rhagoriaeth y Bardd' Dafydd's superiority as a lover over his rival is illustrated by the amount of tears he claims to have shed during his endless vigils:

> Ni ddyry ar ei ddeurudd
> O ddwfr brwd o ddifri brudd
> Gymaint lifnaint eleni,
> Eigr y serch, ag a rois i.
> (*GDG* 54.39–42)

(He will not shed on his cheeks this year, in grave solemnity, as many torrents of ardent water as I have shed, Eigr of love.)

A lively *sérénade* including a humorous dialogue, which is attributed to Dafydd ap Gwilym but is probably the work of Gruffudd Llwyd[22] (*fl. c.*1380–1420), includes what might easily be a comic application of Amors's advice:

---

[21] Cf. *Origines*, 197. Examples in *BDG* include XCVI.7–14, CLII.9–12, and CXXXI.23–4 (Gruffudd Llwyd?): 'Pa un wyd yn penydiaw | Dy glwyf o fewn od a gwlaw?' For a classical parallel see Barsby, *Ovid's Amores*, 169.

[22] In another dialogue-*cywydd* (*CIGE* XLVIII) he visits a widow's home by night claiming to be an angel who has seen her husband's ghost. Chotzen has shown that he was probably drawing on a widely known *motif de conte*, common in the French fabliaux and older humorous tales (*Recherches*, 287). Compare 'Yna y mae f'enaid glân, | A'm ellyll yma allan' (*GDG* 89.39–40); these lines, and more obviously the dialogue in *GDG* 91.11–16 in which the girl asks the shivering poet 'Ai dyn wyd, er Duw o nef?', may be understood as parodying the widespread medieval genre of the debate between body and soul, attested in Welsh at least as early as the 12th cent. (cf. *LlDC* nos. 5, 24; *BBCS*, 2, 127–30; 3, 119–22; R. M. Jones, 'Ymryson ac Ymddiddan Corff ac Enaid', *YB* 5 (1970), 44–61). See Eurys Rowlands, 'Rhamant Hanes y Beirdd', *YB* 3 (1967), 30–2, where it is argued that *GDG* 91 echoes the similar genre of the dialogue between the dead and the living; see also n. 35 below.

Tuchan yn daer wrth gaer galch,
A gruddfan am Eigr ruddfalch!
        (*BDG* CXXXI.7–8)

(Groaning insistently beside a whitewashed fortress, and moaning for proud, red-haired Eigr!)

The final sentence of the French passage cited above calls to mind the Welsh love-poets' references to their thankless nocturnal wanderings, a motif which is given an ironic twist in Llywelyn Goch's elegy (ll. 65–8). In particular, the lines 'Icis venirs, icis alers, | Icis veilliers, icis parlers' (ll. 2,543–4) may be compared with the assertion in 'Rhagoriaeth y Bardd' 'that he will not suffer as much rain and snow as I have suffered to seek you ([all] pomp [stripped] naked!) neither here nor there, all those times I have gone on a bold, persistent journey to the place where you were'—

        ... Na oddef ef ... O law na gwynt ...
        A oddefais i'th geisiaw,
        Amnoeth rwysg, yma na thraw,
        Y sawl waith ar lewdaith lud
        Ydd eddwyf hyd lle'dd oeddud.
                (*GDG* 54.25–30)

A further parallel with the *Roman* is provided by *GDG* 64 ('Y Ffenestr'),[23] and by *GDG* 40 ('Amnaid'), the only *sérénade*-type *cywydd* in which Dafydd does not actually seek admittance into the house. In both poems the lover furtively skirts the walls of the house in search of a window at which he may greet the girl. Similar advice is given in the *Roman* (ll. 2,518 ff.), with the difference that there the lover should only listen at the window or any other convenient aperture to ensure that the occupants are asleep.

Given the various other parallels with the *Roman de la Rose* in Dafydd's poetry, it is not unlikely that he had the God of Love's advice in mind when composing his *sérénade*-type poems. We must, however, agree with Dafydd Johnston's conclusion that, in view of his humorous treatment of the theme, and, with the exception of *GDG* 40, his hopes of physical fulfilment: 'If Dafydd's other serenades bear any relationship to the French passage it can only be as parodies.'[24] The analogues identified here, suggestive though they

---

[23] A possible Ovidian or French source for the scenario of this poem is suggested by Helen Fulton, *DGEC* 250 n. 24.
[24] 'The Serenade and the Image of the House . . .', 5.

are, can by no means be adduced as conciusive proof of his knowledge of the passage in question. We should bear in mind too that he
may have been familiar with more-popular versions of the *sérénade*
from this period which have not survived, and which would presumably have reflected several of the motifs elaborated by Guillaume
de Lorris.[25] It is noteworthy that the widespread motif of the lover's
climatic discomforts is found in a tantalizing English fragment which
clearly resembles the genre, preserved in a sermon written down
around 1300:

> So longe ic haue lauedi
> yhoued at þi gate
> þat mi fot is ifrore faire lauedi
> for þi luue faste to þe stake.[26]

Of course, we must not rule out the possible influence of contemporary English verse on the early *Cywyddwyr*, verse which may itself
have reflected Continental models. But the primary significance for
the present inquiry of this fragment, so fortuitously preserved, is that
it is suggestive of the currency of such lyrics at a popular level before
the *Cywyddwyr*'s time, whether they were composed in English,
French, or even, quite possibly, in Welsh, in the unrecorded verse of
the *Clêr*.

While it seems extremely likely that a *cywydd* such as 'Dan y
Bargod' was influenced, directly or indirectly, by the Continental
lyric tradition, the Welsh love-serenades also have a curious affinity
with various kinds of begging songs belonging to native folk culture.
These songs, known in manuscripts from the late sixteenth century
onwards under such names as 'carol gwirod', 'canu gwasail', 'carol
yn drws', and 'carol tan bared', were sung mostly around Christmas

[25] The opening section of Guillaume's passage finds a suggestive parallel in a considerably later popular song from the Vendée region:

> J'ai bien fait un rêve qu'elle net là,
> Et qui tenais ma mie entre mes bras
> I sautis en pllace, frais comme in gllas,
> I prenis ma culotte et mon chapia,
> A la porte à ma mie, dret y m'en va.

There follows an exchange in which the poet pleads with her to let him in, but without success (cited by Jeanroy, *Origines*, 150 n. 1).

[26] R. H. Robbins, 'Middle English Lyrics: Handlist of New Texts', *Anglia*, 83
(1965), 47; cf. Dronke, *The Medieval Lyric*, 147. Johnston supposes 'that the serenade
was common in popular tradition throughout the Middle Ages, being based upon
actual customs of wooing.' ('The Serenade and the Image of the House . . .', 2). Cf.
R. Geraint Gruffydd, 'Marwnad Lleucu Llwyd . . .', 132; *Recherches*, 285–6.

and the New Year. There were the Christmas festive songs ('canu gloddestol'), songs reflecting the custom of 'Y Fari Lwyd' at the New Year, and those accompanying the hunting of the wren ('Hela'r dryw') in the period centring on Epiphany; similar songs were sung in the Candlemas period, generally in honour of the Virgin, and around May-day ('Calan Mai'), the beginning of summer in the old Celtic calendar.[27] We may compare also the 'pwnco priodas', a kind of poetic contest between the groom's party and that of the bride, which, like the wassailing songs, involved a dialogue between those inside the house and those outside seeking admittance. The customs which the wassailing songs reflect have their origin in primitive fertility rites, as the parading of the ritual horse 'Y Fari Lwyd' and the sacrificing of the wren suggest; and while this function was no doubt on the whole recognized by the wassailers, as, for instance, when they wished prosperity on the household and its crops, several apparent allusions to ancient customs have been reduced to no more than half-understood formulaic jingles.[28] Similar begging songs are well attested throughout Western Europe. In France, for instance, the so-called *Aguilaneuf* songs celebrating the New Year and the May-day *Trimazô* songs were widespread up to the present century.[29] It has been suggested that these songs represent a survival of customs reflected by the most ancient begging songs known, the Greek New Year songs or 'swallow songs' of 2,000 years ago, whereby parties of singers solicited gifts or money in the name of the swallow, harbinger of spring, rather than the May Queen or the Virgin Mary.[30] Whether or not there is in fact a direct link with antiquity, the handful of Greek songs preserved, which appear for the most part to be of popular provenance, serve to indicate the timeless and widely popular nature of such songs.

[27] On the various types of Welsh 'wassail songs' see Rhiannon Ifans, *Sêrs a Rybana: Astudiaeth o'r Canu Gwasael* (Llandysul, 1983).

[28] Meredydd Evans has drawn attention to some apparent reflections of animal guising in the wassail songs ('Y Canu Gwasael yn *Llawysgrif Richard Morris o Gerddi*', *LlC* 13 (1974–81), 224 ff.). The pagan origins of the related customs are discussed by Rhiannon Ifans, *Sêrs a Rybana*, 19 ff.; as she remarks (p. 143) the very fact of being allowed entry into a house may be symbolic of fertility.

[29] C. B. Lewis, 'The "Aguilaneuf" and "Trimazo" Begging Songs and their Origin', in J. A. de Rothschild and M. Williams (eds.), *A Miscellany of Studies in Romance Languages and Literatures presented to Leon E. Kastner* (Cambridge, 1932), 308–41; cf. J. Tiersot, *Histoire de la chanson populaire en France* (Paris, 1889), 188 ff. See also Rhiannon Ifans's chapter 'O'r Tir Pell', in *Sêrs a Rybana*, 222–43.

[30] C. B. Lewis, 'The "Aguilaneuf" and "Trimazo" Begging Songs . . . .'.

As in the rest of Western Europe, however, folk-poetry of this kind was not written down in Wales until the close of the Middle Ages. The majority of Welsh wassailing songs are first recorded in seventeenth- and eighteenth-century manuscripts, the most important source being the collection of *canu gwirod* made by Richard Morris of Anglesey, mostly between 1716 and 1718. Most of these songs belong to an oral folk tradition, and their functional nature is reflected in their general artlessness. But although they are for the most part anonymous, as the editor of the manuscript, T. H. Parry-Williams, has observed, with a few exceptions (such as a carol 'to be sung around the Christmas chair') as they stand most of the songs do not appear to be considerably older than the manuscript itself.[31] It may be significant that this carol is composed in the *cywydd deuair fyrion* or *carol deuair* metre, an archaic metre which, it has been suggested, may have been employed by the *Clêr* from an early period. Indeed, several of the songs from this manuscript which appear to have the greatest claim to a long period of oral transmission are composed in the same metre. A song given the heading 'Carol Gwirod yn Drws', which the editor considers to be one of the oldest in the manuscript, is an unusual adaptation of the *carol deuair*, and is composed of diverse elements which the transcriber does not seem to have entirely understood. These include the obscure forms 'wala dwuniaid wala dwuniaid' and a rather curious reference to holly, as in English Christmas carols:

> holin weithan agor yn llydan
> y drws imi rwi ymron rhynnu yn canu.[32]

(*Holin*, open wide the door to me now, I'm nearly frozen singing.)

This type of verse inevitably calls to mind Gruffydd Robert's reference in the late sixteenth century to the unskilled folk with their 'carolau, a chwndidau, ne rimynnau gwylfeudd',[33] their feast-day or holy-day rhymes. Given the ancient origins and widespread nature of the wassailing tradition, it may well be that similar songs reflecting

[31] *LlRMG* p. lxxxii. One of the songs is ascribed in another MS to the 16th-cent. poet Huw Llwyd Cynfal (see *DCRh* 28). On the marked difference between the two versions due to oral transmission see Meredydd Evans, 'Y Canu Gwasael . . .', 211. He notes too (p. 222) the wassailers' emphasis on observing an old tradition—'y cosdwm su', 'y mae'n gostwm o hen ffassiwn' (*LlRMG* 185, 199).

[32] *LlRMG* 185. The poem is discussed by Meredydd Evans, 'Y Canu Gwasael . . .', 231–2. On 'holin' and its variants in *LlRMG* see ibid. 207, 212. Related folk traditions are discussed by Brinley Rees, *DCRh* 28–31.

[33] *Gramadeg Cymraeg gan Gruffydd Robert*, ed. G. J. Williams (Cardiff, 1939), 279.

similar customs had already formed part of the Welsh folk culture for some time before these words were written. Some of these customs and the early prototypes of the songs discussed above, if they existed, are perhaps reflected in certain allusions in the work of the strict-metre poets. The word 'calennig', the New Year gift solicited in the begging songs, is commonly used by the *Cywyddwyr* with the general meaning of 'a gift', as in *GDG* 133.17, where it describes a kiss. But in one of Dafydd ap Gwilym's poems to Ifor Hael, in which he thanks him for a pair of gloves, it is perhaps significant that the word is followed by a closing couplet which blesses the patron's home:

> Fy mendith gwedy'i nithiaw
> I dai Ifor Hael y daw.[34]
> (*GDG* 9.61–2)

(My purest blessing shall come to the court of Ifor Hael.)

In the line 'Kalandyd pandel. kelennic digel' (*RP* 1,254.12–13), 'on New Year's day, when a notable gift is bestowed', from Gruffudd ap Dafydd ap Tudur's poem requesting the gift of a bow, 'calennig' is specifically associated with 'Dydd Calan' (although, of course, it must not be thought that these professional poets actually composed begging songs of the wassailing type). In *GDG* 92 ('Achau Hiraeth') the personified 'hiraeth', or love-longing, which is sent by the girl to visit the poet as he is about to fall asleep, greets Dafydd with the request: 'Agor y ddôr' (l. 16), 'open the door'. His reply: 'Paddyw? Neu pwy a ddywaid?' (l. 18)—'To whom, or who is it that speaks'—may be compared with Iolo Goch's 'Pa gyfaillt, pwy a'i gofyn?' (*GIG* XIV.10), 'Who is the friend that asks it?', the body's conventional answer to the soul which awakens it from a drunken sleep,[35] and this

---

[34] It is noteworthy that a courtly version of a Christmas *chanson de quête* is attributed to the 13th-cent. French trouvère Adam de la Halle, in which a household is blessed in the manner of the later, popular verse:

> Dieus soit en cheste maison,
> Et biens et goie a fuison
> Nos sire noveus
> Nous envoie a ses amis,
> Ch'est as amoureus
> Et as courtois bien apris,
> Pour avoir des pairesis
> A nohelison. . .

(Raynaud, *Recueil de motets français des XIIe et XIIIe siècles* (Paris, 1881–3), ii. 113–14.)

[35] Dafydd's dialogue with his shadow (*GDG* 141) is also clearly a clever parody of the *altercatio animae et corporis*; cf. Bromwich's remarks in *SP* 202.

question-and-answer formula is, as one might expect, paralleled in the later *canu yn drws* or *canu tan bared*.[36] The wassailers sometimes claim to have been sent by God, Christ, or the Virgin Mary. It is therefore noteworthy that in the opening lines of 'Dan y Bargod' Dafydd urges the girl to show herself 'for the sake of God'—'Er Duw hael dangos dy hun' (*GDG* 89.4)—and a reference to the Virgin Mary in the next couplet may conceivably be understood as an allusion to the so-called 'gwirod Mair' carols sung during Candlemas ('Gŵyl Fair y Canhwyllau'). In a fifteenth-century *sérénade* by Dafydd ab Edmwnd the girl is blessed with the words 'nawdd duw[n] dygylch', 'may God's protection surround you', and in the line 'dy fin fal diod o fedd',[37] 'your lips like a drink of mead', there is perhaps an allusion to the ritual drink 'gwirod Mair', although the simile was common in fifteenth-century poetry, an example, it has been argued, of the influence of the cult of the Virgin and of the 'Song of Songs' on the love-poetry of the period.[38] In a passage from the same *cywydd*—

> deffro vvn differ venaid
> duw dyn blin sy dan dy blaid
> dyro ti a gai deiran
> dy wisc dy gardod i wan
> dy lety dy law ataf
> dy dec korff dywaid ai kaf . . .
>
> (ll. 9–14)

(Awake, my sweetheart, save my soul; by God, it is a weary man that is beneath your wall. Pray give—you shall have three parts [in return](?)—your clothes, your alms to a wretched one, your lodging, your hand [outstretched] towards me, your fair body,—say whether I shall be granted this.)

---

[36] Cf. *LLRMG* 5, 152, 175; in particular, compare the lines: 'Attolwg pwy sydd yna yr amser hyn o'r nos, | A'r drysau wedi eu bario a'u bolltio fynu'n glos, | A minnau yn fy ngwely . . .' (cited p. cvi). DG may have had in mind the popular Celtic story motif of the dialogue with the gatekeeper, such as that between Culhwch and Glewlwyd Gafaelfawr—' "Agor y porth." "Nac agoraf." . . .'—and the closely related 9th- or 10th-cent. poem 'Pa ŵr yw'r Porthor?' (*LlDC* no.31). See R. Bromwich and D. S. Evans (eds.), *Culhwch and Olwen*, pp. xxxiv–xxxvi, 4 ff.; Brynley F. Roberts, 'Rhai o Gerddi Ymddiddan Llyfr Du Caerfyrddin', in *Astudiaethau ar yr Hengerdd*, 296 ff. In the poem the naming of Arthur's companions is a condition of entry, just as the wassailers must solve riddles or face other difficulties before being admitted into the house.
[37] *Gwaith Dafydd ab Edmwnd*, I.40, 16; IV and XXXVII are also love-serenades.
[38] Gilbert Ruddock, 'Rhai Agweddau ar Ganu Serch y Bymthegfed Ganrif', in *DGChSOC* 108.

the word 'cardod' ('alms') is perhaps used ironically, suggesting the
marked similarities which exist between the love-serenade and the
popular begging songs.

Among the pieces of doubtful authenticity printed by Thomas
Parry in his edition of the poetry of Dafydd ap Gwilym is a curious
dialogue poem of uncertain age and imperfect *cynghanedd*, which in
the early seventeenth-century manuscript in which it is preserved
bears the heading 'Yr ymddiddan rhwng Dafydd ap Gwilim ar wrach
am y modd y gwneir y blawd keirch', 'the dialogue between Dafydd
ap Gwilym and the witch about how to make oatmeal'. The opening *englyn*, in which the poet asks a girl for admittance into her
house, is presumably part of a love-serenade:

> Agor y ddor er kariad / ar Vair
> yfory ir af im gwlad
> yma ydd wyf ynn ymddifad
> ys da air dan blas dy dad.
> (*GDG*, p. 420)

(Open the door for the love of Mary, tomorrow I go to my [own] land. Here
I stand, destitute—a true word—beneath your father's house.)

In the remaining stanzas, however, the girl is forgotten (which suggests that the *englyn* may have stood alone at some stage, whoever
its author may have been), and an old hag refuses entry until the poet
has answered a kind of enigma concerning the baking of bread,
which he proceeds to solve. These stanzas would appear to be related
to the request in the opening line that the door be opened 'for the
love of Mary', since they clearly belong to the same tradition as the
enigmas and riddles which the wassailers must answer in a number
of the songs in Richard Morris's collection.[39]

Several of the manuscript's Candlemas songs reflect the custom of
placing a young girl in a chair in the middle of the room once the
wassailers had been admitted. The girl represented the Virgin, and a
so-called 'carol cadair' would be sung in her honour. The ceremo-
nial wassail bowl, which sometimes had lighted candles around its
rim, would be presented to her, and after she had drunk from it the
wassailing party would sing while carrying the vessel around the

---

[39] *LlRMG* 8–9, 12–14, 37–8, 100–2, 149–51, 152–3. For the part which such riddles
(*dychmygion*), along with feats of memory and cumulative *canu gorchest*, played in
the singing contests of the wassailing tradition see Meredydd Evans, 'Y Canu Gwasael
. . .', 216 ff., where some English parallels are cited; cf. *LlRMG* pp. lxxxvi ff.

chair, each member in turn drinking to the maiden's health.[40] It is likely that the ritual drinking would originally have formed part of a fertility rite—the festival, celebrated on 2 February, was also known as 'Gŵyl Fair Forwyn ddechre gwanwyn', 'the festival of the Virgin Mary at the beginning of spring'. It seems, in fact, that the *carolau gwirod Mair* are an example of the way in which the Church had taken over earlier pagan festivals, in this case the Festival of Light, celebrated at the beginning of February half-way through the six winter months, which would account for the emphasis on celebration and drink, and also on light, in many of these songs. It is possible that the words 'myn goleuad Crist', 'by the light of Christ', in *GDG* 132.4 ('Cyfeddach')—comparable, for instance, with the epithet 'Tad y Goleuni', 'Father of the Light', in one of the Candlemas songs[41]—would have had a special connotation, since the *cywydd* is a curious hybrid of drinking-song and love-poem, in which a girl is regaled in a tavern with an endless supply of wine. It is at least worth considering whether Dafydd's audience might have been aware of a parallel here with Candlemas folk-customs,[42] and possibly with songs which reflected these customs, particularly if the *cywydd* was performed at this time of year. The words 'Petem Ddyw Pasg yng Ngasgwyn' (l. 11), 'were we in Gascony on Easter Day', imply that it may indeed have been composed during the Easter period, when, according to the later evidence, similar customs were practised. One of these customs involved the placing of a special crown on a young girl's head, upon which would be laid three cups of 'bragget' with lighted candles between them. The wassailers must then attempt to drink from the crown without burning themselves.[43] In Dafydd ab Edmwnd's description of a girl's hair:

> mae dros i iad yn gadair
> lliw mil o ganwyllav mair

(The colour of a thousand marigolds forms a cluster upon her head.)

[40] See Rhiannon Ifans's chapter 'Mair a'i haur Gadair', in *Sêrs a Rybana*, 150–88; she remarks (p. 168) that before the end of the 14th cent. the Virgin was rarely portrayed standing up.

[41] Ibid. 183; cf. 'Agorwch chwi y drws cavad | fal dyma Fair ai golevad' (*LlRMG* p. lxvi), and ibid., pp. lxvii–lxviii, lxxi.

[42] Cf. Gruffudd Llwyd's fabliau-style *cywydd*, where the widow questions the poet who has appeared beneath her window about her dead husband: 'A fyn roi diod o fedd,|Neu roi rhan, cusan be caid, | O win er lles i'w enaid?' (*CIGE* XLVIII.44–6). The drinking-song as a genre, as found, for instance, in medieval Latin goliardic poetry, is poorly attested in Wales; see *LlRMG* pp. xliv ff. where it is argued that it does not really belong to the realms of folk-poetry.

[43] Rhiannon Ifans, *Sêrs a Rybana*, 175.

while the primary meaning of 'canwyllau Mair' is 'marigold', the association of 'Mary's candles' with the girl's head, and also the use of the word 'cadair' ('chair'), are certainly suggestive.[44]

A final early reference to wassailing traditions is found in the poem from the Red Book of Hergest by Iocyn Ddu fab Ithel Grach:

> Goruwch Clawdd Offa da y digonais,
> Goris Aberryw dryw a drewais,
> Dyrnawd graen â maen, y mae'n glais—a chlwyf,
> Ni wn nas lladdwyf neu a'i lleddais.
>
> (BBBGDd 70.17–20)

(Above Offa's Dyke I acted valiantly, beneath Aberryw I struck a wren, a grim blow with a stone, it is bruised and wounded—I know not whether I might kill it or whether I have killed it.)

Here is an unmistakable reference to the once-widespread custom of the hunting of the wren.[45] The mention of 'diw Ystwyll' (Epiphany) further in the poem is consistent with the Welsh evidence concerning the custom from the seventeenth century onwards. Iocyn's humorous account of the hunt is paralleled in the later folk-songs, according to which the wassailers used stones and sticks to kill the wren—often, like Iocyn, it appears, with great difficulty—before parading the dead bird from house to house in a wooden 'coffin' decked with ribbons. Since there are references in the poem to Iocyn's sexual exploits, it is noteworthy that the killing of the wren, 'king of the birds', was meant to symbolize a sacrificial killing for the sake of the fertility of the neighbourhood, as is reflected in the fact that the wassailers would always visit newly married couples.

If wassailing songs were sung in medieval Wales then the Cywyddwyr would have had every opportunity to become acquainted with them. In her article 'Y Canu Gwaseila a'r

---

[44] Gwaith Dafydd ab Edmwnd, XXII.37–8. It is possible too that in his sérénade already cited there is a play on words alluding to the custom of encircling the maiden's chair: 'digon kayad yw dogylch | dyn dec wyd nawdd duw[n] dygylch' (I.39–40). With his request for a kiss in the next couplet compare the carol gwirod in LlRMG 179 : 'Mae yn weddus cin cychwun roi cusan ir forwun | rhag ofn im bun achwun . . .' (The word 'cylch' (meaning 'circuit') also occurs in 'Cyfeddach' (GDG 132.25)).

[45] See Rhiannon Ifans's chapter 'Hela'r Dryw Bach', in Sêrs a Rybana, 136–49, also 228–32. Brian O Cuív suggests that some such custom was current in medieval Ireland ('Some Gaelic Traditions about the Wren', Éigse, 18 (1980–1), 48, 53). On its ancient origins see E. A. Armstrong, The Folklore of Birds (London, 1958), 161–6. For a fuller discussion of this stanza see H. M. Edwards, ' "Rhodiwr fydd clerwr": Sylwadau ar Gerdd Ymffrost o'r Bedwaredd Ganrif ar Ddeg', Y Traethodydd (Jan. 1994), 53–4.

Gyfundrefn Farddol', among the parallels which Rhiannon Ifans draws between the wassailers and the professional poets is that they were both active over roughly the same holiday periods, they both travelled from household to household seeking reward for their songs, laying great emphasis on the provision of food and drink and satirizing the ungenerous, and that they both performed on the occasion of a marriage.[46] She also touches on another, more directly relevant parallel concerning the *sérénade* convention—the element of obstruction provided by the locked door and inclement weather as the wassailers and *Cywyddwyr* alike request the company of a young girl. The serenaders' complaints of the cold, rain and snow are paralleled in the *canu tan bared* in phrases such as 'ymron rhynnu', 'yn rhynnu yn yr eira', and 'ymron sythu'.[47] The wassailers are heard addressing the women of the household, and the exclusively male parties frequently seek the company of a young maiden (who, in the 'gwirod Mair' carols, represents the Virgin):

> agor y drws fy rhien feindlws
> a gollwng fi ir tu rwi ymron rhynnu.[48]

(Open the door, my fair slender maiden, and let me in—I'm about to freeze.)

The connection with love-poetry is unmistakable here, as it is in conventional descriptions of the maiden as 'fy rhien feindlws ara', 'lodes lan', 'maen [sic] i hael', 'fine-browed girl', and the like, and in one song 'tyrd. . . i agori i mi o gariad', 'come and open to me for love', is the wassailer's request.[49] The song referred to earlier, with its mention of 'holin', is a curious blending of a love-song and *carol gwirod*, and the following lines are from a seventeenth-century Christmas carol, in which the wassailers request candles and a blazing fire and cups of beer . . .

> . . . A chael llances o liw'r gwawn/ Yn llawen iawn i'w llenwi
> Nad âi yn sarrug yn y man/ Er gofyn cusan iddi. . .

---

[46] *YB* 15 (1988), 142–73. She draws attention too to the May-day customs reflected in *GDG*, and to Gruffudd ab Adda's *cywydd* to the birch which became a maypole at Llanidloes (*DGG* LXV).

[47] *LlRMG* 185, 112, 9. With the colloquial phrase 'ymron sythu' compare 'Sythais gymaint a seithawr' from the humorous *sérénade*, *BDG* XCVI.12.

[48] *LlRMG* 87; cf. 'Filles, femmes, qui dormez | Nous prions d'vous réveiller' (C. B. Lewis, 'The "Aguilaneuf" and "Trimazo" Begging Songs . . .', 319).

[49] *LlRMG* 178, 11, 173; 9.

Egorwch, na rusiwch,/ Ertolwg! feinir ferch,
Ni fedra i mo'r canu,/ Rwyf fi wedi synnu o'i serch[50]

(. . . and to have a maiden fair as gossamer to fill them merrily, one who would not suddenly turn sour having been asked for a kiss. . . Open up, be not afraid, I prithee, slender maid, I cannot sing [any longer]—I am smitten with her love.)

Although the themes and language of love-poetry in these folk-songs almost certainly owe something to the influence of the love-serenade upon them, it may be suggested that if the *sérénade* did not actually grow out of earlier prototypes of such begging songs, which are the common inheritance of Western Europe, it may at least have been influenced by them at an early stage. It does seem likely that Dafydd ap Gwilym was familiar with the Continental version of the *sérénade*, either directly—from the *Roman de la Rose* or from lost French verse—or indirectly, through English or through the verse of the *Clêr*. (With regard to the latter, however, we should bear in mind that although the free-metre poets make several references to the custom of wooing 'dan y pared',[51] surprisingly few love-serenades have been preserved from the early *canu rhydd* period.)[52] But if the *carolau tan bared* were indeed part of the sub-literary culture of medieval Wales, any external influence would surely have been modified by the poets' knowledge of these songs, and thus been given a distinctly native flavour. Any affinity it may have had with a popular wassailing tradition and its accompanying songs can only have enriched the cultural context and irony of a *cywydd* such as Dafydd's 'Dan y Bargod'.

The element of obstruction in these folk-songs is not confined to the familiar motifs of the locked door and harsh weather. Rhiannon Ifans touches on a further parallel with the *cywydd* tradition, drawing an analogy between the *Cywyddwyr*'s humorous treatment of the theme of the difficult journey and the wassailers' self-mocking, often

[50] *Sêrs a Rybana*, 75. The 'love' element is again paralleled in the French begging songs; cf. C. B. Lewis, 'The "Aguilaneuf" and "Trimazo" Begging Songs . . .', 320–1.
[51] Cf. *CRhC* 14.9; 26.13; 42.14; 58.87; p. 252.
[52] Some of the *hen benillion* which reflect the genre, such as the well-known 'Titrwm, tatrwm, Gwen lliw'r wy' (composed in the old *awdl-gywydd* metre), may belong to the 16th or 17th cents. (*HB* 451–61). *CRhC* 14 is a kind of narrative serenade in which the poet sends the girl's servant to wake her but receives a cold welcome. The popular motif of the maid features in Madog Benfras's fabliau-type 'Cywydd yr Halaenwr' (*DGG* LXIX), and in the *sérénade*-type *cywyddau BDG* XCVI, CXXXI and *CIGE* XLVIII, which all include dialogue.

burlesque accounts of their wanderings from house to house.[53] Given
the ancient origins of many of the wassailing traditions it is quite
likely, as she suggests, that the use of this widespread motif in the folk-
songs has its roots in pagan mythology reflecting the journey from life
to death. The merry wassailers would no doubt have been unaware of
any such significance, as they sought to gain the sympathy of those
inside the house by complaining in their *carolau gwirod* of the extreme
hardship of their journey across hills and valleys and rivers on a cold
winter night, and of the misfortunes which befell them, often caused
by drunkenness—the effects of the hallowed 'gwirod Mair' itself.[54] If
such songs were popular in the Middle Ages they may have had a
bearing on some of Dafydd ap Gwilym's *cywyddau rhwystr*, in which
he presents himself in the familiar role of the frustrated lover. The 'difficult journey' motif is reflected most notably in GDG 65 ('Y Fiaren'),
GDG 68 ('Y Niwl'), GDG 71 ('Y Don ar Afon Dyfi'), and GDG 127
('Y Pwll Mawn'), and GDG 83 ('Taith i Garu') may also be compared,
an account of a tiring journey to meet Morfudd across the hills and
rivers of Dafydd's native area through wind, rain, and snow. In lines
which recall Dafydd's plea to the swollen River Dyfi the theme is paralleled by Llywelyn Goch, who decides to stay with his two nephews
until the summer since the snow prevents him from crossing the Dyfi
to Ceredigion in the south (DGG LXXXV.29–34).[55] It is Dafydd's
humorous depiction of his journeys which is most reminiscent of the
carolau gwirod. There are, however, a couple of more precise parallels in the *cywyddau* which, although probably no more than mere
coincidence, may conceivably bear some relation to folk tradition. The
briar which ensnares Dafydd, inviting a cascade of virulent *dyfalu*, is
a common hindrance in the *canu gwasail*:

> mae nghydymeth wrth y nghefn
> nid gwell i drefn na mine
> wedi ir mieri gripio i draed
> a thynnu i waed yn bipra [56]

---

[53] 'Y Canu Gwaseila a'r Gyfundrefn Farddol', 160–2.

[54] Cf. *LlRMG* 11, 102–3, 108, 118, 170, 174–5, 177–8.

[55] Further instances of the crossing of rivers in the poetry of DG and his contemporaries are cited by D. J. Bowen, 'Nodiadau ar Waith y Cywyddwyr', *BBCS* 25
(1972), 24–5; as he suggests, it seems to be yet another of those common themes which
characterize the early *cywyddau* (see *GDG*[1], pp. xcviii–ix). This should be borne in
mind with regard to Rachel Bromwich's nevertheless interesting suggestion that 'Y
Don ar Afon Dyfi' is influenced by Ovid's *Amores*, III.6 (*APDG* 72).

[56] *LlRMG* 170; cf. 174, 177.

(My companion is just behind, in no better state than I, since the brambles scratched his feet and caused his blood to flow.)

And the peat-bog into which Dafydd and his horse fall on a dark night in unfamiliar territory may be compared with the wassailers' watery ditches:

> roedd hi yn dowull Iawn dros ben
> wrth glawdd y nhalcen trewis
> ag a syrthis yn y ffos
> ag eithim dros y ngwregis
>
> ag ar i waelod mi rown dro
> dan ymgribo ar dorlan
> wedi gwlychu yn wlub gin ddwr
> yn siwr mi ddoethim allan [57]

(It was very dark indeed; I struck my head against a hedge and fell into the ditch right up to my waist.

And in its depths I twisted, clambering up on to the bank; soaked to the skin I came out safely.)

Dafydd often associates the subjects of his *cywyddau rhwystr* with the dark world of Annwfn and its legendary king, Gwyn ap Nudd. The peat-bog, for instance, is 'Pysgodlyn i Wyn . . . | Fab Nudd . . .', 'a fish-pond for Gwyn ap Nudd', and 'Plas yr ellyllon a'u plant', 'the place of fiends and their children' (*GDG* 127.29–30, 32), and the mist is described as 'Tyrau . . . | Tylwyth Gwyn . . .', 'the towers of the family of Gwyn', and 'Ennaint gwrachïod Annwn', 'ointment of the witches of Annwfn' (*GDG* 68.31–2, 44).[58] This may be compared with the later *cywyddau* which reflect the 'difficult journey' motif, in which the poets tell how they lost their way and encountered the king of Annwfn or his fairy-people, 'y tylwyth teg'.[59] In the

[57] *LlRMG* 177; cf. 170, 174.

[58] See Eurys Rowlands, 'Cyfeiriadau Dafydd ap Gwilym at Annwn', *LlC* 5 (1958–9), 122–35, and Ch. 2 above, p. 63. Cf. 'Mwg ellylldân o Annwn', 'Hir barthlwyth y Tylwyth Teg', and similar allusions in another *cywydd* to the mist, the 'apocryphal' *DGG* XXXIX, which is partly an imitation of *GDG* 68. The theme could have been suggested to DG by the 'enchanted mist' episode in the romance of Geraint fab Erbin (R. M. Jones, *Llyfr Gwyn Rhydderch: y chwedlau a'r rhamantau* (Cardiff, 1973), cols. 448 ff.), of which his 'Cae nïwl hir feddwl' (*GDG* 109.14) is probably a conscious echo (cf. *APDG* 136). Magic mist is a common motif in Celtic folklore. *GDG* 68 finds a partial parallel in an 18th-cent. Irish poem in which the poet meets a beautiful fairy-girl after wandering through a magic mist (S. Ó Tuama and T. Kinsella, *An Duanaire 1600–1900: Poems of the Dispossessed* (Mountrath, 1981), no. 59). The mist motif appears too in a Scottish Gaelic love-poem cited in *Carmina Gadelica*, ii. 325; cf. also ibid. 232–4.

[59] See Brynley F. Roberts, 'Gwyn ap Nudd', *LlC* 13 (1980–1), 284–5.

'apocryphal' 'Cywydd y Sêr' (*DGG* XL), probably composed in the fourteenth century, the poet describes in some detail his arduous journey across the mountains and marshland of Gwynedd to meet his beloved in Anglesey at dawn. He, too, comes to a certain 'dinas ellyllon', 'fiends' stronghold' (ll. 21–2), and later feels it necessary to make the sign of the cross.[60] The motif, which is reflected in at least one of the wassail songs, in which one of the hindrances to be overcome is a fight with ghosts,[61] could have been familiar to Dafydd ap Gwilym and his contemporaries in earlier popular verse which gave humorous accounts of the difficult journey.

The best-known of Dafydd's *cywyddau rhwystr*, GDG 124 ('Trafferth mewn Tafarn'), invites yet another comparison between the *Cywyddwyr* and the wassailing tradition. Here, the bungling poet is impeded by various items of furniture in his attempt to reach a girl's bed at an inn, causing the dogs to bark and waking the ostler who rouses the other guests. The theme bears an intriguing resemblance to that of a sixteenth-century song with the heading 'karol/i/yru rhai oddidan y pared./a fytho yn kanu/' ('a carol to send away those who sing under the eaves'), in which the householder, unimpressed by the wassailers' bad singing, warns that if any of them should enter they will encounter all kinds of daunting impediments:

> Y kynta honoch /i/ mewn a ddel./
> rhaid iddo fo ochel llithro./
> ond e fo syrthif ar /i/ drwyn./
> lle /i/ darfu ir forwyn bisso./
>
> pan elloch /i/ ben vcha/r tu/
> Mae yno gi yn y lludw./
> ef a mafel yn ych ffer./
> dyna /i/ chwi arfer hwnw./[62]

(Whichever one of you comes in first, he must be careful not to slip, otherwise he'll fall nose first where the maid has pissed.

When you reach the far end of the house, there is a dog in the ashes, and he will seize you by the ankle—to that he's well accustomed.)

---

[60] Cf. *DGG* XXXIX, one of the poems to the mist, where the poet comes to a hell-like marsh, 'Lle'r ydoedd ymhob gobant | Ellyllon mingeimion gant' (ll. 49–50); also 'Cywydd y Celffaint' by the 14th-cent. poet Ithel Ddu (*BBBGDd* 69), in which he and his servant, while returning to Gwynedd from the south, are frightened by rotten oak-stumps which they mistake for mounted soldiers.

[61] See Rhiannon Ifans, *Sêrs a Rybana*, 64.

[62] *DCRh* 225; this is the song referred to in n. 31 above.

The remaining eleven stanzas list still more unpleasant and danger-
ous objects which lie in wait in the house and its garden, such as a
washboard, a beehive, a spade, a scythe, and a mallet. In another
'answering song' (*LLRMG* 5) a man warns the singers to stay away
on account of his intimidating wife and ferocious cat! More closely
analogous with 'Trafferth mewn Tafarn' is a free-metre poem entitled 'Cerdd y Carwr Trwstan' ('The Poem of the Clumsy Lover'), in
which the lover, like Dafydd, arranges to meet his girl under cover
of night, and with similar consequences:

> . . . Mynd at ddrws fy nghangen eurfrig,
> Roedd y Sarn yn anian lithrig,
> A mine a'm Sgidie heb eu Clytio,
> Clamp o gwymp a gefais yno.
>
> Codi i fynu yn lledfeddod
> A minne a'm Talcen ar y Rhiniog,
> Gwthio'r drws yn ddwys a'm hysgwydd,
> A hwnnw'n gwichian fel Ceiliagwydd.
>
> A chan ddwysed roeddwn yn gwthio,
> Roedd y cŵn i gyd mewn cyffro,
> O fy nghwmpas yn fy mrathu;
> Syrthiais ar fy mhen mewn Brecci.
>
> Mi fum yno yn yslotian
> Yn hir iawn mewn Brecci a Succan,
> Gwn na wydde Drî mo'm hanes,
> Mewn twr o ludw Mawn mi syrthiais . . .[63]

(I approached the door of my fair-haired sweetheart—the path was ever-so
slippery; since my shoes had not been mended I took a very nasty fall.

Up I got, stunned, my forehead on the threshold; I shoved my shoulder
heavily against the door, which squeaked like a gander.

So heavily was I shoving that the dogs were in uproar all around, snap-
ping at me, and I fell head first into soaking malt.

There I was for a good while quaffing malt and gruel; no one (?), I know,
knew what had befallen me—I tumbled into a pile of peat ash.)

While the poem seems to betray the author's familiarity with
'Trafferth mewn Tafarn', and perhaps with other *cywyddau* composed in the fabliau mode, it also clearly has a certain affinity with

---

[63] Cited in *LlRMG* p. cxv. According to a note in the MS seven of the remaining
stanzas were added to 'the old song' by Richard Morris in 1736; these are similarly
reminiscent of the fabliau-type *cywyddau*, the lover receiving a clubbing from the man
of the house who believes him to be a thief.

the humorous 'answering song' cited above, and may therefore have been inspired in part by one of the conventions of the wassailing tradition. It is noteworthy that the same theme was known in Ireland, judging by a popular poem in which a girl lists to her lover a number of obstructions which will not be in his way when he visits her home; and here, in contrast to the Welsh poems, the dog will remain silent.[64] It was probably Dafydd ap Gwilym who introduced the theme of the physical hindrances and that of the difficult journey into the *cywydd serch*. Whether or not these had already been incorporated into love-poetry in the verse of the *Clêr* we shall never know. Dafydd's other *cywyddau rhwystr*, however, in which a love-tryst is unexpectedly disturbed by a particular object or creature, have no obvious affinity with popular tradition. Poems such as GDG 61 ('Y Cyffylog'), GDG 66 ('Y Cloc') (where it is an erotic dream which is interrupted, rather than a tryst), GDG 125 ('Y Rhugl Groen'), and GDG 130 ('Y Garreg Ateb'), find no significant parallels in the *canu rhydd*.[65] Even the later *Cywyddwyr*, few as they are, who composed on this theme seem to have been imitating the master to some degree.[66] One is thus inclined to suspect that this particular type of *cywydd rhwystr* is very largely a product of Dafydd's own fertile imagination, yet another vehicle for his portrayal of the frustrated lover.

The early *Cywyddwyr*'s debt to the popular culture of their time is graphically illustrated in the poems by Dafydd ap Gwilym (GDG 50) and Iolo Goch (GIG XXVI) which are based on the game known as 'Cnau i'm llaw' ('Nuts in my hand'). The purpose of the game, which has been discussed in detail elsewhere,[67] was to determine whether or not one of the players was loved. An odd number of nuts in his (or her) partner's hand was, it appears, considered a good

[64] *An Duanaire*, no. 83.

[65] To my knowledge, the only pieces which are remotely similar to DG's theme are the *hen benillion* HB 667 and 668, the first of which reads: 'Dau lanc ifanc aeth i garu, | Gyda'r afon ar i fyny, | Un â'i wn a'r llall â'i gledde,— | Cysgod bedwen 'trodd hwy adre.'

[66] Cf. DGG XLVII ('Cywydd y Daran' by Maredudd ap Rhys) and BDG CLIX ('Cywydd y Dylluan' by Robin Leia), both of which, inevitably, are also attributed to DG, and see Eurys Rowlands's remarks in 'Canu Serch 1450–1525', BBCS 31 (1984), 38–9.

[67] D. Machreth Ellis, 'Chwarae "Cnau Mewn Llaw" a Rhai Chwaraeon Eraill', LlC 5 (1959), 185–92; see also GDG, pp. 485–6, 557, and GIG, p. 329. The only other *cywydd* which is based on the game is CIGE LXXVI by Ieuan ap Rhydderch (*fl.* c.1430–70), who was clearly familiar with Dafydd's poem.

omen, not unlike the well-known child's game 'She loves me—she loves me not' which is commonly played with daisies. The two poets' descriptions of the game itself, which clearly followed a fixed formula, have much in common, but their development of the theme could not be less alike. Dafydd, having played successfully, goes on to lavish praise on the portents of the girl's love by means of *dyfalu*. Iolo, however, takes no part in the game since it was he who sent the nuts to Eiddig and his wife, and, with vivid use of direct speech, he tells of the argument which ensues, satirizing the jealous husband who, as in many a fabliau, threatens to beat his wife with a stick. Dafydd's 'crefydd ni'n cred' ('men of religion do not believe us'), and his ironic reference to 'gwarae gau' ('a false game') (*GDG* 50.41, 15), suggest that the custom would have been among the many popular superstitions condemned by the Church. If we are to believe Iolo Morganwg, versions of the game were still popular in Glamorgan in the eighteenth century, though he makes no mention of love.[68] It is therefore somewhat surprising that no folk-songs appear to have survived based on the custom, whose slick, memorable, question-and-answer formula, as it appears in the *cywyddau*, would seem to lend itself to expression in simple folk-rhymes. The traditional association of nuts with fertility and their well-known sexual symbolism, implicit in the *cywyddau*, are, however, much in evidence in the *canu rhydd*, where the familiar euphemism 'hela cnau' or 'cneua' (nut-gathering) appears, for instance, in the lines:

> llanckess heinist a wencha
> myned yn vynych y gneya
> (*CRhC* 62.125–6)

(A lusty lass desires to go gathering nuts often),

or in the *pennill telyn*:

> F'anwylyd, lliw'r can gwenith,
> 'Ddoi di i gneua i'r Gelli Lefrith,
> Lle mae'r adar bach yn pyncio,
> A phob cneuen yn gwisgïo?
> (*HB* 496)

---

[68] One of his descriptions reads: 'Cnau mewn llaw—i'm dwrn y daw—pa sawl un? | Tair—pedair &c. &c. a'r colledydd yn Talu'r pwyth. | Talwch y pwyth, medd yr ennillwr.' (D. Machreth Ellis, 'Chwarae "Cnau Mewn Llaw" . . .', 186). 'Talu'r pwyth', by which is meant that a player must pay the difference if he guessed incorrectly, may have been a traditional element in the game, or else Iolo could have derived it from *GDG* 50.55–8: 'Minnau fy hun o'm lluniaeth | O gnau . . . | I'w glwysbryd . . . | A dalaf bwyth ffrwyth y ffridd.'

(My darling, white as wheat flour, will you come nutting to Gelli Lefrith, where the little birds are singing, and every nut falling ripe from its husk?)

But the only clear reflection of the 'chwarae cnau' of which I am aware in free-metre verse occurs in a sixteenth-century love-carol by Richard Hughes:

> Ir glas lwyni kyll tan irddail
> llei mae/r/ knau yn brigdrymu/r/ gwiail
> tyrd a hel or knau gweskia
> a chadw dair heb dori/n/ gyfa.
>   (CRhC 1, I.57–60)

(To the green hazel groves, under lush foliage, where the nuts weigh down the twigs, come and gather from the ripest nuts, and keep three unbroken, whole.)

The girl is asked to keep three nuts—the 'amnifer' or odd number of the *Cywyddwyr* (Dafydd does not specify the number, but Iolo speaks of nine nuts, and in the fifteenth-century 'chwarae cnau' *cywydd* by Ieuan ap Rhydderch the number is seven). As in *GDG* 50 the hazelnuts signify the promise of a love-tryst, and a pun is no doubt intended in the final line—'a chadw d'air. . .', 'keep your promise without breaking it'. 'A chadw. . .' reminds one of the formula 'gad yna. . .' which is used by all three *cywyddwyr* to state the required number of nuts, and the words 'heb dorri'n gyfa' may also be compared with Dafydd's assurance that the nuts shall not be broken by teeth or stones (ll. 51–4). Could this have been another of the conventions of the 'chwarae cnau' or of the more widespread folklore to which the custom is related?

Though we cannot be certain that the *Cywyddwyr* would have had knowledge of any folk-rhymes deriving from the custom, Iolo Goch's poem does contain a passage which seems clearly to reflect the idiom of popular verse. This is how Eiddig accuses his wife of having been with the poet:

> Fo a'th welad nos Ŵyl Fair,
> Ti ac ef, mewn tŷ a gwair,
> Ac a'th welad nos Ynyd,
> Ti ac ef, mewn tŷ ac ŷd.[69]
>   (GIG XXVI.29–32)

---

[69] Cf. the lines 'Gwyl y Grog i gil y gwrych' and 'Gwr a bolld dan gẁr y berth' in the 'apocryphal' *BDG* CCX.40, 44, the dialogue with the cuckoo discussed in Ch. 4 above. Note that the first and third lines cited from *GIG* XXVI lack *cynghanedd*,

(You were seen on St Mary's eve, you and he, in a barn with hay, and you were seen on Shrove eve, you and he, in a barn with corn.)

Similar use of incremental repetition with variations is, as one might expect, common in the *canu rhydd*, as, for instance, in the peculiar early free-metre poem 'Ow ow tlyse', which ends:

> Ar gwr yn y brwyn ar gwr yn y llwyn ar gwr yn y ros
> Ar gwr echnos ar gwr gynne yn y llwyn llysie
> Tilyli: a thilili, Tilyli fabli.[70]
>
> (CRhC 2, VII.19–21)

(And the man in the rushes and the man in the bush, and the man on the moor, and the man the night before last, and the man just now in the vegetable patch—*Tilyli . . .*)

The device is especially favoured by the authors of those simple *traethodlau* relating a story which are falsely attributed to Dafydd ap Gwilym. The following is a typical passage from the '*Traethodl* of the Ant and the Grasshopper':

> Dyw-c'langauaf, y bore
> Fe a droes y gwynt o'i le,
> I odi, ac i luchio,
> Oddiar lechwedd Moel Eilio,
> I luchio, ac i odi,
> Oddiar ystlys Eryri.[71]
>
> (BDG CXCII.9–14)

(On the morning of All Saints' Day the wind changed its course, so that the snow fell and drifted from the face of Moel Eilio, drifted and fell from the side of Snowdon.)

This almost conversational style of composition clearly belongs to the same world as the words which Iolo Goch puts into the mouth of Eiddig, words which I believe to be particularly suggestive of the influence of contemporary popular verse on early *cywydd* poetry.

GDG 87 ('Hwsmonaeth Cariad') shows Dafydd ap Gwilym at his masterful best, conveying intense emotion through an extended

---

although the *cywydd* contains as many as fourteen such lines, nearly all of which are the first lines of couplets (a feature of some other 14th-cent. *cywyddau*).

[70] The poem probably belongs to the mid-16th-cent. Anglesey poet Llywelyn ap Hwlcyn, who uses a similar device in CRhC 2, IV.19–22. Cf. also CLlC, vol. III, no. XII, and *Cerddi Rhydd Cynnar*, no. 80 (a carol gwirod).

[71] Cf. ll. 43–52; BDG CLXXXI.25–8, CLXXXV.29–32, CLVIII.47–50 (a *cywydd* often lacking *cynghanedd*).

image which is sustained throughout the poem. In January he
ploughs the field of his own bosom[72] and then plants the seeds of
love, which during the three spring months take root and cause him
great anxiety. On May Day he encloses the crop, and while
Morfudd's love thrives and ripens within him he prepares for the
harvest—but all to no avail: a violent storm arrives from the west
and all the wheat is lost, drowned by Dafydd's tears. It was Chotzen
who first drew attention to an analogous husbandry image in the
Roman de la Rose:[73]

> Je resemble le païsant
> Qui gete en terre sa semence
> Et a joie quant el commence
> A estre bele et drue en herbe;
> Mes avant qu'il en coille gerbe,
> L'empire, tel hore est, et grieve
> Une male niele qui lieve
> Quant li espi doivent florir,
> Si fait le grain dedens morir,
> Et l'esperance au vilain tost,
> Qu'il avoit eüe trop tost.
>
> (ll. 3,960–70)

(I am like the peasant who casts his seed on the earth and rejoices when it
begins to be fair and thick when it is in the blade; but before he collects a
sheaf of it, the weather worsens and an evil cloud arises at the time when
the ears should sprout and damages it by making the seed die within and
robs the wretch of the hope that he had had too soon.)

Rachel Bromwich has remarked that Dafydd's image 'is so closely
paralleled in the work of Guillaume de Lorris that I find it impres-
sive as evidence for his actual knowledge of the French poem'.[74]
Once more, in view of other possible indications of Dafydd's knowledge of the *Roman* the resemblance is indeed suggestive, though it

---

[72] Compare the rather different 'ploughman' image of *GDG* 93.17–26 and the erotic
metaphor of *GDG* 79.12, and also that of sowing the seed of love which becomes a
'crop of anguish' (*GDG* 102.5–7). The metaphor of love as a seed which takes root
and grows in the poet's heart is fairly common in French; as in *GDG* 102, the image
may be brief—cf. S. N. Rosenberg and H. Tischler (eds.), *Chanter m'estuet: Songs of
the Trouvères* (London, 1981), 39.43–6—or it may become a significant extended
metaphor, cf. Chichmaref (ed.), *Poésies lyriques de Guillaume de Machaut*, ii. 364
(XI.67–80).

[73] *Recherches*, 331–2; note also Jean de Meun's use of extended 'ploughing'
metaphors to describe love-making, ll. 19,543 ff, 19,709 ff.

[74] *APDG* 74.

extend to the kind of verbal echoes which might betray actual direct imitation. If Dafydd was influenced by this passage it can only have acted as a catalyst for his own, more expansive imagination. He develops the image in far greater detail, internalizing it to correspond to his emotional and psychological state, whereas Guillaume objectively compares the lover with the disappointed peasant. He also makes use of a wealth of technical language, and unlike Guillaume lays great emphasis on the changing seasons, perhaps to correspond to real events. It is, of course, quite possible that the image is Dafydd's own spontaneous creation, perhaps, as has been suggested, inspired by particularly violent storms such as those which are known to have occurred in 1363.[75] Whether or not he was indebted to any precise literary source, such a context would certainly have made the *cywydd* particularly poignant for a contemporary audience. A similar metaphor is found in the 'apocryphal' *cywydd* BDG CC, given by its editors the title 'Arddwriaeth y Bardd' ('The Poet's Husbandry'), a poem which should perhaps be added to our collection of fourteenth-century *cywyddau*.[76] Here is possibly yet another instance of the early *Cywyddwyr*'s liking for composing on similar themes, but although this poet may well have been familiar with Dafydd's poem he shows little sign of imitation. Indeed, he develops his image with considerable originality and wit: to the girl's insistence that she will marry none but a diligent farmer, the poet replies that he is Meirionnydd's foremost husbandman—'Prif hwsmon ar Feirion wyf'[77] (l. 13)—and goes on to equate the composing of love-poetry with ploughing and the preparation of love's harvest. Thus he speaks of 'Aradr o serch anerchion' ('a plough of love-tidings'), 'swch o

[75] See D. J. Bowen's note in *BBCS* 25 (1972), 25–6. Since the image derives from everyday experience it is liable to occur in its basic form in any place at any time. Cf. the *pennill telyn*: 'Medi gwenith yn ei egin | Yw priodi glas fachgennyn, | Wedi ei hau, ei gau, a'i gadw, | Dichon droi'n gynhaeaf garw.' (*HB* 32; cf. 508, 142).

[76] See *GDG*[1], p. clxxiii. It is attributed to DG and Iolo Goch, no doubt due to its similarity to *GDG* 87 and the fact that Iolo has a, albeit very different, *cywydd* to the Ploughman (*GIG* XXVIII). In one MS it is attributed to Gruffudd Hiraethog (cf. D. J. Bowen (ed.), *Gwaith Gruffudd Hiraethog* (Cardiff, 1990), 471), but its language and style clearly are not those of the 16th cent. Although its expression is on the whole relatively unadorned—DG and his contemporaries could compose in this manner when they so wished—some sentences do extend over several couplets and are peppered with *sangiadau* (esp. ll. 31–6, 49–56). The percentage of *cynghanedd Sain* is as high as 36%; the intricate *cynghanedd Sain* of ll. 27 and 47 seem to me to be characteristic of 14th-cent. verse-craft, as is the unusual *Sain gadwynog* of l. 13.

[77] Llywelyn Goch Amheurig Hen is therefore one possible candidate. The reference to Ovid in l. 28 is in keeping with the early *cywyddau serch*.

wawd' ('a ploughshare of praise'), 'Ieuau o amodau mad' ('yokes of fine promises'), 'A thidau cerdd blethedig' ('and chains of woven poetry'), and so forth[78] (ll. 17–26); Ovid's (i.e. the poet's) *llatai* or love-messenger is the shouter ('geilwad'), and the poet himself the farmer ('amaeth') (ll. 27–30). Unlike *GDG* 87, the *cywydd* ends on an optimistic note: once he has reaped the wheat and stored it safely in the barn, the poet hopes to invite the girl to share with him in love's harvest.

In discussing the love-poets' use of the husbandry image we should bear in mind that the art of husbandry, especially the acts of plough-ing and sowing, have timeless erotic connotations. In popular tradi-tion the ploughshare in particular is commonly regarded as a symbol of the male sexual organ, which pierces 'Mother Earth' and makes her fertile.[79] Some of the less pristine free-metre poets used this age-old concept to good effect, as is illustrated by the following extract from an anonymous free-metre poem in which the conventional roles of the girl and poet in the *pastourelle* are comically reversed:

> '*Gwrando ar gwynfan llances landeg*
> *sydd â'i thir yn colli ei adeg,*
> *a minna sydd yn ofni glybwr,*
> *ac yn sicir yn ddiswcwr.*
> *Mae'n ddrwg 'y nghyflwr*
> *o eisie cael at hwn lafurwr.*'
>
> Minna atebais fy mun gryno,
> 'Nid wy' chwaith arfer â llafurio.
> Gwnïo 'ngwŷdd ni fedra' i o'r gore,
> fy mun beredd, hwyr na bore,
> na hwylio ei hwylie
> i hollti'r ddwygwys fel y dyle.'
>
> '*Od oes ond hynny yn dy drwblio*
> *nid rhaid iti fyth mo'r rhusio.*
> *Os yw dy swch mewn chwant i'r cwusa,*

---

[78] For European parallels with this 'allegorical' style of composition see Ch. 6.

[79] Cf. Rhiannon Ifans, *Sêrs a Rybana*, 23 and *passim*; Dafydd Johnston, 'The Erotic Poetry of the *Cywyddwyr*', 74 n. 33, and the references cited there. Improbable though it may seem, it is conceivable that Iolo Goch's *dyfalu* of the plough contains conscious echoes of DG's notorious *cywydd* to his penis: with the unexpected 'Ceiliagwydd erwi gwyddiawn' cf. DG's 'ceiliagwydd | yn cysgu yn ei blu blwydd'; with 'Yn estyn gwddw anystwyth' cf. 'llun asgwrn gwddw gŵydd' (*GIG* XXVIII.47, 60; *CMOC* 1.13–14, 38).

byth nid yngan dan y cynga,
mae ffordd o'r gora,
galw di, mi ddaliaf inna.'

'Mae fy swch, os coeliwch gwengu,
yn un glwydan eto heb g'ledu,
a minna sydd yn llanc diweddar
ei awch dirio at eich daear,
i ymgemio'n gymar,
rhag i chwi hogan chware'n hagar.'

('*Listen to the complaint of a lovely lass whose land is missing its season, and I am afraid of wetness, and indeed I'm without succour. I'm in a bad state in need of a ploughman for this land.*'
I answered my fine maid, 'I'm not used to ploughing either. I can't weave my plough in and out very well, my sweet maid, by night or morning, nor guide its thrusts to part the two sods as it should.'
'*If that's all that's troubling you there's no need at all for you to hesitate. If your ploughshare is inclined to the furrow, it'll make no sound under the burdock, there's a perfectly good way, you call [the oxen], and I'll hold [the plough].*'
'My ploughshare, if you'll believe me sweetheart, is a mere flake which hasn't yet hardened, and I'm a backward lad in desire to thrust towards your earth, to sport with you as a mate, for fear that you play dirty, lass.')[80]

The poem may not be much older than the early eighteenth-century manuscript in which it is recorded, but it is difficult to believe that similar material had not formed part of the repertoires of the popular poets for many centuries. In the 'apocryphal' *cywydd*, while the husbandry image is not overtly erotic, lines such as these surely contain a degree of sexual innuendo:

Braenaru cylch bron eirian,
A chlod teg, ar âr ach lân;
A thynu'n hy fry ar fron,
Cwysau cydweddaidd cyson;
A'm bryd inau i hau had,
A geiriau mwyn o gariad.
(*BDG* CC.37–42)

[80] Ed. and trans. Dafydd Johnston, ibid. 16 (from *LlRMG* 75). It is discussed by Johnston, 'The Erotic Poetry of the *Cywyddwyr*', 74–5, and by E. G. Millward in 'Delweddau'r Canu Gwerin', *Canu Gwerin*, 3 (1980), 13, an article which considers various types of erotic imagery in free-metre verse. For similar examples of the 'ploughing' metaphor in French popular verse see *Chansons des XVe et XVIe siècles*, LXVII, and Tiersot, *Histoire de la chanson populaire en France*, 88.

(Fallowing the curve of the fair breast of a hill on arable land, good and thorough; and boldly ploughing on a hillside yonder regular, well-proportioned furrows; and it is my intention to sow the seed with tender words of love.)

Although Dafydd ap Gwilym's use of the husbandry image is not intended to be in any way sexually suggestive, he may have been familiar with ambiguous and more ribald interpretations of similar imagery in the popular tradition. While bearing in mind that the *cywydd* might easily have been the fruit of his own imagination, I would tentatively suggest that Dafydd had either seen or heard the passage in the *Roman*, and that he, and subsequently another *cywyddwr*, possibly a contemporary, elaborated the image in a highly original manner. But for their application of the husbandry theme to erotic poetry they may also have found a rather less refined precedent in the verse of the *Clêr*.

Another of Dafydd's more significant extended metaphors drawn from the natural world is his portrayal of the hare in *GDG* 46 ('Serch fel Ysgyfarnog'). The first section of the *cywydd* (ll. 1–42), which could easily stand as an independent poem, consists of a well-observed description of the hare's appearance and behaviour, and of its outwitting of hunter and hound. Dafydd then applies the image to his own plight, equating the evasive animal with the girl's love, since it too escapes the 'luckless huntsman' and returns to its lair; and the combination of 'neutral' and pejorative descriptions of the hare, it has been suggested,[81] symbolizes the fickleness and the essential duality of women's love in the poet's experience. Many of the epithets in this *cywydd* have received attention from A. S. C. Ross in his edition and discussion of an English poem which bears the Anglo-Norman heading 'Les nouns de vn leure en engleis'.[82] The poem, which is preserved in a late thirteenth-century hand in a manuscript which by the early fourteenth century was closely associated with Shropshire, opens with a peculiar ritual to be observed on encountering a hare. Whoever should do so should lay down whatever he happened to be carrying . . .

> . . . And blesce him wiþ his helbowe.
> And mid wel goed devosioun
> He shal saien on oreisoun

---

[81] John Rowlands, 'Delweddau Serch Dafydd ap Gwilym', *YB* 2 (1966), 63–5.

[82] 'The Middle English Poem on the Names of a Hare', *Proceedings of the Leeds Philosophical and Literary Society*, vol. 3, Part vi (1935), 347–77.

> In þe worshipe of þe hare;
> þenne mai he wel fare . . .

This 'oreisoun', a list of seventy-seven abusive epithets, forms the central section of the poem, and the closing section ends with a final address to the hare:

> Haue nou godnedai, sire hare!
> God þe lete so wel fare,
> þat þou come to me ded,
> Oþer in ciue [onions], oþer in bred! Amen.[83]

The hare has long been the subject of a great many folk beliefs, one of the most common of which, well attested in Wales and England, is that a hare seen crossing one's path is a bad omen, even a pre-monition of imminent death.[84] It is no doubt a similar superstition which explains the (nevertheless amusing) ritual of the poem. Ross considers the tenour of the poem as a whole to be a product of con-temporary folklore, and he makes the interesting suggestion that

Welsh influence is very clear in the poem. This can be seen both in the gen-eral style and in the names themselves. The poem is in fact written in some-thing very reminiscent of the Welsh *dyfalu* ('epithetical') style . . . This Welsh influence agrees well with the localisation in Shropshire.[85]

He shows that many of the poem's terms of abuse describing the hare display a striking similarity to Dafydd's *cywydd* and to other terms relating to the animal in Welsh tradition: 'wodecat', for instance, he would derive from 'cath y coed', and 'fursecat' from 'cath eithin', and he compares also Dafydd's 'gath ynfyd' and 'cath hirdaith' (ll. 18–19).[86]

Although Welsh influence on the English poem is by no means

---

[83] Ibid. 350–1.

[84] The appearance of a hare could be either a good or a bad omen, according to its colour and movements. See the beliefs noted by Marie Trevelyan, *Folk-lore and Folk-stories of Wales* (London, 1909), 77–8, and Elias Owen, *Welsh Folk-Lore* (Oswestry and Wrexham, 1896), 343–5. Cf. the girl's reaction on seeing the hare in *GDG* 46 var.: 'Ofnodd fod fal y dywod hi | Gwrthwyneb a gwarth inni' (*GDG*, p. 126). For similar beliefs recorded in England see *Folk-Lore*, 64 (1953), 293–4. According to A. H. Krappe there may be 'some connection between the widespread aversion to or avoidance of the hare and the well-nigh universal association of the rodent with the moon' ('Old Celtic Taboos', *Folk-Lore*, 53 (1942), 201).

[85] 'The Middle English Poem on the Names of a Hare', 348.

[86] Ibid. 361; he adds, however, that the use of cat-names for the hare is both very common and very natural.

proven, it is not unlikely that its author knew of similar verse which
was current in thirteenth-century Wales, based on a well-known
stock of popular beliefs. While Dafydd ap Gwilym makes no obvious reference to folk-customs relating to the hare (although his pejorative language and the challenge 'Her, gethinfer gath ynfyd!' (l. 18),
'Shoo! short, ugly, mad cat!', may reflect its association with evil
spirits and with bad luck in general),[87] it may be that his detailed
depiction of the animal is an intricate elaboration of earlier descriptions or, perhaps, simply 'name-calling', in the native oral verse tradition. Hare-coursing, which remained popular into the present
century, was a much-loved sport among the fourteenth-century
nobility. There survives a fairly detailed account of the custom as it
was practised in the time of Twiti, huntsman to King Edward II,[88]
and in the Welsh hunting text 'Y Naw Helwriaeth' (Nine Kinds of
Hunting), compiled in the sixteenth century, hare-coursing is one of
the 'tair helfa ddolef', the 'three clamorous hunts'.[89] Although hunting was essentially an élite-led sport, until the close of the Middle
Ages it was legally accessible to all levels of society.[90] It is noteworthy that in Ulster, for instance, where neighbouring farmers still
gather to go, with the hunt followers, 'in search of a hare' on foot,
each hunt area has its own hunt song.[91] While there is, not surprisingly, no evidence for the existence of popular hunting songs of this

[87] Cf. also 'Gwn dynghedfen lawdrwen lwyd' (l. 12), 'I know the destiny of the
white-hosed grey one'. In light of the epithet 'þe der þat nomon nedar nemnen' (the
animal that no one dare name) (ibid. 351), it may be significant that DG does not mention the hare by its name in GDG 46, unlike his other poems to birds and animals.
(However, GDG 60 begins: 'Ysgyfarnog yng nghartref . . .', though the language here
is not abusive).

[88] The Art of Hunting, ed. B. Danielsson (Stockholm, 1977); see also G. E. H.
Barret-Hamilton, A History of British Mammals (London, 1913), ii. 254 ff. Even for
Chaucer's monk, 'huntyng for the hare | Was al his lust . . .' (Works (ed. Robinson),
p. 19, ll. 191-2). The animal may have been sacred among the Celts (Elias Owen,
Welsh Folk-Lore, 343); especially in central Europe the hare-hunt attained a symbolic
significance, reflected in stone carvings found in churches (C. Roth, 'Folklore of the
Ghetto', Folk-Lore, 59 (1948), 77).

[89] See William Linnard, 'The Nine Huntings: A Re-examination of Y Naw
Helwriaeth', BBCS 31 (1984), 119-32.

[90] Compare the 14th-cent. English poem Gawain, where the great lord hunts a fox,
'And alle the rabel in a res [rush] ryght at his heles' (l. 1,899) shouting abuse at the
animal (Sir Gawain and the Green Knight, ed. R. A. Waldron (London, 1970), ll.
1,690 ff.).

[91] R. Morton (ed.), Folksongs Sung In Ulster (Cork, 1970), 73-4. In pre-industrial
Wales hunting rabbits was a popular pastime on Christmas Day, and fox-hunting on
Boxing Day (Trefor M. Owen, A Pocket Guide: The Customs and Traditions of Wales
(Cardiff, 1991), 67).

kind in medieval Wales, in view of the fact that the hare and related
folklore may have received the attention of Welsh poets as early as
the thirteenth century we cannot ignore the possibility that such
songs would have formed the background for a *cywydd* such as
'Serch fel Ysgyfarnog'. But whether or not this was in fact part of
the poem's contemporary context, Dafydd's complex and meaningful interpretation of the image of the hunt is clearly entirely his own
creation.

GDG 99 ('Pererindod Merch') is one of Dafydd's more light-
hearted love-poems. He fancifully imagines that an unnamed girl (a
nun, according to the opening couplet) must go on a pilgrimage
from Anglesey to St David's in Pembrokeshire as a penance for having killed the lovesick poet, or, as one writer puts it, 'for sinning
against him by not sinning with him'.[92] The poem would no doubt
have been interpreted by a contemporary audience as a witty burlesque of the excesses of courtly love. On another level, the poet's
mock-ritualistic invocations to each of the rivers which the girl must
cross during the course of her journey may be understood as a parody of the popular medieval tradition of protective charms, which
is reflected too in poems by Iolo Goch and Llywelyn Goch, again in
relation to journeys.[93] Gruffudd Gryg's *cywydd* to the wave (DGG
LXXIII) is based on his voyage to the important shrine of Santiago
de Compostela in Northern Spain. There are several later *cywyddau*
which describe the pilgrim's arduous sea voyage from Santiago and
Rome,[94] but to my knowledge GDG 99 and the poem by Gruffudd
Gryg are the only *cywyddau serch* which are based on the idea of a
pilgrimage. There is, however, no lack of evidence concerning the
notorious frivolity and dubious motives of some pilgrims in
medieval Europe.[95] A common theme in thirteenth-century

[92] H. E. Lewis, 'Welsh Catholic Poetry of the Fifteenth Century', THSC (1911–12),
25. GDG 82 seems to reflect a similar context: here DG pleads for his life with a girl
from Anglesey, and both Anglesey and St David's (Mynyw) are mentioned in ll. 33–4.

[93] GIG XVII, BBBGDd 58. See Brynley F. Roberts, 'Rhai Swynion Cymraeg', BBCS
21 (1965), 197–213. The convention of blessing the *llatai* before it sets off on its journey (discussed in Ch. 4 above) may also be compared.

[94] See the 15th-cent. poems cited by G. Hartwell Jones, 'Celtic Britain and the
Pilgrim Movement', Y Cymmrodor, 23 (1912), 255 ff., and Thomas Roberts,
'Cywyddau Pererindod', Y Traethodydd, 99 (1944), 28–39. On pilgrimages in general,
both to domestic and foreign shrines, see Glanmor Williams, The Welsh Church from
Conquest to Reformation (Cardiff, 1962), 265–6, 488–503.

[95] In the Roman de la Rose the Jaloux suspects his wife of making 'noviaus peleri-
nages | Selonc les anciens usages' (ll. 9,351–2); for further references see Recherches,
119–20 n. 6.

Portuguese poetry is that of the young girl who uses the pilgrimage as a pretext for meeting her lover, against her mother's will. Although the theme seems to be peculiar to this region, Jeanroy suggests that these poets may have been inspired by songs analogous with popular *couplets de pèlerinage* of a later date, and that such songs may indeed have been sung by travelling pilgrims.[96] While there is no reason to believe that similar 'young girls' songs' would have been heard on the lips of a medieval *clerwr*, it would be surprising if among the Welsh pilgrims there were not those who whiled away the hours with simple love-songs and scurrilous verse, as well as story-telling and other forms of entertainment. The pilgrimage to St David's—two journeys were deemed by the Church to be equivalent to a pilgrimage to Rome, and three to a pilgrimage to Jerusalem—would have provided a natural breeding-ground for the oral verse tradition of medieval Wales.[97] Some of this verse may conceivably have combined with the love element the theme of the pilgrimage itself. An intriguing thematic parallel for *GDG* 99 is found in a sixteenth-century free-metre poem probably composed by the irrepressible Llywelyn ap Hwlcyn:

> Crychv r cowrsi mynd J garv
> Codi r Capp gwyn ar y Coryn
> Codwch yn rwydd ar ych yscwydd
> Egoriad coch am a wyddoch
> A chais di ffonn bert o linon
> A dos ddyn fain tva Rvffain
> Yna J gofyn y Pab J hvn
> Pa ddrwg benna ath ddvg di yma
> Ai mab a fv gynt Jth garv
> Yno Jr eddv gwenn lygaid ddv
> mai hi a wnaeth fy marfolaeth
> Yno J wiscir rrawn am finir
> J ddwyn penyd dros J bowyd
> O daw gofyn pwy a gannodd hynn
> mab a chalon gowir ffyddlonn
>
> (*CRhC* 2, VI)

---

[96] *Origines*, 325–6; see also ibid. 163–4.

[97] Cf. Hartwell Jones, 'Celtic Britain and the Pilgrim Movement', 299. The popular belief in the value of the pilgrimage to Tyddewi is expressed in a simple verse, which resembles a Latin stanza reported to have been found there in the 13th cent.: 'Dôs i Rufain unwaith | Ac i Fynyw ddwywaith, | A'r un elw cryno | A gei di yma ag yno.' (S. Baring-Gould and J. Fisher, *The Lives of the British Saints*, vol. 2 (London, 1908), 315 n. 3).

(Crimping the coif, going courting, raising the white cap on to the head. Raise on to your shoulder with ease a red key for what you know; and fetch a fair pikestaff, and go Romewards, slender girl. There, the Pope himself will ask: 'What wickedness above all else brought you here? Did you have a boy to love you?' Then the dark-eyed maid will admit that it was she that caused my death, and they will put a hair shirt on her as a penance for her life. If anyone should ask who made this song—a lad of faithful heart and true.)

Despite the poem's thematic resemblance to the *cywydd*, it is clearly an independent creation with its own concise narrative style. An obvious difference is that here, armed with the traditional palmer's symbols of staff and key, the girl goes on a pilgrimage not to St David's but to Rome, and close scrutiny does not reveal a single verbal echo of GDG 99.[98] It may be that Llywelyn borrowed the theme from the *cywydd* and developed it according to his own fancy, and in his own inimitable style. This seems probable, but we must also bear in mind that he could have found his models in the pre-existing popular-verse tradition, perhaps composed in the same *cywydd deuair fyrion* metre, and that similar verse was possibly known to Dafydd ap Gwilym some 200 years earlier.

The humour in GDG 47 ('Bargeinio'), one of Dafydd's more 'uncourtly' poems, is less subtle. His persona here is cynical yet playful, as he negotiates with a girl of loose morals the price to be paid for her services. Her starting price for her 'confession', as Dafydd ironically calls it, is six pounds, but the knowing poet, having opened with an offer of a pound, gradually decreases the amount to a mere penny. It eventually becomes clear that he has no money at all, and that, in any case, he has no intention of paying for something which, in his eyes, should be offered freely in the woodland. He ends the poem with the sarcastic assurance that he will be at her service another time if she so desires. In contrast, a *cywydd* by Llywelyn Goch ends abruptly with a straightforward offer of money—'hwde bunt i'th law' (DGG[2] LXXXIV.28), 'here's a pound in your hand', all other means of persuasion having apparently failed. The theme of GDG 47 is more closely paralleled in two 'apocryphal' *cywyddau* which are probably later than the fourteenth century. The final section of BDG CXCVII, in which the girl demands 100 shillings and

---

[98] In a later version in one of Iolo Morganwg's MSS, where it is attributed to the fictitious Glamorgan poet Rhys Goch ap Rhiccert, the final lines are clearly an imitation of GDG 99! (See Taliesin Williams (ed.), *Iolo Manuscripts* (Liverpool, 1888), 240, and cf. Ifor Williams, 'Rhys Goch ap Rhiccert', *Y Beirniad*, 3 (1913), 241).

the poet is finally forced to admit that he has but a 'small penny', is partly an imitation of *GDG* 47, although this, unlike Dafydd's *cywydd*, is a dialogue poem. The author of *BDG* CLI, which is also a dialogue poem, arranges a tryst but is determined not to part with his money, and makes various excuses to avoid paying the sum which the girl demands. Finally, she submits and agrees to accept his poems as sufficient payment for her love. Chotzen has suggested that *GDG* 47 and Dafydd's other poems which reflect the worlds of tavern and town may have been influenced by the bourgeois poetry of Northern France and Flanders.[99] He might have drawn attention with regard to this particular poem to the words of Jean de Meun's Vieille in the *Roman de la Rose*, who advises young girls never to be generous with their hearts

> . . . Mes vendés le bien chierement
> Touz jours par enchierissement;
> Et gardés que nulz qui l'achat
> N'i puisse fair bon achat . . .
>
> (ll. 13,041–4)

(. . . but sell it very dearly and always to the highest bidder. See that he who buys it can never get a bargain . . .)

However, Dafydd was clearly familiar with life in the recently established boroughs, and the theme of this *cywydd* might easily have occurred to him spontaneously, perhaps in part as a veiled expression of his contempt, as a member of the native *uchelwyr* class, for the commercial preoccupations of the mainly English bourgeoisie. Yet it may once more be significant that the *cywyddau* discussed here find a striking parallel in a later free-metre poem. In an anonymous *carol deuair* of uncertain date, recorded, strangely enough, among Richard Morris's collection of wassail songs, the girl fixes the price, but the man makes excuses, offers her a paltry sum, and eventually admits that he is penniless:

Am fi yn brwuna	doeth mab atta
gofynnodd imi	gae o fy ngharu
cewch yn ddifai	os oes gynnoch i dda
oes gini dda	ped fawn gartre
par faint leia	ach bodlona
tair punt ar ddeg	ag ychwaneg

---

[99] *Recherches*, 163 ff; see also Ch. 7 below.

| mae gini ddime | ped fawn gartre |
| mae r̄ goriade | nis gwubod ymhle.[100] |

(While I was gathering rushes a lad approached me; he asked me if he could love me. 'You may indeed, if you have money.' 'Yes, I have money, were I back home. What's the least you'll accept?' 'Thirteen pounds and more.' 'I have a ha'penny, were I back home. Where the keys are I know not.')

It is not difficult to imagine that closely similar verse, based on this simple formula of a witty dialogue between a man and a woman, had been a popular form of entertainment for many centuries. If this was the case, it is not unlikely that the *Clêr* provided some of the inspiration for Dafydd's *cywydd* and for the later dialogue poems which so closely resemble it.

These dialogue poems have an obvious affinity with the Continental genre of the *pastourelle*, of which some 200 examples survive from twelfth- and thirteenth-century France alone. In these lyrics a wandering knight, often with the promise of riches, attempts to seduce a humble shepherdess, and is either repulsed or gets his way, by force if necessary.[101] But there is nothing in the Welsh verse tradition which can be said to correspond precisely to the Continental genre,[102] and the existence in the *canu rhydd* and the Dafydd ap Gwilym 'apocrypha' of a particular type of humorous dialogue poem which need not necessarily include the narrative introduction of the *pastourelle* suggests a well-established native verse tradition uninfluenced by external models.[103] This type of verse

---

[100] *LlRMG* 117. Cf. the early free-metre poem 'Crys y Mab', composed in the *traethodl* metre (*CRhC* 28). Here a stranger arrives on horseback and asks a girl to sell him her lover's shirt which she is washing under Cardigan Bridge. She answers that she would not give it away 'ir kan pvnt nac ir kanpwn | nac ir lloned y ddwy vron | o vyllt a defed gwnion . . .', and so forth. Despite the superficial resemblance, the poem, which unusually is narrated by the woman, seems to me to bear little or no relationship to the Continental genre of the *pastourelle*. It may be related to a traditional Celtic folk-tale motif; see Gwenan Jones, 'A Washer at the Ford', *Aberystwyth Studies*, 4 (1922), 105–9.

[101] Among the most useful surveys are W. P. Jones, *The Pastourelle: A Study of the Origin and Traditions of a Lyric Type* (Cambridge, Mass., 1931); M. Zink, *La Pastourelle: poésie et folklore au moyen âge* (Paris and Montreal, 1972); Jean-Claude Rivière, *Pastourelles: Introduction à l'étude formelle des pastourelles anonymes françaises des XIIᵉ et XIIIᵉ siècles*, 2 vols. (Paris, 1974–5).

[102] The pieces which most closely resemble the medieval *pastourelle* are some of those free-metre poems listed by Brinley Rees, which have the conventional *chanson d'aventure* openings, 'Am fi . . .', 'Fal yr oeddwn . . .', and the like. See *DCRh* 55–82, where he shows that many of these are probably influenced by contemporary English verse.

[103] Cf. *CRhC* 1,I; *CLlC*, vol. V–VI, p. 11; Evans, 'Iaith a Ieithwedd . . .', ii. 203–4;

is not, of course, confined to Wales. Simple dialogues occur also, for instance, in French popular verse,[104] where, as in some of the Welsh poems, the girl often replies with playful mockery or even abuse, even if she yields eventually to the man's advances. And it is not unlikely, as has been suggested,[105] that earlier verse of this kind contributed to the formation of the essentially courtly genre of the *pastourelle* in the twelfth century. The 'apocryphal' *BDG* CLIV is a fine example of the theme of the comic encounter between a girl and an old man, which is also found in the *canu rhydd*,[106] and the *cywydd* reads, in fact, as a conscious parody of the *pastourelle*. In the narrative opening the poet, who portrays himself as an ageing prelate, arrives on horseback as do the French gallants, but unlike the *pastourelles* it is the man who here resists before finally yielding to the girl's enticement. The explicit reference to the sexual act at the end of the poem is particularly reminiscent of the French *pastourelles*. The prelate's replies reflect the popular motif of comically improbable excuses, which occurs in other Welsh dialogue poems, most notably in the 'apocryphal' fabliau-type *cywydd* *BDG* CLVIII. Dafydd ap Gwilym uses a similar device in his denial of the breaking of dawn in *GDG* 129 ('Y Wawr'), although, as shall be seen in the final chapter, it seems probable that he is drawing here on one of the conventions of the popular French dawn-songs. It would be surprising if Dafydd were not also familiar with the far more widespread genre of the *pastourelle*, perhaps with English versions[107] as well as their French models. The *cywydd* which most resembles the genre is *GDG* 41 ('Merch Gyndyn'), which consists of a narrative

LlRMG 74–5, 117. The 'apocryphal' *cywyddau* include *BDG* CLIV, CLXXX, CXCVII, and two others not included in *BDG*, which have been edited by Dafydd Johnston, *CMOC* 12 and 15. Cf. also *The Cefn Coch MSS.*, 54–6 (Thomas Prys).

[104] Cf. *Chansons des XVe et XVIe siècles*, XLII, LXXXI; for an earlier example see F. Gennrich (ed.), *Rondeaux, Virelais und Balladen, Gesellschaft für Romanische Literatur*, 43 (Dresden, 1921), no. 356. Cf. also the English poem cited by Chaytor, *The Troubadours and England*, 125.

[105] Cf. Jeanroy, *Origines*, 1–44; Pierre Bec, *La Lyrique française au moyen âge . . .*, i. 119–36.

[106] *CLlC*, vol. V–VI, p. 11. For a French example see the moralistic dialogue poem 'Marguet convertie', in A. Jubinal (ed.), *Nouveau recueil de contes, dits, fabliaux et autres pièces inédites des XIIIe, XIVe et XVe siècles*, vol. 1 (Paris, 1839), 317–26. Ifor Williams has drawn attention to a striking Provençal parallel for the unusual scenario of the 'apocryphal' *cywydd*, in 'Dafydd ap Gwilym a'r Glêr', 122–3; see also Chotzen, 'La "Querelle des Femmes" au Pays de Galles', *Revue Celtique*, 48 (1931), 82–3.

[107] For a fine example of the genre composed before DG's time see Brook (ed.), *The Harley Lyrics*, no. 8; cf. also the dialogue poem 'De Clerico et Puella' (no. 24).

introduction with the conventional opening phrase, 'Fal yr oeddwn' ('As I was . . .'), a chance meeting with a girl (as opposed to the usual pre-arranged tryst), and a dialogue. However, the girl's vague promise of a tryst is not among the conventional *dénouements* of the *pastourelle*, and it seems to me that the scenario of this *cywydd* might easily have occurred to the Welsh poet with little or no external stimulus.[108]

The native tradition of humorous dialogue poems, which may well pre-date the earliest *cywyddau* at a sub-literary level, may bear some relationship to the *pwnco priodas*[109] referred to earlier in the discussion of wassailing customs. These verse dialogues between the parties of the bride and groom,[110] with their essential element of obstruction in the form of the locked door, are quite possibly derived ultimately from ancient folk customs such as the *anoethau* or difficult tasks imposed on Culhwch in his quest for Olwen.[111] The well-known custom of obstructing the groom on his way to church may also be compared. It is quite possible, then, that some form of *pwnco priodas* played a part in the popular wooing and marriage customs of medieval Wales, and there is at least one *cywydd* which may reflect such a convention. The 'apocryphal' BDG CLXXX, which has no narrative introduction, is a kind of verbal contest in which the girl and her suitor speak in alternate lines or couplets. Each of the poet's advances is fended off with the provocative wit which

[108] Cf. Bromwich, APDG 96–7, SP 65. Also relevant here are Brinley Rees's remarks in DCRh 50–1: 'Eto i gyd y mae'n ddigon tebyg fod defodau tebyg i'r rhai sydd i'r tu ôl i'r *pastourelle* i'w cael yng Nghymru ac Iwerddon ar un adeg a dichon fod *aisling* (cerdd freuddwyd) y Gwyddyl, a'r chwedlau Cymraeg a Gwyddeleg am arwr yn cyfarfod â merch wrth ffynnon neu ryd, i'w holrhain iddynt.' While it is unlikely that these traditions had any direct bearing on the poems discussed here, they do serve to illustrate the universality of the essential theme of the *pastourelle*.

[109] Jeanroy compares the analogous French folk-songs with the *contrasto* or dialogue poem, which he regards as one of the literary antecedents of the *pastourelle* (Origines, 323); see also Tiersot, *Histoire de la chanson populaire en France*, 202 ff.

[110] See the examples cited by Rhiannon Ifans, *Sêrs a Rybana*, 210 ff., where it is suggested that the tradition is related to the primitive custom of inducing fertility through song; see also her discussion in 'Y Canu Gwaseila'r Gyfundrefn Farddol', 166 ff. On marriage customs in general see Trefor M. Owen, *Welsh Folk Customs* (Cardiff, 1959), 159–72; Dafydd Ifans, 'Lewis Morris ac Arferion Priodi yng Ngheredigion', Ceredigion, 8 (1977), 193–203; Catrin Stevens, *Welsh Courting Customs* (Llandysul, 1993).

[111] These are discussed by Rachel Bromwich and D. Simon Evans, *Culhwch and Olwen*, pp. xlvii ff. See also the motifs listed by Stith Thompson under 'Suitor Tests' in his *Motif-Index of Folk-Literature*, vol. 3 (Copenhagen, 1956), 398–408. The widespread folk-motif of 'the impossible tasks' appears in the Welsh wassailing songs, e.g. LlRMG 88–9.

characterizes this type of dialogue poem, but the girl eventually yields at the offer of marriage. The exchange in Dafydd's dawn-poem is the only instance in the established canon of this kind of humorous repartee which is common in the 'apocryphal' *cywyddau* and free-metre verse alike, and extended dialogues with the beloved such as we find in *GDG* 33 ('Y Bardd yn Onest') are an exception. But if any precedents were needed for Dafydd's use of dialogue in his love-poems, he would surely not have had to turn to the Continental lyric tradition to find them.

Finally, *GDG* 66 ('Y Cloc') explores yet another literary theme which is well attested in Wales as on the Continent, that of the erotic dream. Dafydd's other dream poem, *GDG* 39 ('Y Breuddwyd'), reflects the mythological image of the hunt of the white doe, a widespread motif in earlier Celtic tradition as well as in European literature.[112] The dream or vision genre, whose antecedents in verse go back as far as Ovid and other classical poets, is well represented in Welsh in the prose tales *Breuddwyd Maxen Wledig* and *Breuddwyd Rhonabwy*, and the former has been drawn upon in some detail in the vision which forms the basis for Iolo Goch's eulogy to Syr Hywel y Fwyall of Cricieth Castle (*GIG* II).[113] Maxen's vision of an unknown girl in a far-off land also offers various verbal and thematic parallels with both of Dafydd's dream poems, but the form which the dream motif takes in *GDG* 66 has little in common with the prose tale. It has even less in common with 'Y Breuddwyd', despite the unexpected introduction into both poems of the *llatai* motif (in *GDG* 66 Dafydd sends the dream itself as a *llatai* to his beloved, whereas in *GDG* 39 it is the huntsman's hounds which are interpreted as his love-messengers). The *cywydd*'s affinities lie, rather, with a type of verse described by Brinley Rees in his discussion of the various kinds of dream poems in the *canu rhydd*,[114] in which the dreamer sees the normally indifferent girl approaching or even caressing him. In this type of poem the poet commonly awakens to find, to his distress,

---

[112] Chotzen long ago drew attention to analogous poems by Ovid and the 13th-cent. French poet Thibaut de Navarre (*Recherches*, 215, 257). See also Rachel Bromwich, 'Celtic Dynastic Themes and the Breton Lays', *Études Celtiques*, 9 (1960–1), 439–74, and her remarks in *APDG* 76–7.

[113] See A. Cynfael Lake, 'Breuddwyd Iolo Goch', *YB* 15 (1988), 109–20. 'Awdl y Breuddwyd' (probably 13th- or 14th-cent.), which contains a detailed description of a girl seen in a dream, is also heavily influenced by this and other Welsh prose tales. See T. Gwynn Jones, 'Cerdd Freuddwyd Gymraeg', in *Britannica. Max Forster zum sechzigsten Geburstage*, ed. B. Tauchnitz (Leipzig, 1929), 143.

[114] *DCRh* 76.

that the girl is not by his side, as in *GDG 66* (ll. 17–20). The author of *BDG* CXI, probably a fifteenth-century poem, may well have known of Dafydd's *cywydd* to the clock.[115] The themes of the two poems are certainly very similar, although in the 'apocryphal' *cywydd* a long *dyfalu* passage is devoted to the sleep itself which provided the poet with his wondrous vision, whereas Dafydd's *dyfalu* is purely abusive, applied to the clock which disturbs his sleep. As in *GDG 66* the girl is clearly inaccessible in reality, and the poet rejoices in his dream, only to be disappointed in the cold light of day.

It is a theme which is also found in the troubadour love-lyric, as, for instance, in the work of Folquet de Romans:

> Que la nueit, quan soi endurmiz,
> s'en vai a vos mos esperiz;
> donna, ar ai eu tan de ben
> que quan resvelh e m'en soven,
> per pauc no·m volh los olhz crebar
> quar s'entremetton del velhar;
> e vauc vos per lo leich cerchan,
> e quan no·us trob, reman ploran;
> qu'eu volria toz temps dormir,
> qu'en sonjan vos pogues tenir.

(For at night, when I am asleep, my spirit goes forth to you; lady, then such happiness is mine that when I wake and memory returns, I scarce believe my eyes, for they struggle to wake; and I search through the bed for you, and when I find you not, I abide weeping; for I would like to sleep ever so that I might hold you in my dream.)[116]

The opening lines of this passage, which reflect the medieval explanation of dreams, may be compared in particular with *GDG 66*, since Dafydd's soul (or 'angel') also leaves his body and goes forth to the beloved (ll. 14–16); and the troubadour's wish to sleep forever calls to mind the Welsh poet's praise of his 'sweet sleep' in *BDG* CXI. Among the 'troubadour commonplaces' which Chaytor identifies in a fifteenth-century English love-poem is the following passage:

---

[115] The poem is attributed to three 15th-cent. poets as well as to DG (see *GDG*[1], p. clxxxii). It is certainly no slavish imitation, but there may be a conscious verbal echo of the earlier *cywydd* in the words 'Hun o nef fry' (l. 35). Richard Cynwal (d. 1634) has a *cywydd* on the same theme (Cwrt Mawr MS 27, 393).

[116] Text and translation from Chaytor, *The Troubadours and England*, 139. For further external parallels with *GDG 66* see Ch. 6 below, n. 44, and Ch. 7, pp. 247–8.

> Whan Reste And slepe y shulde haue noxiall,
>   so sodeynly Renyth in my mynde
> your grete bewte! me thynketh than y fynde
>   you as gripyng in myn armes twey;
>   Bute whan y wake, ye are away.[117]

However, the same motif is fairly common in trouvère poetry,[118] and it is equally likely, if not more so, that it was introduced into the English lyric tradition from Northern France. We may postulate a similar provenance for the motif in the work of Dafydd ap Gwilym and in later Welsh poetry. On the other hand, it is possible that this is among those widespread and timeless elements in love-poetry which may arise spontaneously in courtly and popular traditions independent of each other. An enigmatic allusion to an erotic dream in a poem from the Black Book of Carmarthen (written c.1250) suggests that it may have been an established theme in the unrecorded native verse tradition well before Dafydd's time:

> Breuduid a uelun neithwir.
>   ys celuit ae dehoglho.
> Ny ritreithir y reuit.
>   nis guibit ar nuy g[u]elho . . .
> Neur uum y dan un duted
>   a bun dec liu guanec gro.
>   (LIDC 2.1–8)

(I saw a dream last night, expert is he who can interpret it. Its lewdness will not be disclosed; he who cannot see it cannot know it . . . I have been under the same blanket as a fair maid of the colour of a wave on a shingly beach.)

The poem is incomplete, and consists for the most part of a series of proverbs whose relevance to the dream vision is not immediately apparent. But the nature of the poet's vision is unmistakable, although, of course, it lacks the elements of awakening and consequent disillusionment which characterize the particular form of the dream motif with which we are concerned.

A typical example of the type of free-metre dream poetry described by Brinley Rees reads as follows:

> Pan vythwy /n/ brevddwydio //
> hi a vydd rhwng vy nwylo //
> a minne /n/ i embrasio /

---

[117] The Troubadours and England, 137.
[118] Some examples are cited in Recherches, 318; see also Origines, 319.

hi yn llawen./
pan ddarffo i mi ddeffro //
vo gyll vy mvn evrdro //
am dagre ine /n/ syrthio //
am veinwen [119]
(CRhC 6.201–8)

(Whenever I dream she lies in my arms, and joyfully do I embrace her. When I wake my fair maid disappears, and on my sweetheart's account my tears flow.)

The convention is also very common in English, especially in poems of the early Tudor period such as that already cited, and an English origin rather than a Welsh one has in fact been suggested for its occurrence in this poem.[120] However, while we must admit the possibility that this stanza and other free-metre poems which resemble it were influenced to some degree by English literary fashions, it is clear that the poets of the *canu rhydd* did not need to look outside Wales for their inspiration. They could have inherited the theme from the *Cywyddwyr*, but it may also have been present in earlier popular verse. Even if it is to be traced to French and, ultimately, to Provençal influence, the convention may have been assimilated into the native sub-literary tradition before Dafydd ap Gwilym's time. It may well be that, as, for instance, in the case of the bird-messenger motif, an analogous element already established in the native sub-bardic tradition was given new impetus by the pervasion of external literary trends. It is these external trends, and the extent of their influence on the poetry of the early *Cywyddwyr*, which we must now examine in greater detail.

[119] Cf. *Cerddi Rhydd Cynnar*, no. 52; Evans, 'Iaith a Ieithwedd . . .', ii. 4; *LlRMG* 184.

[120] O'Sullivan, 'Developments in Love Poetry . . .', 225. The poem as a whole, with its numerous Classical allusions, is suggestive of English influence; cf. ibid. 215 and *DCRh* 36–7. For examples of the motif in English see nos. 28, 29, and 38 in the collection of poems from a 16th-cent. MS in *Anglia*, 31 (1908), 309–97.

6

External Influences and Analogues: I

Attention to the poetry of Continental Europe in the preceding chapters has for the most part been confined to comparisons with elements in the *cywyddau*, such as the 'bird-messenger' motif and the *sérénade*-type poems, which have been considered as analogous but essentially native developments, drawing on a rich vein of popular tradition. It has been seen also that some signs of external influence may be perceived in the work of poets who flourished a generation or so before the time of the early *Cywyddwyr*, and in the work of Gruffudd ap Dafydd in particular. The aim of this and the final chapter is to examine the significance of the *Cywyddwyr*'s debt to this wider European lyric tradition, not only in terms of their general response to the pervasive influence of the courtly love movement, but more especially by drawing attention to a number of themes, motifs, images, and poetic genres which may be related to a literary culture quite different from that of medieval Wales. To what extent did these external borrowings expand the repertoire of the Welsh poets and enrich the fabric of their lyrics? Some of the analogues identified may appear somewhat trivial when examined in isolation, but seen in the wider context of a considerable body of cumulative evidence even the most minor parallels acquire a more powerful suggestiveness.

The truism that the search for literary sources and influences rarely leads to any absolute truths or indisputable conclusions may certainly be said to apply to Dafydd ap Gwilym and his contemporaries. There is, of course, no question of their seeking, in the manner of their contemporary Chaucer, to translate, to adapt, or even to imitate closely whole works or even whole passages by the celebrated poets of France and Italy;[1] and it would be absurd to imply that the influence of the troubadours and the trouvères on the *cywydd serch*

---

[1] On Chaucer's debt to poets such as Boccaccio, Jean de Meun, and Guillaume de Machaut see Charles Muscatine, *Chaucer and the French Tradition* (Berkeley, Calif., 1957); J. I. Wimsatt, *Chaucer and the French Love Poets: The Literary Background of the Book of the Duchess* (Chapel Hill, NC, 1968); id., *Chaucer and his French Contemporaries: Natural Music in the Fourteenth Century* (Toronto, 1991).

was as immediate or as formative as it was, for instance, on the Italian or German love-poets.[2] Any enquiry into literary influences must at all times take into account the author's capacity for invention—a consideration which is particularly relevant to a poet of Dafydd ap Gwilym's individuality—as well as the existence, in a predominantly oral culture, of a mass of material, including possible intermediary versions, which has not been preserved. Needless to say, thematic or verbal similarities are not a priori signs of literary influence and, with a few rare exceptions, any specific foreign work referred to will not be claimed as a direct textual source. The prime significance of such a correspondence will be to indicate the possibility of the eventual transmission into *cywydd* poetry of one of the conventional elements of the wider European lyric tradition. In the case of Northern French poetry, from which the great majority of analogues are drawn, this lyric tradition encompasses poets as varied as the courtly trouvère, wandering *jongleur*, bourgeois poet, and popular singer, for, if their social contexts and therefore their poetic registers may vary considerably, they were to a large degree drawing on a common stock-in-trade of conventions and formulae. Some analogues are drawn from the work of Anglo-Norman court-poets, and although in comparison with the mass of religious and didactic material preserved in the manuscripts very little lyric poetry is extant in that language, it may be presumed that much has been lost,[3] and it must be considered one of the more likely sources of influence.

We may postulate, with Rachel Bromwich, that some of the characteristic elements of Continental verse had already been assimilated by the *Clêr* as early as the thirteenth century. But in addition we must reckon with the possibility of more direct channels of influence, not only at an oral level, but also from sources of a more literary character, a very likely instance of which, it will be seen, is provided by the *Roman de la Rose*. Though there is no evidence of direct literary contact of the kind which existed between medieval England and Continental Europe, opportunities for cultural interaction were

[2] See *Origines*, pt. 2: 'La Poésie Française à l'Étranger'; Olive Sayce, *The Medieval German Lyric, 1150–1300: The Development of its Themes and Forms in their European Context* (Oxford, 1982).

[3] Cf. M. D. Legge, *Anglo-Norman Literature and its Background* (Oxford, 1963), 332–61. See also the recently published anthology *The Anglo-Norman Lyric*, ed. and trans. D. L. Jeffrey and B. J. Levy (Toronto, 1990), esp. nos. 44–52, and B. Constance West, *Courtoisie in Anglo-Norman Literature* (New York, 1966).

not lacking.[4] These were primarily military, in the form of expeditions during the course of the Hundred Years War (in which, according to *GDG* 75, some of Dafydd's friends and relatives took part); religious, in the form of pilgrimages and of fairly recently established monasteries;[5] and commercial—and in this respect we must not underestimate the cosmopolitan nature of the bustling Norman boroughs, with which Dafydd, at least, was evidently acquainted.[6] Whether Dafydd actually understood Anglo-Norman or Continental French we shall never know, but there is no reason why this should not be the case. Anglo-Norman was the main language of the legal and of a great deal of the civic and official affairs of England and Wales until well into the fourteenth century; and it would be surprising if, for instance, Dafydd's uncle and mentor Llywelyn ap Gwilym, as constable of Newcastle Emlyn, did not need at least a basic knowlege of the language to carry out the Crown's business.[7] It has been suggested, albeit perhaps somewhat controversially, that a considerably greater proportion of the words of Romance origin in Dafydd's work than was previously thought are derived directly from Anglo-Norman rather than Middle English, and most of these loanwords are the earliest, if not the only, examples attested in Welsh.[8]

[4] See *Recherches*, 96–139. The whole question of cross-cultural contact has more recently been discussed by A. T. E. Matonis, 'The Harley Lyrics: English and Welsh Convergences', *Modern Philology*, 86 (1988–9), 1–21; see esp. 1–6, and the historical studies cited there. As she remarks: 'Military alliances, intermarriage, commercial exchanges, monastery and baronial court, market towns, and fairs would have promoted cultural transmission' in the 13th and 14th centuries.

[5] See F. G. Cowley, *The Monastic Order in South Wales, 1066–1349* (Cardiff, 1977), esp. chs. 3 and 6.

[6] See D. J. Bowen, 'Dafydd ap Gwilym a'r Trefydd Drwg', *YB* 10 (1977), 190–220. On the Norman boroughs see R. Rees Davies, *The Age of Conquest: Wales 1063–1415* (Oxford and New York, 1991), esp. parts IV–V; M. Beresford, *New Towns of the Middle Ages* (London, 1967).

[7] Daniel Huws suggests that another of DG's patrons, Rhydderch ab Ieuan Llwyd, who, as a legal expert in the king's service, must have known both French and English, may have seen collections of French romances of the type then fashionable at the royal court ('Llyfr Gwyn Rhydderch', *CMCS* 21 (Summer 1991), 17). The linguistic complexity of the period is discussed by Matonis, 'Harley Lyrics . . .', and D. J. Bowen, 'Beirdd a Noddwyr y Bedwaredd Ganrif ar Ddeg', *LlC*, 17 (1992), 80 ff. See also Ceridwen Lloyd-Morgan, 'French Texts, Welsh Translators', in Roger Ellis (ed.), *The Medieval Translator II* (London, 1991), 45–63; D. A. Trotter, 'L'Anglo-français au Pays de Galles: une enquête préliminaire', *Revue de Linguistique Romane*, 58 (1994), 461–87.

[8] Marie E. Surridge, 'Romance and Anglo-Saxon Elements in the Poetry of Dafydd ap Gwilym', *Proceedings of the First North American Congress of Celtic Studies*, Ottawa, 1986 (Ottawa, 1988), 531–43. On DG's imaginative use of these linguistic borrowings see *APDG* 8–9, 83–4.

We must bear in mind also that Dafydd was familiar with the Norman stronghold of Glamorgan, home to his friend and patron Ifor Hael—and home also to a manuscript of the *Roman de la Rose*[9]— where he could easily have come into contact with the Anglo-Norman and the Gallo-Norman nobility. It is pertinent to recall in this regard Saunders Lewis's claim that: 'We shall not get a proper idea of the cultural climate of the late Middle Ages in Britain unless we recognize that Anglo-French and Middle English and Welsh were all cheek by jowl in the Welsh Marches and Crown Lordships.'[10] If we add to these the language of the Church and of so much learned writing, from the love-poems of Ovid to the lyrics of his medieval emulators, the Latin scholars, we shall begin to understand the multilingual and thoroughly multicultural character of fourteenth-century Wales. The early *Cywyddwyr*, and Dafydd ap Gwilym more than any, were inevitably exposed to potential influences from several directions, and the modes of transmission were no doubt many and various.

It is important to emphasize that the *cywyddau serch* are for the most part far removed in tone and spirit from the earnest declarations which characterize the poetry of *amour courtois*. The *Cywyddwyr* rarely assume that posture of adoring servility which one associates with so many of the trouvères, and their desire for physical fulfilment is more explicitly expressed. Their poems are more dynamic, less rigidly formalized than those of the French love-poets. Most of Dafydd's love-poems, if they do not provide some kind of narrative development, consist of a vigorous dramatic monologue; and that subtle blend of light-hearted humour, wit, and irony which is one of his distinctive hallmarks in fact has more in common with Ovid than with the courtly *chanson*, or with the French lyric tradition in general. Without entering into unnecessary detail, it is patently clear that the *Cywyddwyr* did not attempt to adapt for their own purposes the troubadours' and trouvères' interpretation of love as a philosophic concept with its own language and its own set of precepts which could only be fully understood and appreciated by an élite circle of adherents. Chaytor's remarks in relation to the Middle

[9] See *Recherches*, 110; G. J. Williams, *Traddodiad Llenyddol Morgannwg*, 146; *APDG* 73–4; D. J. Bowen, 'Beirdd a Noddwyr . . .', 81 and n. 149.
[10] 'Dafydd ap Gwilym', *Blackfriars*, 34 (1963), 133; this concise article, which lucidly emphasizes the European context of DG's poetry, is reprinted in *Presenting Saunders Lewis*, ed. A. R. Jones and Gwyn Thomas (Cardiff, 1973), 159–63.

English love-lyric are also, by and large, relevant to the poetry of
Dafydd and his contemporaries:

Many of the features most characteristic of the Provençal *canso* are wanting
in the Middle English lyric. There is no technical vocabulary of love: equiv-
alents for *joi, cortesia, solatz* etc., do not appear. The attempts at psychological explanations of love's beginning and progress are not made. Absent
also are the ideas of love as a service which improves those who loyally bear
its burden, and the pains of which are in reality a supreme delight. The
English lyric is more direct in expression and more genuine in sentiment than
the troubadour poems . . .[11]

It is true that, as Helen Fulton has made clear,[12] the idea of service
and reward, in the form of the metaphor of the praise-poet who
expects repayment, is a recurrent theme in Dafydd's love-poetry. But
the analogy is superficial, and there is certainly no explicit portrayal
of love, or of love's service, as an ennobling force. Despite the ten-
dency to reject the idea of 'courtly love' as a rigidly defined and uni-
form 'system' of values,[13] the work of those poets associated with the
movement does nevertheless reveal a number of more or less consistent, if not homogeneous characteristics. Its dominant feature is the
lover's patient and long-suffering service of his *dame* and of the god
Amors as a source of moral and spiritual enhancement. It is a concept which is most commonly expressed through the interrelated
metaphors of the feudal order, the chivalrous code of conduct, and
religious worship. The first two had little relevance to fourteenth-
century Wales, and although, as will become apparent, there are
instances in Dafydd's work of the blending of erotic and religious
experience, there is nothing which can be said to amount to an
'erotic religion' which, in the words of C. S. Lewis, 'arises as a rival
or a parody of the real religion and emphasizes the antagonism of
the two ideals'.[14] Also notable by its absence is the familiar mythology of this 'erotic religion': there is no God of Love, no Venus, no
divine commandments, and no 'Garden of Love', the earthly paradise
of the trouvères and of the *Roman de la Rose*, where all is governed

[11] *The Troubadours and England*, 118–19.
[12] See her chapter on 'The Court-poetry of Dafydd ap Gwilym', *DGEC* 106–44.
[13] See, for instance, F. X. Newman (ed.), *The Meaning of Courtly Love* (Albany,
NY, 1968); L. T. Topsfield (ed.), *Troubadours and Love* (Cambridge, 1975); G. D.
Economou and J. M. Ferrante (eds.), *In Pursuit of Perfection: Courtly Love in Medieval
Literature* (New York, 1975); R. Boase, *The Origin and Meaning of Courtly Love: A
Critical Study of European Scholarship* (Manchester, 1977).
[14] *The Allegory of Love*, 18.

by the noble etiquette of *courtoisie*. Absent too are some of the more widespread motifs such as the burning heart, or the departure of the lover's heart to his beloved, images which are particularly salient in the poetry of Dafydd's illustrious contemporary, Guillaume de Machaut.

In a poem such as *GDG* 102 ('Cystudd y Bardd'), or in some of the poems to Dyddgu, Dafydd does achieve a degree of serenity which comes close to a kind of sublimation of love. It must be admitted, however, that the loftier preoccupations and much of the essential imagery of *amour courtois* are noticeably lacking in the *cywydd serch*. But what there is, not unlike what is found in the slightly earlier English 'Harley Lyrics',[15] is a variety of motifs and conventions made fashionable by the Continental poets, some of which have been seen to penetrate Welsh love-poetry from at least the beginning of the fourteenth century. It should also be borne in mind that universally attested elements, such as love-sickness and sleeplessness, are already present in the work of the Poets of the Princes as early as the mid-twelfth century. Images of captivity and bondage are common in Dafydd's poetry, and although he several times explicitly refers to himself as his beloved's captive, as in *GDG* 103.16—'Dy gaeth wyf'—the feudal connotations of the French and Provençal 'language of love' are not present.[16] It is conceivable, however, that his description of himself as a subject or vassal of painful love—'Yn ddeiliad cariad y cur' (*GDG* 90.6)—is an isolated echo of the courtly lover's homage to the God of Love.[17] Similarly, his single reference to the commandment of 'love's law'—'Cyfraith serch y sy'n erchi' (*GDG* 96.39)—possibly recalls the French poets' numerous allusions to the

---

[15] See G. L. Brook's introduction to his edition of the poems, *The Harley Lyrics*, 6–14; Elinor Rees, 'Provençal Elements in the English Vernacular Lyrics of MS. Harley 2253', *Stanford Studies in Language and Literature* (1941), 81–95; A. K. Moore, *The Secular Lyric in Middle English* (University of Kentucky Press, 1951), 41–75. Since Ifor Williams's important study, 'Dafydd ap Gwilym a'r Glêr', *THSC* (1913–14), various scholars have drawn attention to parallels between the Harley Lyrics and the early *cywyddau*. The subject has been discussed most notably by A. T. E. Matonis, 'An Investigation of Celtic influences on MS. Harley 2253', *Modern Philology*, 70 (1972–3), 91–108, and 'Harley Lyrics . . .', 1–21; and by Helen Fulton, 'The Theory of Celtic Influence on the Harley Lyrics', *Modern Philology*, 82 (1984–5), 239–54.

[16] Cf. also 'Gwanfardd . . . | Oeddwn gynt iddi yn gaeth'; 'Am ladd ei gwas dulas dig' (*GDG* 53.11–12; 99.9), and *GDG* 50.7; 81.37; 86.7; 89.27–8.

[17] *Deiliad* may simply mean 'one who holds or supports', but the sense of 'vassal, tenant, subject' does appear to be attested earlier than the 14th cent. (see *GPC* s.v. *deiliad*, *deiliadaeth*).

'loi d'amor' or 'amoureuse loy' which all courtly lovers must obey.[18] Dafydd also reflects the convention of the secrecy of courtly love which, according to Dronke, springs not so much from a context of adultery as from 'the universal notion of love as a mystery not to be profaned by the outside world, not to be shared by any but lover and beloved'.[19] It is the 'serch dirgeledig' ('secret love') of GDG 78.2 ('Serch Dirgel'), in which love is said to have made its nest in the security of the poet's heart, never to be revealed;[20] and it is the 'cariad cêl' ('concealed love') mentioned by Iolo Goch in his mock-elegy to his fellow poet Ithel Ddu (GIG XXIII.45). Llywelyn Goch also speaks of the need to conceal a love-tryst (DGG² LXXXIV.14). Although the general impression is that the Cywyddwyr's secrecy is determined more by practical than by spiritual motives,[21] there is some notion of the inviolability of love, especially where Dafydd speaks of his silent concealment as part of his 'mynud' (GDG 104.13–16), his 'courtliness' or 'propriety'. The idea of love as a sickness is as old as the Greek physicians, and that of its 'bitter-sweet' quality can also be traced back to classical writings; but the latter did not become a widespread commonplace until the Middle Ages. References to love's sweet pains ('doux maux') and the like may be found in the work of almost any medieval French love-poet, expressing the lover's suffering in the hope of future joy, and the Roman de la Rose devotes a rather contrived passage (ll. 4,293–340) to this essential paradox of the 'courtly love' philosophy. This particular type of paradox plays no significant part in the cywydd serch, but it is perhaps reflected in Dafydd's use of certain compound forms such as 'gwiwglaf', 'fine invalid', 'rhyfelnwyf', 'love's/passion's war', 'Saeth . . . wychloes', 'an arrow bringing delectable pain', and

---

[18] Cf. Chichmaref (ed.), Poésies lyriques de Guillaume de Machaut, vol. 1, CCLXV.14; vol. 2, p. 345, IX.19; Roman, l. 10,368; Romania, vol. 57, p. 363, LXXIX.30; Gennrich, Rondeaux, Virelais und Balladen, no. 281.3.

[19] MLRELL, i. 48; cf. ibid. 322–3. See also A. R. Press, 'The Adulterous Nature of Fin' Amors: A Re-examination of the Theory', Forum for Modern Language Studies, 6 (1970), 327–41.

[20] I am aware of no significant parallels for this delightful image, but with ll. 11–20 and the similar passage in GDG 104.25–8, cf. Guillaume de Machaut's '. . . Car en mon cuer vueil celer | Et porter | Ceste amour couvertement, | Sans requerre alfgement . . .' (Poésies lyriques, vol. 1, CLXXVII.16–19).

[21] Similarly, E. T. Donaldson observes that the secret or derne love of the 'Harley' poets has more to do with self-protection than with courtly ideals, and that 'by the fourteenth century at least, the aim and end of courtly love was sexual consummation, however idealized it may have been made to appear' (Speaking of Chaucer (New York, 1970), 17, 20).

possibly also in a similar reference to 'wayw llon', 'joyous spear'[22]
(*GDG* 121.28; 101.13; 100.7; 95.43). The arrow which afflicts the
lover with a 'delectable pain' is one instance among many of
Dafydd's fondness for the extremely widespread motif of love's
weaponry, a convention which is, of course, already reflected in the
work of his predecessor Gruffudd ap Dafydd ap Tudur.

Not surprisingly, Dafydd makes use of the associated convention
of the dying lover, as in the final couplet of *GDG* 118 ('Yr Wylan')—

> Oni chaf fwynaf annerch,
> Fy nihenydd fydd y ferch.[23]
> (ll. 29–30)

(Unless I receive a most gentle greeting, this girl shall be my death.)

although his pleas are not as impassioned as those of the trouvères.
He also often portrays the lady as the lover's enemy, an attitude
which, it has been seen, was implicit in the love-poems of his immediate predecessors. He speaks, for instance, of 'gelynboen' (*GDG*
98.55), 'hostile pain', and of love's pains as his enemies—'fy nge-
lynion' (*GDG* 84.7). It may be objected that the ubiquitous wounding arrow or fatal spear may easily be derived from Ovid or that it
could have arisen more or less spontaneously as a natural metaphor
for the pangs of love. In fact it does appear also in Dafydd's elegies:
his distress at the death of Ifor Hael and his wife Nest afflicts him
like an arrow's point—'fal blaen saeth' (*GDG* 11.2); and in his elegy
to Angharad of Glyn Aeron the memory of her is a piercing spear
('gwayw')—'woe for my eye!' (*GDG* 16.73-4).[24] A sure sign that
Dafydd was familiar with this type of imagery as developed by the
Continental love-poets is his use of their somewhat unexpected,
though very widespread metaphor of the lady's eyes as her lover's

[22] *Llon* here may be translated as 'agitated' or 'excited', as in *GDG* 109.26, but in
view of the conventional paradox its more familiar meaning—'gay, joyous'—may also
be present. Cf. also 'Mau boen gwych' (*GDG* 135.12), though this is not a specific
reference to the poet's love.

[23] With DG's variation on this motif—'Nid wyf glaf, ni fynnaf fod, | Nid wyf iach
. . . | Nid wyf farw . . . | A Duw a farn nad wyf fyw' (*GDG* 36.17–20), cf. Guillaume
de Machaut : 'Mais Amours, qui à son grant tort | Me het trop fort, | Si tost ne vuet
mie ma mort | Ne ma vie joieuse . . .' (*Poésies lyriques*, vol. 2, p. 375, XII.109–12); cf.
ibid., vol. 1, XLVII.28–30, XLVIII.17–18, CXLI.3, CLXII.8.

[24] In view of the fact that the 'courtly love' poem *GDG* 140 ('Caer rhag Cenfigen')
was composed for the same Angharad, DG's use of the motif is probably no coincidence. His complaint: 'Deuruddlas fain was wyf yn wael—er gwen' (l. 25) is also reminiscent of love-poetry.

slayers, most notably in the following passage from *GDG* 78 ('Serch Dirgel'):

> Ef aeth ei drem, gem Gymry,
> A'i chariad, ehediad hy,
> Dyn fain wengain ewyngorff,
> Drwy 'mron a'm calon a'm corff,
> Mal ydd âi, gwiw ddifai gofl,
> Gronsaeth drwy ysgub grinsofl.[25]
>
> (ll. 41–6)

(Her glance—jewel of Wales—and her love (a bold flight)—fair slender girl of the foam-hued body—went through my heart and soul and body, as a round arrow would go—fine, flawless darling—through a sheaf of dry stubble.)

These lines have countless external parallels, but a single passage, the work of an anonymous trouvère, will suffice to show their striking affinity with the Northern French lyrics:

> Vostre oeil m'i toldront la vie
> Qui me sont venu ferir
> Et je ne me sai couvrir:
> Il scevent trop d'escremie;
> Devant eulz ne puis fuïr,
> Ains m'i couvendra perir
> Se merci ne vous em prie. [26]

(Your eyes, which came and struck me, will take away my life, and I am unable to defend myself: they are too adept at fencing; before them I cannot flee; rather, I shall have to die there if I do not ask for your mercy in the matter.)

Another fine example of the motif is found in a *cywydd* by a young contemporary of Dafydd ap Gwilym, Sypyn Cyfeiliog (*fl.* *c.*1350–1400):

> . . . A llygaid fy mun lliwgalch
> (Fo'm llas, forwyn feinlas falch)
> Fal gloywder dau bederyn
> Muchudd goruwch deurudd dyn.
> Ac erioed ni las gŵr iach
> Na dugiaid ag arf degach!
>
> (*CIGE* LXXII.13–18)

---

[25] Cf. also *GDG* 30 ('Yr Adarwr'). The motif also appears in later *cywydd* poetry, cf. *CIGE* XLIX.17–22 (Gruffudd Llwyd); *BDG* CXLVIII.5–8; *CSTB* XXXII.11–14.

[26] *Romania*, vol. 44, p. 470. For further examples of the motif in Provençal, French, Latin, and Middle English see *Recherches*, 325.

(And the eyes of my chalk-hued sweetheart (I have been slain, proud maiden, pale and slender) like the brightness of two beads of jet above the girl's cheeks. And never was any healthy man or duke slain with a fairer weapon!)

The unambiguous allusion here to love's pleasant weapons is another of the paradoxes dear to the French poets: it is the 'tres douce lance' of Thibaut de Champagne, the 'douce armeüre' of Guillaume de Machaut,[27] and there can be little doubt that it is from the Continental lyric tradition that the motif is ultimately derived.

This, and the other *cywydd serch* attributed to Sypyn Cyfeiliog (*CIGE* LXXI), may be read as parodies of the excesses and the intrinsic artificiality of the courtly love ideal, which, once devoid of its original social and cultural context, was always open to ridicule. These poems are an assembly of hackneyed formulae: the girl is described as 'gelynes gwanfardd', 'enemy of a feeble poet'(*CIGE* LXXII.43); he cannot sleep or laugh; he approaches his death 'without a wound from any weapon' (another conventional phrase among the French poets, as has been seen in Chapter 3), and he claims that her love has penetrated his side 'like daggers'. His audience would surely have been amused by a statement as overtly hyperbolic as 'Lliw ei grudd . . . | Wnâi i lwys fardd lysu'i fwyd!', 'the colour of her cheek would cause a fair poet to reject his food!' Dafydd ap Gwilym's handling of borrowed conventions, although generally of a more subtle and ironic nature, is as often as not similarly parodistic in its intent. It will become evident when we come to discuss poems as varied as *GDG* 100 ('Saethu'r Ferch'), *GDG* 53 ('Breichiau Morfudd'), *GDG* 58 ('Merch yn Edliw ei Lyfrdra'), and *GDG* 129 ('Y Wawr'), that, at the level of poetic genres as well as themes and motifs, his response to the European literary fashions of his time was highly individualistic, a response coloured to a large degree by the provocative humour which informs his outlook as a poet. Whether there was a comparable response among the other early *Cywyddwyr* it is difficult to judge, since so little of their love-poetry has survived. But as one might expect, there are indications that the same pervasive influences did affect their work to some degree, although, of course, the extent of Dafydd's influence on his contemporaries is equally difficult to assess. Llywelyn Goch's *cywydd llatai* (*DGG* XXXIII) contains such commonplaces as 'saeth o hiraeth', 'an arrow

---

[27] *Les Chansons de Thibaut de Champagne, Roi de Navarre*, ed. A. Wallensköld (Paris, 1925), X.38; *Poésies lyriques*, vol. 1, CXXII.2.

of longing', 'eres fy myw', 'it is a wonder that I live', and a reference
to the jealous husband (ll. 38, 42, 26); and in his *awdl* to Rhydderch
of Glyn Aeron and his friend Llywelyn Fychan descriptions such as
'Rydderch gaethserch' (*lit.* 'Rhydderch whose love is captive'), and
'Brenhinedd y serch, byr iawn hunynt', 'kings of love, very little do
they sleep' (*BBBGDd* 58.6,42), are suggestive of both the poet's and
his patrons' preoccupation with the new kind of *cywydd serch*.
Bearing in mind that there must once have been a number of poems
to the Lleucu Llwyd of the famous elegy, it is significant that
Llywelyn himself is elegized by Iolo Goch as 'Prifeistr cywydd Ofydd'
(*GIG* XXII.43), 'foremost master of Ovid's *cywydd*'. Gruffudd ab
Adda ap Dafydd, in a *cywydd* in which he portrays himself as a
'thief' of illicit love (*DGG* LXVI), speaks of 'glwyfiaith glau', 'loud
pronouncement of injury', 'clwyf i'm clymu', 'a wound that binds
me', 'rhyfelglo' (*lit.* 'war-bondage'), and 'boen efyn', 'fetter of pain'
(ll. 1, 19, 15, 32), and in the form 'purserch' (l. 28), 'pure love', there
is perhaps a suggestion of idealized love. Although Madog Benfras's
description of a noble girl in *DGG* LXVIII is traditional in every
detail, the words 'Bwyf farw o serch' (l. 33), 'that I may die of
love'—and perhaps also his 'cawddnwyf cu' (l. 28), 'precious, sorrowful passion/love', expressing love's paradox—may be less so, and
in *DGG* LXVII he provides yet another allusion to the fatal effect of
the spear of love (l. 20). It should be borne in mind too that 'Cywydd
yr Halaenwr' (*DGG* LXIX), his account of his ingenious outwitting
of the jealous husband, is more reminiscent of the French fabliaux
than any of Dafydd ap Gwilym's narrative poems.[28] Iolo Goch is primarily a praise-poet, and his more considerable poetic canon
includes only three poems concerned with love. These are the technical *tour de force* of *GIG* XXIV ('I Ferch'), XXV ('I'r Farf'), and
XXVI ('Chwarae Cnau i'm Llaw'), none of which can be said to
reflect the Continental conventions of courtly love. The latter, however, is based on the wife–husband–lover scenario common in the
French fabliaux and *chansons de malmariée*, and it will be seen in the
final chapter that the *cywydd* does have some affinity with the *malmariée* genre.[29]

---

[28] There are no specific parallels for the lover's disguise as a saltman, but the 'disguise' motif is common in the fabliaux and the popular-tale tradition (cf. *Recherches*,
287).

[29] His only other references to Eiddig are in *GIG* XXXIV, where the Grey Friar is
described as 'Llwdn troednoeth a ddoeth yn ddig | Lle'r oedd wraig llawer Eiddig' (ll.
17–18). Matonis has argued that some of Iolo's praise-poetry, like that of his younger

If Iolo shows little sign of welcoming the fashions of Continental love-poetry, then the Anglesey poet Gruffudd Gryg seems almost to have rejected them completely. He does make a token reference to Eiddig, but in an elegy (*DGG* LXXXI.60). Although Dafydd ap Gwilym's fictitious elegy to Gruffudd (which this passage closely resembles) contains several references to his love-poetry, including an allusion to Ovid in the term 'Ofyddiaeth' (*GDG* 20.60), the poems to women attributed to him, few though they are, reflect none of the usual distinctive motifs which one associates with *amour courtois*. The theory that Gruffudd, hailing as he did from the stronghold of the *Gogynfeirdd* bardic tradition, consciously rejected the pervasion of European literary trends seems to be supported by the evidence of his poetic dispute with Dafydd ap Gwilym.[30] In *GDG* 147 he ridicules the unashamed exaggeration of the South Walian's love-poetry, specifically satirizing Dafydd's use of the Continental poets' most characteristic motif, that of the 'weapons of love', and accusing him of blatant insincerity. The attack may be aimed in particular at Dafydd's most conspicuous use of the motif, *GDG* 111 ('Y Gwayw'), since in several manuscripts this *cywydd* actually precedes the debate. It is tempting to postulate that the dispute forms part of the exciting literary climate of the 1330s,[31] shortly after the compiling of the Bardic Grammar, when the poets sought not only a new metrical form but also new subject-matter and new styles to satisfy the tastes of some of their less traditionally-minded *uchelwyr* patrons. Dafydd's response to Gruffudd's accusations is a proud defence of his new kind of love-poetry, his 'geuwawd o gywydd', '*cywydd* of false praise', or 'Cywydd gwiw Ofydd', 'Ovid's fine *cywydd*' (*GDG* 148.6, 8), in the tradition of Ovid and the love-poets of medieval Europe. Dafydd ap Gwilym embraced that tradition

contemporary, Gruffudd Llwyd, shows a familiarity with the chivalric ideals of Western Europe ('Traditions of Panegyric in Welsh Poetry: The Heroic and the Chivalric', *Speculum*, 53 (1978), 667–87).

[30] On the *Ymryson*, and its importance as a kind of literary manifesto of the time, see Bromwich, *APDG* 46–50, 68–70. Matonis shows it to be analogous in its central argument and, for instance, in its rhetorical use of personal satire, with the poetic debates of Continental Europe. However, as she rightly observes, the phenomenal influence of 'courtly love' is likely to have induced a conservative response wherever it appeared; and since bardic disputes are well attested in Celtic tradition, the French genres of the *tenson* and *jeu-parti* are unlikely to have had any significant influence on the *Ymryson* ('Barddoneg a Rhai Ymrysonau Barddol Cymraeg yr Oesoedd Canol Diweddar', *YB* 12 (1982), 157–200).

[31] Cf. D. J. Bowen's remarks in 'Dafydd ap Gwilym a Datblygiad y Cywydd', *LlC* 8 (1964), 10–12.

more fully than any other contemporary Welsh poet. Because of this fact, and because of the comparative importance of his poetic canon, it is natural that most of what follows is concerned with his work.

One of the more likely sources of influence on Dafydd's love-poetry is the *Roman de la Rose*, one of the formative works of its time. Begun around 1230 by Guillaume de Lorris, of whom very little is known, as a kind of synthesis in allegorical form of the ideals and conventions of the love-poets of his age, it was continued some fifty years later, in a manner which its original author could scarcely have thought possible, by the liberal-minded Parisian man of letters Jean Chopinel, or Jean de Meun. In the hands of Jean de Meun the allegorical framework of the *Roman* became little more than a use-ful vehicle for a work almost encyclopaedic in its range, which at its best is lively and entertaining, at its worst inconsistent and long-winded. It is the work of an exceptionally well-read man, whose aim was partly that of a popularizer. Jean was evidently well versed in Ovid and the classics; he was also able to draw at will from sources as disparate as the philosophical writings of Alain de Lille, and the courtly, bourgeois, and scholastic traditions of his own century; and the attitudes expressed range from courtly idealism to bourgeois real-ism. The *Roman* was extremely widely read, and its influence on the literature and thought of the late Middle Ages cannot be overstated. The following passage is from C. S. Lewis's *The Allegory of Love*:

> The *Romance of the Rose* is one of the most 'successful' books, in the vul-gar sense, that have ever been written. It exists in 300 manuscripts; it was paraphrased and moralized in prose; it was 'answered'; it was translated or imitated in German, English and Italian . . . The poems that derive from it constitute the most important literary phenomenon of the later Middle Ages. As a germinal book during these centuries it ranks second to none except the Bible and the *Consolation of Philosophy*.[32]

It is well known that at least one manuscript of the French poem found its way to early fourteenth-century Wales, and there is noth-ing improbable in the suggestion that Dafydd ap Gwilym may have been among the many poets influenced by it.

The possibility that he may have been familiar with the *Roman*

---

[32] *The Allegory of Love*, 157. On the *Roman*'s influence on European literature see also E. Langlois (ed.), *Le Roman de la Rose*, vol. 1 (Paris, 1914), 32–41; F. Lecoy (ed.), *Le Roman de la Rose*, vol. 1 (Paris, 1968), pp. xxviii–xxxv; Pierre-Yves Badel, *Le Roman de la Rose au XIVᵉ siècle. Étude de la réception de l'œuvre* (Geneva, 1980); Heather M. Arden, *The Romance of the Rose* (Boston, 1987), ch. 4.

has been touched upon in previous chapters, most notably in relation to the husbandry image and the *sérénade* scene, both the work
of Guillaume de Lorris. The determining of literary sources is at best
a hazardous venture, but the *Roman* does contain at least one passage which is so closely analogous with one of Dafydd's *cywyddau*
as to encourage the search for further echoes, direct or indirect, of
this vast and highly influential poem in the poet's work. The *cywydd*
in question is *GDG* 50 ('Chwarae Cnau i'm Llaw'), in which Dafydd
introduces his description of the rustic love-game by recommending
that the lover should seek the aid and advice of a kindred spirit—in
this case probably his friend and fellow poet Madog Benfras—with
whom he may share his secrets:

> Salm yw 'nghof o lyfr Ofydd;
> Serchog anniferiog fydd,
> Heb gael cydymddaith dan llaw
> I addef pob dim iddaw.
> Mae un fal y damunwyf,
> Brawd-ddyn ym o brydydd nwyf;
> Cymhorthiad i'm cariad caeth,
> Cynghorwr cangau hiraeth . . .
>
> (ll. 1–8)

(My memory is a psalm from Ovid's book; a lover will always be naïve
unless he has a companion at hand to whom he may tell everything. There
is one such as I would wish for, a kindred soul of a love-poet; an aid to my
captive love, an advisor on the various branches of longing . . .)

Chotzen has compared these lines with a passage in the *Roman*
which speaks of Amis, the dreamer's confidant[33] (though he wrongly
attributes it to Jean de Meun, who does, however, keep an important place for this character in his continuation of the *Roman*).[34] A

---

[33] He cites ll. 3,100–10, remarking: 'Entre ces vers et ceux de Dafydd il y a des cor-
respondances qui sont presque littérales' (*Recherches*, 259–60). The figure of the friend
is rare in the *cywydd serch*, although he does appear in the *trioedd serch*; cf. 'Trri [*sic*]
anhepcor serchoc, llygaid i wilio, a Thavod i wadu, a chydymaith i esgusodi' (printed
in John Williams (Ab Ithel), *Dosparth Edeyrn Davod Aur* (Llanymddyfri, 1856), p. cvi,
from Cardiff MS. 60).

[34] See ll. 7,281 ff., where Jean's more worldly version of Amis presents the lover
with a catalogue of advice largely based on Ovid's *Ars Amatoria*. Dafydd Johnston
has recently drawn attention to parallels with this section of the *Roman*, and with ll.
12,987 ff. (the Old Woman's advice to the girl), in two *cywyddau* in which the advice
'is the same as that given by the friend in the *Roman*, the use of force to take the girl
despite her protests' ('The Erotic Poetry of the *Cywyddwyr*', *CMCS* 22 (Winter 1991),
64–5). These are *CMOC* 8, in which the little-known 15th-cent. poet Ding Moel

more remarkable parallel is to be found in Guillaume's earliest reference to Amis, in the commandments of the God of Love to the
lovesick dreamer:

> Or te lo et vueil que tu quieres
> Un compaignon sage et celant
> A qui tu diras ton talant
> Et descouvreras ton corage;
> Cis te fera grant avantage.
> Quant ti mal t'angoisseront fort,
> Tu iras a lui por confort,
> Et parlerés andui ensemble
> De la bele qui ton cuer t'emble,
> De sa biauté, de sa semblance,
> Et de sa simple contenance.
> [Tout ton estre li conteras,
> Et conseil li demanderas]
> Comment tu porras chose faire
> Qui a t'amie puisse plaire . . .
>   (ll.2,686–700)

(Now I advise and wish that you seek out a wise and discreet companion,
one to whom you can tell all your desires and reveal your whole heart. He
will be a great help to you. When your troubles wring you with anguish, you
will go to him for comfort, and the two of you will talk together about the
beautiful lady who, with her beauty, her appearance, with her mere countenance, is stealing your heart. You will tell him your whole situation and will
ask his advice on how you can do something which might be pleasing to
your sweetheart.)

And just as Dafydd assures us (l. 11) that his friend shall not deceive
him (though these words may also be taken to apply to the girl),
Guillaume has the God of Love declare: 'Si n'avras pas poor qu'il
muse | A t'amie ne qu'il t'en ruse' (ll. 2,707–8), 'you will not fear that
he will try to take your love away nor expose you'. All this is not
easily explained as mere coincidence, and tends to suggest that
Dafydd may have had direct knowledge of the *Roman de la Rose*.
Ovid in fact discourages the lover from confiding in a friend,[35] and

advises a friend; and *CMOC* 7, an 'apocryphal' *cywydd* in which the poet seeks the
advice of an older woman. See also Chotzen's discussion of these poems in relation
to the precepts of Ovid and his imitators (*Recherches*, 256–8).

[35] Cf. ibid. 259. Chotzen notes, however, that in one of the medieval French adap-
tations of the *Ars Amatoria* the lover does receive the aid of a confidant (*La Clef
d'Amours*, ed. A. Doutrepont (Halle, 1890), ll. 1,201–20).

the source of Guillaume's Amis would seem to be the medieval code of love *par excellence*, Andreas Capellanus' *De Arte Honeste Amandi*—of which the *Cywyddwyr* provide no obvious echoes—where the courtly lover is more than once advised to avail himself of a *secretarius* or confidant.[36] Dafydd's 'llyfr Ofydd', 'Ovid's book', is a phrase not uncommon in the work of the fourteenth- and fifteenth-century *Cywyddwyr*, where it seems to denote some imagined, or perhaps real authority in the matters of love, not necessarily the *Ars Amatoria*.[37] In the present context Dafydd may well have had in mind the *Roman de la Rose* itself, a work firmly in the Ovidian tradition, and one passage in particular.

Two of Dafydd's poems whose subject-matter has, naturally enough, invited comparison with the *Roman* are GDG 80 ('Tri Phorthor Eiddig') and GDG 140 ('Caer rhag Cenfigen'). The theme of the three porters who guard Eiddig's home recalls the gatekeepers appointed by Jalousie—a character variously interpreted as the girl's outraged relatives and the jealous husband himself—to guard the castle which he has built to protect the Rose. (Guillaume in fact mentions four gatekeepers—Dangier, Honte, Poor, and Malebouche (ll. 3,869 ff.), but Jean de Meun, significantly, speaks of 'ces trois portiers' (l. 7,562), as in his continuation Malebouche supervises the three others.) However, Dafydd's hag, hound, and creaking door are far removed from their allegorical counterparts, as is the humorous tone of the *cywydd* in general. The Ovidian figure of the hag, ubiquitous in medieval fabliau-type literature, plays an important part in the *Roman* in the form of the Vieille who guards Bel Acueil in the castle tower, though, as was seen in Chapter 2, Dafydd's lively portrayal of his sickly, sleepless old hag bears as close a resemblance to Ovid's prototype as to any of her French descendants which I have come across. Before we leap to the conclusion that it was the *Roman* which suggested to Dafydd the scenario of his poem, we should bear in mind the native 'triads of love' material to which the poem has

---

[36] See P. G. Walsh, *Andreas Capellanus on Love*, esp. 247–9, and cf. E. Langlois, *Origines et sources du Roman de la Rose* (Paris, 1891), 30, 37.

[37] Other references include GDG 58.20 (cf. 'llyfr o gariad', GDG 43.45, BDG CLXVIII.10); BBBGDd 77.55; BDG X.25, LXIV.22, CLXIII.17, CLCIX.4; CIGE LIII.35, LXXVI.1; CSTB XVII.45; cf. a Latin poet's allusion to the 'libri dictator amoris' (Raby, *Secular Latin Poetry*, ii. 244). That 'llyfr Ofydd' could be used to describe any work pertaining to love is illustrated in the words 'Llyma lyfr a elwir Llyfr Ovydd', which precede a text of the Welsh translation of Richart de Fourneval's *Bestiaire d'Amour* (*A Welsh Bestiary of Love*, ed. Graham Thomas (Dublin, 1988), 11).

been seen to be related (which may conceivably pre-date the *cywydd* tradition), and also the suggestion that it was perhaps a triad from the White Book of Rhydderch referring to 'Tri phorthawr Gwaith Perllan Fangor' (i.e. the Battle of Chester, 616) which provided the original idea, with Dafydd's 'assault' on the husband's 'fortress' providing an ironic parallel with the historic battle.[38] Yet Dafydd's tongue-in-cheek martial imagery further strengthens the parallel with the *Roman de la Rose*, since Jean's continuation revolves around the besieging and final conquering of the castle of Jalousie by the army of Amour.[39] A large portion of his work is concerned with what to the modern reader are rather tiresome accounts of warfare in allegorical terms, each weapon having its own abstract, moral significance. It is thus tempting to read the lines:

> Saethais drwy'r mur, gur gywain,
> Saethau serch at y ferch fain.
> Saethodd hon o'i gloywfron glau
> Serch ymannerch â minnau.
>
> (*GDG* 80.51–4)

(I shot through the wall—garnering of pain—arrows of love towards the slender girl. She, from her bright, honest bosom, shot love-tidings to me.)

as a conscious parody of Jean's allegorical warfare. Dafydd need not be echoing any passage in particular, but the idea of an archer shooting tidings of love finds suggestive analogues in lines such as these—

> . . . (Car il n'i entra onques fust
> Qui touz de promesses ne fust
> D'un fer ferrees fermement
> De fiance et de serement) . . .
>
> (ll.15,815–18)

---

[38] R. Geraint Gruffydd, 'Cywyddau Triawdaidd Dafydd ap Gwilym', *YB* 13 (1985), 171.

[39] Cf. Dafydd Johnston, 'The Serenade and the Image of the House in the Poems of Dafydd ap Gwilym', *CMCS* 5 (Summer 1983), 6. He draws attention, too, to Ovid's analogy between lover and soldier in *Amores*, i. 9.19–20; cf. ll. 27–8 of the same poem: 'custodum transire manus uigilumque cateruas | militis et miseri semper amantis opus' ('To pass through bands of guards and troops of watchmen is ever the soldier's task and the poor lover's') (Barsby, *Ovid's Amores*); cf. also ibid. 6.29–30. If DG was familiar with these poems, however, *GDG* 80 shows no signs of direct imitation. A further parallel is provided by the 12th-cent. romance *Eneas*, where the hero declares that neither tower nor fortress can defend him from Love, who would 'shoot his arrow through seven walls and wound on the other side . . .' (see Muscatine, *Chaucer and the French Tradition*, 20).

(. . . for no wood ever went into them that was not made entirely of
promises; the arrows were tipped firmly with points made of oaths and
assurances . . .)

or this similar image from the same passage—

> Cil drecent au chatel perrieres;
> Granz caillos de pesans prieres
> Por les murs rompre lor envoient.
> (ll.15,803–5)

(The attackers set up catapults against the castle and shot large pebbles of
weighty supplications in order to break down the walls.)

By indulging in allegory the authors of the *Roman de la Rose* were
continuing a well-established literary fashion, but their contribution
to determining the form of French erotic allegory was enormous, and
their influence on French love-poetry phenomenal.[40] The descriptive
technique favoured by Guillaume, and to a greater extent by Jean de
Meun, became the common heritage of French poets, especially
prevalent in descriptions of allegorical castles, of the weaponry of
love, and of the dress and accoutrements of the God of Love and his
adherents. Thus, in a *dit* by the thirteenth-century trouvère Jacques
de Baisieux true lovers will be aptly armed against their enemies—

> Haubert de loialté aront,
> De parler sagement raront
> Hyaume, et s'aront escut et lance
> D'avenandise et de plaisance . . . [41]

(They shall have a coat of mail of loyalty, they shall also have a helmet of
wise speech, and a shield and lance of graciousness and pleasantness . . .)

Dafydd's contemporary Guillaume de Machaut, to whose elegant
formalism this technique was so well suited, demands in an *envoi*:

---

[40] Cf. Langlois, *Origines et sources . . .*, 46 and *passim*. On the *Roman*'s place in
the wider allegorical tradition see C. S. Lewis, *The Allegory of Love*, esp. ch. 2; H. R.
Jauss, *Genèse de la poésie allégorique française au moyen âge* (Heidelberg, 1962); J.
Batany, *Approches du 'Roman de la Rose'* (Paris, 1973), ch. 2. Interpretations of the
Roman as allegory include A. M. F. Gunn, *The Mirror of Love: A Reinterpretation of
'The Romance of the Rose'* (Lubbock, Texas, 1952); J. V. Fleming, *The Roman de la
Rose: A Study in Allegory and Iconography* (Princeton, NJ, 1969); J. Dufournet (ed.),
Études sur le Roman de la Rose de Guillaume de Lorris (Paris, 1984); Per Nykrog,
'L'Amour et la Rose', Le grand dessein de Jean de Meun (Harvard, 1986).
[41] A. Scheler (ed.), *Trouvères Belges du XIIe au XIVe siècle*, vol. 1 (Brussels, 1876),
p.198, ll. 487–90.

> Princes, veuillés d'un chapiaus de soucie,
> Flouri de plours et boutonné d'amer,
> Moy et mon chant, s'il vous plaist couronner . . .[42]

(Prince, if you please, crown me and my song with a garland of worry [or marigold], adorned with flowers of tears and buttoned with [or bedecked with buds of] bitterness . . .)

As early as the mid-thirteenth century Thibaut de Champagne imagines his heart imprisoned and guarded by three gatekeepers—Biau Senblant, Biautez, and Dangier[43]—and the allegorical figures of the *Roman*, kept alive by countless poets, assumed a kind of reality in the minds of medieval Frenchmen. As one might expect, these faceless conventions had no impact on the more concrete poetic universe of Dafydd and his contemporaries (where even the all-conquering God of Love of the Continental erotic tradition plays no part), or for that matter on the work of his successors. But the basic technique of allegorical description does seem to have influenced a small number of Dafydd's poems. In much of the French poetry of the late Middle Ages, according to Huizinga: 'Finding symbols and allegories had become a meaningless intellectual pastime, shallow fancifulness resting on a single analogy', and he cites as an instance Jean Froissart's *Li Orloge amoureus*, which compares aspects of love to the various parts of a clock.[44] It is essentially the same technique which is employed by Dafydd, though less laboriously, in his description of the harp played by his deceitful mistress:

> Y delyn a adeilwyd
> O radd nwyf, aur o ddyn wyd;
> Mae arni nadd o radd rus,
> Ac ysgwthr celg ac esgus.
> Ei chwr y sydd, nid gwŷdd gwŷll,
> O ffurf celfyddyd Fferyll.
> Ei llorf a'm pair yn llwyrfarw
> O hud gwir ac o hoed garw.

---

[42] *Poésies lyriques*, vol. 1, XLVIII.51–3.

[43] *Les Chansons de Thibaut de Champagne*, XXXIV.19–27.

[44] *The Waning of the Middle Ages* (Harmondsworth, 1955), 210; cf. 317 ff. It has been suggested that the French poem influenced GDG 66 ('Y Cloc'); see Iorwerth C. Peate, 'Dafydd ap Gwilym a Jean Froissart', *LlC* 5 (1958–9), 119–21. This is quite possible, but the resemblance between the two poems is superficial, and it is more likely, as Bromwich remarks, that 'any similarity in their themes arises from the fact that the two 14th century poets were similarly fascinated by a recent scientific invention' (*SP* 123).

> Twyll yw ebillion honno
> A thruth a gweniaith a thro.
> (*GDG* 84.53–62)

(Of love's excellence was the harp built—you are a golden girl; there is on it a carving of agitation's [musical] scale (?), and an engraving of deceit and pretence. Its side—no crude wood—is of the form of Virgil's art. Its column causes my complete demise from genuine enchantment and harsh longing. Its pegs are deception, falsehood, flattery, and inconstancy.)

Would such a description have been composed were it not for the example of the *Roman* and the conventions of French love-poetry? It is possible, but although Dafydd ap Gwilym's high degree of poetic originality is not in doubt, it seems to me that this particular mode of composition is essentially alien to the native poetic tradition.[45]

The extended metaphor of *GDG* 140 ('Caer rhag Cenfigen'), where the poet's body is represented as a fortress which he defends with God's aid against the scandalmongers of a certain parish, brings us closer to the imagery of the *Roman de la Rose*, although there, of course, the castle is that of Jealousy, not of Love. While the image of the castle is widespread in medieval erotic literature,[46] it is equally prominent in the sermon literature of the period. It seems ultimately to be of a religious origin, and is particularly common in the English tradition, where from *Beowulf* to *Piers Plowman* the body or soul is often compared to a castle or fortress.[47] It appears, significantly, in an *awdl* by the thirteenth-century monk-poet Madog ap Gwallter, the device of a preacher, it has been argued, which perhaps marks the entry of the image into Welsh poetry:

> Corff a'e pump synnwyr, llwyr y llywych,
> Caer ureu y doreu ual daear sych.
> Kaeadeu pareu perych yn y bronn,
> Gwiryon borthoryon a berthynych.[48]

---

[45] Another fine example is the 'apocryphal' *BDG* CC, discussed in the previous chapter, which equates the various parts of the plough with love and other abstract qualities.

[46] See Chaytor, *The Troubadours and England*, 131.

[47] Cf., for instance, *Ancrene Wisse, Parts Six and Seven*, ed. Geoffrey Shepherd (Manchester, 1972), 10; Derek Pearsall (ed.), *Piers Plowman* (London, 1978), 141, and the references cited.

[48] Henry Lewis (ed.), *Hen Gerddi Crefyddol* (Cardiff, 1931), XLIII.25–8. The poem is discussed by Andrew Breeze, 'Madog ap Gwallter', *YB* 13 (1985), 93–100, who compares this and other topoi in the poet's work with English Franciscan literature of the same period.

(The body and its five senses, may You guide it completely, a brittle-doored fortress like dry earth. May You ensure that there are bulwarks of spears in its breast, may You bestow it with true gatekeepers.)

The poem may have been known to Dafydd—it is notable that as in GDG 140 the body's 'fortress' is guarded by gatekeepers and is under God's command. But as D. J. Bowen has suggested, he may have borrowed the image directly from the preaching friars,[49] and its provenance may therefore be of a more popular, sub-literary nature. The poem, courtly in tone, would surely have contained an element of parody for a contemporary audience, just as GDG 49 ('Merch yn Ymbincio') ironically echoes the preachers' diatribes against women.[50] In a thirteenth-century Anglo-Norman allegorical poem, heavily influenced by the Roman de la Rose, the poet's heart is imprisoned in the lady's body, a tower which has twelve guardians, Franchise being the marshal, Duzur the chamberlain, Curteysie and Largesce the treasurers, and so forth.[51] Guillaume de Machaut, again employing the kind of allegorical figures made popular by the Roman, provides a fine example of the courtly metaphor of Love as a castle which must be defended against its nameless enemies: Amours, Esperence, Souvenirs, and Dous Pensers are the poet's defences and weapons against the onslaught of Tristece.[52] The affinity of such poems with GDG 140 is given added significance by Dafydd's use once more of the allegorical device of juxtaposing the concrete and the abstract. We may compare, in particular, the couplet

> A gofynag yn fagwyr
> O gariad Angharad hwyr
> (ll. 31–2)

(And the hope of gentle Angharad's love is the defensive wall)

[49] 'Y Cywyddwyr a'r Noddwyr Cynnar', YB 11 (1979), 106–7; cf. his remarks in LlC 14, 198–9. Although the evidence for the popularity of sermons in Welsh in the Middle Ages is sparse (cf. Glanmor Williams, The Welsh Church from Conquest to Reformation, 508), some of the wandering friars must have addressed their audience in its native tongue.

[50] Cf. Recherches, 234; D. J. Bowen, 'Dafydd ap Gwilym a Datblygiad y Cywydd', LlC 8 (1964), 21 n. 156.

[51] Edited by P. Meyer in 'Les Manuscrits Français de Cambridge, II', Romania, 15 (1886), 242–6; cf. M. D. Legge, Anglo-Norman Literature . . ., 336. Chotzen suggests that Dafydd might have been familiar with the most famous courtly adaptation of the allegory, the fragmentary Provençal poem 'Chastel d'Amors', in one of its French or Anglo-Norman versions (Recherches, 264 n. 2).

[52] Poésies lyriques, vol. 1, p. 259, ll. 97 ff.; cf. ibid., p. 274, ll. 33 ff.

with Machaut's

> Et Amours m'iert donjons, tour et deffense
> Contre Tristece . . .[53]

(And Love will be my keep, tower and defence against Sorrow.)

In fact, the game of 'Castel of love' became an amusement in courtly circles, a series of riddles to be answered in the style of Machaut's poem. Huizinga gives the following example:[54]

> Du chastel d'Amours vous demant:
> Dites le premier fondement!
> —Amer loyaument.
>
> Or me nommez le mestre mur
> Qui joli le font, fort et seur!
> —Celer sagement.
>
> Dites moy qui sont li crenel,
> Les fenestres et li carrel!
> —Regart atraiant.
>
> Amis, nommez moy le portier!
> —Dangier mauparlant.
>
> Qui est la clef qui le puet deffermer?
> —Prier courtoisement.

(Of the castle of Love I ask you: tell me the first foundation!—To love loyally.

Now name the principal wall which makes it fine, strong and sure!—To conceal wisely.

Tell me what are the loopholes, the windows, and the stones!—Alluring looks.

Friend, name the porter!—Ill-speaking authority.

Which is the key that can unlock it?—Courteous request.)

This is not all that far removed from Dafydd's allegorical portrayal of his castle:

> A gofynag yn fagwyr
> O gariad Angharad hwyr;
> A maen blif o ddigrifwch,
> Rhag na dirmyg na phlyg fflwch;
> A llurug ddiblyg ddybliad
> Gorddyfn hedd Gwirdduw fy Nhad . . .
> (*GDG* 140.31–6)

---

[53] Ibid. p. 259, ll. 99–100.   [54] *Waning of the Middle Ages*, 122.

(And the hope of gentle Angharad's love is the defensive wall; and a catapult-stone of pleasantness against either scorn or complete humiliation; and
a smooth two-ply coat of mail of the constant peace of the true God my
Father . . .)

Although it has no descriptions of the castle itself comparable with
Dafydd's allegorical portrayal—Guillaume de Lorris's detailed
description is a literal one (ll. 3,797 ff.)—the *Roman* does provide
intriguing analogues. With Dafydd's 'catapult-stone of pleasantness'
compare, for instance, Jean de Meun's 'Granz caillos de pesans
prieres' (l. 15,804), 'large pebbles of weighty supplications', and with
the coat of mail made of God's lasting peace, the lines

> Escu de pez, bon sans doutance,
> Tretout bordé de concordance.
>
> (ll.15,595–6)

(A shield of peace, unquestionably good, bordered all around with agreement.)

Such imagery may or may not have influenced Dafydd directly, but
in his use of a certain allegorical style of composition in this poem
he is, I believe, following a European convention. He has of course
made the image his own. It would be fruitless to search for specific
parallels for all the details of his particular version—the eyes as
watchman, the ears as interpreter, the tongue as gatekeeper, the
rather strange detail of his hands and feet as an outwork, and God
himself as provider in case of siege. However, the *cywydd*, while at
the same time suggesting an undertone of religious parody, clearly
belongs to the wider European courtly love tradition. It is worth noting in this respect that the scandalmongers which are central to it
have been considered to be the nearest equivalent in Dafydd's poetry
to those ever-present enemies of the Continental love-poets—the
lauzenjadors of the troubadours and the *lausengiers* or *médisants* of
the trouvères.[55] The Angharad of the *cywydd*, believed to be the wife
of Ieuan Llwyd of Glyn Aeron, would doubtless have been greatly
flattered to receive such a poem, belonging as she did to a family

---

[55] *Recherches*, 264. On the whole, however, there is no need to attribute the presence of slanderers (*athrodwyr*) in Dafydd's poetry and in the *cywyddau serch* in general to Continental influence. They appear frequently, and quite naturally, in both
courtly and popular literature, cf. Dronke, *MLRELL*, i. 48 and *passim*. On the shadowy slanderers and rivals of the French poets see E. Baumgartner, 'Trouvères et *losen-
giers*', *Cahiers de Civilisation Médiévale*, 25 (1982), 171–8.

which in the second quarter of the fourteenth century appears to have embraced wholeheartedly the new kind of love-poetry.

A further possible influence on Dafydd's poetry has been suggested by Rachel Bromwich, who draws attention to the fact that

his simile of the Bird-Catcher (GDG 30), in which he presents himself as caught by a girl's eyes like a bird trapped in bird-lime beside a pool, has a striking parallel in the image of the fountain of Narcissus, also representing the girl's eyes, by which the lover is entrapped at the beginning of the Roman.[56]

The possibility of foreign influence was considered long ago by Chotzen, who compares this and a similar image from a cywydd which has since been rejected from the canon (BDG CLV.41–2), with two instances of the bird-catcher motif in the poetry of the troubadour Peire Vidal.[57] He cites also a somewhat superficial parallel in Ovid (Amores, I, 8.69), but concludes, since the same image is also attested in the work of an ancient Hindu poet, that it is in fact universal and could have occurred quite naturally to Dafydd as to any other love-poet. Chotzen might have added that instances are indeed to be found in Welsh and Irish popular verse, as in the following stanza from an early free-metre poem:

> Dal yr adar am y glyd
> Kwrs y byd yw hynny
> o bydd heddiw yn wr rrydd
> ni wyr a vydd yfory.[58]

(Entrapping the birds in the glue—that is the way of the world. He who is a free man today cannot know what tomorrow brings.)

As one might expect, the image is not absent from Northern French lyric poetry either. A certain Herbert compares the unfortunate lover to an ensnared bird, exclaiming:

---

[56] APDG 74. The passage referred to is Roman, ll. 1,537–614; further parallels are noted by Patrick Sims-Williams in 'Riddling Treatment of the "Watchman Device" . . .', SC 12/13 (1977–8), 103 n.13.

[57] Recherches, 329–30. Another 15th-cent. cywydd of uncertain authorship provides a closer parallel for DG's image: 'hedydd a vydd hvdodd vi | yn y glyd yn vn gledi | a rroi a goel ar y gwielyn | a fo glew fwyfwy i glyn' (Peniarth 76, ed. E. Stanton Roberts and W. J. Gruffydd (Cardiff, 1927), 69).

[58] Evans, 'Iaith a Ieithwedd y Canu Rhydd Cynnar', ii. 16; cf. CRhC 66.44. For a partial analogue in Irish see An Duanaire, no. 40.

Lais! cheüs seux en iteil lais
Dont vis ne porai eschapeir.[59]

(Alas! I have fallen into just such a snare, from which I shall not be able to escape alive.)

Analogous images could no doubt be multiplied from the love-poetry of various languages and cultures. The importance of the passage by Guillaume de Lorris is that in his allegory the wondrous well, or rather the two crystals, the 'deus pierres de cristal' (l. 1,538) at the bottom of the well in which the dreamer sees the reflection of the Garden of Love, clearly represent the beloved's eyes. Dafydd makes a similar analogy—

Ffynhonnau difas glasddeigr,
Yw gloywon olygon Eigr . . .
(GDG 30.21–2)

(Deep fountains of blue tears are the shining eyes of Eigr . . .)

and it is the water's brightness which first entices the bird, the unfortunate lover. It should be noted that while Dafydd's bird is trapped by lime-covered twigs ('gwiail glud') placed beside the water, Guillaume has the more picturesque detail of coloured grain, the seeds of Amors sown by Cupid, who has also set his fatal snares beside the fountain of Narcissus. Furthermore, Dafydd's metaphor is more complex, the snow which surrounds the springs representing the girl's white face, and the twigs her enchanting eyebrows. His treatment of the image is more homely—the bird, for instance, is captured after crossing to nearby Anglesey—and lacks the mythological context of the allegory. But despite the absence of any precise verbal affinities of the type encountered in the description of Amis, the Roman de la Rose, directly or indirectly, must be considered a likely source of inspiration for GDG 30.

It is Jean de Meun who provides the parallel for GDG 60 ('Anwadalrwydd'), in which the exempla of the hare, the squirrel, and the roebuck,[60] which all return to the wild in defiance of man's attempt to tame them, serve to illustrate the girl's thankless rejection

---

[59] Romania, vol. 56, p. 72; cf. vol. 57, p. 390. Cf. also vol. 45, p. 365 where, as in a passage by Jean de Meun (Roman, ll. 21,491 ff.), the bird (or lover) is enticed by the bird-catcher's sweet sounds.

[60] From the 15th and 16th cents. cf. CSTB X.31–4 (Bedo Aeddren), and The Cefn Coch MSS., 45–7 (Thomas Prys).

of the poet who, we are told, has 'nurtured' her from the age of 18.[61] Once more, one would hardly expect to discover a precise source for the poem, but it is perhaps significant that in the *Roman* also a series of examples based on the same theme—'Toute creature | Vuet retorner a sa nature' (ll. 14,027–8), 'every creature wants to return to its true nature'; 'Nature passe norreture' (l. 14,038), 'Nature surpasses nurture'—serve to illustrate women's innate infidelity, be they married or unmarried:[62]

> Aussi sachiés que toutes fames,
> Soient damoiseles ou dames,
> De quelcunque condicion,
> Ont naturel entencion
> Que cercheroient volentiers
> Par quex chemins, par quex sentiers
> A franchise venir porroient,
> Car touz jors avoir la vorroient.
>
> (ll. 13,959–66)

(In the same way, you should know, all women of every condition, whether girls or ladies, have a natural inclination to seek out voluntarily the roads and paths by which they might come to freedom, for they always want to gain it.)

Franchise and Nature are not, of course, treated by Dafydd as philosophic concepts, and the only exemplum which is at all comparable with *GDG* 60 is that of the bird of the forest—'Li osillons du vert bocage' (l. 13,941)—which yearns to leave its cage for its natural habitat.[63] The same motif appears in a fifteenth-century love-song:

---

[61] Cf. *GDG* 104 in which Dafydd humorously personifies his love as an awkward foster-son, demanding repayment for having nurtured it over a long period of time (the same image is used in *GDG* 96.1–8). It has been suggested that the image is derived from Ovid's *Amores*, ii. 9 (cf. Stern, 'Davydd ab Gwilym . . .', 236). Chotzen suggests the possibility of French influence, but reasonably concludes that the image could very easily have been suggested by one of the familiar features of medieval noble society (*Recherches*, 329).

[62] *Roman*, ll. 13,923 ff. Cf. also the fables of Odo de Chériton, probably translated during the 14th cent.: the cuckoo kills the bird which fostered it, and the moral reads: 'Velly y mae llawer o'r bobyl yn erbyn ac yn anhiryon y gwnant drwc ac anhiryonrwyd y'r rei a'e magassant, ac a wnaethant udunt da yn eu gwendyt, a'e tlodi' (*Chwedlau Odo*, ed. Ifor Williams (Wrexham, 1926), 21). The same exemplum is used in the early 14th-cent. poem *La Messe des oiseaux* by Jean de Condé (Jacques Ribard (ed.), *La Messe des oiseaux et le Dit des Jacobins et des Fremeneurs* (Geneva, 1970), p. 25, ll. 384 ff.).

[63] The source for this passage is Boethius's *De Consolatione*; see Langlois, *Le Roman de la Rose*, iv. 285. Jean's '. . . Et vodroit sus les arbres estre, | Ja si bien nel

> J'ay bien nourry sept ans ung joly gay
> En une gabiolle
> Et quant ce vint au premier jour de may
> Mon joly gay s'en vole . . .

(For seven years I nurtured well a pretty jay in a cage, and when the first day of May arrived my pretty jay flew away . . .)

The bird is promised gold and silver, but to no avail—

> . . . Le gay vola aux bois tout droit;
> Il feict bien sa droiture,
> Ne retourner ne doit par droit:
> Franchise est sa nature.[64]

(The jay flew directly to the woods; it is its right to do so, nor, by right, must it return: freedom is its nature.)

It is quite conceivable, then, that Dafydd acquired his basic theme, directly or indirectly, from the Continental verse tradition, perhaps from the *Roman* itself.

There are a number of other, more minor, motifs which could have been suggested by the *Roman*. In *GDG* 70 ('Noson Olau') Dafydd portrays himself as a thief of love (as does Gruffudd ab Adda in *DGG* LXVI), and curses the moon as Eiddig's accomplice whose light foils his night-time excursions. When Jean de Meun's Fausemblant advises that the lover should try to reach the tower in which Bel Acueil is imprisoned under cover of night, it must not, he says, be a moonlit night—

> Car la lune, par son cler luire,
> Seult as amans mainte fois nuire.
>   (ll. 12,513–14)

(for the moon's clear light is very often an annoyance to lovers.)

But this is a rather insignificant detail in the sprawling vastness of Jean's work, and it is just the kind of theme which might very easily have occurred spontaneously to the Welsh poet, along with all

---

savra l'en pestre' (ll. 13,949–50) may be compared with Dafydd's 'Gwiwair, o châi frig gwial, | Gwaeth oedd i'r tadmaeth y tâl' (*GDG* 60.9–10), though the resemblance is no doubt coincidental.

[64] *Chansons du XVe siècle*, XXVI.1–4, 13–16. The metaphor was also dear to the medieval German love-poets; see Jeanroy, *Origines*, 173–4; Dronke, *The Medieval Lyric*, 113–14.

the other impediments which are the subjects of his *cywyddau rhwystr*.[65]

Leaving Dafydd ap Gwilym for a moment, Llywelyn Goch's elegy to Lleucu Llwyd, which has been seen to be related to the *sérénade* convention, also contains a passage which provides a parallel with the *Roman de la Rose*, and with the wider tradition of French love-poetry:

> Cymyn f'anwylddyn fun fu;
> Ei henaid, grair gwlad Feiriawn,
> I Dduw Dad, addewid iawn,
> A'i mwyngorff, eiliw mangant,
> Meinir i gysegrdir sant . . .
> A da byd i'r gŵr du balch,
> A'i hiraeth, cywyddiaeth cawdd,
> I minnau a gymynnawdd.
> (*DGG* LXXXVII.78–86)

(This was my dear sweetheart's legacy: her soul—Meirionnydd's treasure—to God the Father, a true vow; and her fair slender body—[she of] the colour of fine flour—to sacred consecrated earth . . . and the world's wealth to the proud dark man; and her longing—song of grief—she bequeathed to me.)

For the French poets it is the dying courtly lover, wounded by the *dame*'s indifference, who makes his last will and testament. Thus, at the beginning of Jean de Meun's continuation the despairing dreamer makes his confession to Amors:

> A vous, Amors, ains que je muire . . .
> Sans repentir me fais confés,
> Si cum font li loial amant,
> Et vueil faire mon testament:
> Au departir mon cuer li lez,
> Ja ne seront autre mi lez.
> (ll. 4,214–20)

(I make my confession without repenting to you before I die, O Love, as do all loyal lovers, and I wish to make my testament: at my departure I leave him my heart; I have no other goods to bequeath.)

(The reference is to Bel Acueil, who in Jean's version of the allegory has all but replaced the Rose as the dreamer's beloved.) In a

---

[65] It may have been among the traditional motifs of popular verse. In the early free-metre adaptation of the *trioedd serch*, cited at the beginning of Ch. 5 above, 'a filthy, short moonlit night' is one of the lover's three hindrances.

thirteenth-century song from an Anglo-Norman manuscript, the lover's executors are to be the 'amerus' and the 'chavalerus', his suffering is to be left to the 'medisant' and the 'vilein jelos', and

> A cele pur ki me moer
> Cors e alme e tut mun quer
> Comand tut a sun pleisir.[66]

(To her on whose account I die, body and soul and all my heart I bequeath at her pleasure.)

The 'will' motif takes its place quite naturally in Llywelyn's elegy, but its affinity with one of the minor conventions of medieval French love-poetry is none the less striking.

When Guillaume de Lorris's God of Love, having followed the dreamer through the garden, shoots him with his five fatal arrows, the victim is able each time to remove the shafts; but the barbed arrowheads remain embedded in his heart, never to be removed, as in the following passage:

> Et tant tirai que j'amené
> Le fust o moi tout empené,
> Mes la saiete barbelee
> Qui Biautés estoit appellee
> Fu si dedens mon cors fichie
> Qu'ele n'en puet estre errachie,
> Ains remest ens, encors l'i sans,
> Car il n'en issi onques sans.
>
> (ll. 1,713–20)

(I pulled so hard that I drew out the feathered shaft, but the barbed point called Beauty was so fixed inside my heart that it could not be withdrawn. It remains within; I still feel it, and yet no blood has ever come from there.)

It is generally accepted that the 'weapons of love' motif in the *cywydd serch* is derived from the Continental tradition. But Dafydd ap Gwilym's most conspicuous use of the theme, *GDG* 111 ('Y Gwayw') (where the *dyfalu* description of the spear is, however,

---

[66] *Romania*, vol. 15, pp. 252–3; cf. ibid. 255; in the 14th cent. cf. Guillaume de Machaut (*Poésies lyriques*, vol. 1, CCXXIX.9–14):

> Mon cuer vous lais et met en vo commant,
> Et l'ame à Dieu devotement presente,
> Et voist où doit aler le remanant:
> La char aus vers, car c'est leur droite rente;
>   Et l'avoir soit departi
> Aux povres gens . . . .

entirely in the native mould), provides an interesting analogue with this specific detail in the *Roman*. Dafydd, like the dreamer, cannot remove the spear which is embedded in his heart. He complains:

> Nis tyn dyn dan wybr sygnau,
> I mewn y galon y mae.
>
> (ll. 15–16)

(No man under the stars of heaven can draw it out, within the heart it is.)

a couplet which recalls in particular Guillaume's words:

> . . . Si que par l'oel ou cors m'entra
> La saiete, qui n'en istra
> Jamés, ce croi, par homme né . . .
>
> (ll. 1,743–5)

(. . . so that the arrow entered my heart through my eye, and no man born, I believe, will ever dislodge it from there . . .)

We find similar expressions in the lyric poetry, such as 'Dieu! si ne sai qui le fer m'en traie',[67] 'God! I know not who will draw the point from within me', and Thibaut de Champagne has a poem in which he implores his *dame* to remove love's 'dart' from his heart, although the fatal point has broken inside him.[68] As well as the familiar imagery of *amour courtois*—the more common motifs such as the lover's sleeplessness, sickness, and imminent death, and the general spirit of courtly love poetry—the *Roman de la Rose* contains various elements which have their counterparts in no doubt pre-existing features of the Welsh poetic tradition, and which may therefore conceivably have enriched that tradition in the poems of the early *Cywyddwyr*. Such are Guillaume's depiction of birds as courtly poets and musicians (ll. 492 ff., 631 ff., 701 ff.); his *reverdie* opening in which the earth dons anew its fine garments after the winter's bareness (ll. 45 ff.);[69] and the numerous references to garlands of flowers, typically the *chapel de roses* (e.g. ll. 829–30), which are

---

[67] G. Raynaud (ed.), *Recueil de motets français des XIIᵉ et XIIIᵉ siècles* (Paris, 1881), vol. 1, LXIX.24; cf. vol. 2, p. 1. Note also that in GDG 111, as so often in troubadour and trouvère poetry, it is on seeing the girl for the first time that Dafydd is mortally wounded.

[68] *Les Chansons de Thibaut de Champagne*, VI.29–40; cf. Raynaud, *Recueil de motets français*, vol. 2, p. 15.

[69] For a similar description see A. Scheler (ed.), *Dits et contes de Baudouin de Condé et de son fils Jean de Condé*, vol. 1 (Brussels, 1866), XVIII.20 ff. Examples of DG's 'clothing' imagery, which pervade his nature descriptions, are noted by John Rowlands, 'Delweddau Dafydd ap Gwilym', 255–7.

comparable to the *cae bedw* and other love tokens which adorn the *cywyddau* of Dafydd ap Gwilym in particular. Jean de Meun, in his evocation of a golden age when all were equal and women spared the tyranny of marriage, gives a description of the greenwood which, in its 'domestic' imagery—the trees covering the lovers with their 'pavilions and curtains', protecting them from the sun (ll. 8,435–8)—is akin to Dafydd's recurrent metaphor of the *deildy* as an *uchelwr*'s court. In Jean's continuation, too, the Ovidian figure of the watchful husband is one of the stock characters through whose eyes love and marriage are explored.

Both Jean and Guillaume are admirers of women's natural beauty, which does not need to be enhanced by artificial means. *Biautés*, says Guillaume, is clear as the moon and needs no cosmetic enhancement, and Jean, characteristically, discusses the subject at length, making the Jealous Husband rail against women's *coquetterie* (ll. 992 ff., 8,889 ff., 9,039 ff.). The beauty of fine garments and jewels, he argues, lies in the things themselves and adds nothing to woman's 'biauté naïve', and thus when a woman seeks attention through expensive finery she despises God's gift:

> Et certes, qui le voir en conte,
> Mout font fames a Dieu grant honte,
> Comme foles et desvoïes,
> Quant ne se tiennent a poïes
> De la biauté que Diex lor donne.
> Chascune a sor son chief coronne
> De floretes, d'or ou de soie,
> Et s'en orguillist et cointoie
> Quant s'en va moustrant par la vile . . .
> (ll. 9,039–47)

(And certainly, if the truth be told, women give great shame to God. Straying fools, they do not consider themselves rewarded with the beauty that God gives them. Each one has on her head a crown of flowers, of gold, or of silk. She preens herself and primps as she goes through the town showing herself off . . .)

It is the theme of *GDG* 49 ('Merch yn Ymbincio'), a poem which, like Jean's continuation and the work of numerous medieval poets, reflects the anti-feminist movement and in particular the attacks on women's pride which form such a strong current in the sermon literature of the period.[70] Dafydd and his contemporaries would no

---

[70] Cf. the works cited by Chotzen, *Recherches*, 233–5; he discusses the tradition

doubt have been familiar with the themes and conventions of this widespread and deep-rooted tradition—compare Madog Benfras's satire of the mirror which is the cause of a girl's pride (*DGG* LXVII)—and his sermon-like exempla find no parallels in the *Roman*.[71] His affectionately mocking description of girls prettifying themselves on the morning of a fair[72] is nevertheless vaguely reminiscent of Jean de Meun, and a perhaps more significant analogue is to be found in Jean de Condé's *La Messe des oiseaux*, the poem which has been suggested as a source for the description of the woodland mass in *GDG* 122 ('Offeren y Llwyn'). The closing couplet of *GDG* 49—

> Gwell wyd mewn pais wenllwyd wiw
> Nog iarlles mewn gwisg eurlliw.

(Better are you in a good grey-white smock than a countess in a robe of gold.)

calls to mind the lines

> On voit. I. païsant de vile
> Avoir une aussi biele file
> En povre cote depannee
> K'une roÿne couronnee
> Ki est paree a son endroit.[73]

(One may see that a mere townsman has a daughter who is just as beautiful, in a poor, torn dress, as a crowned queen who, for her part, is all dressed up.)

The affinity of expression here may well be fortuitous, but its special context makes this passage all the more intriguing. Chotzen, who first drew attention to the relevance of the French poem to *GDG* 122, does not actually suggest direct influence, and Rachel Bromwich declares herself 'very doubtful as to whether Jean de Condé's poem

---

more fully in 'La "Querelle des femmes" au Pays de Galles', *Revue Celtique*, 48 (1931), 42–93, in relation to later Welsh literature.

[71] For a specific analogue in a preacher's exemplum see D. J. Bowen, 'Dafydd ap Gwilym a Datblygiad y Cywydd', 21, n. 156. The image of the gilded old bow has parallels in later Welsh verse, cf. *BBCS* 31, 43; *CRhC* 36.21–4; *Cerddi Rhydd Cynnar*, no. 35.

[72] For examples of satires of women's minute attention to appearance see E. Ritter (ed.), *Poésies des XIVe et XVe siècles* (Geneva, 1880), 422, and Nigel Wilkins (ed.), *One Hundred Ballades, Rondeaux and Virelais from the Late Middle Ages* (Cambridge, 1969), no. 60.

[73] Ribard, *La Messe des oiseaux* . . ., p. 47, ll. 1,109–13.

can properly be regarded as a source for Dafydd's treatment of the same theme'.[74] The poem, the full title of which is *La Messe des oiseaux et li plais des chanonesses et des grises nonains* ('The bird-mass and the complaint of the canonesses and the grey nuns'), is essentially a 'court of love' poem. The lengthy description of the bird-mass, which is itself preceded by a *reverdie* opening introducing the poet's vision, forms a preliminary to an allegorical feast and to the court of love itself, presided over by Venus; then comes the 'senefiance', the interpretation of the allegory. This makes for a work of almost 1,600 lines, described by its editor as an anthology of traditional themes and procedures.[75] Not the least of these procedures is religious parody, a genre made fashionable by the songs of the Latin scholars, and the idea of a religion of love is of course inherent to the ethos of *amour courtois*. The notion of the lovers' mass is therefore a quite natural development, and is indeed suggested in the *Roman*, in the words

> Car en tex leus tient ses escoles
> Et chante a ses desciples messes
> Li dieu d'Amors et les deesses.
> (ll. 13,526–8)

(For in such places the god and goddesses of Love keep their schools and sing mass to their disciples.)

I am inclined to disagree with the opinion of Chotzen and Bromwich, who assert that Jean de Condé's treatment of the theme is more irreverent or less exalted than that of the *cywydd*. In fact, in the 'senefiance' the meaning of the bird-mass is earnestly explained, and the love which the poet recommends is that which is 'raisounable', meaning marriage with God's blessing; men of religion are allowed only 'the true love, that of God which lasts forever' (ll. 1,564–5), for worldly love is but a dream, transitory as the blowing wind. However, as one would expect in such a long poem, the account of the service with its many parts is much more complete than that of the *cywydd*, though significantly there is nothing which corresponds to Dafydd's 'cloch aberth'—the sacring-bell represented by the nightingale's song.[76] It is true that in both poems it is the nightingale

---

[74] *APDG* 77; cf. *Recherches*, 187–8, and see also R. Geraint Gruffydd, 'Sylwadau ar Gywydd "Offeren Y Llwyn" Dafydd ap Gwilym', *YB* 10 (1977), 187–8.

[75] Ribard, *La Messe des oiseaux . . .*, p. xiii; see also his discussion of the poem in *Un Ménestrel du XIVᵉ siècle: Jean de Condé* (Geneva, 1969), 376–81.

[76] As Chotzen observed (*Recherches*, 188), the host of the French poem is a rose,

which officiates, but Venus commands that it be accompanied by numerous other birds which fulfil different functions. One might, if pressed for a more or less precise correspondence, compare the following couplet describing the thrush—

> Darllain i'r plwyf, nid rhwyf rhus,
> Efengyl yn ddifyngus.
>
> (ll. 23–4)

(Reading the gospel distinctly to the parish, without excessive excitement.)

with the lines

> Et li mauvis, c'on ot eslut,
> Tantost aprés l'Epistle lut
> Au plus haut que lever le pot . . .
>
> (ll. 159–61)

(and the song-thrush, which had been chosen, immediately afterwards read the Epistle as loudly as it possibly could . . .)

But on the whole, it is clear that *GDG* 122 is not a direct imitation of *La Messe des oiseaux*; the latter should not, as Bromwich rightly suggested, be regarded as a precise 'source' for the *cywydd*. Taking into account the medieval liking for religious parody, and in particular Dafydd's recurrent depiction of birds as poets and preachers, the poem may be seen as a development of his own poetic vision of the natural world. Yet given the underlying similarity in theme between the two poems, we should not discard the possibility that it was Dafydd's knowledge of the French poem, which cannot be much earlier than the *cywydd*,[77] which inspired his own, more lyrical depiction of a woodland mass.

Another of Dafydd's poems which has affinities with the work of Jean de Condé is the *traethodl GDG* 137 ('Y Bardd a'r Brawd Llwyd'). This, and Dafydd's other quarrels with the mendicant friars (nos. 136–9), along with those by Iolo Goch (*GIG* XXXIV–V)

whereas DG has a leaf—'Afrlladen o ddeilen dda' (l. 26). Note, however, that Jean's nightingale detaches from the flower three leaves, but the rose (i.e. the host) remains whole (on the theological significance of the image see Ribard, *La Messe des oiseaux* . . ., 84–5).

[77] Jean de Condé lived until around 1345, and his latest editor considers this poem and another of his most accomplished works—*Li Dis des Jacobins et des Fremeneurs* (discussed below)—to be the products of his artistic maturity. The two poems do not, however, appear to have been widely known: they are preserved in only two of the five MSS which contain the poet's work, written in the early and mid-14th cent. (ibid., pp. xvi–xvii).

and Madog Benfras (*BDG* CCXVII), belong to a larger European
family, best represented on the Continent by the great Parisian *jongleur* Rutebeuf, who composed in the second half of the thirteenth
century when the controversy between poets and friars was at its
height. The early *Cywyddwyr*'s satires of the friars' begging, their
lechery, their gluttony, and their general hypocrisy have plenty of
parallels outside Wales,[78] as does Dafydd's defence of the opposite
sex with which he answers the anti-feminist preachings of the
Franciscan friar. When Dafydd retorts:

> Merch sydd decaf blodeuyn
> Yn y nef ond Duw ei hun.
> O wraig y ganed pob dyn
> O'r holl bobloedd ond tridyn.
> (*GDG* 137.43–6)

(A maiden is the fairest flower in heaven, except God himself. Amongst all
peoples every man was born of a woman, except three.)

he is echoing two of the period's most common arguments in defence
of women: the example of the Virgin Mary and the fact that all men
are born of women. The very same arguments are employed by
countless poets, including Jean de Condé:

> . . . Car nulle honnours n'em puet venir
> En ce c'om mesdie de femme,
> Si n'iert fors pour la haute gemme,
> La roïnne des cieus Marie . . .
> Et tout de femmes issu sommes,
> Si leur devons honnour porter . . .[79]

(For no honour can come of speaking ill of women, if it were only on
account of the high jewel, Mary, queen of heaven . . . And we are all issued
from women, therefore we must treat them honourably . . .)

When Iolo Goch, in defence of carnal love, impresses upon a Grey
Friar the necessity for procreation (*GIG* XXXV.23–6), he is express-

[78] Matonis, 'Medieval Topics and Rhetoric . . .', 263 ff., compares these satires with
similar attacks by Middle English and Latin poets; cf. *Roman*, ll. 10,919 ff. See also
A. Serper, *Rutebeuf: poète satirique* (Paris, 1969), ch. 4; N. F. Regalado, *Poetic
Patterns in Rutebeuf: A Study* (New Haven and London, 1970), chs. 2 and 3; Arnold
Williams, 'Chaucer and the Friars', *Speculum*, 28 (1953), 499–513; and for a comprehensive survey, P. R. Szittya, *The Antifraternal Tradition in Medieval Literature*
(Princeton, NJ, 1986).
[79] Scheler, *Dits et contes . . .*, vol. 2, XXXVI.254–65; cf. vol. 3, LVIII ('Pourquoi on
doit femes honorer'). For further examples, mainly French and Latin, see *Recherches*,
235–7.

ing yet another *lieu commun*, most eloquently supported by Jean de Meun.

All this—the satire of monks, the arguments for and against women and the love of women—was, as Chotzen has shown, common currency, and this weakens the case for direct influence of a literary kind.[80] However, one of Jean de Condé's poems addressed to friars, *Li Dis des Jacobins et des Fremeneurs*, contains a number of elements whose relevance to *GDG* 137 may be more than merely accidental. Both poems are a kind of poetic manifesto, a defence of profane song against the constant and vehement accusations by the Church, and by the friars in particular. Essentially, both Dafydd and Jean de Condé uphold the value of poetry as entertainment. The Frenchman, rather more pompously, stresses also the upholding of good morals, and claims, as a professional *menestrel* attached to a great court, to represent his noble profession, dissociating himself (rather like Gruffudd Llwyd later in the century) from entertainers of a lower order such as magicians, jugglers, and the like.[81] Chotzen has drawn attention to the fact that both poets cite the example of the harpist King David in defence of secular song.[82] According to Dafydd,

> A chywyddau i Dduw lwyd
> Yw sallwyr Dafydd Broffwyd.
> (ll. 59–60)

(And the psalms of the prophet David are but *cywyddau* to holy God.)

Jean, who relates how David cured King Saul by his harping (ll. 9–26), expresses the idea in similar terms, in the lines

> David commanda ou sautier,
> En une psaume, en aucuns vers,
> Dieu a loer en sons diviers
> D'estrumens, que il nome la . . .
> (ll. 54–7)

(David commanded in the psalter, in a psalm, in some verses, that God be praised in various sounds of instruments, which he names there . . .)

---

[80] See esp. *Recherches*, 240–1.

[81] 'Teus sermons que vous en retraites, | Fu dite pour les enchanteurs | Et pour les faus entrejeteurs. . .' (Ribard, *La Messe des oiseaux*. . ., p. 10, ll. 282 ff.). For Ieuan Llwyd's reaction to the *Elucidarium* see Ch. 1 above, n. 47.

[82] *Recherches*, 240.

The invoking of the authority of 'li roys Davis' is not uncommon, and the *Cywyddwyr* were themselves fond of citing the example of 'Dafydd Broffwyd' in relation to love and the poetry of love.[83] As Rachel Bromwich has observed, it is the context of the passages by Jean de Condé which makes them particularly significant[84] (though it is noteworthy that his younger contemporary Guillaume de Machaut, in his defence of the art of music, similarly refers to 'David li prophetes', who pleased God with his harp, and his 'Hympnes, psautiers et orisons', 'hymns, psalms and prayers').[85] Dafydd follows his reference to Dafydd Broffwyd with another biblical reference, strengthening his case by echoing the Book of Ecclesiastes. Jean de Condé, too, uses the device of citing scriptural exempla, boasting to the mocking Dominicans and Franciscans (the very friars who are the butt of the early *Cywyddwyr*'s satire) his knowledge of the sacred book.

> Vous, Jacobin et Cordelois,
> Je sai. I. petit des. II. lois,
> De la viés et de la nouvele . . .
> (ll. 135–7)

(You, Jacobins and Grey Friars, I know a bit about the two laws, the old and the new . . .)

he asserts proudly, in the same conversational, almost familiar, tone which characterizes *GDG* 137. A pleasant poem, argues Jean, brings joy to all who hear it—

> Car par menestreus, bien le di,
> Qui resbaudissent les ostés,
> Est tamains cuers d'anui ostés . . .
> (ll. 128–30)

(For, if truth be told, many a heart is raised from sorrow by minstrels, who gladden the gatherings . . .)

precisely the sentiment expressed in the couplet

---

[83] To *GIG* XXII.83–4 and a reference by Rhys Goch Eryri, cited by Chotzen, *Recherches*, 240, may be added *DGG* XXI.25–8: 'Gorweddaf lle bu Ddafydd | Broffwyd teg braff, i oed dydd; | Gwr a wnaeth er lliw gwawr nef, | Saith salm, tad syth i Selef.' Cf. also *CRhC* I, IV.21–4. A goliardic example of the motif is also cited by Chotzen, and a further Continental parallel is provided, once more, by Jean de Condé (Scheler, *Dits et contes . . .*, vol.3, LIX. 83 ff.).

[84] See her note on 'Dafydd Broffwyd' in *BBCS* 29 (1980), 81.

[85] *Poésies lyriques*, vol. I, pp. 11–12, ll. 235 ff.

Cerdd a bair yn llawenach
Hen ac ieuanc, claf ac iach.[86]
(ll. 51–2)

(A poem makes happier the old and young, sick and well.)

Dafydd reminds the frowning friar that there is a time for joy or entertainment as for preaching—

Ac amser i bregethu,
Ac amser i gyfanheddu.
(ll. 65–6)

Likewise Jean de Condé remarks:

Joie est a la fois en saison
Qui est faite courtoisement.
(ll. 72–3)

(Joy which is courteously brought is sometimes appropriate.)

A further, albeit relatively minor, parallel with Dafydd's poetry is provided by Jean de Condé's *Li Dis de la pelote*.[87] This is a long and somewhat contrived poem in which mutual love between two hearts is compared with the game of *pelote*, the analogy being that, as in the similar game of tennis, the ball should be returned to the person who struck it. In one of his more bitter love-poems, GDG 93 ('Y Cariad a Wrthodwyd'), Dafydd uses a similar image, likening Morfudd, whom he accuses of alternating her affections between her poet and her husband, to a ball which is thrown from hand to hand:

Mal y gwnair, gurair gerydd,
Chwarae â phêl, fy chwaer ffydd,
Hoff wyd, dilynwyd dy lun
O-law-i-law, loyw eilun.
(ll. 27–30)

---

[86] D. J. Bowen makes a similar comparison between the two poems in *Dafydd ap Gwilym a Dyfed* (Llandysul, 1986), 27–8. Jean's emphasis on 'les boinnes gens solacier', 'Dou bien noncier, dou mal celer', and on despising the 'jougleres | U menestrés d'autre maniere' (Scheler, *Dits et contes . . .*, vol. 2, XXXVI.186 ff.) has much in common with the precepts of Einion Offeiriad's slightly later Bardic Grammar; cf. Saunders Lewis, 'Dafydd ap Gwilym', *Presenting Saunders Lewis*, 160. His father, Baudouin de Condé, had already warned against unedifying or vituperative verse, urging poets to compose 'pour la gent deduire' (Scheler, *Dits et contes . . .*, vol. 1, XIX.40 ff.). 'Ac amser i gyfanheddu' (GDG 137.66) may be a deliberate echo of GP 17.9–10, where 'kyuanhedu' (entertainment) is noted as a function of the *teuluwr*; cf. Bromwich, *SP* 163.

[87] Scheler, *Dits et contes . . .*, vol. 2, XXVIII.

(Just as a ball—painful word of rebuke—is played with, my sister in the faith—so dear are you—your form has been pursued from hand to hand, dazzling image.)

This unusual image may easily have occurred to Dafydd quite naturally from everyday life, and this is probably the case. It is noteworthy that here, in total contrast to Jean de Condé's poem, it signifies infidelity. On the other hand, one must bear in mind the possibility that Dafydd was acquainted with the Frenchman's work, and the case for foreign influence is strengthened by Jean de Meun's description of Fortune, which cares nothing for deceit or loyalty, estate or royalty, but treats them as a ball-game, as it were, like a foolish young girl—'s'en joe a la pelote | Comme pucele nice et sote' (*Roman*, ll. 6,557–8).

Moreover, it is surprising to find that two other images illustrating the girl's infidelity in this *cywydd* also have parallels in French poetry. First, Morfudd is compared to a ploughman who has two pairs of oxen which he alternates, just as she passes as it pleases her from husband to lover (ll. 17–26). The sexual innuendo which is probably intended here is more explicitly expressed in an analogous husbandry image by the thirteenth-century Champenois poet Robert de Reims, who wickedly suggests that his beloved's 'land' 'will never be well ploughed as long as she has only one ox to her plough'—

> . . . Ne ja n'ert bien sa terre costoïe,
> Tant comme el n'a qu'un buef à sa charrue.[88]

Morfudd's behaviour is also reminiscent of one of the minor themes of the *malmariée* genre, expressed in the familiar refrain in which the wife assures her husband—

> Soufrés, maris, et si ne vous anuit;
> Demain m'arés et mes amis anuit.[89]

(Have patience, my husband, and do not be annoyed; you'll have me tomorrow, and my lover tonight.)

---

[88] P. Tarbé (ed.), *Les Chansonniers de Champagne aux XIIe et XIIIe siècles*, (repr. Geneva, 1980), 49.20–1. On this poem, which belongs to a genre which deliberately parodies the conventional *grand chant courtois*, see A. Langfors (ed.), *Deux recueils de sottes chansons* (Helsinki, 1945), 22, and the works referred to there.

[89] Raynaud, *Recueil de motets français*, ii. 129 (the theme is discussed by Pierre Bec, *La Lyrique française . . .*, i. 71; on the *malmariée* poems see also Ch. 7 below). Cf. Guillaume de Machaut: 'Et si devés amer, j'en suis tous fis, | Vo mari com vo mari | Et vostre amy com vostre doulz ami. . .' (*Poésies lyriques*, vol. 1, CCXXXI.12–14), lines which find a Welsh analogue in *CSTB* XXVIII.39–48.

Secondly, Dafydd likens his fate as a rejected lover to that of a faithful squire, who, despite having faced peril in place of his knight, remains unrewarded (ll. 33–6). The parallel with this yet more unusual image is provided by Baudouin de Condé, father of Jean de Condé, who in his *Contes dou Wardecors* draws an analogy between the *gardecorps* (a long close protective garment) and the faithful vassal who is willing to defend his lord's very body in battle:

> Quant li sires est em bataille
> Entre ses anemis morteus,
> Si li est cius wardecors teus,
> Qu'il le garandist de la mort . . . [90]

(When the lord is in battle amongst his mortal enemies, this *gardecorps* serves him in such a way as to protect him from death . . .)

Although *Li Contes dou Wardecors*, a long moral poem which stresses the importance of fidelity, nobility, and honour, is on the whole far removed from the *cywydd*, the relevance of this particular passage (in which the 'wardecors' is meant to represent the faithful servant) is readily apparent. And it is not impossible that Dafydd's specific reference to the squire's close-fitting garments—'A'r rhain cyn dynned â'r rhisg', 'and these as tight as bark'—is an echo of the French poem's central metaphor.

The work of the same poet provides a parallel for the image of the uncertain lover as a ship at sea in *GDG* 37.19-26 ('Caru Merch Fonheddig'). Chotzen has shown (in relation not to *GDG* 37 but to the similar image of the 'llong foel' in the 'apocryphal' *BDG* CXLVIII (probably fifteenth-century)) that the image is common in Continental love-poetry, both Latin and vernacular, where it is perhaps derived from Ovid.[91] A French poet complains in a motet—

> Hé Diex! je n'i puis durer
> Pour celle cui je tant ain,
> C'onkes marinier de mer
>   N'ot si grant fain
> Por tormente d'arriver
>   A son droit port
> Con j'ai de celle ke j'ain avoir deport . . .[92]

[90] Scheler, *Dits et contes . . .*, vol. 1, ll. 218–21.

[91] *Recherches*, 331; cf. Fulton's note on *GDG* 37, *DGEC* 241. On the legend of the 'llong foel' and further references to it in 15th- and 16th-century poetry see Brynley F. Roberts, 'Ystori'r Llong Foel', *BBCS* 18 (1960), 337–62.

[92] Raynaud, *Recueil de motets français*, ii. 15.

(Dear God! I cannot go on on account of her whom I love so much, for no storm ever gave any sailor a desire to reach his own true port as great as my desire to receive joy from the one I love . . .)

The ship's arrival at port signifies here, as for Dafydd, the lady's eventual acceptance of the suffering lover. As one might expect, in longer poems, as in Baudouin de Condé's *Li Contes de la rose*, the image received a more expansive and more allegorical treatment,[93] but it is its fusion in this poem with the theme of the inaccessibility of the lady due to her social status which makes it particularly striking. It is, of course, the central theme of *GDG* 37—with which we may compare the *cywydd* to 'Y fun uchel o fonedd' attributed to Gruffudd Gryg (*DGG* LXXII)—reminiscent of occasional complaints by the troubadours and trouvères that they have set their sights too high. Baudouin de Condé is resigned to the fact, and warns others:

> . . . Amant, vous qui manés
> En dangier por mierchi atendre,
> Gardés vous de si haut à tendre
> Que vous n'i puissiés avenir.
>   (ll. 286–9)

(Lovers, you who remain in judgement in order to await mercy, take care not to aspire so high that you cannot reach your goal.)

A similar thought is expressed by Dafydd:

> Oddyna y bydd anawdd
> Disgynnu rhag haeddu cawdd.
>   (ll. 17–18)

(From there it is difficult to come down for fear of earning resentment.)

The couplet refers to his image of the animal which climbs to the safety of a high branch, just as the poet claims to have been accused of venturing too high when he sang the praise of the noble Dyddgu.

Baudouin de Condé's description of the lark, which opens the dream-vision poem entitled *La Voie de Paradis*, has affinities with the excellent *GDG* 114 ('Yr Ehedydd'):

> Quant voi de son orguel marchir
> L'iver et le temps esclarchir,

---

[93] Scheler, *Dits et contes . . .*, vol. 1, X.230 ff. Cf. id., *Trouvères Belges*, ii. 266–7, where the winds which blow the ship off course represent 'La parole de fauses gens', the ever-present *médisants*.

> Chanter le malvis et l'aloe,
> Qui en son dous chant le temps loe,
> Tent ses eles contre le ray
> Du soleil et dist: 'or le ray,
> 'Le dous termine qui m'agrée,
> 'Que printemps à mon vueil m'agrée;'
> S'en merchie Deu en son chant.
> Ainssi va sa joie nonchant
> En l'air, où ele monte à tour
> Et rent grasses au creatour . . .[94]

(When I see Winter overthrown from its pride and the weather brightening, the song-thrush sings and the lark, which praises the season in its sweet song, extends its wings against the sun's light and says: 'Now it is mine once more, the gentle season which pleases me so—how spring fills me with pleasure;' for this it thanks God in its song. Thus it goes announcing its joy in the sky, where it encircles its way upwards, giving thanks to the Creator . . .)

Dafydd's lark, too, described as 'April's gatekeeper', sings the praises of God, the Creator, as it rises majestically into the sky, and the imagery, as in the French poem, is that of poetry and worship:

> Pan ddelych i addoli,
> Dawn a'th roes Duw Un a Thri . . .
>
> (ll. 35–6)

(When you may come to worship, God One and Three has given you a gift . . .)

The lark is described as a preacher and a singer from God's chapel— 'Cantor o gapel Celi' (l. 27), as well as a love-poet—'Modd awdur serch' (l. 23), who sings his songs by the 'rampart' of the stars. In another *cywydd*, again set at the beginning of April, he draws a similar picture of the lark, in the lines

> A'r ehedydd, lonydd lais,
> Cwcyllwyd edn cu callais,
> Yn myned mewn lludded llwyr
> Â chywydd i entrych awyr . . .
>
> (GDG 63.11–14)

(And the calm-voiced lark, dear, grey-cowled bird of wise speech, languidly ascending with a *cywydd* to the heights of the sky . . .)

---

[94] Scheler, *Dits et contes . . .*, vol. 1, XVIII.1–12. It is Baudouin's depiction of the spring awakening in the lines which follow, with its 'clothing' imagery, which is referred to in n. 69 above.

Dafydd's portrayal was long ago compared with a poem by the troubadour Bernart de Ventadour which captures the ecstasy of the lark's
ascent at dawn.[95] As A. T. Hatto has more recently shown, the
depiction of the lark by Chaucer's 'great and more rhapsodic contemporary' has many other external parallels. The convention, which
is especially widespread in medieval Latin writings, is largely
explained by the fact that: 'The flight of [Dafydd's] lark to Heaven's
Gates (like that of other mediaeval larks) is further sustained by the
implicit pun *alauda* ("lark": *lauda* "praise!")',[96] a pun which works
in French as well as Latin. Whether or not the poem by Baudouin de
Condé had any direct bearing on the imagery of *GDG* 114—which,
admittedly, would be surprising considering the currency of the
motif—it is clear that in this *cywydd* Dafydd is once more exercis-
ing his remarkable descriptive powers within the context of the wider
European lyric tradition.

[95] W. Lewis Jones, 'The Literary Relationships of Dafydd ap Gwilym', *THSC*
(1907–8), 137; see Moshé Lazar (ed.), *Bernard de Ventadour : troubadour du XIIe siècle* (Paris, 1966), 31.1–8, and the editor's note, p. 274.

[96] A.T. Hatto, *Eos: An Enquiry into the Theme of Lovers' Meetings and Partings at
Dawn in Poetry* (The Hague, 1965), 812; for a further example in French verse see
Rosenberg and Tischler, *Chanter m'estuet*, 17.1–4.

7

External Influences and Analogues: II

The *cywydd* to the lark discussed in the previous chapter is one of
the finest illustrations of Dafydd ap Gwilym's deep religious rever-
ence for the natural world as God's creation and a manifestation of
God on earth. It is a feeling which pervades his nature poetry, and
the view that a poem such as *GDG* 122 ('Offeren y Llwyn') is, as Ifor
Williams suggested long ago,[1] an irreverent parody of the established
religion comparable with the outrageous burlesques of the Latin
scholars cannot, I think, be justified. The phrase 'caregl nwyf a
chariad' (*GDG* 122.34), 'a chalice of passion and love', is audacious
in the extreme, but despite the element of parody the spirit of the
holy service is not actually undermined. Dafydd's celebration of love
in terms of the sacrament is a challenge, not to religion as such, but
to the kind of extreme asceticism preached by the mendicant friars.
His answer to the doom-laden warnings of the Grey Friar—that
'God is not as cruel as old men claim' (*GDG* 137.37–8), is a terse
reminder that the religion of self-denial is not for everyone, and that
the worship of God in and through his Creation, of which feminine
beauty and earthly sensuality are essential parts, is equally valid. The
image of the woodland love-mass is, of course, reminiscent of the
notion of a 'religion' of love which is so dear to the troubadours and
trouvères; but while the poems of Dafydd and his contemporaries
are, inevitably, filled with the language and imagery of religious
experience, unlike French and Provençal love-poetry there is no
coherent 'system' with its God of Love, its earthly paradise, and its
recurrent metaphor of repentance, penitence, and salvation.
However, Dafydd ap Gwilym's *cywyddau serch* do contain a number of concepts and images drawn from the world of religion which
are analogous with Continental love-poetry.

GDG 52 ('Gofyn Cymod'), in which the poet seeks reconciliation
with his mistress, is another of those poems which are redolent of the
rhetorical style of the preacher. It may be that a light parody is
intended of the *awdlau dadolwch* composed by the *Gogynfeirdd* (a

---

[1] 'Dafydd ap Gwilym a'r Glêr', *THSC* (1913–14), 152–3.

genre which is represented in Dafydd's time by a *cywydd* by Gruffudd Gryg seeking appeasement with the seven sons of Iorwerth ap Gruffudd of Anglesey, *DGG* LXXX); but the poet's humble request for reconciliation with his *dame* is also a fairly common theme in Continental love-poetry.[2] The troubadour Raimbaut d'Orange, like Dafydd, uses a religious comparison in his plea for his lady's mercy, referring to God's mercy shown to the penitent thief.[3] Similarly, Dafydd reminds Morfudd first of the legend of Longinus, according to which the blind soldier, after wounding Christ on the cross, had his sight restored by the divine blood, and secondly of the Virgin Mary's forgiveness when Christ was mocked. A medieval Latin poet warns lovers of the sinfulness of anger, one of the Seven Deadly Sins, with a sermon-like catalogue of its evil effects; 'frequent anger is madness', he says, 'long-lasting anger a crime',[4] and Dafydd has similar advice for Morfudd:

> Nid oes bechawd, methlgnawd maith,
> Marwol mwy ei oferwaith
> No thrigo, mawr uthr ogan,
> Mewn llid, eiliw Enid lân.
>
> (ll. 47–50)

(There is no mortal sin—long ensnaring of the flesh—more vain than to dwell (great terrible scorn) in anger, you of the colour of fair Enid.)

Chotzen has shown in relation to *GDG* 48 ('Merched Llanbadarn') that the motif of lovers meeting in church is well attested not only in Continental literature but also in the popular verse of the Celtic nations, although he admits that the situation described here need not necessarily be related to any received literary convention.[5] Having seen his shameless flirtations flatly rebuffed by the two girls attending the service behind him, Dafydd proclaims that he might as well renounce love and become a hermit (*GDG* 48.39–40). It is one of Dafydd's more humorous poems, and this is the spirit in which

---

[2] Cf. Chichmaref (ed.), *Poésies lyriques de Guillaume de Machaut*, vol. i, XLIII; Scheler (ed.), *Trouvères Belges*, i. 75–7; ii. 42; E. Winkler (ed.), *Die Lieder Raouls Von Soissons* (Halle, 1914), no. 14.

[3] W. T. Pattison, *The Life and Works of the Troubadour Raimbaut d'Orange* (Minneapolis, 1952), nos. 11, 23.

[4] *MLREL*, ii. 448–9. Cf. John Morris-Jones and John Rhŷs (eds.), *The Elucidarium ... from Llyvyr Agkyr Llandewivrevi* (Oxford, 1894), 143: 'Ac na chattwo dyn lit odigassed gantaw vrth ygymodawc' (the MS was probably written in 1346).

[5] *Recherches*, 269–70. For an enlightening discussion of *GDG* 48 see D. J. Bowen, 'Cywydd Dafydd ap Gwilym i Ferched Llanbadarn a'i Gefndir', *YB* 12 (1982), 77–122.

the couplet must be understood. It is possible to regard this, and the magpie's advice to the ageing poet—'. . . dos yn feudwy . . . ac na châr mwy' (*GDG* 63.69–70), 'become a hermit, and love no more'— as ironic echoes of one of the minor conventions of the courtly love lyric. Gontier de Soignies, for instance, declares the extent of his devotion with the words 'Bien saice pour li irai en hermitaige . . .', 'let her be assured that I shall enter a hermitage on her account',[6] and a fifteenth-century poet, after cursing all jealous husbands, concludes, with equal earnestness:

> Adieu, ma dame . . .
> Pour Dieu, ayez ung souvenir
>   D'un amoureulx
> Qui pour vous va ses jours finyr
> En l'ermitage douloureux.[7]

(Farewell, my lady . . . For the sake of God, preserve a memory of a lover who because of you is going to end his days in the distressing hermitage.)

It will be remembered too that, before Dafydd's time, Iorwerth Fychan also compared the sufferings of the lover with those of a hermit.[8] The notion of the lover as martyr, however, which is a natural development of the wider religious metaphor in the poetry of *amour courtois*, is not explicitly reflected in the early *cywyddau*.

In *GDG* 66 ('Y Cloc'), which tells of a pleasant dream, Dafydd expresses the age-old poetic ideal of finding heaven here on earth:

> Cael ydd oeddwn, coel ddiddos,
> Hun o'r nef am hanner nos,
> Ym mhlygau hir freichiau hon . . .[9]
>   (ll. 39–41)

(I was having (a true portent *or/and* a snug embrace) a heaven-sent sleep at midnight, in the folds of her long arms . . .)

The passage is closely paralleled in French poetry. The author of a motet maintains that 'he who sleeps in his love's arms has indeed found paradise'—'Cil qui dort es braz s'amie | A bien paradis trové', and with similar audaciousness another poet proclaims:

---

[6] Rosenberg and Tischler, *Chanter m'estuet*, 122.35.

[7] G. Paris (ed.), *Chansons du XVᵉ siècle* (Paris, 1875), XV.33–40.

[8] See above Ch. 3, p. 92. In the 15th cent. cf. Llywelyn ab y Moel: 'Yr wyf o haint ar fy hyd | Ym mhoen fal ancr ym mhenyd' (*CIGE* LXIV.17–18), and *BDG* CLXVIII.13–14.

[9] Cf. the lines 'Os nef a geisiwn ofyn, | Fy nef oedd weled fy nyn', which refer to the poet's dream in the 'apocryphal' *BDG* CXI.25–6.

> . . . mils qu'en paradis lassus
> ameroie entre ses dous bras . . .[10]

(better than in paradise above would I love between her sweet arms.)

The motif is also reflected in the Harley Lyrics, in 'The Fair Maid of Ribblesdale' (a poem which, as will be seen, provides a number of other analogues with early *cywydd* love-poetry):

> He myhte sayen þat Crist hym seȝe
> þat myhte nyhtes neh hyre leȝe,
> heuene he heuede here.[11]

Dafydd also hints at the idea of heaven on earth in such a seemingly innocuous phrase as 'lle nef yma' (*lit.* 'a place of heaven here'), which describes the idealized woodland of *GDG* 119 (l. 36) ('I Wahodd Dyddgu'); and although the suggestion that his soul might enter heaven ('nef i'm enaid') if he were to win a girl's favours occurs in the light-hearted context of *GDG* 47 (l. 33) ('Bargeinio'), it is nevertheless reminiscent of the more earnest declarations of the trouvères. Gontier de Soignies declares, with reference to his lady's beauty:

> Et se je muir en cest pensé,
> Bien cuit m'ame avoir sauvée.[12]

(And if I die in this thought, I truly believe that I will have saved my soul.)

and it is not uncommon for these poets to assert that they would willingly forsake Paradise itself for their lady's love. Thibaut de Champagne, for instance, proclaims:

> Si me vaudroit melz un ris
> De vous qu'autre paradis.

(More would I value a smile from you than any other paradise.)

and again—

> . . . estre ne voudroie
> En Paradis, s'ele n'i estoit moie.[13]

(I would not care to be in Paradise if she weren't mine there.)

---

[10] Raynaud, *Recueil de motets français*, ii. 102; N. H. J. van den Boogaard, 'Les Chansons attribuées à Wilart de Corbie', *Neophilologus*, 55 (1971), 137.

[11] Brook, *The Harley Lyrics*, 7.82–4; cf. 5.39–40: 'heuene y tolde al his | þat o nyht were hire gest.'

[12] Scheler, *Trouvères Belges*, ii. 13 (no. 6.21–2).

[13] Wallensköld, *Les Chansons de Thibaut de Champagne*, XXI.53–4, XXV.13–14; cf. XLI.53–4. Cf. also Scheler, *Trouvères Belges*, i. 10 (no. 4.4–9); *Chanter m'estuet*, 194.25–8; and the Latin and Provençal examples cited in *Recherches*, 301.

Gillebert de Berneville is verging on blasphemy with his defiant

> Ja mes grez
> N'iert que j'aie bien nul jor
> Nes paradis
> Sanz la bele Biatriz.[14]

(I shall never be satisfied with any good that comes to me a single day, or even paradise, without fair Beatrice.)

This is a thought which finds a notable analogy in the final couplet of *GDG* 77 ('Amau ar Gam'):

> Na chaffwyf dda gan Dduw fry,
> O chei 'modd, o chymyddy.
>   (ll. 27–8)

(May I not have wealth from God above, if you please me, if you'll be reconciled.)

Finally, the thought expressed in the following passage from *GDG* 101 ('Merch Fileinaidd')—

> Pei prytwn, gwn gan henglyn,
> Er Duw a brydais er dyn,
> Hawdd y gwnâi erof, o hawl,
> Fyw o farw, fwyaf eiriawl.
>   (ll. 35–8)

(Were I to compose—I know a hundred *englynion*—for God as many poems as I have composed for a girl, easily for my sake, by right, would He raise me from the dead, most intense entreaty.)

may be compared with Thibaut de Champagne's

> Dame, se je servisse Dieu autant
> Et priasse de verai cuer entier
> Con je faz vous, je sai certainement
> Qu'en Paradis n'eüst autel loier . . .[15]

(Lady, had I served God as well and implored with all my loyal heart as I implore you, I know for sure that there would not be such payment [for me] in Paradise.)

While some of these correspondences are in themselves striking enough, the unavoidable imprint of religion on the medieval mind makes it all but impossible to infer whether external influence may

---

[14] *Chanter m'estuet*, 170.45–8.
[15] Wallensköld, *Les Chansons de Thibaut de Champagne*, XXI.21–4.

be detected in any particular case. Yet the cumulative evidence is rather suggestive of foreign contact, as are a variety of further themes, images, and motifs, most of which are once more taken from the poems of Dafydd ap Gwilym. Although it would again be foolish to claim as a direct source the work of any particular French, Anglo-Norman, or Latin poet referred to here, the parallels identified will at least serve to indicate the possibility of influence in terms of some of the more minor conventions of the European love-lyric in general. We must, at the same time, constantly bear in mind our ignorance of the native popular verse tradition in this period, and be prepared to admit the quite natural possibility of coincidence in matter and tone, and even in seemingly significant details of expression, which may arise in part from what may be termed a certain community of spirit between two poets. This last consideration certainly applies to the marked correspondences which exist between Dafydd's vivid portrayal in *GDG* 110 ('Difrawder') of a girl who flatters to deceive—a theme treated in similar fashion in *GDG* 56 ('Campau Bun')—and a passage by the Artois trouvère Gontier de Soignies:

> En losenges et en biaus dis
> M'en a cortoisement blandi;
> Onques de s'amor ne fui fis
> Ne del tot ne m'en escondi.[16]

(With false praise and fine words she flattered me courteously; I was never certain of her love, yet neither did she refuse me completely.)

Dafydd's beloved, likewise, is not lacking in fine words and kindness—

> Ni symud mynud meinir
> Na'i gwên er celwydd na gwir . . .
>   (ll. 27–8)

(The girl's courtesy does not change, nor her smile, because of lies or truth . . .)

If he happens to become impatient she promptly reassures him with a kiss and pleasant laughter (ll. 35–40) and, like her French counterpart, while she does not actually accept the poet as a lover, neither does she reject him (ll. 31–2). These paradoxes find a further analogue in an anonymous poem, again from the thirteenth century, in

---

[16] Scheler, *Trouvères Belges*, ii. 67 (no. 29.31–4).

which we are told that the lady has broken her promise and taken another lover:

> Or vuelt ma dame, ores ne me vuelt mie,
> Or ai s'amour, et or n'ai rienz conkis . . .
> Si me promet, et deisai lai truix vainne,
> Si suis ameis, et deisai suis haïs . . .[17]

(One moment my lady wants me, the next she doesn't want me at all; one moment I have her love, the next I haven't gained a thing . . . She makes me promises, and then I find her false; I am loved, and then I am detested . . .)

Almost equally striking are the parallels in French love-poetry with *GDG* 100 ('Saethu'r Ferch'), a witty and easily intelligible burlesque of one of courtly love's most distinctive conventions, that of the arrow of love. The stricken poet wishes the same fate on his beloved, but on condition that the arrow does not pierce her skin or as much as a stitch of her smock! With tongue firmly in cheek he then expresses concern for her well-being, and concludes that he much prefers her alive, 'because of her goodness'! This is reminiscent of the troubadours' and trouvères' numerous passages of repentance,[18] which often take the form of a rhetorical self-questioning after some outspoken reference to the lady's cruelty not in keeping with the conduct of a courtly lover. These poets occasionally wish that the *dame* should herself have a taste of the affliction which she causes so that she may have mercy on them, as in the motet 'Mal d'amors, prenés m'amie . . .'.[19] Raoul de Soissons, who, like Dafydd, is 'dying of love', implores the God of Love to strike his lady also:

> Et puis qu'ensi m'estuet la mort souffrir
> De la dolor dont sa biauté me blece,
> La puist Amors par mi le cors ferir,
> S'iert conpaingne de ma douce destrece![20]

(And since I must thus suffer death from the pain with which her beauty wounds me, may Love strike her through her body—she will be a companion to my sweet distress!)

Then, almost inevitably, comes the rhetorical 'Las, qu'ai je dit?', 'Alas! What have I said?', and the poet realizes that if he is to serve

---

[17] *Romania*, vol. 57, p. 364, LXXX.7–12; cf. vol. 56, p. 57, XL.29–35.
[18] Cf. S. N. Rosenberg and S. Danon (ed. and trans.), *The Lyrics and Melodies of Gace Brulé* (New York and London, 1985), *passim*, and see Charles Payen, *Le Motif du repentir dans la littérature française médiévale* (Geneva, 1968), 231–77.
[19] Raynaud, *Recueil de motets français*, vol. i, CXIV.
[20] Winkler, *Lieder*, 7.19–22.

Love faithfully he must suffer alone in the hope of future joy. The *cywydd* may also be compared with a stanza by Le Châtelain de Coucy, in which he claims to have been wounded by the 'pleasant lance' of his lady's eyes, and seeks a fitting vengeance—

> . . . Mout volontiers en preïsse vengance
> —Par Dieu le Creatour!—
> Tel que mil foiz la peüsse le jour
> Ferir u cuer d'autretele savour . . .[21]

(Willingly would I take revenge upon her—by God the Creator!—so that a thousand times a day I might strike her heart with exactly the same sensation . . .)

In its concentration on a single aspect of the girl's body, *GDG* 53 ('Breichiau Morfudd'), like *GDG* 73 ('Gwallt Morfudd'), is in sharp contrast to the conventional *descriptio puellae* as described in the medieval poetic treatises, a convention adhered to in poems by both Iolo Goch and Gruffudd Gryg.[22] But the real subject of this ironically humorous poem is the common motif of the lover's captivity, of which Morfudd's clasping arms are a potent symbol. Dafydd has been held in a corner of the *deildy* by a stifling embrace, and it is the concept of bondage which predominates. An unexpected parallel for the image is provided by this simple *rondel* by Guillaume de Machaut:

> Quant Colette Colet colie,
> Elle le prent par le colet.
>
> Mais c'est trop grant merencolie,
> Quant Colette Colet colie.
>
> Car ses .ij. bras à son col lie
> Par le dous samblant de colet.
> Quant Colette Colet colie,
> Elle le prent par le colet.[23]

(When Colette embraces Colet, she takes him by the neck. But there is too much melancholy when Colette embraces Colet.

---

[21] F. Ferrand and E. Baumgartner (eds.), *Poèmes d'amour des XIIe et XIIIe siècles* (Paris, 1983), XIII.25–8.

[22] *GIG* XXIV; *DGG* LXXI. These are discussed in their European context by A. T. E. Matonis, 'Nodiadau ar Rethreg y Cywyddwyr: y *descriptio pulchritudinis* a'r Technegau Helaethu', *Y Traethodydd*, 133 (1978), 155–67. Dafydd Johnston, however, suggests that Iolo, in his ordered description of the girl from head to foot, was not necessarily consciously following the rhetorical convention (*GIG* 319).

[23] *Poésies lyriques*, vol. 1, CCXXXVII.

For she ties both her arms around his throat with all the fair semblance of a noose (or necklace). When Colette embraces Colet, she takes him by the neck.)

As in the *cywydd*—'Ddwylo mwnwgl . . . Ydd aeth' (ll. 7–8)—it is the lover's neck which is clasped, and the idea of bondage is clear, particularly in the image of tying. The words 'dous samblant' denote a lying embrace, and Morfudd's treacherous deceit is clearly expressed in the images of enchantment—'Hydwyll y'm rhwymodd hudawl' (l. 39), 'deceitfully did a magician bind me'—and intoxication—'Meddw oeddwn, mau ddioddef' (l. 49), 'I was drunk, suffering was my lot'. Moreover, the word-play in the *rondel* is a device which is dear to the *Cywyddwyr*—compare, for instance, Dafydd's play on 'Mynwyd, Mynwyn, Mynwes, Mynwair' in the final lines of this poem. The correspondence between the two poems is noteworthy, especially since Machaut was an older contemporary of Dafydd ap Gwilym. On the other hand, *GDG* 53 is wholly consistent with Dafydd's portrayal of love's inherent duality, and its theme need not necessarily have been suggested by any external source.

The subject of *GDG* 133 ('Cusan') was naturally well known to the Provençal and Northern French poets, who commonly implore their lady to grant them a single kiss or even as much as a pleasant look. Here, however, the gift has been granted, and the *cywydd* is a celebration, devoted entirely to the kiss itself, a theme which reappears a century or so later in as many as three poems by Dafydd ab Edmwnd.[24] I know of only one French poem in which the kiss is a subject in itself, a *dit* by the aptly named Jacques de Baisieux entitled *C'est des fiez d'Amours*,[25] where, in contrast to the *cywydd*, the act is attributed a grand moral significance:

> Or vos dirai, sans mesaisier,
> Do baisier la senefiance.
> Li baisiers nos fait demostrance
> D'amors, de pais et de concorde . . .
>   (ll. 452–5)

(Now I will tell you, without causing embarrassment, the significance of the kiss. A kiss bears witness to love, peace, and harmony . . .)

The lines which follow—

---

[24] *Gwaith Dafydd ab Edmwnd*, XXVI–XXVIII; cf. *CIGE* XLVII.45–58 (Gruffudd Llwyd); *CSTB* IV.1–8.

[25] Scheler, *Trouvères Belges*, i. 183–204.

> Li baisiers doit estre li corde
> De coi li doi cuer sont lié
> A un . . .
>
> (ll. 456–8)

(The kiss should be the cord by which the two hearts are tied together as one . . .)

may be compared with Dafydd's 'Cwlm hardd rhwng meinfardd a merch' (l. 26), 'a fair knot between a slim poet and a girl', and 'Cwlm cariad' (l. 35), 'a love knot', a rather obvious image admittedly, and only one element in the poem's many *dyfalu*-type metaphors.[26] There is also a certain resemblance between the more unusual image of a fortress which encircles the poet's lips ('Cwmpasgaer min', l. 36) and Jacques de Baisieux's comparison of the joining of two hearts in love by means of a kiss with the cementing together of separate stones to form a sturdy wall (ll. 200–15). But on the whole the two poems are so dissimilar as to make any connection between them highly improbable.

Comparisons of the lady's beauty with the sun are also common in the Continental lyric, as in the love-poetry of all periods, and Dafydd ap Gwilym is no exception. His many epithetical similes and metaphors continue the *Gogynfeirdd* tradition of 'light' imagery, but there is little, either in Wales or elsewhere, to compare with the exceptionally well-sustained metaphor of GDG 42 ('Morfudd fel yr Haul'). Having opened the poem with conventional comparisons with the girl's radiance, Dafydd then develops the analogy, once more exploring the essential duality of love: Morfudd is elusive, fickle—she appears one moment and is gone the next, just as the sun may be concealed by a dark cloud, and as it rises and sets in a continuous cycle. When the sun sets out of sight no one may lay a hand on it, and when night falls Morfudd disappears under the roof of the jealous husband. The poem closes with the delightful fancy that if the sun came out in the daytime and Morfudd at night there would be no night, such is Morfudd's radiance. She is in fact brighter than the sun itself (ll. 59–60), a common conceit, which appears, for instance, in the Harley Lyrics:

---

[26] Compare DG's recently discovered *englynion* on the same theme (edited by R. Geraint Gruffydd, '*Englynion y Cusan* by Dafydd ap Gwilym', CMCS 23 (Summer 1992), 1–6), esp. the line 'Diwenydd rhwym dau anadl', 'joyful was the bond of two breaths'.

> Hire hed when ich biholde apon,
> þe sonnebéém aboute nóón
>   me þohte þat y seȝe . . .
> þe mone wiþ hire muchele maht
> ne leneþ non such lyht anaht
>   (þat is in heouene heȝe)
> ase hire forhed doþ in day . . .[27]

Peter Dronke sees in this poem the 'image of the beloved's universal sovereignty, of her irradiating power over all lands',[28] and in his discussion of sun and moon imagery in the German *Minnesang* he refers to the work of the late twelfth-century poet Heinrich von Morungen which, in its use of extended metaphor, is comparable with *GDG* 42. Here, the moon and sun represent respectively the poet and his beloved. As Dronke explains:

> To be capable of (this) ascent of his heart to the sun . . . the lover must accept the whole of the moon's cycle, the joy and the sorrow, the moon's experience of deprivation in the sun's rising as well as of light in the sun's setting . . . But because of wicked tongues, the lover cannot often hope for the *coucher du soleil*.[29]

The well-developed images of the Welsh and German poems, then, though by no means identical, provide a fine example of the way in which two exceptional poets, composing on a similar theme, may create works which have much in common. Both poets have made highly original use of conventional imagery, and the German poems are as close a parallel as we are likely to find for *GDG* 42.

The Middle English poem cited above follows the conventional pattern of the *descriptio puellae*, as, it has been seen, does Iolo Goch's *cywydd* in praise of a girl, *GIG* XXIV,[30] and it is noteworthy that both poets use the same images for the girl's neck and breasts. With Iolo's 'Tagell hir . . . Alarchwedd' (ll. 31–2), 'a long throat like a swan's', compare 'swannes swyre [neck] swyþe [very] wel ysette,| a sponne lengore þen y mette . . .' (ll. 43–4), and with 'bron afaldwf' (l. 34), 'apple-shaped bosom', the lines 'Hyre tyttes aren anvnder bis [under fine linen] | as apples tuo of Parays . . .' (ll.

---

[27] Brook, *The Harley Lyrics*, 7.13–22. On this poem see Marion Glasscoe, 'The Fair Maid of Ribblesdale: Content and Context', *Neuphilologische Mitteilungen*, 87 (1986), 555–7.

[28] *MLRELL*, i. 123.   [29] Ibid. 132–4 (texts are cited with translations).

[30] The two poems are compared by Matonis, 'Nodiadau ar Rethreg y Cywyddwyr . . .', 160–1.

58–9). It is also interesting to note that the idea expressed by Iolo in the passage

> Pwy a allai, pei pensaer,
> Peintio â chalch pwynt fy chwaer?
> Duw a'i gwnaeth, arfaeth eurfab,
> Myn delw Bedr, ar fedr ei fab.
>
> (ll. 57–60)

(Who, even if he were a master craftsman, could paint with chalk my 'sister''s countenance? God made her—golden son's purpose—by Peter's image, for His son.)

is to be found in the French love-lyric:

> . . . car nuns hons portraire
> ne porroit mie sa per,
> tant sëust estudïeir.
>   Trop i ait a faire;
> car Deus la fist per maistrie
> de sa sainte main polie.[31]

(. . . for no man could ever draw her equal, however much he might be able to study. There would be too much work to do; for God formed her to perfection with his elegant sacred hand.)

In the *chanson de mal mariée*, a genre which will be examined in more detail presently, the husband, as often as not, is represented as being not only old and ugly, but also wealthy—a parvenu who remains essentially a *vilain*—and the opposition between wealth and true love is naturally a common motif in these poems. A typically defiant *malmariée* exclaims:

> S'aim trop melz un pou de joie a demener
> Que mil marz d'argent avoir et puis plorer.

(I much prefer a little joy than to have a thousand silver marks, and then weep.)

Another asks:

> Cuidë il por son avoir
> Metre en prison cuer joli?

(Does he believe that he can emprison a joyous heart on account of his wealth?)

---

[31] Gennrich, *Rondeaux, Virelais und Balladen*, 213.18–23.

and then concludes: 'Nus ne doit avoir | Ami por avoir . . .',[32] 'no one should take a lover for the sake of wealth'. Equally proverbial is Dafydd ap Gwilym's

> Rhagor mawr, gerddawr gordderch,
> Y sydd rhwng golud a serch.
> (GDG 31.39–40)

(There is a great difference, sweetheart's poet, between wealth and love.)

a rebuke to Iorwerth ab y Cyriog, who, we are given to understand, has demanded material reward in return for singing a girl's praise. Here, as, for instance, in *La Messe des oiseaux*, where love motivated by the pursuit of wealth is flatly condemned,[33] the contrast is not directly linked with the figure of the jealous husband, but in Dafydd's most complete treatment of the theme, GDG 76 ('Rhag Hyderu ar y Byd'), Eiddig plays a very central role.[34] It is explicitly claimed that it is he, Morfudd's husband, who is somehow responsible for the poet's poverty, and in words which call to mind the moralizing *cywyddau* to the World attributed to his contemporary Gruffudd Gryg (*DGG* LXXVI–LXXVII), Dafydd warns of the transience of worldly wealth, which comes and goes like the ebb and flow of a tide.[35] There are none so content as the careless birds and the humble rhymesters, and he himself has never shed a tear for wealth, though he weeps bitterly on account of his beloved Morfudd. A similar sentiment is expressed by an Anglo-Norman poet who denounces those who court the 'grant dames' purely for their material wealth:

---

[32] *Chanter m'estuet*, 33.60–1; 157.21–7; cf. ibid., no. 202; Paris, *Chansons du XVe siècle*, XV, CXVII. Whether a woman should take a rich or a poor lover was a subject of courtly debate, as for instance in the *débat* in *Chanter m'estuet*, no. 31. The theme is also reflected in many of the *pastourelles* in which the humble shepherdess resists the worldly temptations of the wealthy *chevalier*.

[33] Ribard, *La Messe des oiseaux* . . ., p. 48, ll. 1,118–35; cf. also GDG 95.31–6.

[34] GDG 51 ('Rhagoriaeth ei Gariad') also, it appears, refers to Eiddig (ll. 43–54):

> Poed â'r gyllell hirbell hon | Y cordder gwâl ei galon
> A'i cymerai yn hyfryd, | A maddau bun, meddu byd . . .
> Pa les i minnau, wyrda, | A maddau'r dyn, meddu'r da?
> Nid oes obaith eleni | I'r dyn a fo hŷn no hi.

Cf. further *BDG* LXVI (addressed to a *malmariée*), CLXXIX, CXCVII, and CC, in which the girl, to the poets' chagrin, will marry none but a wealthy man.

[35] Cf. '. . . o achos vot yn kynnhebic golut dayarawl y lanw athrei herwyd anwadalrwyd', from a text in *Llyfr yr Ancr* (Morris-Jones and Rhŷs, *Llyvyr Agkyr Llandewivrevi*, 131.1–2).

> Cil k'eyme par tel desir
> N'estut ja d'amur languir
> Ne le gref dulur sentir
> Ke li fin amant en sent . . .[36]

(He who loves with such a desire as this never has to pine away with love, nor feel the grievous pain that the courtly lover experiences . . .)

This dissociating of sincere love from the pursuit of material gain, of spiritual from material values, may occur to any poet at any time. Ovid, for instance, maintains that a girl should be more pleased with an immortal song than with expensive gifts,[37] and the opposition of love and money is fairly common in Welsh free-metre verse,[38] partly, no doubt, in imitation of the *cywydd serch*. But since the theme is particularly recurrent in medieval French love-poetry, in keeping with the courtly notion of love as a noble and ennobling force, it is not altogether unlikely that its appearance in Dafydd's poems again owes something to the wider European lyric tradition.

The tone is anything but courtly in the famous passage in *GDG* 85 ('Siom') in which Dafydd vents his anger at having regaled Morfudd with fine poems and jewellery and wandered from tavern to tavern presumably singing her praise, all to find that she has become pregnant by another man. Chotzen, who discusses under the heading 'Chansons de taverne' this and other poems such as *GDG* 124 ('Trafferth mewn Tafarn') and *GDG* 132 ('Cyfeddach'), comparing them with the non-courtly poetry of Northern France and Flanders, concludes that if they owe anything to external models, these models should be sought in the poetry composed in bourgeois circles rather than in the courtly lyric or in the verse of the Latin scholars.[39] With *GDG* 85 he compares, for instance, the lines

> Bien me remembre
> De vostre grant deloialteit.
> Acolei m'avez
> Par faucetei
> Tant ke donei
> Vos ai tout, n'an dout mie.[40]

[36] *Romania*, 15 (1886), 249.

[37] *Amores*, I, 10.59–62. These lines contrast with the old woman's advice to the girl in 8.57 ff.

[38] Cf. *CRhC* 1, VII.33–6; 16.9 ff; 22.17 ff; *LlRMG* 47, 110; in Irish cf. Douglas Hyde, *Love Songs of Connacht* (London and Dublin, 1893), pp. 61, 105, 111.

[39] *Recherches*, 170.

[40] A. Jeanroy and A. Langfors (eds.), *Chansons satiriques et bachiques du XIIIᵉ siècle* (Paris, 1921), XXXVI.42–7; cf. also Ferrand, *Chansons des XVᵉ et XVIᵉ siècles*, LXXV.

(I remember well your great disloyalty. Deceitfully you embraced me, so that I gave you everything, I do not doubt.)

A characteristic *jongleur*'s song of carefree love, though lacking the bitterness of *GDG* 85, is particularly striking:

> La tousete es blons muteax,
>   es chevox lons,
> celi donrai mes joiaus
>   et mes granz dons;
>   sejornons,
> ensi s'en va mes avoirs a grant bandon;
>   or maingons,
> et bevons et solaçons et deportons.[41]

(The long-haired lass with the white thighs, to her I shall give my jewels and my generous gifts; let us tarry, thus my wealth departs with great abandon; now let's eat, let's drink, have fun and be merry.)

Also relevant is another anonymous *jongleur*'s song, a vivid lament of present poverty and desperation caused by the poet's lecherous life-style: he has lost everything—his friends, his home, and, like many a Latin scholar, even most of his clothes have been lost at dicing. As he ruefully admits: 'J'ai plus despendut d'avoir | An folie c'an savoir', 'I have spent more money in folly than in wisdom.' He too has put his trust in women, and at great cost—

> Les femes m'ont asoteit
>   Ou je me fioie:
> Cent livres m'ont bien costeit
>   De bone monoie.[42]

(I have been besotted by women in whom I put my trust: they have indeed cost me a hundred pounds of good money.)

These lines recall Morfudd's behaviour towards Dafydd:

> Ymddiried ym a ddaroedd;
> Er hyn oll, fy rhiain oedd,
> Ni chefais, eithr nych ofal,
> Nid amod ym, dym o dâl . . .
>   (ll. 25–8)

---

[41] *Origines*, 504; cf. *Recherches*, 168. Fulton compares the poetry of the 13th-cent. professional minstrel Colin Muset, which similarly reflects the so-called register of *la bonne vie*, with some of the poems of DG (*DGEC* 177–80; cf. ibid. 55–8).

[42] *Chanter m'estuet*, 86.43–4, 33–6.

(I was trustful; despite all this (she was my girl) I received, except for pining's anguish—not with my consent—no payment . . .)

Although Dafydd is here probably expressing his very real disappointment at Morfudd's marriage to Y Bwa Bach, his treatment of
the subject does have a certain affinity with *jongleresque* songs such
as these, which, despite their comparative rarity in the manuscripts,
must have circulated widely in non-courtly and probably also in
courtly circles.[43] At the same time we must bear in mind that the cosmopolitan Welsh boroughs may also have known similar minstrel-
songs in English, perhaps reflecting French models. While there is no
need to accept Chotzen's argument that those *cywyddau* with a background of tavern life necessarily reflect the bourgeois and semi-
popular literature of Northern France, there may well be some truth
in the suggestion that this particular *cywydd* owes something to
external influence.

It may be said that the tone of GDG 97 ('Angof') (like that of
several other poems by Dafydd which consist of a kind of dramatic
monologue) is equally 'uncourtly', in the sense that, far from adopt-
ing the servile posture of the pining lover, he addresses his beloved
on equal terms, even to the point of offering timely advice and
reminding her of the satirical side of the bardic coin. The theme of
the lady's neglect of her poet is not uncommon in the poems of the
trouvères, although they are very rarely as outspoken as the Welsh
poet. Expressions such as 'mettre en oubli' are fairly common,
for instance, in the poems of Guillaume de Machaut, and his
rondel 'Quant ma dame ne m'a recongneü'[44] may be compared
with Dafydd's accusation in this *cywydd* that the girl has pretended
not to recognize him (ll. 7–8). The author of an anonymous
thirteenth-century poem fears that his lady's neglect has been
caused by *médisants*, or perhaps that she has laid her affections
elsewhere:

---

[43] Cf. Pierre Bec's remarks on the role of the *jongleur* as performer and creator: 'Il
manie (donc) plusieurs registres, aristocratiques et populaires, narratifs et lyriques,
lyrico-musicaux et lyrico-chorégraphiques . . . montrant ses talents aussi bien sur les
champs de foire qu'à la table du baron ou du prince'; 'Le jongleur était donc l'inter-
médiaire naturel, pour les chansons, les danses, les thèmes et les genres poétiques,
entre l'aristocratie (chevaleresque, courtoise et cléricale) et le "peuple" . . .' (*La
Lyrique française* . . ., i. 25, 28).
[44] *Poésies lyriques*, vol. 1, CLI.

> Or ne sai ce mesdixant,
> A cui po de bien vorroie,
> M'ont esteit vers lei neuxant
> Ou s'autre amor lai maistroie
>   Qui m'i ait greveit,
> Car an moi n'ai rienz troveit
>   Dont savoir me doie
>   Si mal grei
> Con de ceu c'oblieis soie.[45]

(Now I know not whether slanderers, to whom I would wish little good, have discredited me in her eyes, or whether she is in the power of another love which may have harmed my cause, for within myself I have found nothing that warrants such contempt as to be erased from memory.)

Dafydd, too, fears infidelity, demanding 'Na fydd anghywir hirynt' (l. 27), 'do not be unfaithful for long', and the words 'Bai ditiwr' (l. 16), 'the fault of an accuser', suggest the work of a slanderer, though not necessarily the equivalent of the Continental *médisants*. It must not be thought that all French court-poets were willing to suffer their plight in adoring silence. The early trouvère Gautier de Dargies is not averse to condemning his lady's cruelty and deceit, her 'lying countenance', and even her 'felenie et outrage'.[46] One poem in particular, in which he reacts angrily to the *dame*'s scoffing reproof, is akin to GDG 97 in its frankly threatening tone and its effective expression of moral advice and reprobation by means of proverbial statements. He issues the firm rebuke:

> Ne me devroit gaber mie
> Dame de si grant valour:
> Ne doit dire vilenie,
> Quar qui met gent en irour
> Il puet bien oïr folie.
>   (ll. 20–4)

(A lady of such high esteem certainly shouldn't mock me: she should not utter base words, for he who incurs the wrath of others can expect to hear folly himself.)

Then comes a telling proverb :

> Ele avoit tort
> D'esveillier le chien qui dort . . .[47]

---

[45] *Romania*, vol. 57, p. 345, LXIX.19–27.
[46] A. M. Raugei (ed.), *Gautier de Dargies: Poesie* (Florence, 1981), V, XV, XVII.
[47] Ibid., XVIII.20–6; cf. the proverbs in ll. 59–61.

(She was wrong to wake the sleeping dog . . .)

In similar vein, Dafydd warns the Efa of his poem not to deserve satire like the ungenerous (ll. 17–18), and the warnings 'Angof ni wna dda i ddyn' (l. 19), 'forgetfulness does one no good', and 'Terfyn angof yw gofal' (l. 21), 'the result of forgetfulness is care', have a distinctly proverbial ring. Here, then, is another instance of two poets who clearly share a certain 'community of spirit' treating a similar theme in analogous fashion. Gautier's poem is fairly unrepresentative, but it does serve to remind us that even a distinguished trouvère of noble birth could enrich the French lyric tradition with an interpretation which differs considerably from the stylized formality of *amour courtois*.

This poem, with its familiar tone and conscious use of homely language, and especially the songs discussed above reflecting the style of the *jongleur* rather than the trouvère and the worlds of tavern and woodland rather than the noble court, bring us closer to the popular lyric tradition of Northern France. But what of the popular lyrics themselves, that is to say, lyrics which (though they might also be enjoyed, and even imitated, in the noble courts)[48] were not composed primarily for the entertainment of the learned élite of court and town? Do they offer any significant parallels with the poetry of Dafydd and his contemporaries which are not also found in the predominantly aristocratic lyric tradition, centred mainly on the themes and conventions of *amour courtois*? As in much of the rest of Europe, French popular verse was not deliberately recorded until the fifteenth century. It is, however, inconceivable that similar lyrics did not already exist parallel to the main medieval poetic tradition, and perhaps, as Jeanroy and others have postulated, even prior to that tradition, before the great flowering of the courtly love culture under southern influence in the second half of the twelfth century.[49] In his attempt at a typology of genres in twelfth- and thirteenth-century French poetry, Pierre Bec lays great emphasis on the notion of a 'strong lyric current' which must have had a kind of 'underground' existence during the Middle Ages. He speaks of

la masse de la population paysanne, de loin la plus importante au moyen âge, qui s'est indubitablement transmis, pendant des siècles, toute une lit-

---

[48] The two major collections of anonymous verse in the late 15th and early 16th cents. were probably compiled for aristocratic patrons; see Ferrand, *Chansons des XVe et XVIe siècles*, 13 ff.

[49] *Origines*, *passim*; cf., for instance, Dronke, *The Medieval Lyric*, esp. 30.

térature *folklorique*, peu actualisée dans les textes (mais néanmoins présente comme nous le verrons) et dont les littératures orales actuelles peuvent être, dans une mesure toujours délicate à fixer, un dernier reflet.[50]

(the great mass of the peasant population, by far the largest section of medieval society, which unquestionably transmitted across the centuries a whole body of *folk*-literature hardly attested in the texts (yet nevertheless present as shall be seen), of which modern oral literatures may, to an extent that remains difficult to determine, represent a final reflection.)

One of the most significant aspects of his thesis is his belief, hinted at here, that elements of this popular undercurrent surface also in trouvère and *jongleur* poetry (in much the same way as the love and nature poetry of the *Gogynfeirdd* may reflect in part a native popular lyric tradition), a process which is graphically demonstrated by his index of *motifs popularisants*[51] drawn from twelfth- and thirteenth-century texts. He distinguishes between what he terms the *registre aristocratisant* on the one hand, which applies to the genres of the *grand chant courtois*, and on the other the *registre popularisant*, encompassing both the *jongleresque* and the *folklorisant*. This register is characterized, among other things, by a high degree of anonymity and the distinctive imprint of the wandering *jongleur*; by the various manifestations of the *chanson de femme*; by forms which are termed *lyrico-chorégraphiques* (i.e. dance songs, probably ultimately related to the *fêtes de mai*); and by thematic links with the later oral folk tradition. With the exception of the *aube* or dawn-song (of which there are more examples in Provençal poetry), the register applies to genres which are strictly, or primarily, connected with the North, genres such as the *chanson d'ami/de jeune fille*, *malmariée*, *chanson de toile*, *rondet de carole*, and *ballette*. (The *pastourelle*, *reverdie*, and *motet* are among those genres which are regarded as 'hybrid', since they commonly reflect both registers.)[52] Bec reiterates Jeanroy's generally accepted theory of the primitive ancestry of the *chanson de femme*—a theory which has been

---

[50] *La Lyrique française . . .*, i. 24.

[51] Ibid., ii. 183. He follows Faral (*Les Jongleurs en France au moyen âge* (Paris, 1910)) in stressing the importance of the *jongleurs* not only as a vital link between the aristocratic and popular worlds, but also as active promoters of popular tradition: 'Il n'était pas, au moyen âge, de fête publique, de réjouissances populaires où les jongleurs ne fussent en activité . . . Mais, de plus, les jongleurs orchestraient, et recueillaient aussi sans doute, toute une littérature orale et folklorisante (danse, musique, contes, chansons) dont ils devenaient ainsi les véritables détenteurs' (i. 26).

[52] Ibid., i. 33 ff.

considerably vindicated by the fairly recent discovery of the Mozarabic *khardjas*—but goes further than Jeanroy in regarding the large corpus of *refrains* in twelfth- and thirteenth-century texts as actual 'parallel manifestations of a more traditional oral literature'.[53] He seeks to demonstrate the *interférences registrales* which characterize the popular register—features of the *malmariée*, for instance, are particularly widespread in the other lyric genres—and also the interaction which occurs between the two main registers. The large body of medieval motets provides a fine example of such intertextuality, since the genre, although learned in origin, reflects a wealth of themes and refrains from popular tradition, while at the same time displaying a preoccupation with *fin' amors* more akin to the courtly *chanson*.

A reciprocal movement becomes apparent, which Bec describes as 'un double courant constant du peuple à ce que nous appellerons pour simplifier l'élite et de l'élite au peuple.'[54] The now widely accepted principle of the constant interaction of the 'aristocratic' and 'popular' lyric traditions is certainly relevant to the fine collection of almost exclusively Northern and predominantly Norman songs from a late fifteenth-century manuscript which has been edited by Gaston Paris.[55] The types of love-lyrics represented are by and large what one would expect to find in a partly folk-orientated poetry: there are *pastourelles*, dance-songs, and songs of love and love's despair composed from a woman's standpoint, such as the *chansons de jeune fille* and the *malmariées*. But many of the songs are coloured by the conventional language and preoccupations of *amour courtois*, albeit in an 'extended' and simplified form, which, partly no doubt through the intermediacy of the *jongleurs*, have inevitably seeped downwards from the contexts of noble court and bourgeois *puy* to reach a wider and less exclusive audience. However, in contrast to the courtly

[53] *La Lyrique française* . . ., i. 40–3, 57–68. For a comprehensive collection of *refrains* see N. H. J. van den Boogaard, *Rondeaux et refrains du 12e siècle au début du 14e* (Paris, 1969). On the *khardjas*, women's love-songs in a Romance dialect which form the final verses of a number of Arabic and Hebrew poems composed between 1000 and 1150, see Dronke, *The Medieval Lyric*, 86 ff; Pierre Le Gentil, 'La Strophe Zadjalesque, les Khardjas et le problème des origines du lyrisme roman', *Romania*, 84 (1963), 209–50.

[54] *La Lyrique française* . . ., i. 135. A similar theory of inter-registral contamination is proposed by Paul Zumthor in his influential *Essai de poétique médiévale* (Paris, 1972), 245 ff. and *passim*.

[55] *Chansons du XVe siècle*; for further examples of French popular verse see Ferrand, *Chansons des XVe et XVIe siècles*; E. Rolland (ed.), *Recueil de chansons populaires*, 3 vols. (Paris, 1967).

chanson, perhaps the most striking features of the collection are the woodland trysts, the numerous bird-messengers and love-tokens, and the general background of wild nature in which so many of the lyrics are set. (These elements, as Bec's motif index shows, are to a lesser extent attested in the recorded poetry of the preceding centuries.) In this respect they bear a more than superficial resemblance to the love-poetry of Dafydd ap Gwilym and his contemporaries; and although few of these lyrics, according to their editor, are likely to be much older than the second third of the fifteenth century, it is quite conceivable that earlier sub-literary verse of a similar nature had some bearing on the subject-matter of the early *Cywyddwyr*. On the other hand, as has been argued in previous chapters, it is likely that the *Cywyddwyr*'s fondness for the woodland tryst and related elements such as the *llatai* motif has its origin essentially in the native tradition, and it is, I believe, preferable to regard the fusion of love and nature in French popular verse as an analogous development. If it did have any impact, either directly on the work of the *Cywyddwyr* themselves, or indirectly, through the verse of the *Clêr*, it can surely only have been to enrich a vigorous pre-existing tradition.

Gaston Paris's collection does include one type of poem in particular which has no significant precedents in the French manuscripts of preceding centuries, namely, the account of a humorous incident seen through the eyes of the lover-poet himself. In content and spirit it resembles the fabliaux, but these accounts are briefer, more lyrical, and unlike the fabliaux they are recounted in the first person. In this they are analogous with the humorous narrative poems of Dafydd ap Gwilym and Madog Benfras. Chotzen makes a similar suggestion in relation to a group of *cywyddau* (many of them 'apocryphal') which reflect the theme of the return of the jealous husband:

Il se pourrait qu'en France déjà on eût remanié ces fabliaux très goûtés pour en faire des gabs, et en effet ce procédé est démontrable pour une seule chanson du XVᵉ siècle . . . celle-ci au moins correspond exactement aux cywyddau en question, non seulement pour le fond, mais aussi pour la forme . . . [56]

(It may be that in France these extremely popular fabliaux had already been reworked and turned into 'boasting poems', and this process may in fact be shown in the case of a single fifteenth-century song . . . this song, at least, corresponds exactly to the *cywyddau* in question, as regards form as well as content . . .)

[56] *Recherches*, 290.

The Norman lyric to which he refers is here reproduced in its
entirety, since the situation described and the spirit in which it is told
bear a striking resemblance to GDG 145 ('Caru yn y Gaeaf'):

Je fuz l'aultrier	o la belle sourprins
Du faulx jalloux	dont point ne me guectoye.
Hellas! pourquoy	ne prenoys je la voye
De m'en aller	a travers ces jardrins?
Le faulx jaloux	avoit des gens commys
Pour espier	s'en sa maison iroye:
Certes j'y vins	tout ainsy que souloye;
Incontinant	je fuz saisy et pris.
Il apella	trestouz ses bons amys
Tant qu'ilz ont faict	une grande assemblée;
Ils ont sur moi	faict une grant huée
Comment on faict	au loup quand il est pris.
Croyez de vrai	que je n'eusse pas prins
Cent escutz d'or	ne aultant de monnoye
Pour desployer	une bource de soye!
La mercy Dieu,	j'eschappay et m'en vins.[57]

(The other day I was caught unawares with my sweetheart by the false jealous husband, for whom I wasn't on the lookout at all. Alas! Why did I not
make my getaway across the gardens?

The false jealous husband had chosen some people to watch whether I
would enter his house: indeed, I arrived, just as I always did; unsuspecting,
I was seized and held.

He called together all his best friends so that they formed a huge crowd; they
raised a great clamour against me, as they do to a wolf when it's been caught.

Believe me, I wouldn't have accepted [even] a hundred gold ecus nor an
equivalent sum, since I would have had [to take time] to open a silk purse!
Thanks be to God, I escaped and got away.)

In GDG 145, too, Dafydd is ignominiously chased away by Eiddig
and his friends, the jealous husband having raised the hue and cry
after being awakened by the drunken poet at his window. The
French poet shows a similar willingness to laugh at his own misfortune, and his humorous direct addresses to his no doubt sympathetic
audience in the first and last stanzas achieve an effect comparable to
the ironic 'asides' which Dafydd produces even in his darkest hours.
In particular, his final comment, 'La mercy Dieu, j'eschappay et m'en

---

[57] Paris, *Chansons du XVᵉ siècle*, LVIII. The translation of the somewhat obscure
final stanza is based on the editor's tentative interpretation.

vins', which appears to be a conventional ending in songs of this type,[58] reflecting the widespread conviction that God is on the lover's side, is reminiscent of the typically frivolous closing couplet of *GDG* 124 ('Trafferth mewn Tafarn'):

> Dihengais i, da wng saint,
> I Dduw'r archaf faddeuaint.

(I escaped—it was good that the saints were nearby—of God I ask forgiveness.)

These words, with their ironic suggestion of providential protection, may be compared with the couplet

> Oni'm gwŷl ffel ni'm delir,
> O rhan Duw, ar hyn o dir.

(Unless a sly one sees me I shall not be caught, if God grants, on this piece of land.)

which occurs towards the end of 'Y Wawr' (*GDG* 129.43-4), another of Dafydd's narrative poems.

It is not clear in *GDG* 129 whether the girl is married or unmarried, whether it is from the jealous husband or the girl's unwilling parents that the poet must make good his escape. In *GDG* 135 ('Lladrata Merch'), in which he and the girl manage to sneak out of an inn into the woods nearby when all are in a drunken sleep,[59] it is clearly the girl's parents who must be foiled. Chotzen has shown that the theme could have been familiar from French popular poetry[60]— in the medieval *pastourelles*, including the Latin lyrics, there is frequent mention of the protective mother in particular—or from the fabliaux, although there the enemy is more often than not the stock figure of the jealous husband. A fine example is found in the *pastourelle*-type dialogue, 'De Clerico et Puella' from the Harley Lyrics, in which the girl warns her lover:

> 'þou art wayted day ant nyht wiþ fader ant al my kynne.
> Be þou in mi bour ytake, lete þey for no synne
> me to holde ant þe to slon, þe deþ so þou maht wynne!'
> (24.18–20)

---

[58] Cf. the final lines of a popular narrative poem cited by Tiersot, *Histoire de la chanson populaire*, 49: '. . . Quand mon maître étonné se sauva de ce lieu | Tout en robe de chambre, ainsi qu'il plut à Dieu.'

[59] Cf. *Amores*, I, 4.51 ff., where Ovid asks the girl to ply her husband with wine so that they might deceive him while he lies asleep.

[60] *Recherches*, 260–2.

Chotzen believes that the theme would have been reflected in native popular verse, and he is no doubt right to suggest that Dafydd is here adhering closely to reality and to popular tradition. It is perfectly possible that the situation described in *GDG* 135 is based on an actual event, particularly since the two other *cywyddau* discussed by Chotzen under the heading 'Les Parents' (*BDG* CLII, CXCIII) have since been rejected from the canon.

While I have seen nothing either in the fabliaux or in later French verse which resembles the scenario of this particular *cywydd*, another of Dafydd's humorous poems finds an interesting parallel in song XXXV in Gaston Paris's collection. The French poet, again in the first person, tells of the misfortune which befell him as he waited patiently beneath a bush, as his beloved had requested:

> Un faulx oisel s'assist sur moy,
> Qui commença a m'esgacher,
> Pies et corneilles, sur ma foy,
> Comme si m'y deussent manger.
>
> (ll. 5–8)

(A false bird settled itself on me and began to harass me, magpies and crows, upon my oath, [seemed] as though they were going to eat me.)

In *GDG* 61 ('Y Cyffylog') Dafydd and the girl are similarly disturbed by the noisy woodcock, whose tumult they mistake for the arrival of Eiddig. In *GDG* 63, too, Dafydd is disturbed by the ill-omened magpie as he awaits a woodland tryst, and we may compare also Madog Benfras's crow which in *BDG* LXXXIV is associated with Eiddig and scares away the poet's beloved nightingale. In the French poem the jealous husband, warned by his barking hounds, arrives on the scene with the ambiguous cry: 'Le regnart est a noz poussins!' (l. 12),[61] 'the fox is among our chickens', and the poet manages to deceive his gullible rival by putting him on the trail of an imaginary fox. It is noteworthy that both this poem and *GDG* 61 are introduced by general reflections on love: the French poet states proverbially: 'Jamès amoureulx bien n'aura' (l. 1), 'no good will ever come to a lover', and Dafydd, just as ominously, asks:

---

[61] Compare Eiddig's defiant 'Gwnaethwn ffo i'r cadno coch' in *GIG* XXVI.34, a reference to the colour of Iolo's hair. For another version of the French poem see Ferrand, *Chansons des XVᵉ et XVIᵉ siècles*, CII.

A fu ddim, ddamwain breiddfyw,
Mor elyn i serchddyn syw
Â'r gaeaf, oeraf eiroed,
Hirddu cas yn hyrddio coed?

(ll. 1–4)

(Was there ever anything—hazardous occasion—so hostile to a fine lover as winter—coldest snow-tryst—long, black and hateful, pounding trees?)

Clearly, a certain kind of French popular verse, with regard both to its subject-matter and its personal style, is to a considerable extent analogous with the narrative *cywyddau*. Given the likelihood that such songs were composed earlier than the fifteenth century, it may be that they had at least as much influence on the Welsh poetic tradition as their more notorious cousins, the fabliaux. Although the fabliau as a genre probably pre-dates the more lyrical form, both types of poem provide a likely source for the ubiquitous lover–wife–husband triangle in the early *cywyddau*, and it is somewhat surprising that, as Chotzen's extensive research has shown, in the established canon of Dafydd's poems at least, there are no specific echoes of the 150 or so literary fabliaux which have survived.[62] Of course, there is no accounting for the many hundreds more which have been irretrievably lost to posterity.

One of the surest signs of Dafydd's debt to the pervasiveness of European trends lies in his familiarity with a number of distinctive poetic genres, both popular and courtly in tone, which are associated with the Continental verse tradition. It has been argued in previous chapters that, although he would almost certainly have been aware of genres such as the *sérénade* and the *pastourelle* (conceivably through Latin and Middle English as well as French and Anglo-Norman), it is debatable whether these were a significant influence on his poetry. There can be no such doubt concerning the relationship between GDG 58 ('Merch yn Edliw ei Lyfrdra'), in which Dafydd claims to be a better lover than a soldier, and a relatively small group of poems known as the *débats du clerc et du chevalier*, which have as their subject the respective merits of the clerk and knight as courtly lovers.[63] As a literary theme the debate is probably

[62] The definitive edition is *Nouveau recueil des fabliaux*, ed. N. van den Boogaard and W. Noomen (Van Gorcum, Assen, 1983–). On the genre see Muscatine, *Chaucer and the French Tradition*, ch. 3; Per Nykrog, *Les Fabliaux* (Copenhagen, 1957).

[63] See Charles Oulmont, *Les Débats du clerc et du chevalier dans la littérature*

derived from Ovid (*Amores*, III.8), although it does have a very real bearing upon the social conflicts of twelfth- and thirteenth-century France. The first to draw attention to the correspondence was Ifor Williams, and his remarks have since been elaborated upon by Chotzen and Rachel Bromwich,[64] both of whom emphasize the fact that the genre was known in England, as is clear from the evidence of two thirteenth-century Anglo-Norman poems. One of these poems, the *Geste de Blancheflour e de Florence*, may have been trans-lated from English, and it differs from the other versions, be they Latin, French, or Anglo-Norman, in that the judgement is in favour of the knight. As Chotzen has shown, the argument in favour of the clerk in the other Anglo-Norman poem, *Melior e Ydoine*, contains some striking correspondences with the *cywydd*, and clearly it is this version which is most closely analogous with *GDG* 58. It may be sig-nificant also that, although the argument in this poem takes the usual form of the bird-debate, the poem contains few of the artificial trap-pings of the Court of Love which adorn the other versions—as Langlois remarks, there is no mention of the God of Love, his palace, or the sepulchre of the vanquished girl.[65] On the other hand, the effect of the Continental God of Love and his accompanying mythol-ogy on the *cywydd serch* is so negligible that they might in any case have been consciously rejected by a Welsh poet. In view of the con-ventional nature of the debate, allied to our ignorance of what has been lost, the Anglo-Norman poem should be regarded only as one possible source among many. Whether or not Dafydd is indebted to any specific version, his handling of the genre is typically original in that his only concession to its formal conventions is his sparing use of dialogue; and if, as seems likely, his rival in this poem is

poétique du moyen âge (repr. of the 1911 edn., Geneva, 1974); Edmond Faral, *Recherches sur les sources latines des contes et romans courtois du moyen âge* (Paris, 1913), 191–303. The Latin poems are also discussed by Raby, *A History of Secular Latin Poetry*, ii. 290–7, and the Anglo–Norman versions by Legge, *Anglo-Norman Literature* . . ., ch. 13.

[64] Ifor Williams, 'Dafydd ap Gwilym a'r Glêr', 146–7; *Recherches*, 228–30; *APDG* 75; cf. Bromwich's remarks in *SP* 156, and Fulton, *DGEC* 193–4.

[65] *Origines et sources du Roman de la Rose*, 14. It may be, as Rachel Bromwich has argued (*APDG* 78), that this particular convention in the French bird-debate poems, 'the burial of a victim of love, in a tomb surrounded by birds who sing in perpetual chorus about it', influenced the 'apocryphal' *DGG* XIX ('Claddu y Bardd o Gariad'), which probably belongs to the 14th cent. For a parallel in French popular verse see Tiersot, *Histoire de la chanson populaire* . . ., 19. The theme is also found in the early free-metre poem *CRhC* 30 ('Carol Claddu'r Bardd') (see Ch. 4 above, pp. 122–3 and n.), and in the 'apocryphal' *cywyddau DGG* XXI and *BDG* LII.

Morfudd's future husband, Y Bwa Bach, who, we are told in GDG 75, accompanied Rhys ap Gruffudd on a military expedition to France,[66] then not for the first time his adaptation of a received literary convention is grounded firmly in reality. This echoing of one of the established genres of courtly love poetry must have contributed considerably to the humour of the poem for a learned contemporary audience. However, the lengthy bird-debates of the *débats du clerc et du chevalier* and the French dream-vision poems, a convention which is parodied in Chaucer's *Parlement of Foules*,[67] have no real parallels in the *cywyddau* despite Dafydd's personification of birds and the fact that his cock-thrush (GDG 28), magpie (GDG 63), and woodcock (GDG 115) are all endowed with the power of speech. Although the portrayal of the cock-thrush in GDG 123 as a sheriff, justice of the peace, and court steward who reads from the roll is superficially comparable with the function of birds as officiants in the Continental 'courts of love', this is but one example of Dafydd's recurrent legal imagery, and it need not have been suggested by any external literary sources.

With the *chanson de malmariée* we return to the world of popular verse, or at least to the popular register. For although in the hands of twelfth- and thirteenth-century French poets the genre reflects the spirit of *amour courtois*, which is most evident in the derision of the jealous husband's *vilenie*, it is generally accepted that the essential theme is ultimately derived from popular seasonal festivities. This is most clearly implied by the evidence of the twelfth-century Provençal dance-song 'A l'entrada del tems clar', the song of the April Queen who celebrates the rebirth of spring by joining her young lover in a symbolic dance and rejecting her aged jealous husband, the mythological king of the underworld who represents the old season.[68] It has been convincingly argued that the truly popular *malmariées* which abound from the fifteenth century onwards, with their preference for the woman's monologue, the absence of the poet-narrator,

---

[66] The line 'Brwydr yng ngwlad Ffrainc neu Brydyn' (GDG 58.30) probably refers to the battles of Crécy and Neville's Cross in 1346 (cf. DGG, p.186); GDG 75 may refer to the events of the same year. Y Bwa Bach is probably Dafydd's rival in GDG 54 also, another poem in which he seeks to convince the girl of his superiority as a lover.

[67] See Muscatine, *Chaucer and the French Tradition*, 115 ff.

[68] See J. Bédier, 'Les Fêtes de mai et les commencements de la poésie lyrique au moyen âge', *Revue des deux mondes* (May, 1896), 146–72; Dronke, *The Medieval Lyric*, 196–7. For a survey of the principal theories concerning the origins and evolution of the *malmariée* genre see Bec, *La Lyrique française . . .*, i. 81–90.

and their antithesis not between *vilain* and *courtois* but between
young and old (cf. the 'viellart' and 'bachalar' of 'A l'entrada . . .'),
may be a continuation of a submerged verse tradition which could
have served as a model for the more 'courtly' versions of the trouvères and bourgeois poets.[69] In these medieval versions the narrator
is almost always present: he may set the scene for an argument
between wife and husband, or a conversation between wife and
lover, or in some cases between two women; he may also attempt to
console a *malmariée* whose complaint he overhears. But most often
the poet's role is to introduce the wife's complaint against her jealous husband, and her yearning for the love of her idealized *ami*.

None of the early *cywyddau* are significantly modelled on either
of these scenarios,[70] and there is no instance of the kind of whole-
sale imitation of the genre which occurs in Middle English, as in the
following fragment from a fourteenth-century manuscript:

> Alas hou shold y syng,
> Yloren [lost] is my playnge [pleasure]
> Hou sholdy wiჳ ჳat [*sic*] olde man
> To leuen [remain] and let my leman,
> Swettist of al ჳinge [*sic*].[71]

However, the basic theme of the *chanson de mal mariée*, as well as
some of its characteristic elements, including the opposition between
wealth and true love discussed above, are undoubtedly reflected in
the *cywydd serch*. The typical *Jaloux* of the French *malmariées*, like
the jealous husbands who are the butt of the joke in so many of the
fabliaux, is a wealthy but despicable villein who beats his wife and
is obsessively watchful. His moral and social deficiencies are matched
by his physical shortcomings: as well as being old and often impotent, he is likely to be grotesquely ugly or pox-ridden. All these traits

---

[69] Bec, *La Lyrique française* . . ., i. 89, expresses his broad agreement with this theory as expounded by R. Dähne, *Die Lieder der Maumariée seit dem Mittelalter* (Halle,
1933).

[70] The same is true of the 'apocryphal' poems, in which the basic *malmariée* theme
is not uncommon; cf., for instance, *BDG* LXVI, XC, CLXIII, CXCI. One of the
cywyddau which most closely resembles the French versions is the 15th- or 16th-cent.
BDG CXCVI, a dialogue in which the poet urges the maltreated wife to rebel and beat
her drunkard of a husband. The theme is especially prominent in the poetry of
Gwerful Mechain (*fl.* 1462–1500), the first Welsh female poet whose work has been
preserved; cf. Leslie Harries, 'Barddoniaeth Huw Cae Llwyd ac Eraill', unpublished
MA thesis, University of Wales (1933), 125, no. LXVIII.

[71] R. M. Wilson, *The Lost Literature of Medieval England* (London, 1952), 187; cf.
a married woman's complaint in a *pastourelle*, Brook, *The Harley Lyrics*, 8.37–40.

appear in Dafydd ap Gwilym's various satirical portrayals of Eiddig, but it is the two poems which directly contrast the beloved's beauty with the husband's ugliness, GDG 73 ('Gwallt Morfudd') and GDG 81 ('Llychwino Pryd y Ferch') which come closest to the spirit of the Continental poems. In GDG 81 (probably another *cywydd* to Morfudd, although she is not named), the poet complains that the girl's fair complexion has been ruined by her husband's vile breath, which is compared to peat-smoke—'Anadl fal mwg y fawnen' (l. 21). This unusual theme, which Dafydd develops through a series of highly imaginative and effective images, may well have been suggested by external influence, since in a thirteenth-century woman's monologue a *malmariée* similarly complains that the *Jaloux*'s breath might cause her death. The song, a simple *ballette*, is a fine illustration of the genre, incorporating several of its familiar motifs:

> Au cuer les ai, les jolis malz.
>> Coment an guariroie?
>
> Kant li vilains vait a marchiet,
> Il n'i vait pais por berguignier,
> Mais por sa feme a esgaitier
>> Que nuns ne li forvoie.
> Au cuer les ai . . .
>
> Vilains, car vos traites an lai,
> Car vostre alainne m'ocidrait.
> Bien sai c'ancor departirait
>> Vostre amor et la moie.
> . . .
>
> Vilains, cuidiez vos tout avoir,
> Et belle dame et grant avoir?
> Vos avereiz lai hairt on [*leg.* ou?] col,
>> Et mes amins lai joie.
> . . .[72]

(The pleasant pains are in my heart. How shall I be cured of them?

When the villein goes to market, he does not go to haggle, but to spy on his wife, so that no one may lead her astray. The pleasant pains . . .

Villein, now back away, for your breath might be the death of me. I know full well that your love and mine might yet be parted.

---

[72] *Chanter m'estuet*, no. 2. Cf. *Recherches*, 246. A further analogue is provided by Baudouin de Condé in his *Contes d'Amours*: '. . . Vilain, coustumier|De vilenie, en samblant faire | D'amor, fi! vostre alaine flaire | Si vilainnement vilounie, | Que toute en est avilounie | La terre, sor coi vos marchiés . . .' (Scheler, *Dits et contes . . .*, vol. I, IX.196–201).

Villein, did you think that you had everything, both a beautiful lady and great wealth? You shall have a rope around your neck, and my lover shall have the joy.)

This typical portrayal of the rebellious wife who openly defies her husband finds its closest parallel in the early *cywyddau* in the lively dialogue in Iolo Goch's version of 'Chwarae cnau i'm llaw' (*GIG* XXVI). Here, the poet's beloved denies Eiddig's allegations and claims that Iolo would flee before no man, for which she feels the weight of her husband's stick. Morfudd, despite the remark: 'Gŵyr hi gwatwaru gŵr hyll' (*GDG* 42.10), 'she knows how to mock [her] ugly husband', is not seen directly challenging Eiddig. But one of the few instances of direct speech attributed to her is peculiarly reminiscent of the words uttered by all those *malmariées* whose hatred for the *Jaloux* is contrasted with their love for the *ami*:

> Mwy carwn ôl mewn dolgoed,
> Dibrudd drin, dy ebrwydd droed
> No'm godlawd ŵr priawd prudd,
> Neu a ddeiryd i'w ddeurudd.
>
> (*GDG* 77.15–18)

(More would I love in a wooded dale—foolish conflict—the imprint of your swift foot than my miserable, glum husband, or anything pertaining to his two cheeks.)

Another correspondence in this poem ('Amau ar Gam') is Dafydd's plea to Morfudd to leave her husband, and similar advice is given by Gruffudd Llwyd, one of the second generation of *cywyddwyr*, in his dialogue with a *malmariée* who has suffered the indignity of being fettered to Eiddig's goat (*CIGE* XLVI)! The contrast here between Eiddig and the poet's beloved is similar to that of *GDG* 81—

> Hyhi'n lân, haeddai ganu,
> Efo'n frwnt gyda'i fun fry;
> Hi mewn cariad yn rhadlawn,
> E'n hagr wep anhygar iawn . . .
>
> (*CIGE* XLVI.25–8)

(Clean/fair is she (she deserved poetry), filthy is he with his girl up yonder; gracious and in love is she, ugly-faced and most unamiable is he . . .)

The wish for the husband's death in Gruffudd's closing couplet, a motif which is found in several of the 'apocryphal' *cywyddau* to Eiddig,[73] is also a common feature of the French *malmariées*, exem-

---

[73] See Ch. 2 above, nn. 12, 46.

plified in the final stanza of the *ballette*. It is worth noting that the basic theme of the *malmariées* is suggested by the proverb 'Gwell hir wedaut no drycwrha',[74] 'better long spinsterhood than to wed a bad husband', attested as early as the thirteenth century; but even if the ill-matched marriage was among the indigenous subjects of the Welsh popular poets, there is no doubting the influence of the well-defined conventions of the *chanson de malmariée* on the *cywydd serch*. It is the kind of genre one might expect to have passed into the repertoire of the *Clêr* at an early stage, and thence into the verse of the early *Cywyddwyr*. Whatever the modes of transmission, it appears that Dafydd has once more applied some of the motifs and a great deal of the spirit of French love-poetry to subject-matter which bears a more or less close relationship to reality.

In *GDG* 79 ('Morfudd a Dyddgu') Dafydd compares the two women to whom so much of his love-poetry is devoted: Dyddgu is the epitome of nobility—serene, well-educated, modest, but inaccessible—whereas Morfudd is by nature impulsive and fickle; but above all Morfudd is a married woman, and the opportunity is not lost to belittle the jealous husband. Not surprisingly, the poet's choice falls for Dyddgu, 'if she may be had'. The idea may have occurred to Dafydd quite spontaneously, but the existence in Continental literature of a certain type of poem based on a choice between two women does again raise the possibility that the *cywydd* reflects a conventional theme. Guilhem IX of Aquitaine, famous as the first of the troubadours, in a coarsely suggestive song cannot choose which of two fine horses to mount; he cannot have both since they detest each other, and the two women are eventually named in the penultimate stanza.[75] The medieval Latin poets face similar dilemmas: one poet is undecided between two maidens, one of whom deceives him while the other rejects him (not unlike Morfudd and Dyddgu), and he prays that he may somehow possess both.[76] The subject was deemed

---

[74] *BBCS* 4, 9. The theme is not, however, particularly prominent in the early *canu rhydd*. Brinley Rees, in his chapter on the *chansons d'aventure*, notes that the large collection with which he is concerned contains only two *malmariée* poems (*CRhC* 22; NLW MS. 832,110), both of which are perhaps closer to Dafydd ap Gwilym's *cywyddau* on the same theme than to the corresponding poems in French and English (*DCRh* 62); cf. also *CRhC* 16; i, I.33–6; i, VII.85–8.

[75] A. R. Press (ed.), *Anthology of Troubadour Lyric Poetry* (Edinburgh, 1971), 12–13; see L. T. Topsfield, 'The Burlesque Poetry of Guilhem IX of Aquitaine', *Neuphilologische Mitteilungen*, 69 (1968), 280–302.

[76] *MLRELL*, ii. 493–5; cf. the poem cited by Raby, *A History of Secular Latin Poetry*, ii. 320.

worthy of mock-scholastic discussion in the Northern French *débats*. Richart de Fourneval, having considered the respective merits of loving a married woman and a young girl, like Dafydd, chooses the latter, and in an anonymous *débat* which, again, has a certain similarity to the *cywydd*, the poet's preference is for his true beloved, although she makes him suffer in hope, rather than a girl who is willing to give herself without delay.[77] Dafydd's sudden clear-cut decision in the final couplet also calls to mind the *débat* form. But even if he had no direct knowledge of such poems, here is another theme which may well derive ultimately from the European lyric tradition.

A more familiar theme attested both in Latin and the vernaculars is the conflict between summer and winter, which may, as Raby suggests,[78] have its roots in seasonal festivities and popular song and story. The best-known example is the 'Conflictus Veris et Hiemis' composed by Alcuin in the eighth century,[79] and similar debate poems were composed throughout the Middle Ages. The genre is also reflected in the seasonal descriptions of the lyric poets. It is a fairly widespread convention, which is paralleled in Dafydd's seasonal poetry in his contrast of winter and early summer in *GDG* 69 ('Mis Mai a Mis Ionawr'). His unsonorous evocation of the month of January, or rather, perhaps, November, the 'black month', provides an effective contrast with the lush, leisurely description of May which precedes it:

> Annhebyg i'r mis dig du
> A gerydd i bawb garu;
> A bair tristlaw a byrddydd,
> A gwynt i ysbeilio gwŷdd;
> A llesgedd, breuoledd braw,
> A llaesglog a chenllysglaw,
> Ac annog llanw ac annwyd,
> Ac mewn naint llifeiriaint llwyd,
> A llawn sôn mewn afonydd,
> A llidio a digio dydd,
> Ac wybren drymled ledoer,
> A'i lliw yn gorchuddio'r lloer.
> Dêl iddo, rhyw addo rhwydd,
> Deuddrwg am ei wladeiddrwydd.
>   (ll. 31–44)

---

[77] *Origines*, 472–7; *Chanter m'estuet*, no. 84.
[78] *A History of Secular Latin Poetry*, ii. 282.
[79] Helen Waddell, *Mediaeval Latin Lyrics* (Harmondsworth, 1952), 92–6.

(Unlike the wrathful, black month which rebukes everyone for loving; which causes miserable rain and short days, and wind despoiling the trees; and feebleness—terrifying frailty—and a long cloak and hailstone-rain, and encourages floods and colds, and in streams grey torrents, and a great din in rivers, and makes the day angry and indignant, and a heavy, chill sky, its colour concealing the moon. May there come to him—such a facile vow!—a double evil for his boorishness.)

Compare the opening stanza of one of the *Carmina Burana*, a lovelyric which celebrates the coming of spring:

> Cedit, hyems, tua durities,
> frigor abit; rigor et glacies
> brumalis et feritas, rabies,
> torpor et improba segnities,
> pallor et ira, dolor et macies.

(Now, Winter, yieldeth all thy dreariness, the cold is over, all thy frozenness, all frost and fog, and wind's untowardness. All sullenness, uncomely sluggishness, paleness and anger, grief and haggardness.)[80]

Winter is surly, while May is 'the fairest time of gentilesse', reflecting the common medieval antithesis between the courtly and the rustic. For Dafydd, May is 'Cadarn farchog serchog sâl' (l. 3), 'a strong knight, a lover's boon', while winter is cursed for its boorishness ('gwladeiddrwydd'), just as for Charles d'Orléans, for instance, summer is 'gentil' and winter a 'villain' which should be exiled from the land.[81] In an Anglo-Norman version of the traditional *conflictus*, 'De l'Yver et de l'Esté',[82] two powerful lords vie for mastery. Dafydd, too, commonly personifies summer as a benevolent lord, most notably in GDG 27 ('Mawl i'r Haf'), where summer declares that he is a prince destined to return to Annwfn, the Celtic Otherworld, once his work is accomplished. There are no striking similarities between the Anglo-Norman poem and GDG 69, although there is a certain resemblance between the words spoken by generous summer—

---

[80] Text and trans. from ibid. 222–3. In a poem composed in Latin and German (*MLRELL*, ii. 411–14), the detailed description of the effects of winter—an arrogant, spiteful tyrant who overcomes the earth 'from which verdant April, the giver, made the grass to rise'—is not unlike that of GDG 69; cf. also the passage cited by Raby from an 'Altercatio Yemis et Estatis', *A History of Secular Latin Poetry*, ii. 282.

[81] Wilkins, *One Hundred Ballades*, no. 100.

[82] Jubinal, *Nouveau recueil*, ii. 40–9. It is preserved in the same MS as the English Harley Lyrics, MS. Harley 2253.

> Feynz, formentz, févez, peys,
> Touz sunt norys en mé treis meys . . .
>
> (ll. 109–10)

(Hay, wheat, beans, peas—all are nourished in my three months . . .)

and those of the summer-prince in *GDG* 27, whose destiny it is 'to
come for three months to grow the materials for a multitude of
crops'—'Dyfod drimis i dyfu | Defnyddiau llafuriau llu . . .' (ll.
35–6). But while this *cywydd*, and Dafydd's seasonal poetry in general, no doubt owe more to native mythology and folk-beliefs than
to any borrowed traditions, it is probable that *GDG* 69 does reflect
his knowledge of the foreign debate poems and related conventions.
As usual, his interpretation of the theme is his own, and it would be
futile to search for any specific 'source' in either French or Latin.

Dafydd's burlesque in *GDG* 112 ('Yr Annerch') of the *llatai* convention, which he himself, it has been seen, helped to elaborate, bears
a certain resemblance to a type of parodistic nonsense poetry which
goes back at least as far as Guilhem of Aquitaine. Dafydd's opening
couplet:

> Annerch, nac annerch, gennad,
> Ni wn pwy, gwraig macwy mad.

(Greet, do not greet, messenger, I know not who, the wife of a fine young
lord.)

is reminiscent of Guilhem's parody of the love of a courtly poet for
an inaccessible lady, in which he claims never to have seen his
beloved and is therefore quite free of care.[83] The song is imitated by
another troubadour, Jaufré Rudel,[84] and in the fourteenth century
Guillaume de Machaut has a *ballade* beginning 'Mes dames
qu'onques ne vi', 'My ladies whom I have never seen', of whom he
asks that they intercede on his behalf with a certain 'monsigneur de
Loupi' in return for 'all he has done for them'.[85] Pierre Bec associates poems such as these with the *registre du non-sens*, a register
which is best represented in medieval France by the deliberately irra-
tional, sometimes almost surreal verse of the *fatrasie* and the *resverie*,
genres which flourished in the bourgeois circles of thirteenth-century
Northern France, and which may bear some relation to popular tradition. Bec's criticism, in his discussion of the origins of the *fatrasie*,

---

[83] Press, *Anthology . . .*, 14–17.   [84] See Dronke, *The Medieval Lyric*, 112, 120.
[85] *Poésies lyriques*, vol. I, CCL.1–8.

of the theory which gives precedence to the creative powers of a single poet, while dismissing the influence of any 'transcendent tradition' or pre-existing registral conventions, is relevant to GDG 112. Such a process, he argues, seems a priori extremely hypothetical in the medieval context.[86] Dafydd's poem is certainly unique in the cywydd tradition. Although, as regards subject-matter, it has nothing in common with the bourgeois verse, in its very irrationality it clearly has a certain affinity with these and other French and Provençal 'nonsense poems'. On the other hand, Dafydd is a wholly remarkable poet, and it could be argued that it was his own extraordinary creative faculties that gave him the idea of parodying his own work for the entertainment of an audience of connoisseurs.

Finally, there can be no such doubt regarding the Continental ancestry of GDG 129 ('Y Wawr'). On its generic relationship with the Provençal alba, the Northern French aube, all scholars are agreed. Stern, for instance, while recognizing the international and timeless character of the dawn-song, maintains that the influence of the alba on the Welsh poem is just as likely as its influence on the German Minnesang.[87] It is only Chotzen who, having considered the external parallels, suggests that the theme may have arisen independently in medieval Wales.[88] It has been seen in Chapter Five that the cywydd, with its humorous repartee based on a series of unlikely excuses, has much in common with popular tradition, and as Hatto's invaluable symposium on the subject clearly shows, there can be no doubting the internationality of the basic theme of the parting of lovers at dawn. It is attested in the Greek Anthology and in Ovid;[89] it has indeed been observed that one of two Chinese dawn-songs preserved from the sixth century BC bears a wholly remarkable resemblance to the cywydd [90] (a lesson, if any were needed, in the need for

[86] La Lyrique française . . ., i. 176; see 164–82. Other discussions include L. C. Porter, La Fatrasie et le fatras: Essai sur la poésie irrationnelle en France au moyen âge (Geneva, 1960); P. Zumthor, E. G. Hessing, and R. Vijlbrief, 'Essai d'analyse des procédés fatrasiques', Romania, 84 (1963), 145–70.

[87] 'Davydd ab Gwilym . . .', 241. The genre is more widely attested in medieval Germany than elsewhere. The earliest recorded instance is a woman's song from the Carmina Burana (written down c.1220), which suggests the existence of an older native tradition of dawn-poems; cf. Dronke, The Medieval Lyric, 177 ff; Jeanroy, Origines, 274 ff.   [88] Recherches, 290–4.

[89] See Barsby's remarks, Ovid's Amores, 147, and the Greek parallels cited on 171–2. Apart from the lover's complaint at the break of dawn, Ovid's poem (Amores, I. 13) has little in common with GDG 129.

[90] Recherches, 293; cf. D. J. Bowen's remarks in LlC 7, 247–8, and see Dronke, The Medieval Lyric, 168–9.

caution in the determining of literary influence). There is also some evidence, both in Latin and in the vernaculars, that the theme was familiar in the Romance-speaking areas of medieval Europe considerably earlier than the twelfth century.[91] In his contribution to Hatto's study Woledge considers the possibility of 'similar situations provoking a similar poetic reaction in imaginative minds of different ages',[92] a sentiment with which Chotzen would no doubt have agreed. However, the occurrence in the *cywydd* of certain conventional motifs is hardly explained by coincidence. In fact, the theme seems never to have been popular in the Welsh verse tradition. *GDG* 129, and *BDG* XCVII, an 'apocryphal' *cywydd* falsely attributed to Dafydd, are the only true *aubes* to have survived.[93] Although one of the genre's familiar motifs is echoed in at least two other *cywyddau*—in *BDG* CVII and CLVIII the crow and the lark are praised for enabling the poets to flee from their beloved's arms at daybreak— there is nothing in the *canu rhydd* which remotely resembles these poems.[94] If the theme had ever been widespread in medieval Wales, one might expect the two *cywydd* versions to have been paralleled, or even imitated, in the verse of the early free-metre poets.

It is therefore logical to turn to possible external sources, and in particular to the love-poets of Northern France. Helen Fulton refers to *GDG* 129 as 'a clever parody of the courtly genre of the *aube*', an opinion also expressed by Bromwich.[95] These courtly dawn-songs, the more artistic Provençal *albas* especially, are indeed more serene and more lyrical than the *cywydd* and share little of its narrative quality. The lovers at most merely complain at the coming of dawn—its signs are rarely denied, and they are certainly never treated with the light-hearted humour of the Welsh poet. The tone

---

[91] See ibid., 170 ff; *MLRELL*, ii. 352–3.   [92] Hatto, *Eos . . .*, 357.

[93] Both are discussed by Melville Richards, in ibid. 568–74. Bromwich speaks of 'The other fourteenth-century *aube*' (*APDG* 96); the dating of *BDG* XCVII is uncertain, but it is noteworthy that it does contain a very high proportion of *cynghanedd Sain*, a characteristic of much 14th-cent. poetry. Thomas Parry, in fact, had doubts concerning the authenticity of *GDG* 129; see *GDG*, p.537.

[94] The only significant reflection of the theme known to me is the *pennill telyn*, *HB* 320: 'Ber yw'r nos a buan derfydd, | Buan iawn y cân yr 'hedydd; | Lle bo dau yn caru'n ffyddlon, | Ni chânt hwy siarad hanner digon.' Kenneth Jackson remarks that in Ireland 'the *alba* would seem to have been insignificant among [these] themes imported to Ireland, and as a full-blown type it appears to be quite unknown' (Hatto, *Eos . . .*, 576).

[95] *DGEC* 207; *SP* 161.

of the *cywydd* provides a stark contrast with the refrain of a woman's *aube* attributed to the trouvère Gace Brulé:

> Or ne hais riens tant com le jour,
> Amins, ke me depairt de vos.[96]

(I hate nothing as much as the day, my love, which parts me from you.)

This is one of only five *aubes* attested in Old French (compared to eighteen from Provence), but these, and other fragmentary evidence, suggest that the genre was rather more widespread, and that it remained in France closer to its popular origins than was the case with the Provençal *alba*.[97] One of the two fragments which have been incorporated in motets expresses the popular motif of the lover's denial of the break of dawn—

> Est il jors?—Nenil ancores;
> Vos lou hasteis trop[98]

(Is it day?—No, not yet; you bring it forward too much.)

The motif commonly takes the form of the 'lying bird', as in the thirteenth-century refrain—

> Il n'est mie jours,
> Saverouze au cors gent;
> Si m'aït Amors,
> L'alowette nos mant.[99]

(It is not day, my sweet love of fairest form; in the name of Love himself, the lark lies to us.)

The refrain must have been fairly widely known since it is attested in a variant form, and this particular motif has actually been preserved to this day in various parts of France.[100] In the lively, colloquial dialogue of *GDG* 129 Dafydd's denials are threefold: the rising sun he claims to be the moon and stars; the crow sings not because dawn has broken but because it is troubled by vermin; and most

[96] Rosenberg and Danon, *Lyrics and Melodies of Gace Brulé*, no. 80. See J. Saville, *The Medieval Erotic ALBA: Structure and Meaning* (New York and London, 1972).

[97] See Bec's persuasive arguments, *La Lyrique française. . .*, i. 90–107. For instance, the figure of the *veilleur* or watchman (who plays no part in the *cywyddau*) is common in the 'aristocratic' *albas*, but appears in only one of the French *aubes*; cf. *Origines*, 61 ff.

[98] Raynaud, *Recueil des motets français*, ii. 4.

[99] *Chanter m'estuet*, 15.9–12; cf.the songs cited by Woledge in Hatto, *Eos . . .*, 356–7.

[100] Bec, *La Lyrique française. . .*, i. 104 n. 44; cf. *Origines*, 68–9.

playfully of all, the sound of approaching dogs is claimed to be the barking of the 'hounds of the night', the legendary hounds of Gwyn ap Nudd, king of Annwfn. The first two are paralleled in the 'apocryphal' *cywydd*, with the difference that there it is the crowing of a cock which is denied, and by the woman rather than the man.[101] Remarkably, the same two motifs are paralleled in the early Chinese dawn-song. More relevant to the present discussion is the fact that similar elements occur in French popular verse, as Chotzen was well aware. The denial of the early bird, typically the lark, is very common in French, but compare also the following lines from a poem composed in the Limousin dialect:

> Encara n'es pas jorn,
> Quo es la luna que raia,
> Encara n'es pas jorn,
> Que es la luna d'amor . . .[102]

(The day has not yet dawned, it is the moon that shines; the day has not yet dawned, it is the moon of love . . .)

In a poem recorded in nineteenth-century Brittany, a country more susceptible than most to French influence, both the 'sun-moon' motif and the denial of the cockerel's song are found together.[103] There is reason to believe, then, that the *Cywyddwyr*'s humorous treatment of the theme is not so much a deliberate parody of the courtly dawn-songs of the troubadours and trouvères (of which they may or may not have known) as an elaboration of a set of fixed conventions probably derived from French popular verse. Dafydd especially, as is exemplified in his allusion to the otherworldly hounds of native folklore, develops his subject-matter with characteristic freedom and wit, but the essential theme of *GDG* 129 is unmistakably conventional.

---

[101] As in several of the Continental poems (cf. Bec, *La Lyrique française*. . ., i. 98 n. 28) the dawn is associated here with the jealous husband—'Soniais yn gall . . . | Am y dydd,—amod Eiddig' (ll. 15–16). It is also described as 'jealous' by Ovid and the early Greek poets, cf. Barsby, *Ovid's Amores*, 147.

[102] Bec, *La Lyrique française*. . ., i. 104 n. 47. The motif also appears in a Flemish poem cited in *Recherches*, 293. Further examples of the denial and explaining away of the signs of dawn in the literature of various countries may be found in Hatto, *Eos* . . ., 616 and *passim*.

[103] De la Villemarqué, *Barzaz Breiz: Chants populaires de la Bretagne* (6th edn., Paris, 1867), 236–7. The poem's authenticity, along with that of several others in this collection, is doubtful; but whether or not it is a genuine popular Breton poem, its author was clearly drawing here on a familiar motif.

Dafydd ap Gwilym's debt to the literature of medieval Europe is considerable. Although a proven master of his own proud and time-honoured poetic inheritance, more than any of his contemporaries he was receptive to the pervasive Continental literary fashions of his time. But this was no passive acceptance. Whether he was reflecting some of the more widespread commonplaces of the courtly love movement or exploiting some established genre developed by poets far from his native Ceredigion, his work is never that of an imitator. What was borrowed was remoulded, assimilated with native modes and techniques, and given new life and new meaning. This process often takes the form of creative parody, and in Dafydd's handling of external conventions the ironic smile is seldom far beneath the surface. He was just as accessible to the influence of an indigenous sub-literary culture which is itself likely to have absorbed some of the characteristic features of Continental verse. His rare talent would have flourished at any time in any place, but the various currents that came together in fourteenth-century Wales helped to imbue his verse with a special richness and vigour, a many-sidedness in theme and treatment which is one of the great achievements of medieval literature. What we have in his love-poetry is an exciting synthesis of old and new which bears the unmistakable stamp of a unique poetic personality. Through his artistic ingenuity and powers of imagination he fashioned a new kind of poetry for a new age, thereby enriching not only the Welsh literary tradition but that of Western Europe as a whole. Beyond Wales, that contribution has yet to be fully appreciated.

Bibliography

ARDEN, HEATHER M., *The Romance of the Rose* (Boston, 1987).

AUDIAU, JEAN, *Les Troubadours et l'Angleterre* (Paris, 1927).

BADEL, PIERRE-YVES, *Le Roman de la Rose au XIVe siècle. Étude de la réception de l'œuvre* (Geneva, 1980).

BARSBY, JOHN A. (ed.), *Ovid's Amores, Book One* (Oxford, 1973).

BATANY, J., *Approches du 'Roman de la Rose'* (Paris, 1973).

BEC, PIERRE, *La Lyrique française au moyen âge (XIIe et XIIIe siècles). Contribution à une typologie des genres poétiques médiévaux*, 2 vols. (Paris, 1977–8).

BÉDIER, JOSEPH, 'Les Fêtes de mai et les commencements de la poésie lyrique au moyen âge', *Revue des deux mondes* (May, 1896), 146–72.

—— (ed.), *Les Chansons de Colin Muset* (Paris, 1912).

BERESFORD, M., *New Towns of the Middle Ages* (London, 1967).

BLAUNER, D. G., 'The Early Literary Riddle', *Folk-Lore*, 78 (1967), 49–58.

BOASE, R., *The Origin and Meaning of Courtly Love: A Critical Study of European Scholarship* (Manchester, 1977).

VAN DEN BOOGAARD, N. H. J. (ed.), *Rondeaux et refrains du 12e siècle au début du 14e* (Paris, 1969).

—— 'Les Chansons attribuées à Wilart de Corbie', *Neophilologus*, 55 (1971), 123–41.

—— and NOOMEN, W. (eds.), *Nouveau recueil des fabliaux* (Assen, 1983–).

BOWEN, D. J., 'Gruffydd Hiraethog ac Argyfwng Cerdd Dafod', *LlC* 2 (1952–3), 147–60.

—— 'Sylwadau ar Waith Dafydd ap Gwilym', *LlC* 6 (1960), 36–45.

—— 'Dafydd ap Gwilym a Datblygiad y Cywydd', *LlC* 8 (1964), 1–32.

—— 'Agweddau ar Ganu'r Bedwaredd Ganrif ar Ddeg a'r Bymthegfed', *LlC* 9 (1966–7), 46–73.

—— 'Nodiadau ar Waith y Cywyddwyr', *BBCS* 25 (1972), 19–32.

—— 'Dafydd ap Gwilym a'r Trefydd Drwg', *YB* 10 (1977), 190–226.

—— 'Y Cywyddwyr a'r Noddwyr Cynnar', *YB* 11 (1979), 63–108.

—— 'Cywydd Dafydd ap Gwilym i Ferched Llanbadarn a'i Gefndir', *YB* 12 (1982), 77–122.

—— 'Dafydd ap Gwilym a Cheredigion', *LlC* 14 (1983–4), 163–209.

—— *Dafydd ap Gwilym a Dyfed* (Llandysul, 1986).

—— 'Beirdd a Noddwyr y Bedwaredd Ganrif ar Ddeg', *LlC* 17 (1992), 60–107.

BRAMLEY, KATHLEEN ANNE [née Evans], 'Canu Hywel ab Owain Gwynedd', *SC* 20/1 (1985–6), 167–191.

—— *et al.* (eds.), *Gwaith Llywelyn Fardd, I, ac Eraill o Feirdd y Ddeuddegfed Ganrif* (Cardiff, 1994).

BROMWICH, RACHEL, *Trioedd Ynys Prydein, The Welsh Triads* (Cardiff, 1961).

—— 'Influences upon Dafydd ap Gwilym's Poetry', *Poetry Wales*, 8: 4 (Spring 1973), 44–55.

—— *Dafydd ap Gwilym*, 'Writers of Wales' series (Cardiff, 1974).

—— *Selected Poems of Dafydd ap Gwilym* (Bungay, Suffolk, 1985).

—— *Aspects of the Poetry of Dafydd ap Gwilym: Collected Papers* (Cardiff, 1986).

—— and EVANS, D. SIMON (eds.), *Culhwch and Olwen: An Edition and Study of the Oldest Arthurian Tale* (Cardiff, 1992).

BROOK, G. L. (ed.), *The Harley Lyrics* (4th edn., Manchester, 1968).

BULLOCK-DAVIES, CONSTANCE, 'Welsh Minstrels at the Courts of Edward I and Edward II', *THSC* (1972–3), 104–22.

BURKE, PETER, *Popular Culture in Early Modern Europe* (London, 1978).

CHAYTOR, H. J., *The Troubadours and England* (Cambridge, 1923).

CHICHMAREF, V. (ed.), *Poésies lyriques de Guillaume de Machaut*, 2 vols. (Paris, 1909).

CHOTZEN, T. M., *Recherches sur la poésie de Dafydd ab Gwilym* (Amsterdam, 1927).

CLANCY, JOSEPH P., *The Earliest Welsh Poetry* (London, 1970).

COIRAULT, P., *Formation de nos chansons folkloriques* (Paris, 1953).

CONRAN, ANTHONY (trans.), *The Penguin Book of Welsh Verse* (Harmondsworth, 1967).

COPLEY, F. O., *Exclusus Amator* (Madison, 1956).

COWLEY, F. G., *The Monastic Order in South Wales, 1066–1349* (Cardiff, 1977).

CURTIUS, E. R., *European Literature and the Latin Middle Ages* (New York, 1953).

DAHLBERG, CHARLES (trans.), *The Romance of the Rose by Guillaume de Lorris and Jean de Meun* (Princeton, NJ, 1971).

DÄHNE, R., *Die Lieder der Maumariée seit dem Mittelalter* (Halle, 1933).

DANIEL, R. IESTYN (ed.), *Gwaith Bleddyn Ddu* (Aberystwyth, 1994).

DAVENSON, H. (ed.), *Le Livre des Chansons* (Neuchâtel, 1946).

DAVIES, CENNARD, 'Robin Clidro a'i Ganlynwyr', unpublished MA thesis, University of Wales, 1964.

DAVIES, J. H. (ed.), *Cymdeithas Llên Cymru*, vol. I, *Carolau: gan Richard Hughes* (Cardiff, 1900).

—— *Cymdeithas Llên Cymru*, vol. III, *Casgliad o Hen Ganiadau Serch* (Cardiff, 1902).

—— *Cymdeithas Llên Cymru*, vols. V–VI, *Caniadau yn y Mesurau Rhyddion, gyda rhagymadrodd ar godiad a datblygiad barddoniaeth rydd yn y Gymraeg* (Cardiff, 1905).

DAVIES, J. H. (ed.), 'The Roll of the Caerwys Eisteddfod of 1523', *Transactions of the Liverpool Welsh National Society* (1904/5–1908/9), 87–102.

DAVIES, R. REES, *The Age of Conquest: Wales 1063–1415* (Oxford and New York, 1991) (first published 1987 as *Conquest, Coexistence and Change: Wales 1063–1415*).

DE COUSSEMAKER, E. (ed.), *Œuvres complètes du trouvère Adam de la Halle* (Ridgewood, NJ, 1965; repr. of 1872 edn.).

DONOVAN, P. (ed.), *Cywyddau Serch y Tri Bedo* (Cardiff, 1982).

DRAGONETTI, ROGER, *La Technique poétique des trouvères dans la chanson courtoise* (Brugge, 1960).

DRONKE, PETER, *Medieval Latin and the Rise of European Love-Lyric*, 2 vols (Oxford, 1965–6).

—— *The Medieval Lyric* (London, 1968).

—— 'Serch *Fabliau* a Serch Cwrtais', in John Rowlands (ed.), *Dafydd ap Gwilym a Chanu Serch yr Oesoedd Canol* (Cardiff, 1975), 1–17.

DUFOURNET, J. (ed.), *Études sur le Roman de la Rose de Guillaume de Lorris* (Paris, 1984).

ECONOMOU, G. D. and FERRANTE, J. M. (eds.), *In Pursuit of Perfection: Courtly Love in Medieval Literature* (New York, 1975).

EDWARDS, H. M., '"Rhodiwr fydd clerwr": Sylwadau ar Gerdd Ymffrost o'r Bedwaredd Ganrif ar Ddeg', *Y Traethodydd* (Jan. 1994), 50–5.

ELLIS, ROBERT (Cynddelw) (ed.), *Barddoniaeth Dafydd ab Gwilym o grynhoad Owen Jones, William Owen ac Edward Williams, yn nghydag amryw gyfieithiadau i'r Seisnig* (Liverpool, 1873; original version published 1789).

EVANS, DAFYDD H., 'Yr Ustus Llwyd a'r Swrcod', *YB* 17 (1990), 63–92.

EVANS, H. MEURIG, 'Iaith a Ieithwedd y Cerddi Rhydd Cynnar', unpublished MA thesis, University of Wales, 1937.

EVANS, J. GWENOGVRYN (ed.), *The Poetry in the Red Book of Hergest* (Llanbedrog, 1911).

EVANS, KATHLEEN ANNE, 'Cerddi'r Gogynfeirdd i Rianedd a Gwragedd', unpublished MA thesis, University of Wales, 1972.

EVANS, MEREDYDD, 'Y Canu Gwasael yn *Llawysgrif Richard Morris o Gerddi*', *LlC* 13 (1974–81), 207–35.

FARAL, EDMOND, *Les Jongleurs en France au moyen âge* (Paris, 1910).

—— *Recherches sur les sources latines des contes et romans courtois du moyen âge* (Paris, 1913).

—— *Les arts poétiques du XIIe et du XIIIe siècle* (Paris, 1958).

FERRAND, F. (ed.), *Chansons des XVe et XVIe siècles* (Paris, 1986).

—— and BAUMGARTNER, E. (eds.), *Poèmes d'amour des XIIe et XIIIe siècles* (Paris, 1983).

FLEMING, J. V., *The Roman de la Rose: A Study in Allegory and Iconography* (Princeton, NJ, 1969).

Fulton, Helen, 'The Theory of Celtic Influence on the Harley Lyrics', *Modern Philology*, 82 (1984–5), 239–54.

—— *Dafydd ap Gwilym and the European Context* (Cardiff, 1989).

Gasté, A. (ed.), *Chansons Normandes du XVᵉ siècle* (Caen, 1966).

Gennrich, F. (ed.), *Rondeaux, Virelais und Balladen, Gesellschaft für Romanische Literatur*, 43 (Dresden, 1921).

Gruffydd, R. Geraint, 'Marwnad Lleucu Llwyd gan Llywelyn Goch Amheurig Hen', *YB* 1 (1965), 126–37.

—— 'Sylwadau ar Gywydd "Offeren Y Llwyn" Dafydd ap Gwilym', *YB* 10 (1977), 181–9.

—— 'The Early Court Poetry of South West Wales', *SC* 14/15 (1979–80), 95–105.

—— 'Cywyddau Triawdaidd Dafydd ap Gwilym: Rhai Sylwadau', *YB* 13 (1985), 167–77.

—— 'Dafydd ap Gwilym: Trem ar ei Yrfa', *Taliesin*, 71 (Sept. 1990), 25–40.

—— '*Englynion y Cusan* by Dafydd ap Gwilym', *CMCS* 23 (Summer 1992), 1–6.

Gunn, A. M. F., *The Mirror of Love: A Reinterpretation of 'The Romance of the Rose'* (Lubbock, Texas, 1952).

Harrison, A., 'Tricksters and Entertainers in the Irish Tradition', *Proceedings of the First North American Congress of Celtic Studies*, Ottawa, 1986 (Ottawa, 1988), 293–307.

Hatto, A. T. (ed.), *Eos: An Enquiry into the Theme of Lovers' Meetings and Partings at Dawn in Poetry* (The Hague, 1965).

Hill, D. E. (ed.), *Ovid: Metamorphoses I–IV* (Warminster, 1985).

Hill, R. T. and Bergin, T. G. (eds.), *Anthology of the Provençal Troubadours*, 2 vols. (rev. edn., New Haven, Conn., 1973).

Huizinga, J., *The Waning of the Middle Ages* (Harmondsworth, 1955; first published 1937).

Hull, Vernam and Taylor, Archer (eds.), 'A Collection of Welsh Riddles', *University of California Publications in Modern Philology*, 26 (1942–50), 225–325.

Huot, Sylvia, *'The Romance of the Rose' and its Medieval Readers: Interpretation, Reception, Manuscript Transmission* (Cambridge, 1993).

Huws, Daniel, 'Llawysgrif Hendregadredd', *NLWJ* 22 (1981–2), 1–26.

—— 'Llyfr Gwyn Rhydderch', *CMCS* 21 (Summer 1991), 1–37.

Ifans, Rhiannon, *Sêrs a Rybana: Astudiaeth o'r Canu Gwasael* (Llandysul, 1983).

Jackson, Kenneth (ed.), *Early Welsh Gnomic Poems* (Cardiff, 1935).

—— *Studies in Early Celtic Nature Poetry* (Cambridge, 1935).

Jarman, A. O. H., *The Legend of Merlin* (Cardiff, 1960).

—— 'Telyn a Chrwth', *LlC* 6 (1960–1), 154–75.

—— (ed.), *Llyfr Du Caerfyrddin* (Cardiff, 1982).

JARMAN, A. O. H. and HUGHES, G. R. (eds.), *A Guide to Welsh Literature*, 2 vols. (Swansea, 1976 and 1979).

JAUSS, H. R., *Genèse de la poésie allégorique française au moyen âge* (Heidelberg, 1962).

JEANROY, A., *Les Origines de la poésie lyrique en France* (3rd edn., Paris, 1925).

—— and LANGFORS, A., 'Chansons inédites tirées du manuscrit français 1591 de la Bibliothèque Nationale', *Romania*, 44 (1915–17), 454–510.

—— (eds.), *Chansons satiriques et bachiques du XIIIᵉ siècle* (Paris, 1921).

JEFFREY, D. L. and LEVY, B. J. (eds.), *The Anglo-Norman Lyric* (Toronto, 1990).

JENKINS, DAFYDD (ed. and trans.), *The Law of Hywel Dda*, 'Welsh Classics' series (Llandysul, 1990).

JOHNSTON, DAFYDD, 'The Serenade and the Image of the House in the Poems of Dafydd ap Gwilym', *CMCS* 5 (Summer 1983), 1–19.

—— '*Cywydd y Gal* by Dafydd ap Gwilym', *CMCS* 9 (Summer 1985), 71–89.

—— (ed.), *Gwaith Iolo Goch* (Cardiff, 1988).

—— (ed.), *Blodeugerdd Barddas o'r Bedwaredd Ganrif ar Ddeg* (Llandybïe, 1989).

—— (ed.), *Canu Maswedd yr Oesoedd Canol/Medieval Welsh Erotic Poetry* (Cardiff, 1991).

—— 'The Erotic Poetry of the *Cywyddwyr*', *CMCS* 22 (Winter 1991), 63–94.

—— (ed. and trans.), *Iolo Goch: Poems* (Llandysul, 1993).

JOHNSTON, R. C. and OWEN, D. D. R. (eds.), *Fabliaux* (Oxford, 1965).

JONES, ELIN M. and JONES, NERYS ANN (eds.), *Gwaith Llywarch ap Llywelyn 'Prydydd y Moch'* (Cardiff, 1991).

JONES, NERYS ANN and OWEN, ANN PARRY (eds.), *Gwaith Cynddelw Brydydd Mawr*, vol. 1 (Cardiff, 1991).

JONES, OWEN, PUGHE, WILLIAM OWEN, and WILLIAMS, EDWARD (eds.), *The Myvyrian Archaiology of Wales* (2nd edn., Denbigh, 1870).

JONES, R. M., 'Ymryson ac Ymddiddan Corff ac Enaid', *YB* 5 (1970), 44–61.

—— 'Mesurau'r Canu Rhydd Cynnar', *BBCS* 28 (1979), 413–41.

JONES, T. GWYNN, 'Bardism and Romance: A Study of the Welsh Literary Tradition', *THSC* (1913–14), 205–310.

—— *Rhieingerddi'r Gogynfeirdd* (Denbigh, 1915).

—— 'A "Court of Love" Poem in Welsh', *Aberystwyth Studies*, 4 (1922), 85–96.

—— 'Ein Kymrisches Fluchgedicht', *ZCP* 17 (1928), 167–76.

—— *Welsh Folklore and Folk-Custom* (London, 1930).

JONES, W. P., *The Pastourelle: A Study of the Origin and Traditions of a Lyric Type* (Cambridge, Mass., 1931).

KENNEY, E. J. (ed.), *P. Ovidi Nasonis: Amores, Ars Amatoria, Remedia Amoris* (Oxford, 1961).

KRAPP, G. P. and DOBBIE, E. V. K. (eds.), *The Exeter Book* (Columbia, 1936).

LAFITTE-HOUSSAT, J., *Troubadours et cours d'amour* (Paris, 1971).

LANGFORS, A., 'Mélanges de poésie lyrique française', parts III–V, *Romania*, 56 (1930), 33–79; 57 (1931), 312–94; 58 (1932), 321–79.

—— (ed.), *Deux recueils de sottes chansons* (Helsinki, 1945).

LANGLOIS, ERNEST, *Origines et sources du Roman de la Rose* (Paris, 1891).

—— (ed.), *Le Roman de la Rose*, 5 vols. (Paris, 1914–24).

LAZAR, MOSHÉ, *Amour courtois et 'fin' amors' dans la littérature du XIIe siècle* (Paris, 1964).

LE GENTIL, PIERRE, 'La Strophe Zadjalesque, les Khardjas et le problème des origines du lyrisme roman', *Romania*, 84 (1963), 1–27, 209–50.

LECOY, F. (ed.), *Le Roman de la Rose*, 3 vols. (Paris, 1965–70).

LEE, GUY (ed.), *Ovid's Amores* (London, 1968).

LEGGE, M. DOMINICA, *Anglo-Norman Literature and its Background* (Oxford, 1963).

LEWIS, C. S., *The Allegory of Love* (Oxford, 1936).

LEWIS, CERI W., 'Einion Offeiriad and the Bardic Grammar', in Jarman and Hughes (eds.), *A Guide to Welsh Literature*, vol. 2 (Swansea, 1979), 58–87.

LEWIS, SAUNDERS, 'Dafydd ap Gwilym', *Blackfriars*, 34 (Mar. 1963), 131–5 (repr. in A. R. Jones and Gwyn Thomas (eds.), *Presenting Saunders Lewis* (Cardiff, 1973), 159–63).

—— *Gramadegau'r Penceirddiaid* (Cardiff, 1967).

LLOYD, D. MYRDDIN, 'The Later Gogynfeirdd', in Jarman and Hughes (eds.), *A Guide to Welsh Literature*, vol. 2 (1979), 36–57.

LLOYD-JONES, J., 'The Court Poets of the Welsh Princes', *Proceedings of the British Academy*, 34 (1948), 167–97.

LLOYD-MORGAN, CERIDWEN, 'French Texts, Welsh Translators', in Roger Ellis (ed.), *The Medieval Translator II* (London, 1991), 45–63.

LLWYD, ALAN (ed.), *50 o Gywyddau Dafydd ap Gwilym* (Swansea, 1980).

LOOMIS, R. M., *Dafydd ap Gwilym: The Poems* (New York, 1982).

MATONIS, A. T. E., 'An Investigation of Celtic influences on MS. Harley 2253', *Modern Philology*, 70 (1972–3), 91–108.

—— 'Medieval Topics and Rhetoric in the Work of the Cywyddwyr', unpublished Ph.D thesis, Edinburgh University, 1973.

—— 'Nodiadau ar Rethreg y Cywyddwyr: y *descriptio pulchritudinis* a'r Technegau Helaethu', *Y Traethodydd*, 133 (1978), 155–67.

—— 'Traditions of Panegyric in Welsh Poetry: The Heroic and the Chivalric', *Speculum*, 53 (1978), 667–87.

—— 'Barddoneg a Rhai Ymrysonau Barddol Cymraeg yr Oesoedd Canol Diweddar', *YB* 12 (1982), 157–200.

—— 'The Harley Lyrics: English and Welsh Convergences', *Modern Philology*, 86 (1988–9), 1–21.

MATONIS, A. T. E., 'The Concept of Poetry in the Middle Ages: The Welsh Evidence from the Bardic Grammars', *BBCS* 36 (1989), 1–12.

MERONEY, HOWARD, 'Studies in Early Irish Satire', *Journal of Celtic Studies*, 1 (1950), 199–226; 2 (1953), 59–130.

MEYER, P., 'Les Manuscrits français de Cambridge, II', *Romania*, 15 (1886), 236–357.

MOORE, A. K., *The Secular Lyric in Middle English* (Kentucky, 1951).

MORRIS-JONES, JOHN and PARRY-WILLIAMS, T. H. (eds.), *Llawysgrif Hendregadredd* (Cardiff, 1933).

MORYS, TWM, 'Chwedleu Chwydlyd: Golwg ar Ganu Dychan Llyfr Coch Hergest', *Barddas*, 135–7 (1988), 32–4.

MURPHY, GERARD (ed.), *Early Irish Lyrics* (Oxford, 1956).

MUSCATINE, CHARLES, *Chaucer and the French Tradition* (Berkeley, Calif., 1957).

NEILSON, W. A., *The Origins and Sources of the 'Court of Love'* (New York, 1967; first published 1899).

NEWMAN, F. X. (ed.), *The Meaning of Courtly Love* (Albany, NY, 1968).

NYKROG, PER, *Les Fabliaux* (Copenhagen, 1957).

—— *'L'Amour et la Rose'. Le grand dessein de Jean de Meun* (Harvard, 1986).

OGILVY, J. D. A., 'Mimi, Scurrae, Histriones: Entertainers of the Early Middle Ages', *Speculum*, 38 (1963), 603–19.

O'SULLIVAN, H. J. T., 'Developments in Love Poetry in Irish, Welsh and Scottish Gaelic before 1650', unpublished M.Litt. thesis, Glasgow University, 1976.

Ó TUAMA, SEÁN, *An Grá in Amhráin na nDaoine* (Dublin, 1960).

—— 'Serch Cwrtais mewn Llenyddiaeth Wyddeleg', in John Rowlands (ed.), *Dafydd ap Gwilym a Chanu Serch yr Oesoedd Canol* (Cardiff, 1975), 18–42.

OULMONT, CHARLES, *Les Débats du clerc et du chevalier dans la littérature poétique du moyen âge* (repr. of the 1911 edn., Geneva, 1974).

OWEN, ANN PARRY, 'Rhieingerdd Efa ferch Madog ap Maredudd. Cynddelw Brydydd Mawr a'i cant', *YB* 14 (1988), 56–86.

OWEN, TREFOR M., *Welsh Folk Customs* (Cardiff, 1959).

PARIS, GASTON (ed.), *Chansons du XVe siècle* (Paris, 1875).

PARRY, THOMAS, 'Statud Gruffudd ap Cynan', *BBCS* 5 (1929), 25–33.

—— 'Datblygiad y Cywydd', *THSC* (1939), 209–31.

—— *A History of Welsh Literature*, trans. H. I. Bell (Oxford, 1955).

—— 'The Welsh Metrical Treatise Attributed to Einion Offeiriad', *Proceedings of the British Academy*, 47 (1961), 177–95.

—— (ed.), *The Oxford Book of Welsh Verse* (Oxford, 1962).

—— (ed.), *Gwaith Dafydd ap Gwilym* (2nd edn., Cardiff, 1963).

PARRY-WILLIAMS, T. H. (ed.), *Llawysgrif Richard Morris o Gerddi* (Cardiff, 1931).

—— (ed.), *Canu Rhydd Cynnar* (Cardiff, 1932).

—— (ed.), *Hen Benillion* (2nd edn., Llandysul, 1956).

PEARSALL, DEREK, *Old English and Middle English Poetry* (London, 1977).

PENNAR, MEIRION, 'Syniad "Y Caredd Digerydd" ym Marddoniaeth Gymraeg yr Oesoedd Canol', *YB* 9 (1976), 33–40.

—— 'Dryll o Dystiolaeth am y Glêr', *BBCS* 28 (1979), 406–12.

—— 'Teuluaeth a Maswedd', *YB* 16 (1990), 52–9.

POIRION, D. (ed.), *Le Roman de la Rose* (Paris, 1974).

PORTER, L. C., *La Fatrasie et le fatras: Essai sur la poésie irrationnelle en France au moyen âge* (Geneva, 1960).

PRESS, A. R., 'The Adulterous Nature of *Fin' Amors*: A Re-examination of the Theory', *Forum for Modern Language Studies*, 6 (1970), 327–41.

—— (ed.), *Anthology of Troubadour Lyric Poetry* (Edinburgh, 1971).

RABY, F. J. E., *A History of Secular Latin Poetry in the Middle Ages*, 2 vols (2nd edn., Oxford, 1957).

RAUGEI, A. M. (ed.), *Gautier de Dargies: Poesie* (Florence, 1981).

RAYNAUD, G., *Recueil de motets français des XIIe et XIIIe siècles*, 2 vols. (Paris, 1881–3).

REES, BRINLEY, *Dulliau'r Canu Rhydd 1500–1650* (Cardiff, 1952).

REES, ELINOR, 'Provençal Elements in the English Vernacular Lyrics of MS. Harley 2253', *Stanford Studies in Language and Literature* (1941), 81–95.

RIBARD, JACQUES, *Un Ménestrel du XIVe siècle: Jean de Condé* (Geneva, 1969).

—— (ed.), *La Messe des oiseaux et le Dit des Jacobins et des Fremeneurs* (Geneva, 1970).

RITTER, E. (ed.), *Poésies des XIVe et XVe siècles* (Geneva, 1880).

RIVIÈRE, JEAN-CLAUDE, *Pastourelles: Introduction à l'étude formelle des pastourelles anonymes françaises des XIIe et XIIIe siècles*, 2 vols. (Paris, 1974–5).

ROBERTS, BRYNLEY F., 'Gwyn ap Nudd', *LlC* 13 (1974–81), 283–9.

ROBINSON, F. N., 'Satirists and Enchanters in Early Irish Literature', in D. G. Lyon and G. F. Moore (eds.), *Studies in the History of Religions presented to Crawford Howell Joy* (New York, 1912), 95–130.

ROBINSON, F. N. (ed.), *The Works of Geoffrey Chaucer* (2nd edn., Oxford, 1957).

ROLLAND, E. (ed.), *Recueil de chansons populaires*, 3 vols. (Paris, 1967).

ROSENBERG, S. N. and TISCHLER, H. (eds.), *Chanter m'estuet : Songs of the Trouvères* (London, 1981).

—— and DANON, S. (eds.), *The Lyrics and Melodies of Gace Brulé* (New York and London, 1985).

ROSS, A. S. C., 'The Middle English Poem on the Names of a Hare', *Proceedings of the Leeds Philosophical and Literary Society*, 3 (1935), 347–77.

ROWLAND, JENNY, 'Genres', in Brynley F. Roberts (ed.), *Early Welsh Poetry : Studies in the Book of Aneirin* (Aberystwyth, 1988), 179–208.

—— *Early Welsh Saga Poetry* (Cambridge, 1990).

ROWLANDS, EURYS, 'Cyfeiriadau Dafydd ap Gwilym at Annwn', *LlC* 5 (1958–9), 122–35.

—— 'Cywydd Dafydd ap Gwilym i Fis Mai', *LlC* 5 (1958–9), 1–25.

—— 'Nodiadau ar y Traddodiad Moliant a'r Cywydd', *LlC* 7 (1963), 217–43.

—— 'Rhamant Hanes y Beirdd', *YB* 3 (1967), 28–38.

—— 'Iolo Goch', in J. Carney and D. Greene (eds.), *Celtic Studies: Essays in Memory of Angus Matheson 1912–62* (London, 1968), 124–46.

—— (ed.), *Poems of the Cywyddwyr* (Dublin, 1976).

—— 'Canu Serch 1450–1525', *BBCS* 31 (1984), 31–47.

ROWLANDS, JOHN, 'Delweddau Serch Dafydd ap Gwilym', *YB* 2 (1966), 58–76.

—— (ed.), *Dafydd ap Gwilym a Chanu Serch yr Oesoedd Canol* (Cardiff, 1975).

RUDDOCK, GILBERT, 'Rhai Agweddau ar Ganu Serch y Bymthegfed Ganrif', in John Rowlands (ed.), *Dafydd ap Gwilym a Chanu Serch yr Oesoedd Canol* (Cardiff, 1975), 95–119.

—— 'Amwysedd ac Eironi ym Marwnad Lleucu Llwyd', *YB* 9 (1976), 61–79.

SAVILLE, J., *The Medieval Erotic ALBA: Structure and Meaning* (New York and London, 1972).

SAYCE, OLIVE, *The Medieval German Lyric, 1150–1300: The Development of its Themes and Forms in their European Context* (Oxford, 1982).

SCHELER, A. (ed.), *Dits et contes de Baudouin de Condé, et de son fils Jean de Condé*, 3 vols. (Brussels, 1866–7).

—— (ed.), *Trouvères Belges du XIIᵉ au XIVᵉ siècle*, 2 vols. (Brussels, 1876; Louvain, 1879).

SIDGWICK, F. and CHAMBERS, E. K. (eds.), *Early English Lyrics* (London, 1966; first published 1907).

SIMS-WILLIAMS, PATRICK, 'Riddling Treatment of the "Watchman Device" in *Branwen* and *Togail Bruidne Da Derga*', *SC* 12/13 (1977–8), 83–117.

—— 'Dafydd ap Gwilym and Celtic Literature', in B. Ford (ed.), *Medieval Literature. Part Two: The European Inheritance* (Harmondsworth, 1983), 301–17.

SMITH, J. BEVERLEY, 'Einion Offeiriad', *BBCS* 20 (1964), 339–47.

SOUTHWORTH, J., *The English Medieval Minstrel* (Woodbridge, 1989).

SPEARING, A. C., *Medieval Dream-Poetry* (Cambridge, 1976).

SPEIRS, JOHN, *Medieval English Poetry: The Non-Chaucerian Tradition* (London, 1957).

STERN, L. C., 'Davydd ab Gwilym, ein walisischer Minnesänger', *ZCP* 7 (1910), 1–265.

SURRIDGE, MARIE E., 'Romance Linguistic Influence on Middle Welsh', *SC* 1 (1966), 63–92.

—— 'Romance and Anglo-Saxon Elements in the Poetry of Dafydd ap Gwilym', *Proceedings of the First North American Congress of Celtic Studies*, Ottawa, 1986 (Ottawa, 1988), 531–43.

SZITTYA, P. R., *The Antifraternal Tradition in Medieval Literature* (Princeton, NJ, 1986).

TARBÉ, P. (ed.), *Les Chansonniers de Champagne aux XIIᵉ et XIIIᵉ siècles* (Geneva, 1980; first published 1850).

TAYLOR, ARCHER, *The Literary Riddle Before 1600* (Calif., 1948).

—— (ed.), *English Riddles from Oral Tradition* (Calif., 1951).

THOMPSON, STITH, *Motif-Index of Folk-Literature*, 6 vols. (Copenhagen, 1955–8; first published 1932–6).

THORPE, LEWIS (trans.), *Gerald of Wales: The Journey Through Wales and The Description of Wales* (Harmondsworth, 1978).

TIERSOT, J., *Histoire de la chanson populaire en France* (Paris, 1889).

TOPSFIELD, L. T., 'The Burlesque Poetry of Guilhem IX of Aquitaine', *Neuphilologische Mitteilungen*, 69 (1968), 280–302.

—— (ed.), *Troubadours and Love* (Cambridge, 1975).

TROTTER, D. A., 'L'Anglo-français au Pays de Galles: une enquête préliminaire', *Revue de Linguistique Romane*, 58 (1994), 461–87.

TUPPER, FREDERICK (ed.), *The Riddles of the Exeter Book* (Boston, 1910).

WADDELL, HELEN (ed.), *Mediaeval Latin Lyrics* (Harmondsworth, 1952; first published 1929).

—— *The Wandering Scholars* (6th edn., Harmondsworth, 1932).

WALLENSKÖLD, A. (ed.), *Les Chansons de Thibaut de Champagne, Roi de Navarre* (Paris, 1925).

WALSH, P. G. (ed.), *Thirty Poems from the Carmina Burana* (Reading, 1976).

—— (ed.), *Andreas Capellanus on Love* (London, 1982).

WARREN, F. M., 'The Romance Lyric from the Standpoint of Antecedent Latin Documents', *Proceedings of the Modern Language Association of America*, 26 (1911), 280–314.

WEST, B. CONSTANCE, *Courtoisie in Anglo-Norman Literature* (New York, 1966).

WHICHER, G. F. (ed.), *The Goliard Poets* (New York, 1965).

WILHELM, JAMES J., *The Cruelest Month* (New Haven, Conn, 1965).

—— *Seven Troubadours* (Pennsylvania, 1970).

WILKINS, NIGEL (ed.), *One Hundred Ballades, Rondeaux and Virelais from the Late Middle Ages* (Cambridge, 1969).

WILKINSON, L. P., *Ovid Recalled* (Cambridge, 1955).

WILLIAMS, ARNOLD, 'Chaucer and the Friars', *Speculum*, 28 (1953), 499–513.

WILLIAMS, G. J., *Traddodiad Llenyddol Morgannwg* (Cardiff, 1948).

—— 'Cerddi'r Nant', *BBCS* 17 (1957), 77–89.

WILLIAMS, G. J. and JONES, E. J. (eds.), *Gramadegau'r Penceirddiaid* (Cardiff, 1934).

WILLIAMS, GLANMOR, *The Welsh Church From Conquest to Reformation* (Cardiff, 1962).

WILLIAMS, IFOR, 'Dafydd ap Gwilym a'r Glêr', *THSC* (1913–14), 83–204.

—— and ROBERTS, THOMAS (eds.), *Cywyddau Dafydd ap Gwilym a'i Gyfoeswyr* (Bangor, 1914; rev. edn., Cardiff, 1935).

——, LEWIS, HENRY, and ROBERTS, THOMAS (eds.), *Cywyddau Iolo Goch ac Eraill* (rev. edn., Cardiff, 1937).

WILLIAMS, J. E. CAERWYN, *Traddodiad Llenyddol Iwerddon* (Cardiff, 1958).

—— 'Cerddi'r Gogynfeirdd i Wragedd a Merched, a'u Cefndir yng Nghymru a'r Cyfandir', *LlC* 13 (1974–81), 3–112.

—— *The Poets of the Welsh Princes*, 'Writers of Wales' series (Cardiff, 1978).

—— 'The Nature Prologue in Welsh Court Poetry', *SC* 24/5 (1989–90), 70–90.

—— and LYNCH, PEREDUR I. (eds.), *Gwaith Meilyr Brydydd a'i Ddisgynyddion* (Cardiff, 1994).

WILLIAMSON, CRAIG (ed.), *The Old English Riddles of the Exeter Book* (Chapel Hill, NC, 1977).

WILSON, R. M., *The Lost Literature of Medieval England* (London, 1952).

WIMSATT, J. I., *Chaucer and the French Love Poets: The Literary Background of the 'Book of the Duchess'* (Chapel Hill, NC, 1968).

—— *Chaucer and his French Contemporaries: Natural Music in the Fourteenth Century* (Toronto, 1991).

WINKLER, E. (ed.), *Die Lieder Raouls Von Soissons* (Halle, 1914).

WOOD, G. A., 'The Anglo-Saxon Riddles', *Aberystwyth Studies*, 1 (1912), 9–62; 2 (1914), 1–41.

ZEYDEL, E. H. (ed.), *Vagabond Verse: Secular Latin Poems of the Middle Ages* (Detroit, 1966).

ZINK, M., *La Pastourelle: poésie et folklore au moyen âge* (Paris and Montreal, 1972).

ZUMTHOR, PAUL, *Essai de poétique médiévale* (Paris, 1972).

—— *Introduction à la poésie orale* (Paris, 1983).

——, HESSING, E. G., and VIJLBRIEF, R., 'Essai d'analyse des procédés fatrasiques', *Romania*, 84 (1963), 145–70.

Index